出版说明

人类历史的发展过程也是思想文化不断积累和沉淀的过程。在几千年的人类历史发展长河中，先贤们或在人文社科领域，或在科学技术领域创作出了无数经典名著。这些著作所蕴藏的思想财富和学术价值，早已为世人所熟知，它们无不体现了作者所处的特定时代的思想和文化。通过这些经典名著，读者不仅可以欣赏到流畅的文笔、生动的描述和详细的刻画、深邃的思想，更可以领悟它们各自独特的历史与文化内涵。可以说，这些作品深深地影响了世世代代的读者，也引导着当今的学人以此来充实和丰富自己的头脑。有鉴于此，我们邀请了专门研究世界历史文化的专家学者，精心挑选代表世界历史文化不同领域的经典作品，采取英汉双语对照的形式出版，一方面为读者提供原汁原味的世界经典名著，让读者自由地阅读，在此过程中逐渐提升自己的英语水平；另一方面通过这种阅读，以达到对世界历史文化的整体了解，开阔自己的视野，打开通往世界的心灵之窗，同时又获得思想文化、个人修养、伦理道德等多方面的提升。

我们衷心期待这套书成为大家学习道路上不可或缺的好伙伴！如果您在阅读中发现有疑问或错误之处，请不吝指正，以便我们更加完善这套书。

英国语文 5

（英汉双语）

[英] 托马斯-尼尔森公司⊙编　王　硕　李康康⊙译

THE ROYAL READERS

北京工业大学出版社

图书在版编目（CIP）数据

英国语文. 5：英汉对照 / 英国托马斯–尼尔森公司编；王硕，李康康译. — 北京：北京工业大学出版社，2017.7

ISBN 978-7-5639-5265-6

Ⅰ. ①英…　Ⅱ. ①英… ②王… ③李…　Ⅲ. ①英语－教材　Ⅳ. ①H31

中国版本图书馆CIP数据核字（2017）第060379号

英国语文 5（英汉双语）

编　　者：［英］托马斯–尼尔森公司
译　　者：王　硕　李康康
责任编辑：王　喆
封面设计：同人阁文化传媒·书装设计
出版发行：北京工业大学出版社
（北京市朝阳区平乐园100号　邮编：100124）
010-67391722（传真）bgdcbs@sina.com
出 版 人：郝　勇
经销单位：全国各地新华书店
承印单位：大厂回族自治县正兴印务有限公司
开　　本：787毫米×1092毫米　1/16
印　　张：24.5
字　　数：529千字
版　　次：2017年7月第1版
印　　次：2017年7月第1次印刷
标准书号：ISBN 978-7-5639-5265-6
定　　价：49.80元

译者前言

《英国语文》原名《皇家读本》（The Royal Readers），是20世纪前后由英国著名的教材出版公司托马斯–尼尔森公司编写出版的一套小学语文教材。这套教材共分为六册，分别对应西方英语国家小学一至六年级的语文教学。这套书出版后，在西方英语国家的学校被广泛使用。根据这套书原编者的初衷，是为了引导孩子们对他们所阅读的作品产生真正的兴趣，并通过阅读提升他们的能力，最终将阅读所获得的能力运用到生活实践中去。可以说，这是一套以兴趣为引导、学以致用的教材。

这套书的编写体例非常严谨，一至四册教材的每篇文章后面基本都有课后提问、拼读训练、书写练习等内容，从第五册开始，又增加了单词解释，使学生通过阅读增加词汇量，进一步巩固和加深对文章的印象。

在选文内容上，这套书由浅入深，每一册对应不同年龄段的读者，选文也从简单的儿歌、短文、常用句型开始，逐渐提升为篇幅稍长的作品，再进阶到中长篇的经典著作。从难易程度来看，这套书前三册内容简单浅显，文字朴素简洁，比较适合国内中低年级小学生阅读；后三部分的内容相对繁复深奥，开始有侧重性，有的笔法精妙、描写细腻，有的文风犀利、寓意深刻，比较适合高年级小学生和中学生阅读。总之，这套书的选文内容丰富，从其所选文章涉及的体裁来看，包括了故事、童话、传记、诗歌等；题材涉及旅游、历险、历史、自然、科学等。这些选文体现了英国丰富的历史文化知识和西方国家的道德价值观念，让小读者们在提高文学修养的同时，也可以开阔自己的视野。

这套书的最大特色在于它所包含的内容非常贴近生活，能让小读者们觉得书中讲述的事情就发生在他们身边。而且，这套书所选的文章除了颂扬真、善、美之外，并没有回避生活中的艰难与困苦，突出了困境之下个人的坚守与成长。这样的文章往往更容易引起心灵的共鸣，也将对小读者们的人生观起到正面积极的作用。

我们衷心希望通过这套书的出版，让中国的读者朋友学习地道标准的英语，打开通往世界的心灵之窗；同时还能获得文学知识、个人修养、伦理道德等多方面的提升。

如果您在阅读中发现有疑问或错误之处，请不吝指正，以便我们更加完善这套书的编写。

目录
Contents

Lesson 1 A PERILOUS ADVENTURE

第一课 千钧一发的冒险

Three or four lads are standing in the channel below the great Natural Bridge of Virginia. They see hundreds of names carved in the limestone buttresses, and resolve to add theirs to the number. This done, one of them is seized with the mad ambition of carving his name higher than the highest there! His companions try to dissuade him from attempting so dangerous a feat, but in vain. He is a wild, reckless youth; and afraid now to yield, lest he should be thought a coward, he carves his way up and up the limestone rock, till he can hear the voices, but not the Words of his terror-stricken playmates.

One of them runs off to the village, and tells the boy's father of his perilous situation. Others go for help in other directions; and ere long there are hundreds of people standing in the rocky channel below, and hundreds on the bridge above, all holding their breath, and awaiting the fearful catastrophe. The poor boy can just distinguish the tones of his father, who is shouting with all the energy of despair,—"William! William! don't look down! Your mother, and Henry, and Harriet are all here praying for you! Don't look down! Keep your eyes towards the top!"

The boy does not look down. His eye is fixed towards heaven, and his young heart on Him who reigns there. He grasps again his knife. He cuts another niche, and another foot is added to the hundreds that remove him from the reach of human help from below.

The sun is half way down in the west. Men are leaning over the outer edge of the bridge with ropes in their hands. But fifty more niches must be cut before the longest rope can reach the boy! Two minutes more, and all will be over. That blade is worn to the last half inch. The boy's head reels. His last hope is dying in his heart, his life must hang upon the next niche he cuts. That niche will be his last.

At the last cut he makes, his knife—his faithful knife—drops from his little nerveless hand, and ringing down the precipice, falls at his mother's feet! An involuntary groan of despair runs through the crowd below, and all is still as the grave. At the height of nearly three hundred feet, the devoted boy lifts his hopeless heart and closing eyes to commend his soul to God.

Hark!—a shout falls on his ears from above! A man who is lying with half his length over the bridge, has caught a glimpse of the boy's head and shoulders. Quick as thought the noosed rope is within reach of the sinking youth. No one breathes. With a faint, convulsive effort, the swooning boy drops his arm into the noose.

Not a lip moves while he is dangling over that fearful abyss; but when a sturdy arm reaches down and draws up the lad, and holds him up before the tearful, breathless multitude—such shouting and such leaping and weeping for joy never greeted a human being so recovered from the jaws of death.

Words

ambition, *aspiration.*
attempting, *undertaking.*
buttresses, *supports.*
catastrophe, *event.*
commend, *commit.*
convulsive, *agitated.*
dangerous, *perilous.*
despair, *hopelessness.*
dissuade, *discourage.*
dying, *expiring.*
energy, *vehemence.*
glimpse, *glance.*
greeted, *welcomed.*
involuntary, *unintentional.*
leaning, *stretching.*
multitude, *crowd.*
nerveless, *feeble.*
precipice, *cliff.*
reckless, *rash.*
resolve, *determine.*
seized, *inspired.*
swooning, *fainting.*

Questions

What did the boys see on the limestone rocks? What did they resolve to do? What did one of them propose? Who came to witness his dangerous position? In what did his chance of safety lie? How was he at last saved?

☆ ☆

三四个小伙子站在宏伟的弗吉尼亚自然大桥的桥洞下。他们看到桥墩的石头上刻着许多人名，便决定要把自己的名字也加进去。刻完后，其中一个小伙子心里一直有个疯狂的想法，他想把自己的名字刻得比别人的都高！他的朋友劝解他放弃这样危险的行为，但一点用也没有。他是个桀骜不驯又无所顾忌的年轻人；他怕自己要是现在放弃了，人家就会把他看成是懦夫，于是他决定要一直攀爬上桥墩的石头上，直到听到人们的欢呼声为止，而不是听从他那群胆小的朋友的劝阻。

他其中一位朋友跑到村里头，把他危险的处境告诉了他父亲。剩下的人则四处寻求帮助，不一会儿工夫，就来了上百个人聚集在桥洞下，还有的挤在桥上，屏住呼吸，来观看那惊心动魄的一幕。这可怜的孩子一下子就辨认出了他父亲的声音，他父亲正声嘶力竭地喊着：“威廉！威廉！别往下看！你妈妈、亨利，还有哈利亚特都在为你祈祷呢！别往下看！眼睛往上看！”

男孩没有往下看。他的眼睛紧盯着天空的方向，年轻的心一心想着上帝是那里的主宰。他再一次抓起刀子，又刻下一笔，又攀爬了一步，他本来已经离着地面几百英尺，这样地面上的人们就更加难以帮他了。

太阳已经快要下山了。人们把身子探出桥，手里抓着绳子。但在那最长的绳子能够得到这男孩之前，他还得再刻上五十刀！再过两分钟，一切就结束了！那刀子已经被磨损得只剩下半寸的样子了，而男孩子开始头昏目眩起来。他最后的希望就是即使死去也要完成自己的心愿，而他的生命就完全系在他要刻的下一笔了。那一笔将是他的最后一笔。

当最后一笔刻完的时候，他的刀——他那恪尽职守的刀子——从他那已经毫无感觉的手中掉落了下来，一路滚落下峭壁，落在了他母亲的脚边！油然而生的绝望情绪马上在下面的人群中蔓延开来，但所有人都鸦雀无声，一动不动。在三百英尺的高度，那热忱投入的男孩已经绝望的心升华了起来，他闭上眼睛等待着上帝的召唤。

啊！——一声喊叫从头顶传来！有个人把身子横亘在桥上，抓住了男孩的头和肩膀。说时迟那时快，那带套索的绳子一下子就够到了往下坠的男孩。大家都屏住呼吸。昏昏沉沉的男孩使出吃奶的力气，把胳膊套进了绳套里。

他惊心动魄地悬吊在半空的时候，没有人发出声响；但当用稳稳的手臂托住那孩子，拽他上桥，把他送到满含热泪、屏住呼吸的人群面前的时候——人们爆发出前所未有的欢呼雀跃声和喜极而泣的声音，他们为从死神手中夺回一个毫发无损的生命而喜极而泣。

Lesson 2
THE DESTRUCTION OF SENNACHERIB'S ARMY
第二课 亚述王军队的陨灭

The Assyrian came down like the wolf on the fold,
And his cohorts were gleaming with purple and gold.
And the sheen of their spears was like stars on the sea,
When the blue waves roll nightly on deep Galilee.

Like the leaves of the forest when summer is green,
That host with their banners at sunset were seen;
Like the leaves of the forest when autumn hath blown,
That host on the morrow lay withered and strown.

For the Angel of Death spread his wings on the blast,
And breathed in the face of the foe as he passed;
And the eyes of the sleepers waxed deadly and chill,
And their hearts but once heaved, and for ever were still.

And there lay the steed with his nostrils all wide,
But through them there rolled not the breath of his pride
And the foam of his gasping lay white on the turf,
And cold as the spray of the rock-beating surf.

And there lay the rider, distorted and pale,
With the dew on his brow and the rust on his mail
And the tents were all silent, the banners alone,
The lances unlifted, the trumpets unblown.

And the widows of Asshur are loud in their wail;
And the idols arc broke in the temple of Baal;
And the might of the Gentile, unsmote by the sword,
Hath melted like snow in the glance of the Lord!

—Lord Byron (1788−1824)

Words

banners, *standards.*
distorted, *deformed.*
gasping, *panting.*
gleaming, *sparkling.*
sheen, *brightness.*
silent, *noiseless.*
wail, *lamentation.*
waxed, *became.*
withered, *faded.*

☆ ☆

如野狼一样，亚述人从荒原席卷而来，
他们的队列闪烁着紫色和金色。
戟矛闪亮，如同海上的繁星，
似蓝色的波浪在夜晚向深邃的加利利湖席卷。

如翠绿的盛夏时分树林里的绿叶，
暮色沉沉，军队将领和他们的条幅依稀可见；
像深秋时节树林里的叶子，
朝露振振，军队铩羽，英气不复。

死亡之神，振动羽翼滑翔而过，
把死亡的气息吹拂到其所到之地；
沉睡的人儿双目紧闭，如蜡像一般一动不动，身体冰冷，
他们曾经搏动的心脏永远停止了跳动。

骏马倒地，大张着鼻孔，
它喘息的不再是往日的荣耀，
那曾经的喘息只留下嘴边挂着白沫，
它已经冰冷地躺在了砾石丛生的草原。

还有那马背上的人也躺在了地上，身体扭曲，脸色苍白，
眉心沁汗，信件斑驳，
营地死寂一片，只剩下那独自飘曳的条幅，

无人投掷的长矛，还有那不再吹响的号角。

从亚述人的窗边经过，能听到他们的号啕声动天；
太阳神庙里的神像被捣毁；
那利刃也丝毫触动不得加利利人的权威，
好像被上帝看了一眼的积雪一样，融化不再！

——拜伦勋爵（1788—1824）

Lesson 3 "ABOVE THE CLOUDS"

第三课 在云端

In 1856 an attempt was made, under the auspices of the British Government, to commence a series of observations in some region "above the clouds," where the serene and quiet air would be specially favourable for viewing the heavenly bodies. The island of Teneriffe was selected for this purpose, as combining more of the required advantages than any other mountain within easy reach of Europe.

The expedition was under the direction of Piazzi Smyth, the distinguished astronomer at Edinburgh; who, in a remarkable and interesting work, has since published a narrative of the expedition. In an article contributed to a popular magazine he thus graphically describes the ascent of Teneriffe to a point high "above the clouds:"—

It was only a few days after—on a morning also cloudy, and with north-east cloud too—that the little party set forth from the town of Orotava, on the northern coast of Teneriffe, to climb the great mountain, and put to the only true test of actual practice their hopes of getting "above the clouds." Through long, winding, stony pathways, between vineyards and cactus plantations, between orange groves and fig-trees, they proceeded, always ascending; past gardens, and then past orchards, still ever ascending; past corn-fields and oat-fields, ascending yet higher, and then amongst natural vegetation only—ferns and heath and some few wild laurels; and now, at a height of 3000 feet vertical, they are close under the cloud.

Before entering therein, let us pause for a moment and survey the beauties of creation in the region we are leaving behind. If, for that one purpose of severe astronomy, a position below the clouds is unsuitable, yet what an infinite amount of benefit for man to enjoy, and of beauty for him to contemplate, is connected therewith! Beneath the clouds are kindly rains and gentle dews; and these, assisted by a warm climate, encourage all those exquisite forms of vegetation which we have admired clothing the lower slopes of the mountain. Without these, where were the fruits to support human life; where the buds and blossoms and fading flowers which teach us many a lesson useful to life eternal?

But duty now calls us on our upward way. Before many more seconds are passed, first comes one cold hurrying blast, with mist upon its wings, and then another, and another. Then, in the midst of a constant dense wet fog, all creation is shut out of our view, except the few feet of sloping earth on which we are treading, and that appears of a dull gray; and the occasional spiders' webs seen across our path are loaded with heavy drops of moisture.

For half an hour we must toil on and on through this winding-sheet of gloom; perpetually on the same upward way, but strong in faith and hope of what must in the end be presented to our eyes; on still, and up higher, when suddenly a momentary break appears overhead, and a portion of sky is seen—oh, so blue!—but it is lost again.

In a few minutes, however, another opening, another blue patch is seen; and then another, and another. Before three minutes more are passed, all the hurrying clouds seem blown on one side. Fair sky is everywhere above and around, a brilliant sun is shining, and there, there below us, is the upper surface of the clouds, extending far and wide, like a level plain, shutting out lowland and city and sea all from view, and in their place substituting brilliant reflections of solar light, which make the surface of this new mist-country look winter than snow! Yes, indeed, we are now "above the clouds;" and this view that we have attempted to describe is the first example of the heightened, the advanced, the glorified appearance of even Earth's sombre fog-banks to those who are privileged for a time to look on them from the heavenward side.

"Above the clouds!"—not only no rain, no mist, no dew, but a scorching sun, and an air, both by day and by night, dry to almost an alarming degree. The further we advance, and the higher we ascend, the drier becomes the air; while at the same time the strength of the north-east trade-wind is continually decreasing, and at the height of about six or seven thousand feet has completely died away.

Not that it has ceased elsewhere as well, for the driving clouds below show that it is still in its accustomed violence there. The distant movements of those rollers of white cloud betray that it must yet be raging down there in all its strength, tearing the mist piecemeal, and bowing down the heads of suffering palm-trees, and lashing the sea into foam-crested waves. Heaven grant that no cry of shipwrecked mariners be borne on the breeze; and, more still, that no evil thoughts be engendering in the cities of men.

It was when our party on the mountain were in the fullest enjoyment of their daily and nightly views of the heavens, that their friends in the towns of Teneriffe near the sea-coast wrote to them most sympathizingly:

"Oh! what dreadful weather you must have been suffering! Down here we have had for three weeks the most frightful continuance of storms—constant clouds, rain, and howling winds; and if that was the case with us, what must it not have been with you at the greater height!"

Yet at the greater height, at that very time, the air was tranquil and serene, the sky clear, and bad weather entirely confined to that lower depth in the atmosphere beneath "the grosser clouds."

Words

accustomed, *usual.*

actual, *real.*

alarming, *disquieting*.
ascending, *mounting*.
auspices, *patronage*.
brilliant, *gorgeous*.
commence, *begin*.
completely, *entirely*.
confined, *limited*.
contemplate, *consider*.
continuance, *succession*.
decreasing, *diminishing*.
distinguished, *eminent*.
dreadful, *terrible*.
engendering, *growing*.
expedition, *enterprise*.
exquisite, *dedicate*.
graphically, *forcibly*.
heightened, *elevated*.
hurrying, *fleeting*.
mariners, *seamen*.
momentary, *transient*.
narrative, *account*.
observations, *investigations*.
perpetually, *constantly*.
practice, *expedience*.
privileged, *permitted*.
region, *district*.
serene, *tranquil*.
severe, *accurate*.
substituting, *exchanging*.
survey, *examine*.
sympathizing, *compassionately*.
treading, *walking*.
unsuitable, *inconvenient*.
vegetation, *plant life*.
violence, *vehemence*.

Questions

What place was selected for the astronomical expedition of 1856? Who directed it? At what height was the party close under the cloud? What benefits arise to man from being beneath the clouds? How long was the party in piercing the cloud? What was the state of the sky above it? What was the appearance of the clouds from above? What was the state of the air as they ascended higher? What change did the trade-wind undergo? What showed that it had not ceased elsewhere? What was the state of the weather near the sea-coast? What, above the clouds?

☆ ☆

1856年，在英国政府的资助下，一个太空系列观测项目在部分地区展开。这些地区僻静而天气晴朗，对于观测空中的天体而言再好不过了。特纳利夫岛就是这部分地区中的一个，它得天独厚的条件要胜过所有能够容易到达的欧洲山地。

这次探险活动是在皮亚兹·史密斯的带领下进行的。史密斯是爱丁堡负有盛名的天文学家，他在一本备受追捧且生动有趣的书中，描写了此次探险活动。在一篇写给大众杂志的文章中，他如此形象地描述了特纳利夫山高耸“在云端”：

仅仅过了几天的时间——也是一个多云的早晨，云朵向东北方漂移——小分队从位于特纳利夫岛北海岸的斯特拉瓦出发，向着特纳利夫山攀登，以实现他们到达“云端”的梦想。他们走过那些又长又蜿蜒而且布满砾石的山路，跨过那些葡萄藤和仙人掌盘踞的荒原，又穿过橘子林和无花果树林，仍然向前行进，不停地登攀；他们又过了几个花园，穿过了几个农场，仍然继续前行；接着又过了几片玉米田和麦田，他们攀登得更高，到达了只有原始植被——蕨类、石楠和一些野生月桂树的地方；而现在，在海拔3 000英尺的地方，他们离着云端只有几步之遥了。

在到达前，我们先停下来看看那些生长在我们走过的路途中的美丽生物吧。因为，如果只是为了严肃的天文学的话，攀爬到云端下的地方实在是不值得，但如果能把一路上所闻所见的美丽事物都冥想一番，那该是怎样的一种美妙境界啊！云端下是温和的雨露；它们在温暖的气候下，给所有多姿多彩的植物提供了生长条件，而那些植物，我们多希望它们能点缀海拔低的山坡啊！没有它们的话，哪里有滋养我们的鲜果，哪里有让我们见证花朵从盛开再到花瓣凋零的机会，从而明白了人生的许多道理。

但我们现在肩负重任，必须向前。又过了许多时候，我们先是到了一处荒芜的寒冷之地，迷雾萦绕其间，然后又过了一处，再过一处。之后，在久久不散的潮湿的浓雾中，一切生物都从我们视野中消失不见了，只有脚下的几英尺陡峭的土地发出毫无生机的灰白色，偶尔能看到几处蛛网横结在路上，上面净是水坑。

我们必须继续跋涉，穿越着蜿蜒的晦暗，一直走上半个钟头；我们永远在同样的路上向上攀登，而内心保持着最后会看见美景的强烈信念和希望；然后继续前行，攀登得更高，直到突然头顶出现了一瞬间的闪亮，露出天空的一角——噢，如此湛蓝的天啊！——但不久又看不到了。

不过，过了几分钟，又看到了天空一角，看到那湛蓝的一角；再过几分钟，又看到一处。不出三分钟的时间，所有那些行迹匆匆的流云都被吹拂到一边了。清澈的天空随处可见，呈现在头顶和周围，明亮的太阳在闪耀着，而就在那里，就在我们站立的地方，已经到了云端，它向外无限延展着，取代了那太阳光的明亮的倒影，让这迷雾萦绕的地方更像冬季的雪天！是的，没错，我们现在已经“在云端”了；而我们希望描述的这个场景，是对晦暗的、烟雾萦绕之地的升华的、提升的、光辉的场景的首次描述，把这样的景象描述给曾经有幸仰视过它们的人们听。

“在云端”！这里没有雨水，没有雾气，没有朝露，有的只是灼人的太阳和干燥到几乎令人惊异的空气，昼夜环绕在那里。我们越往前走，越往高处攀登，就发现空气变得越干燥；同时北风的强度也在减小，到海拔六七千英尺的高度，几乎就没什么风了。

这并不是说风停了，因为从下面风卷残云的景象看来，它依然强劲。远处云朵的卷动表明在低处，风一定是在用尽全力呼啸，在迷雾中间撕开口子，让那忍受强风吹拂的棕榈树低下了头，这风还拍打着大海，卷起一波波白沫冠顶的波浪。上天为证，已经葬身海底的、见识到这劲风的船员绝对不会发出哭嚎，而在这里生活的人们心中也没有邪恶的念头。

当我们在山上满心欢喜地庆贺白天和夜晚看到的天空的美景的时候，那生活在海岸边的特纳利夫城的朋友，用最同情的口吻写了一封信：

“哦！你们该遭受了怎样恶劣天气啊！在山下，我们一连经历了三个星期的暴风雪，可怕极了——乌云不散，雨水连连，还有呼啸的风一直吹个不停；如果我们这里都是这样的话，那你们在高处该是怎样一副光景啊！”

但在高处，就在那一刻，气氛静谧而宁和，天空清澈，坏天气完全是在低处缠绵，在那“更潮湿的云朵”之下。

Lesson 4 THE CONDOR OF THE ANDES

第四课 安第斯山脉的秃鹫

In those sterile heights Nature withholds her fostering influence alike from vegetable and from animal life. The scantiest vegetation can scarcely draw nutriment from the ungenial soil, and animals shun the dreary and shelterless wilds. The condor, or South American vulture, alone finds itself in its native element amidst these mountain deserts. On the inaccessible summits of the Cordillera, and at an elevation of from 10,000 to 15,000 feet, this bird builds its nest, and hatches its young in the months of April and May.

Few animals have attained so wide a celebrity as the condor. This bird was known in Europe at a period when its native land was numbered among those fabulous regions which are regarded as the scenes of imaginary wonders. The most extravagant accounts of the condor were written and read; and general credence was granted to every story which travellers brought from the fairy-land of gold and silver. It was only at the commencement of the present century that Humboldt overthrew the extravagant notions that had previously prevailed respecting the size, strength, and habits of this extraordinary bird.

The full-grown condor measures, from the point of the beak to the end of the tail, from four feet ten inches to five feet; and from the tip of one wing to that of the other, from twelve to fourteen feet! This bird feeds chiefly upon carrion; it is only when impelled by hunger that it seizes living animals, and even then only the small and defenceless, such as the young of sheep, vicunas, and llamas.

It cannot raise great weights with its feet; which, however, it uses to aid the power of its beak. The principal strength of the condor lies in its neck and in its feet; yet it cannot, when flying, carry a weight exceeding eight or ten pounds. All accounts of sheep and calves being carried off by condors are mere exaggerations.

The bird passes a great part of the day in sleep,

and hovers in quest of prey chiefly in the morning and evening. Whilst soaring at a height beyond the reach of human eyes, the sharp-sighted condor discerns its prey on the level heights beneath it, and darts down upon it with the swiftness of lightning. When a bait is laid, it is curious to observe the number of condors which assemble in a quarter of an hour in a spot near which not one had been previously visible. These birds possess the senses of sight and smell in a singularly powerful degree.

Some old travellers have affirmed that the plumage of the condor cannot be pierced by a musket ball. This absurdity is scarcely worthy of contradiction; but it is nevertheless true that the bird has a singular tenacity of life, and that it is seldom killed by fire-arms, unless when shot in some vital part.

Its plumage, particularly on the wings, is very strong and thick. The natives, therefore, seldom attempt to shoot the condor. They usually catch it by traps or by the lasso, or kill it by stones flung from slings, or by the bolas.

A curious method of capturing the condor alive is practised in one province. A fresh cow-hide, with some fragments of flesh adhering to it, is spread out on one of the level heights, and an Indian provided with ropes creeps beneath it, whilst some others station themselves in ambush near the spot ready to assist him. Presently a condor, attracted by the smell of the flesh, darts down upon the cow-hide; and then the Indian, who is concealed under it, seizes the bird by the legs, and binds them fast in the skin, as if in a bag. The captured condor flaps its wings, and makes ineffectual attempts to fly, but is speedily secured, and carried in triumph to the nearest village. Live condors are frequently sold in the markets of Chili and Peru, where a very fine one may be purchased for a dollar and a half.

—DR. J. VON TSCHUDI: *Travels in Peru*.

Words

absurdity, *nonsense*.
affirmed, *asserted*.
ambush, *conceal ment*.
assemble, *collect*.
capturing, *seizing*.
celebrity, *distinction*.
commencement, *beginning*.
defenseless, *unprotected*.
discerns, *descries*.
exceeding, *surpassing*.
extraordinary, *wonderful*.
extravagant, *exaggerated*.
fabulous, *legendary*.
fostering, *nourishing*.
frequently, *often*.
impelled, *driven*.
inaccessible, *unapproachable*.
ineffectual, *fruitless*.
particularly, *especially*.
purchased, *bought*.
sharp sighted, *keen eyed*.
singularly, *peculiarly*.
soaring, *flying*.
sterile, *barren*.
summits, *peaks*.
tenacity, *retentiveness*.
triumph, *exultation*.
ungenial, *unfavourable*.

Questions

What other name is given to the condor? Where does it build its nest? What accounts were current before the ‘present’ (i.e. 19th) century? Who overthrew these? What are the dimensions of a full-grown condor? On what does it chiefly feed? Where does its principal strength lie? When does it go in quest of prey? What shows the keenness of its sight and smell? Why do the natives seldom attempt to shoot the condor? How do they kill it? What curious method of capturing it is practised in one province? For what may a live condor sometimes be bought?

☆ ☆

大自然在贫瘠的高海拔地区对其泽养万物的能力做了公正的保留，对植物如此，对动物也一样。零星分布的植物勉强从贫瘠的土地中汲取养分，动物们则对这样荒凉而毫无遮掩的地方避之不及。秃鹫，或者叫南美洲秃鹰，独自生活在这些山区的沙漠上，这里就是它的原生带。在无法企及的科迪勒拉山脉的高峰上，在海拔1万到1.5万英尺的高处，秃鹫在那里筑巢，在4月和5月孵化幼鸟。

几乎没有什么动物像秃鹫一样有名。它曾在欧洲风靡一时，因为它的故乡是想象中一个颇为神秘的国度。人们写了很多描述秃鹫的华丽夸张的辞藻，这些辞藻又传播开来；而人们普遍相信那些远行者从神奇的土地上带回金银的故事。仅仅到了20世纪之初的时候，洪堡才推翻了那些之前流行于人们中间的关于这非凡鸟儿的身形、力量和习性的夸张描述。

成年秃鹫，喙尖到尾端的长度从4英尺10英寸到5英尺不等，而从其一翼的一端到另一翼的一端的宽度则有12到14英尺！秃鹫大多食腐肉，只有在饥饿难耐的情况下，它才会捕捉活的动物，不过即使是那样，它捕捉的也只是些身形娇小、没有反抗能力的动物，比如小山羊、小羊驼和小美洲驼。

秃鹫的脚爪抓不起大重量的动物，因此，它会用喙的力量来协助。秃鹫的主要力量在它的颈部和脚爪上，但飞翔的时候，它不能携带重量超过八磅或十磅的东西。那些秃鹫掠去羊牛的说法都不过是夸张的传言罢了。

白天大部分时候，秃鹫都在睡觉，而清晨和傍晚则是它盘旋空中捕捉猎物的主要时机。秃鹫在人眼难以看到的高度飞翔，用锐利的眼睛观察地上的猎物，然后以迅雷不及掩耳之势一个俯冲下去抓住猎物。当腐肉出现的时候，从来不会只出现过一只秃鹫，而是不出十几分钟就会有一群的秃鹫聚集而来，这是非常有趣的现象。这些鸟儿的视觉和嗅觉都非常厉害。

某些有经验的远行者说，秃鹫的羽毛火枪也打不烂。这样荒谬的说法不值得辩驳，但无论如何，秃鹫的生命力顽强却是不争的事实，它很少会被火枪射杀，除非是被击中了致命的部位。

它的羽毛，特别是翅膀部分的羽毛，又坚硬又厚实。土著人因此几乎不会狩猎秃鹫。他们通常是设下陷阱或用套索来擒得它们，或者用石头砸死，或是用绳索勒死它们。

在某个地方，有一个生擒秃鹫的有趣方法。新剥下的小牛皮，上头粘连着新鲜牛肉的香味，被平铺在一个较高的架子上，有个手里拿绳子的印第安人埋伏在下面，同时，他的帮手也埋伏在附近。秃鹫被肉的味道所吸引，就俯冲向牛皮；然后藏在牛皮下头的印第安人就抓住秃鹫的腿，牢牢地捆住它，就像给袋子扎口一样。被擒得的秃鹫挥动翅膀，梦想要飞走，但总是徒劳，人们马上就把它捉住了，然后胜利昂扬地把它抬到最近的村子。活的秃鹫经常在智利和秘鲁的市场上被贩卖，在那里，一只上好的秃鹫可能会卖上一点五美金。

——J. 冯 · 茨舒狄博士 :《秘鲁游记》

Lesson 5 THE PRAIRIE ON FIRE (I)

第五课 大草原失火记（一）

[The prairies.—Between the Mississippi and the Rocky Mountains there is a vast extent of grassy plains called *Prairies*. The soil is fertile and the vegetation luxuriant; and before their occupation by the white man the tall grass waved in the wind over the wide expanse, resembling the rolling of an emerald ocean. These plains furnished food for countless herds of buffaloes, elks, antelopes, and other animals that feed on herbage. They moved continually to and fro in vast masses, as the seasons changed and the state of the pasture drove them to new fields.

Different regions of the prairies had different characters. The wide undulating plains, frequented by buffaloes and covered with grass, were called *Rolling Prairies*, from their general resemblance to the long, heavy swell of the ocean, when subsiding after a storm; and *Dry Prairies*, because they were generally destitute of water. These were the most common and extensive.

Other regions abounded in springs, and were covered with shrubs and bushes. These were called *Bushy Prairies*.

Lastly, there were the *Alluvial* or *Wet Prairies*, which wore covered with rich verdure and gorgeous flowers, and which in the rainy season were frequently overflowed.

Sometimes a prairie was set on fire, either accidentally or by design. Such a prairie on fire was one of the most terrible things in nature. The ocean of flame rolled onward and onward before the wind, with irresistible might, devouring everything that lay in its path. Droves of wild horses, buffaloes, antelopes, rushed madly before the advancing flames, beasts of prey forgetting their enmities in the midst of the common danger. Crowds of vultures and other birds of prey followed the course of the fire, and seized upon the carcasses which the flames had not completely consumed.]

The sleep of the fugitives lasted for several hours. The trapper was the first to shake off its influence, as he had been the last to court its refreshment. Rising just as the gray light of day began to brighten that portion of the studded vault which rested on the eastern margin of the plain, he summoned his companions from their warm lairs, and pointed out the necessity of their being once more on the alert.

"See, Middleton! exclaimed Inez, in a sudden burst of youthful pleasure, that caused her for a moment to forget her situation, how lovely is that sky; surely it contains a promise of happier times!"

"It is glorious!" returned her husband. "Glorious and heavenly is that streak of vivid red; and here is a still brighter crimson. Rarely have I seen a richer rising of the sun."

"Rising of the sun!" slowly repeated the old man, lifting his tall person from his seat with a deliberate and abstracted air, while he kept his eye riveted on the changing and certainly beautiful tints that were garnishing the vault of heaven. "Rising of the sun!—I like not such risings of the sun. Ah's me! the Indians have circumvented us. The prairie is on fire!"

A PRAIRIE ON FIRE

"Oh, dreadful!" cried Middleton, catching Inez to his bosom, under the instant impression of the imminence of their danger. " There is no time to lose, old man; each instant is a day. Let us fly!

"Whither?" demanded the trapper, motioning him, with calmness and dignity, to arrest his steps. "In this wilderness of grass and reeds, we are like a vessel in the broad lakes without a compass. A single step on the wrong course might prove the destruction of us all. It is seldom danger is so pressing that there is not time enough for reason to do its work, young officer; therefore let us await its biddings."

"For my part," said Paul Hover, looking about him with an unequivocal expression of concern, "I acknowledge that should this dry bed of weeds get fairly into flame, a bee would have to make a flight higher than common, to prevent his wings from being scorched. Therefore, old trapper, I agree with the captain, and say, Mount and run!"

"Ye are wrong—ye are wrong;—man is not a beast, to follow the gift of instinct, and to snuff up his knowledge by a taint in the air or a rumbling in the ground; but he must see, and reason, and then conclude. So, follow me a little to the left, where there is a rising in the ground whence we may make our reconnoitering."

The old man waved his hand with authority, and led the way, without further parlance, to the spot he had indicated, followed by the whole of his alarmed companions. An eye less practised than that of the trapper might have failed in discovering the gentle elevation to which he alluded, and which looked on the surface of the meadow like a growth a little taller than common.

When they reached the place, however, the stunted grass itself announced the absence of that moisture which had fed the rank weeds of most of the plain, and furnished a clew to the evidence by which he had judged of the formation of the ground hidden beneath. Here a few minutes were lost in breaking down the tops of the surrounding herbage—which, notwithstanding the advantage of their position, rose even above the heads of Middleton and Paul—and in obtaining a look-out that might command a view of the surrounding sea of fire.

The examination which his companions so instantly and so intently made, rather served to assure them of their desperate situation than to appease their fears. Huge columns of smoke were rolling up from the plain, and thickening in gloomy masses around the horizon. The red glow which gleamed upon their enormous folds, now lighted their volumes with the glare of the conflagration, now flashed to another point, as the flame beneath glided ahead, leaving all behind enveloped in awful darkness, and proclaiming louder than words the character of the imminent and rapidly approaching danger.

"This is terrible!" exclaimed Middleton, folding the trembling Inez to his heart. "At such a time as this, and in such a manner!"

"The gates of heaven are open to all who truly believe," murmured the gentle wife.

"This resignation is maddening! But we are men, and will make a struggle for our lives!—How now, my brave and spirited friend;—shall we yet mount and push across the flames; or shall we stand here, and see those we most love perish in this frightful manner without an effort?"

"I am for a swarming-time and a flight before the hive is too hot to hold us," said the bee hunter, to whom it will be at once seen that the half-distracted Middleton had addressed himself.—"Come, old trapper, you must acknowledge this is but a slow way of getting out of danger. If we tarry here much longer, it will be in the fashion that the bees lie round the straw after the hive has been smoked for its honey. You may hear the fire begin to roar already; and I know by experience that when the flame once gets fairly into the prairie grass, he is no sloth that can outrun it."

"Think you," returned the old man, pointing scornfully at the mazes of the dry and matted grass which environed them, "that mortal feet can outstrip the speed of fire on such a path?"

"What say you, friend doctor?" cried the bewildered Paul, turning to the naturalist with that sort of helplessness with which the strong are often apt to seek aid of the weak, when human power is baffled by the hand of a mightier Being;—"what say you? Have you no advice to give away in a case of life and death?"

The naturalist stood, tablets in hand, looking at the awful spectacle with as much composure as though the conflagration had been lighted in order to solve the difficulties of some scientific problem. Aroused by the question of his companion, he turned to his equally calm though differently occupied associate, the trapper, demanding with the most provoking insensibility to the urgent nature of their situation—"Venerable hunter, you have often witnessed similar prismatic experiments—"

He was rudely interrupted by Paul, who struck the tablets from his hand with a violence that betrayed the utter intellectual confusion which had overset his equanimity.

Words

abstracted, *absent.*
acknowledge, *admit.*
advantage, *superiority.*
alluded, *referred.*
appease, *allay.*
brighten, *illumine.*
carcasses, *dead bodies.*
clew (or clue), *guide.*
conflagration, *burning.*
deliberate, *calm.*
demanded, *asked.*
desperate, *forlorn.*
destruction, *ruin.*
devouring, *consuming.*
elevation, *rising.*
emerald, *green.*
contours *prodigious.*
environed, *surrounded.*
exclaimed, *shouted.*
experience, *personal proof.*
fashion, *manner.*
frightful, *terrible.*
furnished, *afforded.*
garnishing, *adorning.*
imminence, *neatness.*
influence, *power.*
insensibility, *indifference.*
intently, *eagerly.*
luxuriant, *exuberant.*
margin, *border.*
necessity, *urgency.*
prairies, *meadows.*
reconnoitering, *examinations.*
refreshment, *comfort.*
resemblance, *likeness.*
resignation, *calmness.*
riveted, *fixed.*
scornfully, *reproachfully.*
spectacle, *sight.*
trembling, *quivering.*
undulating, *waving.*
unequivocal, *unmistakable.*
ordure, *greenness.*

Questions

For what did Inez and her husband mistake the red streak on the horizon? Who undeceived them? Whom did he suspect of firing the prairie? For what purpose? What did most of the travellers advise? Who opposed this? Where did he lead the party?

☆ ☆

【大草原——在密西西比河和落基山脉中间，有一片广袤的绿色平原，叫作大草原。那里土地肥沃，植物茂盛，在白人占领那里之前，高高的草在风中摇曳，遍布整个地区，就像一片翡翠般的海洋。这片平原地区为无数的水牛、麋鹿和羚羊以及其他的食草动物提供了食物。这些动物在这广袤的土地上，随着季节的轮转和草木的生长而不断迁徙，去往新的栖息地。

不同地区的大草原有各自特点。广大而连绵起伏的平原，经常被水牛占据，平原上面长满了绿草，这样的平原叫作滚动的大草原，因为在暴风雨之后，它们很像绵长而臃肿的大海的波浪；而干燥的大草原，则是得名于它们通常缺水。这样的大草原是最常见的，分布也最广泛。

还有的草原在春天大量出现，上面被灌木覆盖。这样的草原叫作灌木大草原。

最后，还有冲积大草原或者叫湿地大草原，它们上面长着茂盛的植物和美丽的花朵，而在雨季的时候，这些地方经常被过于繁茂的花朵占满。

有时候，大草原上会失火，这其中有的是意外，有的则是有意为之。大草原失火是自然界最可怕的景象之一。海洋一样的火焰在风的吹动下不断涌动，势不可挡，把出现在它面前的一切都吞噬掉。野马群、水牛群、羚羊群都疯了似的赶在大火到来前逃命。秃鹫和其他的猎食鸟类则跟随着火的方向，伺机抓住那些没有被火完全烧掉的尸体。】

逃亡的人们已经睡了几个钟头了。布置陷阱的人是第一个从睡梦中醒来的，同时他也是最后一个进入梦乡的。天色刚刚泛白，照亮了那位于平原区东部边缘的土丘的时候，他就起身了，他把伙伴们从温暖的洞穴中叫了出来，告诉他们依然要保持警惕。

“看，米德尔顿！”恩兹叫道，她突然发出年轻人似的叫喊，这让她暂时忘记自己的处境，“天空是多么蓝啊，这肯定预示着好日子的到来啦！”

“太美了！”她丈夫回答道。天空中那一抹生动的红，是如此的美丽，如此美好，然后那红色变成了更加明亮的深红色。

“太阳升起来啦！”那老人慢慢重复道，他长长的身子从椅子里坐直了，带有一种庄重和心神不宁的神色，他的眼睛一直死盯着天穹处闪耀的美丽色彩的变幻。“太阳升起来了！我并不喜欢太阳以这样的方式升起。啊，天啊！咱们被印第安人包围了。大草原失火了！”

“哦，太可怕了！”米德尔顿喊道，在危险即将到来时，出于本能，他一把把恩兹拽到怀里。“没时间了，老人家，得争分夺秒了，咱们快逃吧！”

“去哪儿呢？”布置陷阱的人质问道，阻止住他的脚步，平静而不失尊严。”

“在这草木和芦苇丛生的荒野，我们就像失去指南针在大湖上航行的小船一样。只要走错一步就会是灭顶之灾。从没有什么危险紧急到没有时间用理智来思考的地步。所以，年轻的军官，让我们静观其变吧。”

“对于我而言，”保罗·哈维尔说道，他看着他脸上也带着同样的忧虑神色，

“我承认如果这些野草丛生的地方变成了火场，蜜蜂要想不灼伤自己的翅膀也得飞得比以前高才行。因此，年老的布置陷阱的人，我同意上尉的话，我觉得应该向山上逃！”

“你们错了，你们错了，人类不是兽类，只能跟着自己的本能行动，只能通过天色的变化或者地上的一点风吹草动获取；人类必须先观察，然后推理论证，再得出结论。所以，跟我向左边走吧，那里有一片突起的土地，我们可以在那儿做一下观测。”

老人很有威严地挥动了一下手，没有再说其他的话，就领着大家向他说的那个地方走去，所有装备了武器的同伴都跟随着他。要是没有像布陷阱的人那经验丰富的双眼，是很难发现那个不起眼的高地的，那高地从草原横着望过去，不过比平常的草原只高一点点。

然而等到他们到达的时候，发现那里草木矮小，也就是说缺乏水分，而水分都滋养草原大部分地区上的杂草了，同时这帮助他判断了这个地方隐藏在草木下的土地的情况。他们在这里花了几分钟的时间刨开周围的草木——这里位置优越，草木的高度能盖得过米德尔顿和保罗的头——能获取一个观测点来看看周围的火势。

他的同伴一瞬间发出的惊呼声是如此强烈，这叫声与其说能够安抚他们的恐惧情绪，倒不如说是提醒他们自己的处境是多么危急。巨大的烟柱从草原上滚滚而起，在地平线附近变得更加浓厚，形成灰暗的一大片。红色的火光照亮了滚滚烟尘，巨大的烟尘在大火的光亮下变得明显，火光渐盛，火焰匍匐向前，把一切都吞噬在黑暗当中，以无声胜有声之势头宣告着即将到来的危险。

“太可怕了！”米德尔顿喊道，他把瑟瑟发抖的恩兹往怀里抱得更紧了。“到了这样危急的时刻，这样一种吞噬一切的势头！”

“天堂的门对那些对它深信不疑的人们已经开启，”他温柔的妻子说道。

“这种下场实在是太疯狂了！但我们是人类，我们要为自己的生命搏斗一番！就现在吧，我勇敢的充满斗志的朋友，我们是要继续向前，穿过重重火焰呢，还是要坐以待毙，亲眼看着我们最爱的人被这可怕的大火不费吹灰之力地吞噬掉？”“我赞成大家赶紧逃走，趁着蜂巢还没热到容不下我们，”捕蜂人说道。接着心事重重的米德尔顿对他说道：“来吧，年老的布置陷阱的人，你必须得承认，这是一条从危险中缓慢逃生的道路。如果我们在这里耽搁太久，蜜蜂就会在蜂巢被烟熏之后飞到草丛边。你一定已经听到了大火的呼啸声，我从过往的经验知道，只要大火烧到了大草原上的草，一会儿它就能把所有草都烧成灰烬。”

“谢谢，”老人回答道，他轻蔑地指向他们周围的那干燥茂盛的草地，“人的双脚能赶得上大火一路烧去的速度吗？”

“你说呢，医生朋友？”不知所措的保罗叫道，他把头转向那位自然主义者，一脸的无助，那无助情绪经常是弱者从强者那里寻求帮助时，当人类的力量在一个更强大力量面前不知所措的时候才有的，“你怎么说？在这生死存亡的时刻，难道你就没有一点儿建议吗？”

自然主义者站立在那里，手里拿着药片，眼睛看着这可怕的景象，尽可能地保持淡定，好像大火是被点燃来解决什么科学难题似的。听到同伴的提问，他转身面向同样神色镇定，但做着其他营生的，例如布置陷阱的人，用最挑衅的麻木声音对他们当前的紧急处境质问道：“尊敬的猎人，你不是经常见到这样的原始的实验吗？”

他被保罗粗鲁地打断了，保罗把他手中的药片重重打落在地上，将这位因为有药在手而故作镇定的纯正知识分子的困惑暴露出来了。

Lesson 6 THE PRAIRIE ON FIRE (II)

第六课 大草原失火记（二）

Before time had been allowed for remonstrance, the old man, who had continued during the whole scene like one much at a loss how to proceed, though, also, like one who was rather perplexed than alarmed, suddenly assumed a decided air, as if he no longer doubted as to the course it was most advisable to pursue.

"It is time to be doing," he said, interrupting the controversy that was about to ensue between the naturalist and the bee hunter; "it is time to leave off books and moanings, and to be doing."

"You have come to your recollection too late, miserable old man!" cried Middleton. "The flames are within a quarter of a mile of us, and the wind is bringing them down in this direction with dreadful rapidity."

"Anan! the flames! I care but little for the flames! If I only knew how to circumvent the cunning of the Tetons as I know how to cheat the fire of its prey, there would be nothing needed but thanks to the Lord for our deliverance. Do you call that a fire! If you had seen what I have witnessed in the eastern hills, when mighty mountains were like the furnace of a smith, you would have known what it was to fear the flames, and to be thankful that you were spared.—Come, lads, come; 'tis time to be doing now, and to cease talking, for yonder curling flame is truly coming on like a trotting moose. Put hands upon this short and withered grass where we stand, and lay bare the earth."

"Would you think to deprive the fire of its victims in this childish manner?" exclaimed Middleton.

A faint but solemn smile passed over the features of the old man, as he answered, "Your grandfather would have said, that when the enemy was nigh, a soldier could do no better than obey."

The captain felt the reproof, and instantly began to imitate the industry of Paul, who was tearing the decayed herbage from the ground in a sort of desperate compliance with the trapper's direction. Even Ellen lent her hands to the labour; nor was it long before Inez was seen similarly employed, though none among them knew why. A very few moments sufficed to lay bare a spot of some twenty feet in diameter.

To one side of this little area the trapper brought the females, directing Middleton and Paul to cover their light and inflammable dresses with the blankets of the party. Then the old man, crossing to the other side, approached the grass, which still environed them in a dangerous circle, and selecting a handful of the driest of the herbage, he placed it over the pan of his rifle. The light combustible kindled at the flash. Then he placed the little flame in a bed of the standing fog, and patiently awaited the result.

The subtle element seized with avidity upon its new fuel, and in a moment forked flames were gliding among the grass, as the tongues of ruminating animals are seen rolling among their food, apparently in quest of its sweetest portions.

"Now," said the old man, holding up a finger, and laughing in his peculiarly silent manner, "you shall see fire fight fire. Ah's me! many is the time I have burned a path from wanton laziness to pick my way across a tangled bottom."

"But is this not fatal?" cried the amazed Middleton; "are you not bringing the enemy nigher to us, instead of avoiding it?"

"Do you scorch so easily? Your grandfather had a tougher skin. But we shall live to see,—we shall *all* live to see."

The experience of the trapper was in the right. As the fire gained strength, it began to spread on three sides, dying of itself on the fourth for want of aliment. As it increased, and the sullen roaring announced its power, it cleared everything before it, leaving the black and smoking soil far more naked than if the scythe had swept the place. The area in which the fugitives had taken refuge increased as the fire advanced; and by going to the spot where it had been first kindled by the trapper, they avoided the excessive heat. In a very few moments the flames began to recede in every direction, leaving the party enveloped in a cloud of smoke, but perfectly safe from the torrent of fire that was still furiously rolling onward.

The others regarded the simple expedient of the trapper with that species of wonder with which the courtiers of Ferdinand are said to have viewed the manner in which Columbus made his egg to stand on its end,—though with feelings that were filled with gratitude instead of envy.

"Most wonderful!" said Middleton, when he saw the complete success of the device: " the thought was a gift from Heaven."

"Old trapper," cried Paul, thrusting his fingers through his shaggy locks, " I have lined many a loaded bee into his hole, and know something of the nature of the woods, but this is robbing a hornet of his sting without touching the insect!"

"It will do—it will do," returned the old man, who, after the first moment of his success, seemed to think no more of the exploit. "Let the flames do their work for a short half hour, and then we will mount. That time is needed to cool the meadow; for these unshod beasts are tender on the hoof as a barefooted girl."

The veteran, on whose experience they all so implicitly relied for protection, employed himself in reconnoitering objects in the distance, through the openings which the air occasionally made in the immense bodies of smoke, that by this time lay in enormous piles on every part of the plain.

—J. FENIMORE COOPER

Words

aliment, *nourishment*.
apparently, *seemingly*.
avidity, *greediness*.
avoiding, *shunning*.
compliance, *obedience*.
controversy, *dispute*.
deliverance, *release*.
deprive, *cheat*.
device, *plan*.
employed, *occupied*.
enveloped, *enclosed*.
expedience, *contrivance*.
exploit, *achievement*.
features, *countenance*.
fugitives, *wanderers*.
gratitude, *thankfulness*.
implicitly, *confidently*.
inflammable, *combustible*.
occasionally, *sometimes*.
perplexed, *puzzled*.
rapidity, *celerity*.
recollection, *remembrance*.
remonstrance, *expostulation*.
reproof, *rebuke*.
returned, *answered*.
subtle, *wily*.
sullen, *dismal*.
tangled, *intricate*.
veteran, *old man*.
witnessed, *beheld*.

Questions

What did the trapper presently instruct his companions to do? How large a space did they clear? Where did the trapper place the females? What did the trapper do at the other side? What was the result? With what feelings did the others regard the trapper's device?

☆ ☆

已经没时间用来责备诘问了，那老人继续像那不知所措地强调前进的人一样，其实，也像一个与其说是被吓坏了，不如说是感到困惑的人一样，突然间打定了主意，好像不再怀疑接下来要走的路是最佳路线似的。

“是时候行动起来了，”他说到，打断了即将在自然主义者和捕蜂人之间产生的争论，“是时候甩开书本和抱怨，开始行动了。”

“你现在开窍得太晚了，可怜的老人家！”米德尔顿喊道。“大火离着咱们只有不到四分之一英里的距离了，而风把火向着我们这边吹着，速度惊人。”

“啊！大火！我一点儿都不关心大火！如果我知道如何把狡猾的提顿族人包围在中间，就像找知道如何能不让大火吞噬它眼前的猎物的话，那我们不需要做任何事情，只需要感谢上帝对我们的救赎就好了。你把这叫作大火！如果你曾经看见过我在东边山上曾见到的景象，那高山崇岭就像铁匠的火炉一样，你就会知道什么叫对大火的恐惧了，就会知道如何感恩自己逃过一劫了。来吧，孩子们，来吧，是时候行动起来了，不要再争辩了，因为那边卷动的火焰正向这边袭来，就像跑动着的麋鹿一样。动手拔光那些矮小枯萎的草吧，也就是我们站立的地方的草，然后躺在地上。”

“你觉得这样过家家的方式就能让我们躲过这个大劫吗？”米德尔顿喊道。

老人脸上掠过一丝淡淡的但威严的微笑，他答道，“你的祖父会说，当敌近在眼前，遵从命令是士兵最好的选择。”

上尉听出了话里的责备之音，于是马上开始学着保罗，以一种绝望的遵从，顺着布置陷阱的人指出的方向拔着地上的枯萎的草木。艾伦甚至也出力帮忙；不一会儿，恩兹也同样拔起草来，虽然他们没有人知道为什么要这么做。过了好一会儿，他们就有直径二十英尺的地方可以直接躺在地上了。

布置陷阱的人把女人带到这片小地方的一边，指导米德尔顿和保罗把轻盈而易燃的衣物覆盖到毯子上。然后这老人，走到另一边，走近那把他们包围进危险的圈子的草木中，选了一把干草，把它堵在来复枪的枪口上。轻盈的易燃物马上就着起了火。然后他把这小火堆放到了冒起的烟上，耐心等待结果。

柔软的火焰一遇到新燃料的加入就欢腾起来，不一会儿的工夫，火焰就在草丛中蔓延开来，就像在食物中打滚的反刍动物的舌头一样，很显然是在寻找着其中最美味的东西。

“现在，”老人说道，他举起一根手指，笑得奇怪而沉默，“你们即将看到火和火的搏斗。啊，我啊！有许多次我都从那火焰的慵懒中烧出一条纠结的路径。”

“但这样就没事了？”惊奇的米德尔顿叫道，“你这样不是把敌人带得离着我们更近了，而不是避免遇上它？”

“你怎么这么容易发出诘问！你的祖父性格更坚毅。但我们会活着见识到的，我们会活着见识到的。”

布置陷阱的人的经验是对的。当火势很足的时候，火开始时向三个方向弥散，为了获取更多的燃料，便会向第四个方向蔓延。当火势渐猛，那沉闷的吼叫声表明它的力量，它会把一切出现在自己面前的东西都吞噬掉，只留下漆黑的冒着烟的光秃秃的土地，那光秃程度要比镰刀割过之后更彻底。随着大火的到来，逃亡者们藏身之地的范围在变大；当火到达之前被布置陷阱的人点燃的地方的时候，他们躲避过了过高的热浪。不一会儿，每一个方向的火焰都开始减弱了，里头的人被包围在浓烟滚滚之中，但他们却非常安全，不会受到那无情的依然滚滚向前的火焰的吞噬了。

其他人把布置陷阱人的简单的权宜之计看成人类的又一奇迹，就好像菲尔迪南的追随者们说自己曾见过哥伦布让鸡蛋站立时的神情一样——尽管他们心中充满了感恩而不是嫉妒。

“太棒了！”米德尔顿说道，当他看到这个办法完全起了作用：“这简直是神来之笔。”

“年老的布置陷阱的人，”保罗叫道，他把手指从自己破破烂烂的衣兜里伸出来，“我曾经从蜂窝里捕过不少的蜜蜂，我了解树林的特点，但你这么做简直是把蜜蜂的毒刺从它身上摘掉却一点都不沾到蜜蜂身上！”

“成了——成了，”老人家回答道，他在自己成功之后似乎马上想到，不要再做什么了。“让大火再烧上半个钟头吧，然后我们再继续前进。草原需要时间冷却；赤脚的野兽在这样的热土地上用蹄子走路就像光脚走路的小姑娘一样柔弱。”

他们曾如此公开依赖的兽医，曾如此依靠他的经验来保命的兽医，则自顾自地观测着远处的动静，风偶尔从大片的烟堆的缺口吹出来，那大片大片的烟到此时已经遍布草原的各个角落。

——J. 费尼莫尔·库珀

Lesson 7 MARY, QUEEN OF SCOTS

第七课 苏格兰的玛丽女王

I looked far back into other years, and lo! in bright array
I saw, as in a dream, the forms of ages passed away.
It was a stately convent with its old and lofty walls,
And gardens with their broad green walks, where soft the footstep falls;
And o'er the antique dial-stone the creeping shadow passed,
And, all around, the noon-day sun a drowsy radiance cast.
No sound of busy life was heard, save from the cloister dim
The tinkling of the silver bell, or the sisters' holy hymn.
And there five noble maidens sat beneath the orchard trees,
In that first budding spring of youth when all its prospects please;
And little recked they, when they sang, or knelt at vesper prayers,
That Scotland knew no prouder names—held none more dear than theirs;—
And little even the loveliest thought, before the holy shrine,
Of royal blood and high descent from the ancient Stuart line:
Calmly her happy days flew on, uncounted in their flight;
And as they flow, they left behind a long-continuing light.

The scene was changed. It was the court, the gay court of Bourbon,
And 'neath a thousand silver lamps a thousand courtiers throng
And proudly kindles Henry's eye—well pleased, I ween, to see
The land assemble all its wealth of grace and chivalry:—
But fairer far than all the rest who bask on Fortune's tide,
Effulgent in the light of youth, is she, the new-made bride!
The homage of a thousand hearts—the fond, deep love of one—
The hopes that dance around a life whose charms are but begun,—
They lighten up her chestnut eye, they mantle o'er her cheek,
They sparkle on her open brow, and high-souled joy bespeak:
Ah! who shall blame, if scarce that day, through all its brilliant hours,
She thought of that quiet convent's calm, its sunshine and its flowers?

The scene was changed. It was a bark that slowly held its way,
And o'er its lee the coast of France in the light of evening lay;
And on its deck a Lady sat, who gazed with tearful eye
Upon the fast receding hills, that dim and distant rise.

No marvel that the Lady wept,—there was no land on earth
She loved like that dear land, although she owed it not her birth;
It was her mother's land, the land of childhood and of friends,—

HOLYROOD PALACE, EDINBURGH

It was the land where she had found for all her griefs amends,—
The land where her dead husband slept—the land where she had known
The tranquil convent's hushed repose, and the splendours of a throne;
No marvel that the Lady wept—it was the land of France—
The chosen home of chivalry—the garden of romance!
The past was bright, like those dear hills so far behind her bark;
The future, like the gathering night, was ominous and dark!
One gaze again—one long, last gaze—"Adieu, fair France to thee!"
The breeze comes forth—she is alone on the unconscious sea!

The scene was changed. It was an eve of raw and surly mood,
And in a turret-chamber high of ancient Holyrood
Sat Mary, listening to the rain, and sighing with the winds,
That seemed to suit the stormy state of men's uncertain minds.
The touch of care had blanched her cheek—her smile was sadder now:
The weight of royalty had pressed too heavy on her brow;
And traitors to her councils came, and rebels to the field;—
The Stuart *sceptre* well she swayed, but the *sword* she could not wield.
She thought of all her blighted hopes—the dreams of youth's brief day,
And summoned Rizzio with his lute, and bade the minstrel play
The songs she loved in early years—the songs of gay Navarre;
The songs perchance that erst were sung by gallant Chatelar:
They half beguiled her of her cares, they soothed her into smiles,
They won her thoughts from bigot zeal and fierce domestic broils:

But hark! the tramp of armed men! the Douglas' battle-cry
They come!—they come!—and lo! the scowl of Ruthven's hollow eye!
And *swords* are drawn, and daggers gleam, and tears and words are vain—
The ruffian steel is in his heart—the faithful Rizzio's slain!
Then Mary Stuart dashed aside the tears that trickling fell:
"Now for my father's arm!" she said;—" my woman's heart farewell!"

The scene was changed. It was a lake, with one small lonely isle;
And there, within the prison-walls of its baronial pile,
Stem men stood menacing their Queen, till she should stoop to sign
The traitorous scroll that snatched the crown from her ancestral line.
"My lords!—my lords!" the captive said, "were I but once more free,
With ten good knights on yonder shore to aid my cause and me,
That parchment would I scatter wide to every breeze that blows,
And once more reign a Stuart Queen o'er my remorseless foes!"
A red spot burned upon her cheek—streamed her rich tresses down;
She wrote the words—she stood erect—a Queen without a crown!

The scene was changed. A royal host a royal banner bore.
And the faithful of the land stood round their smiling Queen once more.
She stayed her steed upon a hill—she saw them marching by—
She heard their shouts—she read success in every flashing eye.
The tumult of the strife begins—it roars—it dies away;
And Mary's troops and banners now, and courtiers—where are they?
Scattered and strewn, and flying far, defenceless and undone;—
Alas! to think what she has lost, and all that guilt has won!—
Away! away! thy gallant steed must act no laggard's part;
Yet vain his speed—for thou dost bear the arrow in thy heart!

The scene was changed. Beside the block a sullen headsman stood,
And gleamed the broad axe in his hand, that soon must drip with blood.
With slow and steady step there came a Lady through the hall,
And breathless silence chained the lips and touched the hearts of all.
I knew that queenly form again, though blighted was its bloom;
I saw that grief had decked it out—an offering for the tomb!
I knew the eye, though faint its light, that once so brightly shone;
I knew the voice, though feeble now, that thrilled with every tone;
I knew the ringlets, almost gray, once threads of living gold!
I knew that bounding grace of step—that symmetry of mould!
Even now I see her far away, in that calm convent isle,
I hear her chant her vesper-hymn, I mark her holy smile,—
Even now I see her bursting forth upon the bridal morn,

A new star in the firmament, to light and glory born!
Alas, the change!—she placed her foot upon a triple throne,
And on the scaffold now she stands—beside the block—alone
The little dog that licks her hand, the last of all the crowd
Who sunned themselves beneath her glance and round her footsteps bowed!
Her neck is bared—the blow is struck—the soul is passed away!
The bright, the beautiful, is now—a bleeding piece of clay!
The dog is moaning piteously; and, as it gurgles o'er,
Laps the warm blood that trickling runs unheeded to the floor
The blood of beauty, wealth, and power—the heart-blood of a Queen,—
The noblest of the Stuart race—the fairest earth has seen,—
Lapped by a dog! Go think of it, in silence and alone;
Then weigh against a grain of sand the glories of a throne!

—HENRY GLASSFORD BELL

Words

antique, *old-fashioned.*
beguiled, *cheated.*
bespeak, *betoken.*
blanched, *made pale.*
blighted *withered.*
cloister, *convent.*
courtiers, *nobles.*
defenseless, *unprotected.*
descent, *lineage.*
effulgent, *splendid.*
faithful, *loyal.*
firmament, *heavens.*
gleamed, *flashed.*
headsman, *executioner.*
homage, *reverence.*
laggard, *loiterer.*
lapped, *licked.*
marvel, *wonder.*
menacing, *threatening.*
minstrel, *songster.*
ominous, *portentous.*
pertinent, *scroll.*
piteously, *mournfully.*
receding, *retiring.*
remorseless, *pitiless.*
ruffian, *cruel.*
stately, *majestic.*
seminary, *regularity.*
traitorous, *treacherous.*
tranquil, *peaceful.*
tumult, *uproar.*
unconscious, *insensible.*
unheeded, *disregarded.*

☆ ☆

我回头向遥远的过去望去，哦！在明亮的光辉中，
我看见，年岁逝去的样子，就像在梦里一般。
那是一座庄严的修道院，它的墙壁古老而高贵，

而花园里宽阔的绿色的路，上面有轻柔的脚步踏过；
那年代久远的刻度盘石头上，有让人害怕的影子经过，
周遭的一切，都被中午的太阳投上一种昏昏欲睡的光彩。
没有熙熙攘攘的生活的声响，只有那修道院的晦暗，
银铃子的清脆声，或是修女们的圣歌的哼唱。
有五位高贵的女子正端坐在果树下，
在那花骨朵萌生青春的春季里，所有的一切都令人惬意，
苏格兰人知道的最高贵的名字——没有人的名字比她们的更高贵了；
在这神圣的神殿前，甚至几乎没有听到过，
关于皇家血脉和从古老的斯图尔特一脉而衍生高贵后代的最美好的想法：
她幸福的时光静静地倏忽而去，如同白驹过隙一般；
随着它们的流逝，留下了一道久久持续的光。

（场景转换。）宫廷里，在位于波旁王朝欢快的宫廷里，
一千盏银色的宫灯下站立着一千个朝臣，
灯光照亮了亨利的眼睛——我想，能看到他，非常满意的神色，
地上聚集的全是高贵的淑女和勇猛的骑士，
但比所有的人更高贵的则是那在财富的浪涛中沐浴，
在青春的光辉中灿烂的，她，那位新娘！
千万人的效忠尊崇——对一个人的喜欢和深深爱戴，
认为在一个魅力即将绽放的生命身旁跳舞的希冀，
它们照亮了她那栗子色的眸子，照耀在她的脸颊上，
在她那舒展的眉毛上闪亮，诉说着满心的欢喜：
啊！如果仅仅在那天，在那么多的美好时光之后，她还想着
在修道院的安静时光，那里的阳光和花朵，那么应该责怪于谁？

（场景转换。）犬吠声慢慢地从路上传来，
在那位于法兰西海岸边的路的庇荫处，在傍晚的光线下，
有一位小姐坐在露天台上，眼含热泪凝望着那快速退去的群山，隐约闪现。
难怪这位小姐啜泣，世界上没有一片土地像这片土地一样，
让她如此挚爱，虽然它不仅是她的出生地；
这是她母亲的土地，她童年时光和朋友的土地，
这是她所有的忧伤得到疗养的地方，

在这片土地上，她亲爱的丈夫长眠于世了。这片她曾经了解的土地，
安静的修道院悄无声息，王冠光辉闪耀；
难怪这位小姐啜泣，这是法兰西的土地，
骑士选定的家园——浪漫的花园！
过往的岁月都明亮起来，就像那些退到她身后的亲爱的山峦；
而未来，则像乌云密布的夜晚，透着不祥和黑暗的色彩！
再凝望一眼——那长长的，最后的凝望——“永别了，我亲爱的法兰西！”
微风吹拂，她独自一人漂泊在无意识的大海！

（场景转换。）这是满怀原始而坚决的心意的前夕，
在古老的霍利鲁德的高高的炮塔楼室里，
玛丽坐在那里，听着雨的声响，合着风叹着气，
这似乎和暴风雨天气下人们不确信的心情相契合。
关怀的抚摸让她的双颊发白——她的微笑变得更悲伤了，
此时此刻，
皇室的重担向她的双眉压得太重，
还有背叛她的议会的叛徒以及国家的叛乱者。
她很好地挥动着斯图尔特的王权，但却不能挥动宝剑。
她想到所有那些自己枯萎的希望——年少时无忧无虑的日子做得白日梦，
她把里兹奥召唤到身边，让他带上自己的弹诗琴，吟唱诗歌，
她早年挚爱的那些歌曲——那些欢快的纳瓦拉的歌曲；
在往昔，那些歌曲偶尔会被勇敢的夏特利尔吟唱，
他们半哄着她让她能照拂自己，他们安抚她让她微笑，
他们因着那偏执的热情和强烈的国内的如火如荼的情形中赢得了她的心：
然而请听，武装的人踩踏过的声音！道格拉斯的战场上嚎叫的声音！
他们来了！——他们来了！——哦！卢思文空洞的眼睛中的愁容！
剑已经出鞘，匕首在闪亮，泪水和话语都是多余的，
恶棍般的钢铁已经插入他的心脏——忠贞的里兹奥被杀害了！
玛丽斯图尔特热泪盈眶而潸然泪下：
“为了我父亲的左膀右臂，我的心之所属，永别了！”

（场景转换。）这是一个中间有座孤岛的湖泊，
那里，在男爵的监狱高墙内，

壮硕的男人站立着恐吓他们的女王，直到她妥协签字，
叛乱者把她从世代的王位上拽了下来。
“上帝啊！——上帝啊！”被俘虏的女王喊道，“如果我能重获自由，
身边有十位好骑士在那边的海岸帮助我的事业和我，
我会把羊皮纸到处挥舞，挥舞到每一阵吹拂着的风中，
如果我能重新成为斯图尔特的女王，居于我那无情的敌人之上！”
一个红点灼在她脸颊上——顺着她高贵的头发向下流动；
她把这些话写下——站直了身子——就是一个无冕的女王！

（场景转换。）皇家的人举着皇家的旗帜。
对国家忠诚的臣子们再一次围绕在微笑着的女王身边。
她骑着骏马在山上，她看见他们向着这边跋涉，
她听到他们的喊叫声，她从他们闪动的眼睛中看到了成功的色彩。
骚乱的冲突开始了——它怒吼——它消散；
玛丽的军队和战旗呢？去那儿了？
散落在地上，破败不堪，飘零在远处，毫无防备抵抗；
啊！想想她失去的东西吧，想想她的愧疚吧！
去了！去了！你的英勇的骏马一定不会落后；
但是它再快也来不及了，因为你的心脏上中了一箭！

（场景转换。）在街头，一个脸色沉郁的人站立着，
他手中是闪亮的宽斧，不久就会滴血。
一位小姐穿过大厅，踏着缓慢而稳重的步子走过去，
所有人的嘴唇像上了锁链一样闭住呼吸，心脏也无声地跳动着。
我知道这是女王的架势，虽然光线晦暗；
我看见忧伤探出头来，走向坟墓的邀约！
我知道这眼睛，虽然眼神模糊，曾经却如此闪亮；
我知道这声音，虽然现在低弱，曾经却震悚世人；
我知道这指环，几乎发白，曾经却是金光熠熠！
甚至现在我看见她就在远处，在那安静的修道院的小岛上，
我听到她哼唱着圣歌，我看到她圣洁的笑容，
甚至现在我看见她当上新娘的那个早晨，
一颗天空中的新星，耀眼而光明！

啊，一切都变了！她坚持三权为己独尊，
如今站在了断头台上，就在大街旁边，独自一人
小狗舔着她的手，最后的民众
那些她眼神扫过的人们，她脚边的人们
对她鞠躬！
她香颈已断——刀已落下——香消玉殒！
那曾闪耀的美丽的人儿现在成了滴血的一摊泥土！
狗发出可怜的呻吟声，当它叫着，
跪在那滴滴答答在地上弥散着的温暖鲜血里，
那美丽的，拥有财富和权势的人儿的血，世间曾经的最美丽的人儿，
居然被一只狗朝跪！安静想想吧，独自想想吧，
王座的光荣最终敌不过一抔尘土的力量！

——亨利·格拉斯福德·贝尔

Lesson 8 DEATH OF LITTLE NELL

第八课 小妮儿之死

She was dead. No sleep so beautiful and calm, so free from trace of pain, so fair to look upon. She seemed a creature fresh from the hand of God, and waiting for the breath of life; not one who had lived, and suffered death. Her couch was dressed with here and there some winter-berries and green leaves, gathered in a spot she had been used to favour. "When I die, put near me something that has loved the light, and had the sky above it always." These were her words.

She was dead. Dear, gentle, patient, noble Nell was dead. Her little bird—a poor, slight thing, the pressure of a finger would have crushed—was stirring nimbly in its cage; and the strong heart of its child-mistress was mute and motionless for ever! Where were the traces of her early cares, her sufferings and fatigues? All gone. Sorrow was dead, indeed, in her; but peace and perfect happiness were born—imaged in her tranquil beauty and profound repose.

And still her former self lay there, unaltered in this change. Yes, the old fireside had smiled upon that same sweet face; it had passed like a dream through haunts of misery and care—at the door of the poor schoolmaster on the summer evening, before the furnace fire upon the cold wet night, at the still bedside of the dying boy, there had been the same mild and lovely look. So shall we know the angels in their majesty after death.

The old man held one languid arm in his, and the small tight hand folded to his breast for warmth. It was the hand she had stretched out to him with her last smile—the hand that had led him on through all their wanderings. Ever and anon he pressed it to his lips, then hugged it to his breast again, murmuring that it was warmer now; and as he said it he looked in agony to those who stood around, as if imploring them to help her.

She was dead, and past all help or need of help. The ancient rooms she had seemed to fill with life even while her own was waning fast, the garden she had tended, the eyes she had gladdened, the noiseless haunts of many a thoughtful hour, the paths she had trodden as it were but yesterday, could know her no more. "It is not," said the schoolmaster,as he bent down to kiss her on the cheek, and gave his tears free vent—"it is not in *this* world that Heaven's justice ends. Think what it is, compared with the world to which her young spirit has winged its early flight, and say, if one deliberate wish, expressed in solemn tones above this bed, could call her back to life, which of us would utter it?"

She had been dead two days. They were all about her at the time, knowing that the end was drawing on. She died soon after daybreak. They had read and talked to her in the earlier portion of the night; but as the hours crept on she sank to sleep. They could tell, by what she faintly uttered in her dreams, that they were of her wanderings with the old man. They were of no painful scenes, but of those who had helped them and used them kindly; for she often said, "God bless you!" with great fervour. Waking, she never wandered in her mind but once, and that was at beautiful music which, she said, was in the air. God knows. It may have been.

Opening her eyes at last from a very quiet sleep, she begged that they would kiss her once again. That done, she turned to the old man, with a lovely smile upon her face—such, they said, as they had never seen, and never could forget—and clung with both her arms about his neck. She had never murmured or complained, but with a quiet mind, and manner quite unaltered—save that she every day became more earnest, and more grateful to them—faded like the light upon the summer's evening.

The child who had been her little friend came there almost as soon as it was day with an offering of dried Bowers, which he begged them to lay upon her breast. He told them of his dream again, and that it was of her being restored to them, just as she used to be. He begged hard to see her, saying that he would be very quiet, and that they need not fear his being alarmed, for he had sat alone by his younger brother all day long when he was dead, and had felt glad to be so near him. They let him have his wish; and indeed he kept his word, and was in his childish way a lesson to them all.

Up to that time the old man had not spoken once—except to her—or stirred from the bedside. But when he saw her little favourite, he was moved as they had not seen him yet, and made as though he would have him come nearer. Then, pointing to the bed, he burst into tears for the first time; and they who stood by, knowing that the sight of this child had done him good, left them alone together.

Soothing him with his artless talk of her, the child persuaded him to take some rest, to walk abroad—to do almost as he desired him. And when the day came on which they must remove her in her earthly shape from earthly eyes for ever, he led him away, that he might not know when she was taken from him. They were to gather fresh leaves and berries for her bed.

And now the bell—the bell she had so often heard by night and day, and listened to with solemn pleasure, almost as to a living voice—rung its remorseless toll for her, so young, so beautiful, so good. Decrepit age, and vigorous life, and blooming youth, and helpless infancy, poured forth—on crutches, in the pride of health and strength, in the full blush of promise, in the mere dawn of life—to gather round her tomb. Old men were there, whose eyes were dim and senses failing—grandmothers, who might have died ten years ago and still been old—the deaf, the blind, the lame, the palsied—the living dead, in many shapes and forms, to see the closing of that early grave.

Along the crowded path they bore her now—pure as the newly fallen snow that covered it, whose day on earth had been as fleeting. Under that porch where she had sat when Heaven, in its mercy, brought her to that peaceful spot, she passed again; and the old church received her in its quiet shade. They carried her to one old nook, where she had many and many a time sat musing, and laid their burden softly on the pavement. The light streamed on it through the coloured window—a window where the boughs of trees were ever rustling in the summer, and where the birds sang sweetly all day long. With every breath of air that stirred among those branches in the sunshine, some trembling, changing light would fall upon her grave.

"Earth to earth, ashes to ashes, dust to dust." Many a young hand dropped in its little wreath—many a stifled sob was heard. Some, and they were not a few, knelt down. All were sincere and truthful in their sorrow. The service done, the mourners stood apart, and the villagers closed round to look into the grave before the stone should be replaced.

One called to mind how he had seen her sitting on that very spot, and how her book had fallen on her lap, and she was gazing with a pensive face upon the sky. Another told how he had wondered much that one so delicate as she should be so bold; how she had never feared to enter the church alone at night, but had loved to linger there when all was quiet, and even to climb the tower-stair, with no more light than that of the moon rays stealing through the loop-holes in the thick old walls. A whisper went about among the oldest there that she had seen and talked with angels; and when they called to mind how she had looked and spoken, and her early death, some thought it might be so indeed.

Thus, coming to the grave in little knots, and glancing down, and giving place to others, and falling off in whispering groups of three or four, the church was cleared in time of all but the sexton and the mourning friends. Then, when the dusk of evening had come on, and not a sound disturbed the sacred stillness of the place—when the bright moon poured in her light on tomb and monument, on pillar, wall, and arch, and most of all, it seemed to them, upon her quiet grave—in that calm time, when all outward things and inward thoughts teem with assurances immortality, and worldly hopes and fears are humbled in the dust before them, then with tranquil and submissive hearts they turned away, and left the child with God.

—CHARLES DICKENS

Words

assurance, *evidence.*
complained, *repined.*
creature, *being.*
daybreak, *dawn.*
deliberate, *premeditate.*
delicate, *weakly.*
disturbed, *broke.*
favourite, *darlings.*
fleeting, *transient.*
gladdened, *rejected.*
glancing, *looking.*
grateful, *thankful.*
immortality, *deathless.*
imploring, *beseeching.*
languid, *exhausted.*
misery, *wretchedness.*

monument, *memorial*.
nimbly, *actively*.
offering, *present*.
painful, *trying*.
palsied, *paralyzed*.
patient, *endowing*.
pavement, *floor*.
pensive, *thoughtful*.
persuaded, *induced*.
pleasure, *satisfaction*.
profound, *deep*.
repose, *rest*.
restored, *returned*.
sincere, *honest*.
solemn, *serious*.
soothing, *calming*.
stifled, *smothered*.
trembling, *flickering*.
unaltered, *unchanged*.
vigorous, *healthy*.
wandered, *raved*.
wanderings, *journeyings*.

☆ ☆

她死去了。如此美丽而安静的沉睡，如此不受疼痛的困扰，看起来如此漂亮。她似乎是上帝手中刚刚诞生的生命一般，等待着生命的气息吹拂的人，而不是一个已经生活过的，然后死去的人。她的睡椅上到处装饰着冬天的莓果和绿叶，放在她曾经喜欢的地方。“要是我死了，在我身边放上喜欢光且生长在蓝天下的东西。”她曾如是说道。

她死去了。亲爱的、温柔的、耐心的、高贵的妮儿死去了。她的那只小鸟——一只可怜的小东西，只消一个手指的力量就能把它压死——麻木地在自己的笼子里扑棱个不停。它那小主人强健的心脏已经永远静止了，停止了跳动！她曾经的那些关怀，她曾经受过的磨难，她的疲惫不堪都到哪里去了？一切都逝去了。悲伤也死去了，的确，她心中的悲伤，但平静和完美的幸福则诞生了——幻化在她那宁静的美和深沉的静之中。

然而她的身体依然躺在那里，没有丝毫变化。是的，久远的火堆向着同样的一张甜美的脸庞微笑着，好像做了个梦一样，摆脱了痛苦和关怀的萦绕——在一个夏日早晨那可怜的校长家门前，在火炉温暖阴冷的夜晚之前，在那不久于人世的男孩子的病榻前，都曾出现过同样一张温和而可爱的脸庞。因此，我们只有在她们死去才知道天使的伟大。

老人把小妮儿低垂的一只手臂握在自己手里，把那小小的手掌紧紧握在自己怀里温暖着。她最后一次向老人伸出的就是这只手，她的脸上带着最后的笑容——这只手曾带着他走过了所有的颠簸路程。他亲吻了那手，道了永别，然后再一次把它贴近胸膛，喃喃道，手变热了些；他一边说着，一边难过地看着周围站着的人，好像在祈求他们帮帮她一样。

她死去了，没有任何人能帮得了她，也没有帮她的必要了。即使生命渐渐褪色，她也曾经给这古老的房子带来生机，她曾经照料过的花园，她曾经带去笑意的双眼，那许多个无声的深思的时刻，她曾经踏过的小路，就好像昨天一样，再也见不到她了。“并不是，”校长说道，他一边俯下身子去吻她的脸颊，脸上泪水纵横：“并不是在这个世界上，上帝不公正了。想想这是什么，和这个她年轻的灵魂早早飞去的世界相比，如果，如果一个虔诚的许愿，用严肃的口吻在这床边说出，能够让她起死回生，我们中会有谁许下这个愿望呢？”

她已经死去两天了。他们都守在她旁边，知道就要结束了，她在黎明之后不久就去了。他们在刚刚入夜的时候给她读读书，和她说说话，但随着夜渐渐深了，她就陷入了沉睡。他们能从她梦中迷迷糊糊的话语中知道，她在和老人一起流浪。那里没有痛苦，只有那些关心他们和好心帮助他们的人，因为她经常饱含深情地说：“上帝保佑您！”只有一次，她在自己的想法中游荡着，走着，空气中响着美妙的音乐声，她说：“上帝知道。”她最后的时光可能是这样的。

她最后一次从安静的沉睡中睁开眼睛，祈求他们再吻她一次。之后，她转向老人，脸上挂着迷人的笑容——这个模样，他们说，他们从未见过，也不会忘记。老人把她的胳膊挂在自己的脖子上，她没有低声说什么，也没有抱怨什么，但心却很平静，举止并未异样——除了她每天都会对他们真挚地感恩——她的逝去就像夏天傍晚时分的光一样地褪去了。

那个曾经和她是朋友的小孩，几乎在收到干枯的宝禾的那天就马上去看她了，他祈求过他们把宝禾放在自己的胸口。他告诉他们自己的梦，梦中她又活过来了，她就像从前一样。他祈求看看她，说自己不会出声，说他们不必害怕自己的惊慌，因为他在自己弟弟死去的时候一整天都守候在他身旁，他很高兴能守在女孩儿的身边。他们让他如愿，他也的确恪守了自己的诺言，以自己孩子般的方式给他们上了一课。

到那时为止，老人一句话也没有说——除了和她说话——他也没有离开过床边。但当他看到她那小小的最好的朋友的时候，老人被打动了，他们之前没见过他，老人想让他走得更近点。然后，他指着床，眼泪第一次一涌而出，那些站在旁边的人，知道这个孩子曾经对她好过，就让他们独自待在一起了。

老人用那粗糙的言语说着她的故事，安慰着他，那孩子劝他歇息一下，出去走走，做一些他自己希望做的事情。当到了必须得把她移走的日子的时候，当把她尘世间的身体从这世间永远移开的时候，老人让女孩儿的朋友走了，他可能不知道她是什么时候被他从身边夺走的。人们找来嫩叶和莓作为她的睡榻。

而现在铃声响了——她曾日日夜夜经常听到的铃声，快快乐乐地听着的铃声，就好像有生命敲响了毫无怜悯的声响似的，她是如此的年轻，如此的美丽，如此的善良。风烛残年的人、年富力强的人、青春的年轻人以及无助的婴儿，都涌上前来，他们或者健康而精力充沛，或者有大好前程，或者已经进入迟暮之年，都聚集在她的墓旁。老人也去了，他们眼睛低垂，精神低迷——那些可能在十年前就去世的祖母们还在老去——耳聋的，目盲的，脚跛的，瘫痪的——所有活着的人，以各种形态和样子，来看看那英年早逝的孩子。

顺着挤满人的小路，他们抬起了她，她就像初雪一样纯净，在世间短短走过一遭。她曾得上天怜悯，让她坐在安静的门廊下一角，现在他们把她从门廊下抬过去了，古老的教堂接受了她安详的身体。他们把她抬到一个古老的角落，她曾经不止一次坐在那里沉思，人们把她轻轻放在过道上。光线透过彩色的窗子照耀在上头，那窗子到了夏天会有很多树枝窸窸窣窣地摩挲着，鸟儿一整天都在欢唱。阳光下，这些树枝间吹过的每一丝风，都会引起枝丫的颤抖，变化的光线落在她的墓穴上。

“嗟乎，尘归尘，土归土。”许多年轻的手伏在小小的花环上，许多人强忍着啜泣，但是哭出了声。有些人，而且不是少数的几个，跪下身子，所有人的伤悲都真挚而真诚。等到仪式结束了，悼念的人站到一边，村民们围上来看一眼那石头前的墓穴。

有人想起她曾经坐在那里的样子，她的书就搁在膝盖上，她若有所思地看着天空。还有人说道，他曾惊讶像她这样娇弱的人竟会那么勇敢。她从不害怕独自在夜晚走进教堂，她喜欢在那里停留，当一切都静悄悄的，然后爬上塔楼的台阶，除了透过厚实的古墙上的洞洒落进来的月光，都看不见什么光。老人们窃窃私语说，她曾见到过天使，并和他们交谈。当他们想到她曾经的音容笑貌，她的言谈举止，还有她的英年早逝的时候，他们觉得一定是因为见到了天使的缘故。

于是，他们来到墓穴前，看了一眼，让别人再看，三四个人窃窃私语着离去，不一会儿，教堂里就只剩下教堂司事和悼念她的挚友了。尔后，夜幕降临，没有一丝声响搅扰到这里的宁静——明亮的月亮把光线洒向墓穴和墓碑，洒在柱子上、墙上、穹顶上，几乎所有的地方，在他们看来，洒在了她静静的墓室上。在那样一个宁静的时刻，当外界的纷繁和内心的思绪都充满了永恒和不朽，世俗的愿望和恐惧在他们面前都微不足道了，然后，他们怀着宁静而顺从的心，转身离去了，把那孩子交给了上帝。

——查尔斯·狄更斯

Lesson 9 GRACE DARLING

第九课 亲爱的格蕾丝

[Grace darling was a daughter of the lighthouse keeper on Longstone, the largest of the Fame Islands, a group of bare and desolate rocks off the coast of Northumberland. On a dark and stormy night in September 1838, the steamer Forfarshire way wrecked between these islands and the coast; and the fore part, to which some dozen poor wretches clung, was impaled upon a rock. At dawn the next morning, Grace Darling, then a slight maid of twenty-two, descried the fragment of the wreck, and prevailed upon her father to go out with her in the open boat to rescue the survivors. Nine persons were got safely into the boat and landed on the island. Grace at once became one of the most famous of women. She died of consumption in 1841.]

A maiden gentle, yet, at duty's call,
Firm and unflinching as the Lighthouse reared
On the Island-rock, her lonely dwelling-place;
Or like the invincible Rock itself that braves,
Age after age, the hostile elements,
As when it guarded holy Cuthbert's cell.
All night the storm had raged, nor ceased, nor paused,
When, as day broke, the Maid, through misty air,
Espies far off a Wreck, amid the surf,
Beating on one of those disastrous isles;—
Half of a Vessel, half—no more; the rest
Had vanished, swallowed up with all that there
Had for the common safety striven in vain,
Or thither thronged for refuge. With quick glance
Daughter and Sire through optic-glass discern,
Clinging about the remnant of this Ship,
Creatures—how precious in the Maiden's sight!
For whom, belike, the old man grieves still more
Than for their fellow-sufferers engulfed
Where every parting agony is hushed,
And hope and fear mix not in further strife.
"But courage, Father! let us out to sea—
A few may yet be saved." The Daughter's Words,
Her earnest tone, and look beaming with faith,
Dispel the Father's doubts: nor do they lack

The noble-minded Mother's helping hand
To launch the boat; and with her blessing cheered,
And inwardly sustained by silent prayer,
Together they put forth, Father and Child!
Each grasps an oar, and struggling on they go—
Rivals in effort; and, alike intent
Here to elude and there surmount, they watch
The billows lengthening, mutually crossed
And shattered, and re-gathering their might;
As if the tumult, by the Almighty's will,
Were, in the conscious sea, roused and prolonged,
That woman's fortitude—so tried, so proved—
May brighten more and more!

True to the mark.
They stem the current of that perilous gorge,
Their arms still strengthening with the strengthening heart
Though danger, as the Wreck is neared, becomes
More imminent—Not unseen do they approach;
And rapture, with varieties of fear
Incessantly conflicting, thrills the frames
Of those who, in that dauntless energy,
Foretaste deliverance. But the least perturbed
Can scarcely trust his eyes, when he perceives
That of the pair—tossed on the waves to bring
Dope to the hopeless, to the dying, life—
One is a Woman, a poor earthly sister;
Or, be the Visitant other than she seems,
A guardian Spirit sent from pitying Heaven,
In woman's shape. But why prolong the tale,
Casting weak words amid a host of thoughts
Armed to repel them? Every hazard faced
And difficulty mastered, with resolve
That no one breathing should be left to perish,
This last remainder of the crew are all
Placed in the little boat, then o'er the deep
Are safely borne, landed upon the beach,
And, in fulfilment of God's mercy, lodged
Within the sheltering Lighthouse.

Shout, ye Waves!
Send forth a song of triumph. Waves and Winds,

Exult in this deliverance wrought through faith
In Him whose providence your rage hath served!
Ye screaming Sea-mews, in the concert join!
And would that some immortal Voice—a Voice
Fitly attuned to all that gratitude
Breathes out from floor or couch, through pallid lips
Of the survivors—to the clouds might bear—
Blended with praise of that parental love
Beneath whose watchful eye the Maiden grew
Pious and pure, modest and yet so brave,
Though young so wise, though meek so resolute—
Might carry to the clouds and to the stars
Yea, to celestial Choirs, GRACE DARLING'S name!

—WILLIAM WORDSWORTH.

Words

beaming, *globing*.
belike, *probably*.
blended, *mingled*.
celestial, *heavenly*.
Conflicting, *struggling*.
dauntless, *fearless*.
deliverance, *safety*.
descried, *discovered*.
disastrous, *calamitous*.
elude, *evade*.
engulfed, *swallowed*.
exult, *glory*.
fortitude, *endurance*.
fragment, *remnant*.
fulfillment, *accomplishment*.
immortal, *deathless*.
incessantly, *constantly*.
invincible, *unsociable*.
pallid, *death-like*.
perturbed, *disquieted*.
rapture, *delight*.
resolute, *steadfast*.
sustained, *upheld*.
unflinching, *stanch*.
vanished, *disappeared*.

☆ ☆

【亲爱的格蕾丝是法姆群岛中最大岛屿的长石滩上面灯塔瞭望员的女儿。法姆群岛是由诺森伯兰郡一些光秃而荒弃的石岛组成的。在1838年9月一个风高夜黑的晚上，蒸汽船福尔法希尔号在这些石岛和海岸中间触礁，船的前部，也就是十几个穷人在的位置，被一块礁石触穿了。第二天黎明的时候，亲爱的格蕾丝，当时不过22岁的姑娘，描述了沉船的场景，并说服她父亲和她一同乘船去拯救幸存者。有九个人被救到了船上，然后在岛上登陆。格蕾丝马上成为家喻户晓的名字之一，她于

1841年死于肺痨。】

那姑娘，温柔然而，在职责的召唤下，
坚定而不可动摇，在灯塔向后照耀在
岛屿上，她孤单在家。
或者就像坚不可摧的石头一样，
年复一年，战胜危险的因素，
当它守护着神圣的卡斯波特的牢房的时候。
暴风雨呼啸了一整夜未终止，也未停歇，
天亮的时候，这姑娘穿越雾气弥漫，
到达远处的沉船地，在浪涛中间，
浪涛拍打着那可怕的岛屿；
只剩下半条船，半条，再也没有什么了，剩下的
消失不见，被吞噬掉了，
即使曾经徒劳挣扎过，
或者在对岸寻求庇护之所。用望远镜快速看上一眼，
看清是一个女儿和她父亲，
紧紧抓住船剩余的部分，
生命啊，在姑娘的眼中是多么弥足珍贵啊！
和她一样，老人也感到忧伤，
但这种忧伤要逊色于姑娘对被海水吞噬的船员的忧伤，
在那里，所有分离的忧伤都寂然无声，
希望和恐惧不再交融在未来的挣扎中。
“拿出勇气来吧，父亲！咱们一起出海去，
还能再救上几个来。”这是那位女儿的话，
她声音真挚，脸上满是坚贞的神色，
这打消了她父亲的疑虑，他们不缺
那有崇高思想的母亲的帮忙，
把船推下水，在她的祝福的欢呼声中，
那沉默的祈祷深沉而内敛，
他们一起将船向前推，父亲和他的孩子！
俩人各自抓起船桨，奋力向前滑动，
像竞争者一样用力；同样都想

在这里逃脱在那里越过，他们看到
巨浪翻滚，彼此穿越，
彼此击打，重新积蓄着能量；
好像在上帝的意愿下，这骚乱，
在有意识的大海上，发生而延续，
而那姑娘的坚毅——她是如此努力，如此坚定——
会变得愈加光彩夺目！

坚定要到达目的地。
他们趟过水流湍急的危险海峡，
他们的臂膀跟随着坚毅的心在用力滑动着，
虽然危险重重，沉船就在眼前，一切变得
更加迫近——他们靠近的时候没有人不看见。
破裂和各种各样的恐惧，
不断交错，惊吓着那些人，
也就是用无穷无尽体力的人的身体，
让他们提前知道什么是救赎。但那内心较为淡定的人
也几乎不敢相信自己的双眼，当他看到
那对父女来到跟前。他们踏过风浪将
希望带给绝望的人，带给快要死去的人生命。
其中有一个是女人，一个可怜的人世间的姐妹；
或者，比她看起来更像的，是人世间的过客，
悲悯的上天派来的守护者的精神，
在这个女人的身体里萌发。但为什么这个故事这么长，
在这一连串的思绪中加入这么多羸弱的词语，
将这些思绪击退吗？每一次面对的危险，
每一次战胜的困难，用意志力战胜，
没有一个活着的人被留在那里死去，
最后船员中幸存的人都
被安置在这小船上，然后在深深的大海上
有了安全感，他们向着海滩登陆，
而在上帝的仁慈下，到达了
庇护他们的灯塔。

嚎叫吧，浪涛！
发出胜利的歌唱。狂风巨浪，
在信念的锻造下，为这救赎欢欣！
为你的愤怒得到宽恕的上帝而欢欣！
大海的嘶叫声，加入到这欢庆之中！
会不会有那永恒的声音，那声音
是所有感恩声音的融汇
从地上或沙发上的人口中呼出，
问问幸存者苍白的双唇间吐出，对着那云说，
歌颂那在父母的怜爱之下，
在他们关切的眼神下成长的姑娘，
如此虔诚而纯洁，谦逊却又勇敢，
虽然年轻却如此聪慧，虽然温和却如此坚毅。
这歌颂声可能会传到云端，传到星星那里，
是的，传到天庭的唱诗班，那亲爱的格蕾丝的名字！

——威廉·华兹华斯

Lesson 10 THE FRIGATE-BIRD

第十课 海 鸟

What bird is this? It is the little ocean-eagle, first and chief of the winged race, the daring navigator who never furls his sails, the lord of the tempest, the scorner of all peril—the man-of-war or frigate-bird.

Here we have a bird which is virtually nothing more than wings: scarcely any body—barely as large as that of the domestic cock—while his prodigious pinions are fifteen feet in span! The great problem of flight is solved and overpassed, for the power of flight seems useless. Such a bird, naturally sustained by such supports, needs but allow himself to be borne along. The storm bursts; he mounts to lofty heights, where he finds tranquility. The poetic metaphor, untrue when applied to any other bird, is no exaggeration when applied to him: literally, he sleeps upon the storm.

When he chooses to oar his way seriously, all distance vanishes: he breakfasts at the Senegal; he dines in America.

Or if he thinks fit to take more time, and amuse himself on route, he can do so. He may continue his progress through the night uninterruptedly, certain of reposing himself. Upon what? On his huge motionless pinion, which takes upon itself all the weariness of the voyage; or on the wind, his slave, which eagerly hastens to cradle him

Amid the glowing azure of the tropics, at incredible altitudes, almost imperceptible in the dim remoteness, we see him triumphantly sweeping past us—this black, solitary bird, alone in the waste of heaven; or, at the most, at a lower elevation, the snow-white sea-swallow crosses his flight in easy grace!

On looking at him closely, you perceive that he has no feet. At all events, his feet, being exceedingly short, can neither walk nor perch. With a formidable beak, he has not the talons of a true eagle of the sea.

Thence arises his life of uncertainty and hazard—the life of a corsairs and a pirate rather than of a mariner.

The immense and superb apparatus of his wings becomes on land a danger and an embarrassment. To raise himself, he needs a strong wind and a lofty station—a promontory, a rock. Surprised on a sandy level, on the banks, the low reefs where he sometimes halts, the frigate-bird is defenseless; in vain he threatens, in vain he strikes, for a blow from a stick will overcome him.

At sea, those vast wings, of such admirable utility in ascent, are ill fitted for skimming the surface of the water. When wetted, they may over-weight and sink him. And thereupon, woe to the bird!

And yet, what shall he do? His food lies in the waters. He is ever compelled to draw near them, to return to them to skim incessantly the hateful and prolific sea which threatens to engulf him.

Thus, then, this being, so well armed and winged, superior to all others in power of flight and vision as in daring, leads but a trembling and precarious life. He would die of hunger had he not the ingenuity to create for himself a purveyor, whom he cheats of his food. His ignoble resource, alas! is to attack a dull and timorous bird, the noddy, famous as a fisher. The frigate-bird, which is of no larger dimensions, pursues him, strikes him on the neck with his beak, and constrains him to yield up his prey. All this takes place in the air. The noddy drops the fish: but the frigate-bird catches it before ft can reach the water.

—JULES MICHELET.

Words

altitudes, *heights*.
apparatus, *machinery*.
constrains, *compel*.
dimensions, *site*.
embarrassment, *hindrance*.
formidable, *dreadful*.
ignoble, *mean*.
imperceptible, *invisible*.
metaphor, *image*.
precarious, *uncertain*.
prodigious, *vast*.
prolific, *fruitful*.
resource, *expedient*.
solitary, *lonely*.
sustained, *supported*.
tempest, *storm*.
timorous, *cowardly*.
uninterruptedly, *continuously*.
utility, *usefulness*.

Questions

Why does the frigate-bird fly so easily? Where does he go to escape the storm? On what does he repose himself in the night? Why is he helpless on land? Why is it dangerous for him to skim the surface of the water? On what does he feed? How does he procure it?

这是什么鸟？它是海上的小鹰，是飞禽中的佼佼者，是勇敢的引航者，它从不半途而废，它是暴风雨的君主，它蔑视一切危险；它是战士，是海鸟。

我们看到的这鸟儿除了翅膀之外几乎别无其他：几乎没有身体——身体只相当于家鸡那么大——然而它那巨大的翅膀展开来居然有十五英尺之长！如此，飞翔的问题就解决了，因为飞翔的力量似乎是不费吹灰之力的。这样的鸟，生来就有这样的先天优势，需要自己成为独行侠，也只能允许自己这样。暴风雨来到了，它扶摇直上到高处，那里安静平和。诗人那些对别的鸟的不实的比喻，放在它身上却丝毫不夸张。顾名思义，它睡在暴风雨之上。

当它选择奋力飞翔的时候，所有的距离都消失了。它在塞内加尔吃早餐，在美洲进食晚餐。

或者，如果它想再多花一点儿时间，想在路上自娱自乐的话，它也能做得到。它可以继续自己的旅程，整夜飞翔不间断。如果它要歇息一番，靠什么呢？靠它那巨大的不动的羽翼，它们能轻而易举地飞完那疲劳的旅行；或者靠它的努力，风力，因为风力会迫不及待地变成它的摇篮，将它抚慰。

在热带地区蔚蓝的海面上，在高海拔地带，向远处几乎望不到什么，我们却能看到海鸟胜利昂扬地在我们身边掠过。这黑色孤独的鸟儿，独自在广袤的天空中飞着；或者，在大部分的时候，在海拔低一些的地方，它优雅而不费力地飞过白雪一样的海面。

近处观察它的话，你会看见它并没有脚爪。在任何情况下，它那极其短小的脚爪，既不能走路又不能栖息。有了它那骇人的大喙，它就不需要像海鹰那样的利爪了。

之后它的生活就变得不可预测而充满危险了，那是海盗的生活，而不是航海者的生活。

它那巨大而卓越的翅膀，到了陆地上就成了威胁它生命并引起不便的装备。为了能飞起来，它需要强劲的风和一个高地——海角，礁石。让人惊讶的是，它经常停留在平坦的沙地上，或者停在河岸边，或是那些低陷的暗礁上，于是这海鸟就变得毫无防备能力；它徒劳地发出威胁，徒劳地反抗，因为一根棍子的击打就能结束它的生命。

在海上，这巨大的翅膀，在飞翔时如鱼得水，但在水面滑翔的时候则失去优势。当它的翅膀蘸湿的时候，它们会因为过重而让海鸟沉溺。因此，这鸟儿真可怜啊！

然而，它能怎么办呢？它的食物都在水里。它总是不得不靠近水面去捕食，不断地掠过水面，掠过那让它憎恨的多产的海面，而那大海则威胁着要吞掉它。

因此，这生物的装备如此良好，羽翼如此丰满，比其他飞禽都有优势，视野比它们都要开阔，实际上却生活得战战兢兢，如履薄冰。如果它不是聪明地给自己找了个供食者，肯定早就饿死了。从供食者那里，它夺取食物。它那不光彩的食物来源，就是靠攻击木讷而胆小的鸟类，也就是以捕鱼而著名的燕鸥。海鸟的身形实际上并不比燕鸥大，它追逐燕鸥，啄打燕鸥的颈部，迫使燕鸥放弃自己的猎物，这一切都发生在空中。燕鸥捕到的鱼掉下来，但海鸟却能在鱼掉在水里之前把鱼截住。

——朱尔斯·米奇乐

Lesson 11 A MOTHER'S LOVE

第十一课 妈妈的爱

A mother's love!—	妈妈的爱!
how sweet the name!	多么美的名称啊!
What *is* a Mother's Love?—	什么是妈妈的爱呢!
A noble, pure, and tender flame,	是高贵，纯粹而温柔的火焰，
Enkindled from above,	在上天闪耀，
To bless a heart of earthly mould—	祝福那尘世间的人儿，
The warmest love that can grow cold;—	渐而冷却的最温暖的爱;
This is a Mother's Love.	这就是妈妈的爱。
To bring a helpless babe to light,	把一个无助的婴儿带到光明的地方，
Then, while it lies forlorn,	然后，孤单地躺在那里，
To *gaze* upon that dearest sight,	凝视着那最亲爱的眼神，
And feel herself new-born;	感受自己得到新生;
In its existence lose her own,	有了他之后自己就失去了存在，
And live and breathe in it alone;—	只为他而活而呼吸;
Thin is a Mother's Love.	这就是妈妈的爱。
In weakness in her arms to bear,	她虚弱地张开手臂，
To cherish on her breast,	把他珍惜地拥在怀里，
Feed it from Love's own fountain there.	用爱本身的喷泉喂食他。
And lull it there to rest;	哄着他在那里睡着;
Then while it slumbers watch its breath,	然后他睡着的时候，看着他呼吸，
As if to guard from instant death;—	生怕死亡会突然降临似的;
This is a Mother's Love.	这就是妈妈的爱。
To mark its growth from day to flay,	从第一天开始就观察他的成长，
I to opening charms admire,	我羡慕着那毫无保留的爱，

Catch from its eye the earliest ray	从他的眼中捕捉到最初的光彩，
Of intellectual fire;	那智慧的火焰；
To smile and listen while it talks,	当他说话的时候微笑着，聆听着，
And lend a finger when it walks;—	他走路的时候用手扶着；
This is a Mother's Love.	这就是妈妈的爱。
And can a Mother's Love grow cold—	妈妈的爱会不会变冷呢？
Can she forget her boy?	她会忘记自己的孩子吗？
His pleading innocence behold,	他那祈求纯洁的眼睛，
Nor weep for grief—for joy?	不是为忧伤而哭泣，而是因为高兴？
A mother may forget her child,	一个妈妈怎能忘记自己的孩子，
While wolves devour it on the wild;—	当荒野里的狼群把它吞噬的时候，
Is *this* a Mother's Love?	这还是妈妈的爱吗？
Ten thousand voices answer, "No!"	一万个声音答道，“不是！”
Ye clasp your babes and kiss;	你拍打着你的孩子，亲吻他；
Your bosoms yearn, your eyes overflow;	你的胸脯渴望着，你的眼睛流着泪；
Yet, ah! remember this:—	但是，啊！记住吧：
The infant reared alone for earth,	婴儿是为这尘世独自而来的，
May live, may die—	他生，他也会死，
to curse his birth;—	这是他一出生的时候就有的诅咒；
Is this a Mother's Love?	这是妈妈的爱吗？
Blest infant! whom his mother taught	保佑这婴儿吧！妈妈！
Early to seek the Lord,	早早教他找寻上帝，
And poured upon his dawning thought	在他启蒙的想法上，倾注了
The day-spring of the Word:	上帝春日般的话语，
This was the Lesson to her son,—	这是给她儿子的一课，
Time is Eternity begun;—	永恒的时间开始了；
Behold that Mother's Love!	看看妈妈的爱吧！
Blest mother! who in Wisdom's path,	保佑那妈妈吧！她在智慧的路上，
By her own parent trod,	教育她的孩子，

Thus taught her son to flee the wrath,	教她的孩子从愤怒中逃离，
And know the fear of God:	知道对上帝心存畏惧，
Ah, youth!	啊，年轻人！
like him enjoy your prime,—	就像他一样享受自己的风华正茂吧，
Begin Eternity in time,	开始永恒的时间，
Taught by that Mother's love.	这是他妈妈的爱交给他的。
That Mother's Love!—	那就是妈妈的爱！
how sweet the name	多么美的名字啊！
What was that Mother's Love?—	什么是妈妈的爱？
The noblest, purest, tenderest flame,	最高贵，最纯粹，最温柔的火焰，
That kindles from above	在上天闪耀，
Within a heart of earthly mould,—	在一颗尘世的人儿心中绽放，
As much of heaven as heart can hold,—	上天和心灵能承受的极限，
Nor through eternity grows old;—	永远也不会变老，
This was that Mother's Love.	这就是妈妈的爱。
—MONTGOMERY.	——蒙哥马利

Words

admire, *wonder at*.
cherish, *rapport*.
dawning, *opening*.
devour, *consume*.
enjoy, *delight in*.
enkindled, *inflamed*.
eternity, *futurity*.
existence, *life*.
forlorn, *helpless*.
fountain, *spring*.
innocence, *simplicity*.
instant, *Immediate*.
intellectual, *mental*.
reared, *trained*.
remember, *recollect*.
slumbers, *sleeps*.
tenderest, *most susceptible*.
yearn, *long*.

Lesson 12 NELSON AND HARDY

第十二课 纳尔逊和哈代

The life of Nelson abounds with illustrations of naval daring, but most of these are well known. One, however, narrated by Colonel Drinkwater Bethune, the historian of "The Siege of Gibraltar," and an eye-witness of what follows, is as well worthy of general fame as some of Nelson's more splendid achievements. It is the more interesting as, on this occasion, that personal affection for his more immediate followers, which in every case secured their devoted attachment to himself, was the inciting cause of a display of unwonted gallantry.

Commodore Nelson, whose broad pendant at that time was hoisted in the *Minerve*, Captain Cockburn, got under weigh from Gibraltar on the 11th of February 1797, in order to join Sir John Jervis's fleet. The frigate had scarcely cast round from her anchorage, when two of the three Spanish line-of-battle ships in the upper part of Gibraltar Bay were observed also to be in motion. The headmost of the Spanish ships gaining on the frigate, the latter prepared for action, and the *Minerve's* situation every instant becoming more hazardous, Colonel Drinkwater asked Nelson his opinion as to the probability of an engagement. The hero said he thought it was very possible, as the headmost ship appeared to be a good sailer; "but," continued he, looking up at the broad pendant, "before the Dons get hold of that bit of bunting I will have a struggle with them; and sooner than give up the frigate, I will run her ashore."

Captain Cockburn, who had been taking a view of the chasing enemy, now joined the commodore, and observed that there was no doubt of the headmost ship gaining on the frigate. At this moment dinner was announced; but before Nelson and his guests left the deck, orders were given to set the studding-sails. Seated at dinner, Colonel Drinkwater was congratulating Lieutenant Hardy, who had lately been exchanged, on his being no longer a prisoner of war, when the sudden cry of "a man overboard" threw the dinner-party into disorder. There is, perhaps, no passage in naval history of deeper interest than the following account of what then occurred:—

"The officers of the ship ran on deck; I, with others, ran to the stern windows to see if anything could be observed of the unfortunate man. We had scarcely reached them before we noticed the lowering of the jolly-boat, in which was my late neighbour, Hardy, with a party of sailors; and before many seconds had elapsed, the current of the Strait (which runs strongly to the eastward) had carried the jolly-boat far astern of the frigate, towards the Spanish ships. Of course the first object was to recover, if possible, the fallen man; but he was never seen again. Hardy soon made a signal to that effect, and the man was given up as lost.

"The attention of every person was now turned to the safety of Hardy and his boat's crew. Their situation was extremely perilous, and their danger was every instant increasing from the fast sailing of the headmost ship of the chase—the *Terrible*,,—which by this time had approached nearly within gunshot of the *Minerve*. The jolly-boat's crew pulled 'might and main' to regain the frigate, but apparently made little progress against the current of the Strait. At this crisis, Nelson, casting an anxious look at the hazardous situation of Hardy and his companions, exclaimed, 'No, it shall not be; I shall not lose Hardy: back the mizzen-topsall! '

"No sooner said than done. The *Minerve's* progress was retarded, having the current to carry her down toward Hardy and his party, who, seeing this spirited maneuver to save them from returning to their old quarters on board the *Terrible*, naturally redoubled their exertions to rejoin the frigate. To the landsmen on board the *Minerve* an action now appeared to be inevitable; and so, it would seem, thought the enemy, who, surprised and confounded by this daring maneuver of the Commodore's (being ignorant of the accident that led to it), must have construed it into a direct challenge.

"Not conceiving, however, a Spanish ship of the line to be an equal match for a British frigate with Nelson on board of her, the captain of the *Terrible* suddenly shortened sail in order to allow his consort to join him, and thus afforded time for the *Minerve* to drop down to the jolly-boat to pick up Hardy and the crew; and the moment they were on board the frigate, orders were given again to make Bail. Being now under studding-sails, and the widening of the Strait allowing the wind to be brought more on the *Minerve's* quarter, the frigate soon regained the lost distance, and in a abort time we had the satisfaction to observe that the dastardly Don was left far in our wake; and at sunset, by steering to the southward, we lost sight of him and his consort altogether; and Commodore Nelson thus escaped, to share in the Battle of St. Vincent, and win fresh laurels from the Spaniard."

—GIEFARD

Words

achievements, *exploits.*
attachment, *affection.*
challenge, *defiance.*
companions, *mates.*
conceiving, *supposing.*
confounded, *baffled.*
congratulating, *complimenting.*
consort, *partner.*
construed, *interpreted.*
dastardly, *cowardly.*
elapsed, *passed.*
engagement, *combat.*
exertions, *efforts.*
extremely, *highly.*
gallantry, *bravery.*
hazardous, *perilous.*
illustrations ,*examples.*
inciting, *instigating.*
maneuver, *stratagem.*
observed, *remarked.*

occurred, *happened*.
pendant, *banner*.
recover, *rescue*.
retarded, *impeded*.
satisfaction, *pleasure*.
situation, *position*.
suddenly, *unexpectedly*.
unfortunate, *unhappy*.
unwonted, *unusual*.

Questions

When did this incident occur? How many Spanish ships followed the *Minerve*? What caused the latter to stop in its course? Who were placed in grant peril? What order did Nelson give? Whom was he unwilling to lose? What did the *Terrible* immediately do? What did the *Minerve* de when the Jolly-boat's crew was picked up? What was the result?

☆ ☆

纳尔逊的一生几乎是一部海上传奇，而对其中的大部分故事我们都已经熟知。但有一个人，据德恩克沃特·毕思恩上校说，他是“直布罗陀海峡包围战”的历史学家，同时也是那场海战的目击者，他的事迹并不逊色于尼尔森那些最辉煌的战绩。在当时的情形下，就他的直接追随者的个人情感而言，这件事更有趣，这些人不论任何情况，都对他死心塌地追随，正是他们的情感直接激起了这种罕见的英勇行为。

当时，海军准将纳尔逊那宽大的坠饰飘扬在密涅瓦号上，船长库科伯恩在1797年2月11日从直布罗陀海峡出发，去加入圣约翰·杰维斯舰队。护卫舰起航的地方周围鲜有船只，但三艘西班牙战列舰中的两艘，却出现在直布罗陀海湾上部，准备行动。带头的西班牙船只聚集在护卫舰上，剩余的则随时待命，德恩克瓦特上校请示尼尔森将军，问是不是可能会有海战发生。这位英雄将军说他认为非常有可能，因为带头的船是个好手；“但是，”他继续说道，同时抬头看着宽大的坠饰，“在敌人发动撞击之前，我会尽力和他们周旋；之后我们不能放弃护卫舰，我会驾驶它冲向海岸。”

库科伯恩船长看了一眼追逐在身后的敌人，现在也加入了准将的行列，他观察到带头的船只毫无疑问已经逼近护卫舰了。到吃晚饭的时间了，但尼尔森在自己和客人离开船舱之前，就下达了升起补助帆的命令。德恩克瓦特上校端坐在餐桌旁，他正祝贺着哈代中尉，祝贺他获得交换资格，不再是战俘了，这时候突然传来一声“甲板上有个人”的喊叫，把晚餐聚会弄得乱成一团。可能，海军历史上没有比描述当时的场景更有趣的了：

“船上的军官跑上甲板；我和其他人一起也跑到船尾的窗子那儿看能不能看见是不是有什么不走运的人出了什么事儿。还没等我们跑到那儿，就看到小艇在下放，上面坐着的是我从前的邻居哈代，还有几个水手；没过多长时间，海峡的水流（当时是强而有力地往东流动）就把小艇冲向了护卫舰的尾端，向着西班牙船只而去。当然，如果可能的话，最先看到的一定是掉下去的人，但他再也没有被看到。哈代对此马上做了个手势，然后放弃找寻此人，这人就算失踪不见了。

“现在所有人的注意力都集中到了哈代和他船员的安危上。他们当时的处境非常危急，他们因为快速地向着追逐其后的带头的船只航行，而危险时刻在增加。带头的舰船特利波尔号，当时刚刚进入到密涅瓦号的射程中。小艇上的人用力地拉着，想重新占领护卫舰，但很显然因为要对抗海峡的湍流，这几乎没什么作用。在危急时刻，纳尔逊焦虑地看着处在陷阱中的哈代和船员，他喊道：“不，不要这样，我不能失去哈代，快重新用后桅第二层帆！”

“说时迟，那时快。密涅瓦号的航速变慢了，水流将它带向哈代和他的船员那儿，他们看到这样鼓舞人心的调兵遣将，让他们免于回到特利波尔号的老队伍中间，无疑让他们士气倍增，夺下了护卫舰。对于那些在密涅瓦甲板上的人来说，采取行动显得势不可免了；因此，似乎，那惊奇于准将的大胆招数而又因此感到困惑的敌人一定把这个行为看成是直接挑衅了。（其实敌人不知道是因为意外才导致了这个行为）。

“毋庸置疑，西班牙战舰的确能和纳尔逊率领的英国护卫舰分庭抗礼，然而特利波尔号的船长为了让同伴赶上自己，突然拉短了帆的长度，因此就为密涅瓦号停下，让小艇上的哈代和船员登船赢得了时间。他们一登上护卫舰，起航的命令就下达了。在全帆航行下，海峡变得逐渐开阔，这使得风更多吹动在密涅瓦号的右舷，因此护卫舰不一会就甩开了西班牙船只一段距离，我们很高兴地观察到可恶的敌人已经被我们远远甩开了。到日落时分，我们向南转向的时候，就看不到西班牙人和他的舰队了，而纳尔逊准将也就逃脱了一劫，得以加入到圣文森的战役中，并打败了西班牙人，赢得了胜利。

——吉尔法德

Lesson 13 THE SPANISH CHAMPION

第十三课 西班牙战士

The warrior bowed his crested head, and tamed his heart of fire,
And sued the haughty king to free his long-imprisoned sire:
"I bring thee here my fortress keys, I bring my captive train;
I pledge my faith, my liege, my lord—oh! break my father's chain."

"Rise! rise! even now thy father cornea, a ransomed man this day;
Mount thy good steed, and thou and I will meet him on his way:"
Then lightly rose that loyal son, and bounded on his steed;
And urged, as if with lance in hand, his charger's foaming speed.

And lo! from far, as on they pressed, there came a glittering band,
With one that 'mid them stately rode, as a leader in the land:
"Now haste, Bernardo, haste! for there, in very truth, is he,
The father—whom thy grateful heart hath yearned so long to see."

His dark eye flashed, his proud breast heaved, his cheek's blood came and went;
He reached that gray-haired chieftain's side, and there dismounting, bent:
A lowly knee to earth he bent, his father's hand he took;—
What was there in its touch that all his fiery spirit shook?

That hand was cold, a frozen thing—it dropped from his like lead;
He looked up to the face above—the face was of the dead;
A plume waved o'er that noble brow—the brow was fixed and white;
He met at length his father's eyes, but in them was no sight!

Up from the ground he sprang, and gazed; but who can paint that gaze?
They hushed their very hearts who saw its horror and amaze:
They might have chained him, as before that noble form he stood;
For the power was stricken from his arm, and from his cheek the blood.

"Father!" at length he murmured low, and wept like childhood then—
(Talk not of grief till thou hast seen the tears of warlike men—)
He thought on all his glorious hopes, on all his high renown
Then flung the falchion from his side, and in the dust sat down;

And, covering with his steel-gloved hand his darkly mournful brow,
"No more, there is no more," he said, "to lift the sword for now:
My king is false! my hope betrayed! my father—oh! the worth:
The glory, and the loveliness, are passed away from earth!"

Up from the ground he sprang once more, and seized the monarch's rein
A mid the pale and wildered looks of all the courtier train;
And with a fierce, o'ermastering grasp, the rearing war-horse led,
And sternly set them face to face—the king before the dead!

"Came I not forth upon thy pledge, my father's hand to kiss?—
Be still, and gaze thou on, false king! and tell me what is this?
The voice, the glance, the heart I sought—give answer, where are they?
If thou wouldst clear thy perjured soul, send life through this cold clay!

"Into these glassy eyes put light—be still, keep down thine ire!—
Bid these white lips a blessing speak—this earth is not my sire!
Give me back him for whom I strove, for whom my blood was shed!
Thou canst not?—and a king!—His dust be mountains on thy head!"

He loosed the steed—his slack hand fell; upon the silent face
He cast one long, deep, troubled look, then turned from that sad place:
His hope was crushed—his after-fate untold in martial strain—
His banner led the spears no more amidst the hills of Spain!

—MRS. HEMANS (1793–1835).

Words

betrayed, *deceived.*
bounded, *leapt.*
Captive, *enslaved.*
courtlier, *knightly.*
glittering, *sparkling.*
glorious, *splendid.*
grateful, *thankful.*
haughty, *proud.*
horror, *repugnance.*
loveliness, *beauty.*
martial, *warlike.*
mournful, *sorrowful.*
o'ermastering, *overpowering.*
prejured, *forsworn.*
ransomed, *redeemed.*
renown, *celebrity.*
sternly, *auterely.*
troubled, *disturbed.*
wildered, *perplexed.*
yearned, *longed.*

Questions

Who was the "warrior" referred to? Who was the "king"? What did the former beg of the latter? What was his father's name? On what condition had the king promised to deliver up Don Sancho? How did he keep his promise? What effect had this event on Bernardo's future?

☆ ☆

那战士低下自己高贵的头，把心中的火焰抚灭，
向无上的国王祈求释放他那被长期囚禁的父亲：
"我给您带来了我城堡的钥匙，带来了我的俘虏；
我祈求您，我的陛下，我的君王，我的国王——哦！打开我父亲的锁链吧。"

"平身！平身！你父亲马上就来了，今天他就被赎为自由身；
跨上你那骏马，和我一起去迎接他的到来。"
然后那忠诚的臣子轻轻直起身子，跳上自己的骏马；
快马加鞭，好像手中握着长矛似的，他的战马飞驰向前。

天啊！从远处，他们先前走的时候，传来了叮叮当当的队伍的声响，
在他们中间有一个人威严坐在马上，就像这片土地的领袖一样：
"赶快，博尔纳多，赶快！就在那儿，绝对没错，就是他
父亲——你那颗感恩的心一直以来期望见到的人儿。"

他的黑眼睛闪动着，骄傲的胸脯剧烈起伏着，他的脸颊上血液翻涌；
他到达了白发苍苍的领袖身边，从马上下来俯下身子，
他跪在地上，拿起了父亲的手；
他摸到了什么，让他那炽烈的劲头发生动摇？

是冰冷冰冷的手——从他手中垂落；
他抬头望望那张脸——那分明是死去的人的脸庞；
一阵风吹过那苍老的额头——那额头一动不动，颜色惨白；
他终于看到了父亲的双眼，但它们已经毫无光泽！

他从地上一跃而起，凝望着，可是谁能描画

他凝望的神色呢?
看到这神色中的恐惧和惊讶的人们都静默下来,
他们本来可以在这位高贵的勇士站立前把他锁起来;
因为他双臂无力,脸上毫无血色。

“父亲!”他最后低声呢喃,然后向孩子一样哭泣,
(没看到战士的眼泪的话,不要谈悲伤。)
他想到自己所有光荣的希望,所有高贵的名声,
然后从自己身边抽出了刀,坐在地上。

戴着钢丝手套的手搭在他那深色的忧伤的额头上,
“不能再这样了,不能再这样了”,他说道,“现在应该举起剑来;
我的国王是骗子!他夺走了我的希望,我的父亲——
哦!那些价值,光荣和爱戴,都从世间消失了!”

他再一次从地上一跃而起,抓住了君王的缰绳,
在脸色发白,疑惑不解的群臣中间;
他大喘着气,骑着战马飞奔,
让他们面对国王和死去的人!

“我来到这儿为了亲吻我父亲的手,
镇定些,看看你,撒谎的国王!告诉我,
我寻找的是什么声音,什么眼神,什么心?告诉我答案,
它们在哪里?
如果你不把欺骗的性格改掉的话,我就把你埋进这冰冷的泥土里!

“在那明亮的眼睛前点上灯,镇定些,压下你的怒火!
向这苍白的双唇说一下祝福的话语——这土地不是我的父亲!
把我努力寻找的父亲还给我,因为我是他的血脉!
你做不到吗?你还是国王呢!我要把他的骨灰撒落在你的头顶!”

他停下马,他那松懈的手垂下;向着那静静的脸庞,
他投去了悠长、深沉而复杂的眼神,然后离开这个伤心之地。

他的希望都破灭了，在战士们中间，没有人说起他以后的命运，
他引领戟矛的战旗不再飘扬在西班牙山地的上空！

——赫曼斯夫人（1793–1835）

Lesson 14
THE CHEMISTRY OF A CANDLE (I)
第十四课　蜡烛的化学知识（一）

"And now, uncle," asked Harry, who was a favourite with the old gentleman, "can you tell me what you do when you put a candle out?"

"Put an extinguisher on it, you young rogue, to be sure."

"Oh, but I mean, you cut off its supply of oxygen," said Master Harry.

"Cut off its what?"

"He means something he heard at the Royal Institution," observed Mrs. Wilkinson. "He reads a great deal about chemistry, and he attended Professor Faraday's lectures there on the chemical history of a candle, and has been full of it ever since."

"Now, you, sir," said Uncle Bagges, "come you here to me, and tell me what you have to say about this chemical, eh?—or comical, which?—this—comical chemical history of a candle."

"Harry, don't be troublesome to your uncle," said Mrs Wilkinson.

"Troublesome? Oh, not at all. I like to hear him."

"Let us get a wax candle then, uncle. There's one on the mantle-shelf. Let me light it."

"Take care you don't bum your fingers, or set anything on fire," said Mrs. Wilkinson.

"Now, uncle," commenced Harry, having drawn his chair to the side of Mr. Bagges, "we have got our candle burning. Look down on the top of it, around the wick. See, it is a little cup full of melted wax. The heat of the flame has melted the wax just round the wick. The cold air keeps the outside of it hard, so as to make the rim of it. The melted wax in the little cup goes up through the wick to be burned, just as oil does in the wick of a lamp. What do you think makes it go up, uncle"

"Why—why, the flame draws it up, doesn't it?"

"Not exactly, uncle. It goes up through little tiny passages in the cotton wick, because very, very small channels, or pipes, or pores, have the power in themselves of sucking up liquids. What they do it by is called capillary attraction;—just as a sponge sucks up water, or a bit of lump-sugar the little drop of tea or coffee left in the bottom of a cup.

"Now, I'll blow the candle out; not to be in the dark, but to find out what it is.—Look at the smoke rising from the wick. I'll hold a bit of lighted paper in the smoke so as not to touch the wick. But see, for all that, the candle lights again! So this shows that the melted wax sucked up through the wick is turned into vapour, and the vapour burns. The heat of the burning vapour keeps on melting more wax, and that is sucked up too within the flame, and turned into vapour and burned; and so on the wax is all used up and the candle is gone. So the flame, uncle, you see, is the last of the candle; and the candle seems to go through the flame into nothing, although it doesn't, but goes into several things;—and isn't it curious, as Professor Faraday said, that the candle should look so splendid and glorious in going away?

"I dare say that the flame of the candle looks flat to you; but if we were to put a lamp-glass over it, so as to shelter it from the draught, you would see it is round—round sideways, and running up to a peak. It is drawn up by the hot air. You know that hot air always rises, and that is the way smoke is taken up the chimney. What do you think is in the middle of the flame."

"I should say fire," replied Uncle Bagges.

"Oh, no. The flame is hollow. The bright flame we see is something no thicker than a thin peel or skin, and it doesn't touch the wick. Inside of it is the vapour I told you of just now. If you put one end of a bent pipe into the middle of the flame, and let the other end of the pipe dip into a warm bottle, the vapour or gas from the candle will mix with the air there; and if you were to set fire to the mixture of gas from the candle and air in the bottle, it would go off with a bang."

"I wish you'd do that, Harry," said Master Tom, the younger brother of the juvenile lecturer.

"I want the proper things," answered Harry.—"Well, uncle, the flame of the candle is a little shining case, with gas in the inside of it and air on the outside, so that the case of flame is between the air and the gas. The gas keeps going into the flame to burn; and when the candle bums properly, none of the gas ever passes out through the flame, and none of the air ever gets in through the flame to the gas. The greatest heat of the candle is in this skin, or peel, or case of flame."

"Case of flame!" repeated Mr. Bagges. "Live and learn. I should have thought a candle-flame was as thick as my poor old noddle."

"I can show you the contrary," said Harry. "I take this piece of white paper, look, and hold it a second or two down on the candle-flame, keeping the flame very steady. Now, I'll rub off the black of the smoke, and—there—You find that the paper is scorched in the shape of a ring, but inside the ring it is only dirtied, and not singed at all."

"Seeing is believing," remarked the uncle.

"But," proceeded Harry, "there is more in the candle-flame than the gas that comes out of the candle. You know a candle won't bum without air. There must be always air around the gas, and touching it, as it were, to make it burn. If a candle hasn't got enough of air it goes out, or burns badly, so that some of the vapour inside of the flame comes out through it in the form of smoke; and this is the reason of a candle smoking. So now you know why a great clumsy dip smokes more than a neat wax candle: it is because the thick wick of the dip makes too much fuel in proportion to the air that can get to it.

"What should you say now," continued Harry, "if I were to tell you that the smoke that comes out of a candle is the very thing that makes a candle burn with a bright light? Yes; a candle shines by consuming its own smoke. The smoke of a candle is a cloud of small dust; and the little grains of dust are bits of charcoal, or carbon, as chemists call it. They are burned the moment they are made; and the place they are made in is the case of flame itself, where the strongest heat is. The great heat separates them from the gas which comes from the melted wax; and as soon as they touch the air on the outside of the thin case of flame they burn."

"Can you tell me how it is that the little bits of carbon cause the brightness of the flame?" asked Mr. Wilkinson.

"Because they are pieces of solid matter," answered Harry. "To make a flame shine, there must always be some solid, or at least dense, matter in it."

"Very good," said Mr. Bagges; "solid stuff necessary to brightness!"

"Some gases and other things," resumed Harry, "that burn with a flame you can hardly see, burn splendidly when something solid is put into them. Hydrogen gas if blown through a pipe, bums with very little light; but if the flame is blown upon a piece of quick-lime, it gets so bright as to be quite dazzling. If you now send some oxygen on to the flame, the flame gets no brighter, but the lime shines like a little sun. Make the smoke of oil of turpentine pass through the same oxygen, and it gives the flame a beautiful brightness directly. Well, carbon, or charcoal, is what causes the brightness of all lamps, and candles, and other common lights; so, of course, there is carbon in what they are all made of."

"So carbon is smoke, eh? and light is owing to your carbon. Giving light out of smoke, eh? as they say in the classics," observed Mr. Bagges.

Words

answered, *replied.*
beautiful, *lovely.*
brightness, *brilliancy.*
chimney, *smoke-vent.*
clumsy, *coarse.*
comical, *funny.*
commenced, *began.*
consuming, *absorbing.*
contrary, *opposite.*
Curious, *strange.*
dazzling, *blinding.*
directly, *immediately.*
draught, *air-current.*
enough, *plenty.*
exactly, *precisely.*
extinguisher, *cap.*
juvenile, *youthful.*
melted, *dissolved.*
mixture, *Union.*
necessary, *essential.*
noddle, *head.*
observed, *remarked.*
pores, *passages.*
proceeded, *continued.*
properly, *rightly.*
rogue, *rascal.*
scorched, *blackened.*
separates, *disjoins.*

shelter, *protect.*
solid, *substantial.*
splendid, *grand.*
troublesome, *tiresome.*
vapour, *gas.*

Questions

When a candle burns, why does the melted wax go up through the wick? What happens when you hold a bit of lighted paper in the smoke of a candle after it has been extinguished? What does this show? Of what does the flame of a candle consist? What is inside? How can this be shown? Without what will a candle not born? Why does a "clumsy dip smoke more than a nest wax candle"? What in reality la the smoke of a candle? Why la it that the little bits of oar bon cause the brightness of the flame? Illustrate this by the example of the oxy-hydrogen lime-light.

☆ ☆

"现在，叔叔，"哈利，这位老绅士最喜欢的一个侄子问道，"您能告诉我怎样熄灭一支蜡烛吗？"

"你这小家伙，在上面放上灭火的东西肯定就能把它熄灭。"

"哦，但我的意思是，你切断它氧气的来源，"哈利少爷说道。

"切断它的什么？"

"他说的是从皇家学院听到的，"威尔肯森夫人说道，"他读了大量的关于化学的书籍，还参加了法拉德教授在学院办的关于蜡烛化学史的讲座，从那儿以后，他脑子里一定净是这些东西。"

"现在，先生，"巴格斯叔叔说道，"您来我这儿，告诉我关于这种化学物质你有什么看法，嗯？或者关于它的有趣的事情？这个——蜡烛的趣味化学史。"

"哈利，别去烦你叔叔。"威尔肯森夫人说道。

"烦我？哦，一点儿也没有。我喜欢听他说话。"

"那叔叔，咱们先拿出一段蜡烛来。在柜架上就有一段，咱们把它点燃吧。"

"小心别烧到手，也别点着任何东西。"威尔肯森夫人说。

"现在，叔叔，"哈利开始把自己的椅子拖到巴格斯先生旁边，"我们得让蜡烛烧着。低头看看它的顶部，就在烛芯周围。看，那是一湾融化的蜡。火焰的热度融化了烛芯周围的蜡。冷的空气使它外围变得坚硬，从而形成了它的边缘。这一湾融化的蜡从烛芯向上走，被燃烧，和灯油在油灯灯芯中的工作原理是一样的。你觉得是什么让蜡往上走，叔叔？"

"是什么呢——什么呢，是火焰让它往上走的，是不是？"

“不完全正确，叔叔。蜡从棉质的芯子中间的微小的通道向上走，因为那非常非常微小的通道，或管道，或空隙自身有一种将液体吸附起来的力量。这种力量叫作毛细管引力；就像海绵能吸水，或者糖能把杯子里剩余的一点茶或咖啡吸附掉一个道理。”

“现在，我把蜡烛吹灭；不是为了恢复黑暗，而是为了看看究竟是怎么回事。看看从蜡芯那里升起来的烟，我会拿一小片纸放到那冒烟的地方，但不接触到蜡芯。看吧，那蜡烛居然又燃起来了！因此这就表明融化的蜡被从蜡芯中吸起来，变成蒸汽，而蒸汽被点燃了。燃烧的蒸汽的热度会融化更多的蜡，而这些蜡又被吸进了火焰，变成蒸汽燃烧；如此下去蜡就会被烧尽，而蜡烛也就用完了。因此这火焰，叔叔，您看，是蜡烛最后的部分；而通过火焰，蜡烛似乎变不成任何东西，但情况并非如此，蜡烛实际上变成了好几样东西。这不是很奇妙吗，正如法拉德教授说的那样，蜡烛燃烧的时候应该看起来美丽而耀眼吗？”

“我敢说，蜡烛的火焰在您的眼中看来平淡无奇，但如果我们在上头罩上一个玻璃灯罩保护它免得干燥的话，你就会看到它是圆形的——边缘是圆形的，向上形成一个峰状。它是被热空气抽上去的。您知道，热空气上升，这就是烟为什么能从烟囱出去的原理。您认为火焰中间是什么东西？”

“我说是火。”巴格斯叔叔回答道。

“哦，不。火焰是空心的。我们看到的明亮的火焰并不比薄薄的果皮或皮肤厚多少，它也并不和蜡芯接触。它中间是我刚才给您讲的蒸汽。如果你把一段弯折的管子的末端放在火焰中间，让管子的另一端进入一个温暖的瓶子里，那么从蜡烛中蒸发的蒸汽或气体就会和空气在那里混合；如果你将这种由蜡烛蒸汽和瓶子里的空气混合而成的气体点燃，它就马上会发出一声爆炸声。”

“我想让你试试，哈利。”汤姆少爷说，他是哈利的弟弟。

“我想把事情说清楚，”哈利回答道，“好的，叔叔，蜡烛的火焰是一个小小的闪亮的圈子，中间有气体蜡，外面有空气的包围，因此火焰圈是介于空气和气体蜡之间。不断有气体蜡进入火焰中燃烧，当蜡烛燃烧顺利的时候，没有气体蜡从火焰中溢出，也没有空气能进入到火焰中的气体蜡中间。蜡烛温度最高的部分是在火焰的表面，或叫焰表，或是外焰。”

“外焰！”巴格斯先生重复道，“真是活到老学到老。我本来以为蜡烛的火焰就像我这个老笨蛋一样厚实。”

“我可以给您看看，事实恰恰相反，”哈利说道。“我拿出这张白纸，看，把它放在蜡烛的火焰上一两秒钟，让火焰稳定燃烧。现在，我把黑烟的部分弄掉了，然后，你会发现纸被灼烧后呈环状，而环状的内部只不过是发黑，其实并没有被烧透。”

“眼见为实啊。”他叔叔说道。

“但是，”哈利继续说，“蜡烛的火焰产生的不仅仅是气体蜡这一种东西。你知道蜡烛没有空气燃烧不了，气体蜡周围一定要有空气的存在，然后和空气接触才能燃烧。如果没有充足的空气，那么蜡烛就会熄灭，或者燃烧不佳，因此一些火焰内部的蒸汽蜡会从火焰中以烟的形式跑出来；这也就是蜡烛会冒烟的原因。所以现在您知道了为什么一支巨大的火炬冒的烟要比小小的蜡烛产生的烟要少的原因了：那是因为火炬厚实的芯子产生太多的燃料，却没有相当数量的空气可以与之接触。”

“现在您觉得怎么样，”哈利继续说，“是我要告诉您，正是从蜡烛里跑出来的烟让蜡烛燃烧时产生光亮，蜡烛通过消耗掉自身产生的烟而发光。蜡烛的烟是一团小小的灰尘团，这些小的灰尘团，化学家把它叫作木炭或碳。它们一产生就被燃烧掉了，而它们正是在火焰外焰部，也就是最热的地方产生的。高温将它们和由融化的蜡转化而成的气体蜡分离开来，它们只要一接触到薄薄的外焰外面的空气，就马上燃烧起来。”

“你能告诉我，那些小的碳团是怎么产生火焰的光亮的吗？”威尔青森夫人问道。

“因为它们是固态的，”哈利回答道。“使火焰发光，就必须包含有一些固态的，或至少形态紧密的物质。”

“非常好，”巴格斯先生说，“产生光亮，必须有固态的物质！”

“还有一些气体和别的东西，”哈利继续说道，“它们燃烧时的火焰肉眼几乎看不到，只有当一些固态的东西加进去的时候，它们才能绚丽地燃烧。氢气，如果通过一根管子吹进去的话，燃烧的时候会产生很微弱的光；如果火焰是在石灰石上燃烧的话，就会产生让人目眩的光亮。如果你现在输送一些氧气到火焰上的话，火焰并不会变得更明亮，但石灰石却会变得像小小的太阳一样闪耀。在同样的氧气中放上松脂油产生的烟，火焰就会立马变得绚丽耀眼。嗯，碳或者木炭，是让所有的灯、蜡烛和其他常见的灯发光的原因。”

“所以，碳就是烟，而光是因为碳产生的，是从烟当中产生的，对吧？就像人们在经典著作中总结的那样。”巴格斯先生总结道。

Lesson 15
THE CHEMISTRY OF A CANDLE (II)
第十五课 蜡烛的化学知识（二）

"But what becomes of the candle," pursued Harry, "as it bums away? where does it go?"

"Nowhere, I should think. It burns to nothing."

"Oh, dear, no!" said Harry; "everything goes somewhere. You can see it goes into smoke, which makes soot, for one thing. There are other things it goes into, not to be seen by merely looking, but you can get to see them by taking the right means. Just put your hand over the candle, uncle."

"Thank you, my young gentleman, I would rather be excused."

"Not close enough down to burn you, uncle;—higher up. There;—you feel a stream of hot air, so something seems to rise from the candle. Suppose you were to put a long glass lamp-chimney over the flame, and let the flame burn just within the end of it, as if it were a chimney, some of the hot steam would go up and pass out at the top, but a sort of dew would be left behind in the glass chimney, if the chimney was cold enough when you put it on. There are ways of collecting this dew; and when it is collected it turns out to be really water. I am not joking, uncle. Water is one of the things which the candle turns into while burning—water coming out of fire. In some light-houses, Professor Faraday says, two gallons of oil are burned in a single night; and if the windows are cold, the steam from the oil clouds them, and, in frosty weather, freezes into ice."

"Water out of a candle, eh?" exclaimed Mr. Bagges "As hard to get, I should have thought, as blood out of s post. Where does it come from?"

"Part from the wax, and part from the air; and yet not a drop of it comes from either the air or the wax. What do you make of that, uncle"

"Eh? Oh, I'm no hand at riddles! Give it up."

"No riddle at all, uncle. That which comes from the wax is a gas called hydrogen. We can obtain it from water by passing the steam of boiling water through a red-hot gun-barrel which contains a quantity of iron wire or turnings. Part of the steam will mix with the iron turnings, and change them into rust; and the other part, which comes out of the end of the barrel, will be hydrogen gas, and this part of the water we can set on fire."

"Eh?" cried Mr. Bagges. "Upon my word! One of these days we shall have you setting the river on fire!"

"Nothing more easy," said Harry. "When pure hydrogen bums, we get nothing but water. I should like to show you how light this hydrogen is; and I wish I had a small balloon to fill with it and send up to the ceiling; or a pipe full of it to blow soap-bubbles with, and show how much faster they rise than common ones blown with the breath."

"So do I," interposed Master Tom.

"And so," resumed Harry, "hydrogen, you know, uncle is part of water, and just one-ninth part. The other eight parts are a gas also, called oxygen. This is a very curious gas. It won't bum in air at all itself, like gas from a lamp; but it has a wonderful power of making things bum that are lighted and put into it. A lighted candle put into a jar of oxygen blazes up directly, and is consumed before you can say Jack Robinson. Charcoal bums away in it as fast, with beautiful bright sparks; phosphorus burns with a light that would dazzle you to look at; and a piece of iron or steel, just made red-hot at the end first, may be burned in oxygen more quickly than a tick could be in common air. The experiment of burning things in oxygen beats any fire-works."

"How funny that must be!" exclaimed Tom.

"Now we see, uncle," Harry continued, " that water is hydrogen and oxygen united together; that water is got whenever hydrogen is burned in common air; that a candle won't burn without air; and that when a candle burns, there is hydrogen in it burning and forming water. Now, then, where does the hydrogen of the candle get the oxygen, to turn into water with it?"

"From the air, eh?"

"Just so. It is the oxygen in the air that makes things burn; but if the air were nothing but oxygen, a candle would not last above a minute.

"'If a house were on fire in oxygen,' as Professor Faraday said, 'every iron bar, or, rather, every pillar, every nail and iron tool, and the grate itself; all the zinc and copper roofs, and leaden coverings, and gutters, and pipes, would consume and burn, increasing the combustion.'"

"That would be, indeed, 'burning like a house on fire,'" observed Mr. Bagges.

"But there is another gas, called nitrogen," I said Harry "which is mixed with the air; and it is this which prevents a candle from burning out too fast."

"Eh?" said Mr. Bagges. "Well, I do think we are under considerable obligations to nitrogen."

"I have explained to you, uncle," continued Harry "how a candle, in burning, turns into water. But it turns into something else besides that. The little bits of carbon that I told you about, which are burned in the flame of a candle, and which make the flame bright, mingle with the oxygen in burning, and form still another gas, called carbonic acid gas, which is very destructive to life when we breathe it. So you see that a candle-flame is vapour burning; and that the vapour, in burning, turns into water and carbonic acid gas."

"Haven't you pretty nearly come to your candle's end?" said Mr. Wilkinson.

"Nearly. I only want to tell uncle that the burning of a candle is almost exactly like our breathing. Breathing is consuming oxygen, only not so fast as burning. In breathing, we throw out from our lungs water in the form of vapour, and carbonic acid gas, and take oxygen in. Oxygen is as necessary to support the life of the body as it is to keep up the flame of a candle."

"Well," said Mr. Bagges, "any more to tell us about the candle?"

"If I had time, I could tell you a great deal more that Professor Faraday said about oxygen, and hydrogen, and carbon, and water, and breathing; but you should go and hear him yourself, uncle."

"Eh? well I think I shall. Some of us seniors may learn something from a juvenile lecture, at any rate if given by a Faraday. And now, my boy, I tell you what," added Mr. Bagges; "I am very glad to find you so fond of study and science; and you deserve to be encouraged; and so I'll give you a—what-d'ye-call-it—a galvanic battery on your next birth-day; and so much for your teaching your old uncle the Chemistry of a Candle."

Words

blazes, *flames.*
ceiling, *Inside-roof.*
collecting, *gathering.*
combustion, *conflagration.*
considerable, *important.*
deserve, *merit.*
destructive, *injurious.*
encouraged, *stimulated.*
exclaimed, *ejaculated.*
excused, *pardoned.*
experiment, *operation.*
explained, *expounded.*
freezes, *congeals.*
grate, *fireplace.*
increasing, *augmenting.*
joking, *making fun.*
obligation, *indebtedness.*
obtain, *procure.*
prevents, *hinders.*
pursued, *continued.*
quantity, *portion.*
riddles, *conundrums.*
seniors, *old folks.*
support, *maintain.*
suppose, *assume.*
turnings, *flings.*
united, *Joined.*
wonderful, *extraordinary.*

Questions

What are the different things into which the candle goes when it burns? How is the water produced? What is it that prevents the candle from burning too fast? How is the carbonic acid gas produced? Show how the burning of a candle resembles the process of breathing.

☆ ☆

“那蜡烛会变成什么呢？”哈利继续追问，“它燃尽了之后会变成什么了呢？”

“什么也不是，我觉得。燃烧不成什么东西。”

“哦，亲爱的，不是的！”哈利说道，“所有的东西都会变成某种东西。你可以看见它变成了烟，变成烟灰，这是一个例子。它还可以变成其他的东西，但不是通过简单地看就能发现的，而是需要通过适当的方法才行。把您的手放到蜡烛上方，叔叔。”

“谢谢你，我的小绅士，我看还是算了吧。”

“不要太靠近，不会烧到您的，叔叔，举得高点儿，就这样，你会感觉到热空气流，因此似乎是蜡烛里有什么东西在上升。假设您把一个长长的玻璃灯罩，照在火焰上，让火焰在罩子的尾端燃烧，就好像这罩子是烟囱似的，一定会有热流向上走，从罩子的顶端冒出去，而在玻璃罩子中间会留下一点水珠，如果你把罩子放到火焰上的时候，它是凉的话，这些水珠可以通过一些办法来收集；当收集好了之后，它们就会变成真正的水。我不是在开玩笑，叔叔。水是蜡烛燃烧的时候产生的物质之一——从火中产生的水。在一些通亮的屋子里，法拉德教授说，一晚上能烧掉两加仑的油脂；如果窗子是凉的话，因为油脂燃烧产生的水就会笼罩在窗子上，天气寒冷的时候，就会结成霜冻。”

“蜡烛会产生水，嗯？”巴格斯先生惊诧道，“这很不可思议，我原本以为，嗯，这简直像柱子会产生血液那么不可思议。那么水是从哪里来的呢？”

“一部分是来自蜡，一部分是来自空气；但没有一滴是完全来自蜡或者空气的。您想明白了吗，叔叔？”

“嗯，哦，我还是想不明白，我放弃。”

“一点儿也不难，叔叔。蜡产生了一种叫氢气的气体。我们在装有铁线或铁屑的烧得红热的油水分离罐上，放上沸腾水的水蒸气，这样就能从水中得到氢气了。部分水蒸气会和铁屑混合，把它们变成铁锈；而其他蒸气则会从罐子的底部出去，变成氢气，而这部分的水我们则能把它点燃。”

“啊？”巴格斯先生喊道。“我敢说，总有一天你能把河给点燃喽！”

“没那么简单，”哈利说。“当纯氢气燃烧的时候，我们得到的只是水。我想给您展示一下，怎么点燃氢气；要是有一只装满氢气的小气球就好了，把它放飞到天花板那儿；或者有一只管子里头都是氢气，用它来吹出肥皂泡泡，然后我就能给您展示一下它们比装满空气的球或泡泡飞得要快多了。”

“我也能这样做。”汤姆少爷插嘴道。

“因此，”哈利继续说道，“你知道的，叔叔，氢气是水的一部分，而且仅仅占到其中的九分之一。剩余的九分之八的部分也是一种气体，叫作氧气。这是一种很有意思的气体，和灯产生的气体一样，它在空气中不会自己燃烧，但对于那些点燃的，并放置到它中间的东西而言，它有一种强大的使它们燃烧的能力。一支点燃的蜡烛放到一个装满氧气的罐子里，会马上剧烈燃烧起来，在你还没说完杰克·罗宾逊几个字前就烧尽了。木炭在氧气中也燃烧得很快，还会产生美丽的耀眼的火花；磷燃烧的时候会产生一种强光，让人眼睛不能直视；一块铁或钢，一开始末端烧得通红，放到氧气中会快速燃烧，比一段木棍在空气中燃烧得还要快。在氧气中，燃烧物体做的实验，胜过了其他的燃烧实验。”

“那一定有趣极了！”汤姆叫道。

“现在我们明白了，叔叔，”哈利继续说道，“水是由氢气和氧气组成的，只要空气中有氢气燃烧就会产生水，而蜡烛没有空气不会燃烧。当蜡烛燃烧的时候，是里头的氢气在燃烧并形成水。现在，蜡烛中的氢气是如何获取氧气，从而和氧气一同变成水的呢？”

“从空气中，嗯。”

“没错。正是空气中的氧气让东西燃烧；但如果空气中只有氧气的话，一支蜡烛燃烧的时间都不到一分钟。”

“法拉德教授说，‘如果一座房子在氧气中起火了’，‘所有的铁栏杆，或者换种说法，所有的柱子、所有的钉子和铁质工具以及壁炉、全部的锌和铜制的屋顶、铅质的覆盖物、水沟、管道，都会起火燃烧，增加火势。’”

“的确如此，就像整座房子着火了一样，”巴格斯先生评价道。

“但还有另一种气体，叫作氮气，”哈利说，“它混杂在空气中，就是它使得蜡烛不会过快燃烧。”

“哦？”巴格斯先生说。“好的，我真的认为我们欠了氮气好大一个人情。”

“我已经和您解释过了，叔叔，”哈利继续说道，“一支蜡烛是如何在燃烧的过程中变成水的。但除了水之外，它还变成了其他的东西。我之前和您说过的小小碳离子的，它在蜡烛的火焰中燃烧，并使得火焰明亮发光。如果碳和氧气混合燃烧的话，就会形成另外一种气体，叫碳酸气体，人如果吸了这种气体的话，是非常有害的。所以，您明白了蜡烛产生的火焰是因为气体在燃烧；而那种燃烧着的气体，变成了水和碳酸气体。”

“你关于蜡烛的故事，快要讲完了吗？”威尔肯森夫人问道。

“快了。我只想告诉叔叔蜡烛的燃烧就和我们的呼吸几乎是一样的道理。呼吸消耗氧气，只不过赶不上燃烧时消耗氧气的速度。我们呼吸的时候从肺里释放出蒸汽形式的水以及碳酸气体，吸进的则是氧气。氧气对于蜡烛火焰燃烧就和它对于支持生命的作用一样必不可少。”

“好的，”巴格斯先生说，“你还有什么关于蜡烛的知识要说吗？”

“如果我有时间的话，我会告诉您更多法拉德教授讲述的关于氧气的知识，关于氢气、碳、水、呼吸的知识，但您应该去亲自听听他讲的，叔叔。”

“嗯？好我觉得我会去的。我们老年人能从年轻人讲的课中学到一些东西，不管是不是一位叫法拉德的教授讲的。现在，我的孩子，我告诉你，”巴格斯先生补充道，“我非常高兴，你能这么喜欢学习，这么喜欢科学，你值得夸奖，因此我将给你一个——叫什么来着——一块电池作为你明年的生日礼物。你给老叔叔讲的蜡烛的化学知识课就到这里告一段落吧。”

Lesson 16 THE "MAYFLOWER"

第十六课 "五月花"号

On the northern border of Nottinghamshire stands the little town of Scrooby. Here, about the end of the sixteenth century, there were some grave and well-reputed persons, to whom the ceremonies of the Established Church were an offence. They met in secret at the house of one of their number, a gentleman named Brewster. They were ministered to in all scriptural simplicity by the pastor of their choice—Mr. Robinson, a wise and good man. But their secret meetings were betrayed to the authorities, and their lives were made bitter by the persecutions that fell upon them. They resolved to leave their own land, and seek among strangers that freedom which was denied them at home.

They embarked with all their goods for Holland. But when the ship was about to sail, soldiers came upon them, plundered them, and drove them on shore. They were marched to the public square of Boston,and there the Fathers of New England endured such indignities as an unbelieving rabble could inflict. After some weeks in prison, they were suffered to return home.

Next spring they tried again to escape. This time a good many were on board, and the others were waiting for the return of the boat which should carry them to the ship. Suddenly dragoons were seen spurring across the sands. The shipmaster pulled up his anchor, and pushed out to sea with those of his passengers whom he had. The rest were conducted to prison. After a time they were set at liberty. In little groups they also made their way to Holland. Mr. Robinson and his congregation were reunited, and the first stage of the weary pilgrimage from the old England to the New was at length accomplished.

Eleven quiet and not unprosperous years were spent in Holland. The Pilgrims worked with patient industry at their various handicrafts. They quickly gained the reputation of doing honestly and effectively whatever they professed to do; and thus they found abundant employment. Mr. Brewster established a printing-press, and printed books about liberty; which, as he had the satisfaction of knowing, greatly enraged the foolish King James. The little colony received additions from time to time as oppression in England became more intolerable.

The instinct of separation was strong within the Pilgrim heart. They could not bear the thought that their little colony was to mingle with the Dutchmen and lose its independent existence. But already their sons and daughters were forming alliances which threatened this result. The Fathers considered long and anxiously how the danger was to be averted. They determined again to go on pilgrimage. They would seek a home beyond the Atlantic, where they could dwell apart and found a State in which they should be free to think.

On a sunny morning in July 1620, the Pilgrims kneel upon the sea-shore at Delfthaven, while the pastor prays for the success of their journey. Out upon the gleaming sea a little ship lies waiting. Money has not been found to transplant the whole colony, and scarcely one hundred have been sent. The remainder will follow when they can. These hundred depart amid tears and prayers and fond farewells. Mr. Robinson dismissed them with counsels which breathed a pure and high-toned wisdom, urging them to keep their minds ever open for the reception of new truths.

THE "MAYFLOWER" IN CAPE COD BAY

Their little ship, the *Speedwell*, brought them to South-ampton, where they found the *Mayflower*, a ship hired for the voyage, and a small band of Pilgrims from London. At Plymouth the *Speedwell* was pronounced unseaworthy, and was abandoned; and the *Mayflower*, crowded with the whole party (one hundred and two souls), set sail alone.

The *Mayflower* was a ship of one hundred and sixty tons. The weather proved stormy and cold; the voyage unexpectedly long. It was the middle of September when they sailed. It was not till the 11th November that the *Mayflower* dropped her anchor in the waters of Cape Cod Bay.

A bleak-looking and discouraging coast lay before them. Nothing met the eye but low sand-hills, covered with ill-grown wood down to the margin of the sea. The Pilgrims had now to choose a place for their settlement. About this they hesitated so long that the captain threatened to put them all on shore and leave them.

Little expeditions were sent to explore. At first no suitable locality could be found. The men had great hardships to endure. The cold was so excessive that the spray froze upon their clothes, and they resembled men cased in armour. At length a spot was fixed upon. The soil appeared to be good, and abounded in "delicate springs" of water. On the 23rd December the Pilgrims landed—stepping ashore upon a huge boulder of granite, which is still reverently preserved by their descendants. Here they resolved to found their settlement, which they agreed to call New Plymouth.

The winter was severe, and the infant colony was brought very near to extinction. They had been badly fed on board the *Mayflower*, and for some time after going on shore there was very imperfect shelter from the weather. Sickness fell heavily on the worn-out Pilgrims. Every second day a grave had to be dug in the frozen ground. By the time spring came in there were only fifty survivors, and these sadly enfeebled and dispirited.

THE PLLGRIM STONE

But all through this dismal winter the Pilgrims laboured at their heavy task. The care of the sick, the burying of the dead, sadly hindered their work. But the building of their little town went on. They found that nineteen houses would contain their diminished numbers. These they built. Then they surrounded them with a palisade.

Upon an eminence beside their town they erected a structure which served a double purpose. Above, it was a fort, on which they mounted six cannon; below, it was their church. Hitherto the Indians had been a cause of anxiety, but had done them no harm. Now they felt safe. Indeed there had never been much risk. A recent epidemic had swept off nine-tenths of the Indians who inhabited that region, and the discouraged survivors could ill afford to incur the hostility of their formidable visitors.

The Pilgrims had been careful to provide for themselves a government. They had drawn up and signed, in the cabin of the *Mayflower*, a document forming themselves into a body politic, and promising obedience to all laws framed for the general good. Under this Constitution they appointed John Carver to be their governor. They dutifully acknowledged King James, but they left no very urge place for his authority. They were essentially a self-governing people. They knew what despotism was, and they were very sure that democracy could by no possibility be so bad.

The welcome spring came at length, and "the birds sang in the woods most pleasantly." The health of the colony began somewhat to improve; but there was still much suffering to endure. The summer passed not unprosperously. They had taken possession of the deserted clearings of the Indians, and bad no difficulty in providing themselves with food. In the autumn came a ship with a new company of Pilgrims. This was very encouraging; but unhappily the ship brought no provisions, and the supplies of the colonists were not sufficient for this unexpected addition. For six months there was only half allowance to each.

Such straits recurred frequently during the first two or three years. Often the colonists knew not at night "when to have a bit in the morning." Once or twice the opportune arrival of a ship saved them from famishing. They suffered much, but their cheerful trust in Providence and in their own final triumph never wavered. They faced the difficulties of their position with undaunted hearts. Slowly but surely the little colony struck its roots and began to grow.

Words

abounded, *teemed with.*
accomplished, *completed.*
armour, *mail.*
authorities, *magistrates.*
betrayed, *revealed.*
ceremonies, *observances.*
conducted, *led.*
counsels, *advice.*
democracy, *republicanism.*
descendants, *children.*
despotism, *tyranny.*
determined, *resolved.*
discouraging, *uninviting.*
document, *paper.*
dutifully, *loyally.*
eminence, *elevation.*
encouraging, *inspiriting.*
enfeebled, *weakened.*
enraged, *Irritated.*
epidemic, *disease.*
excessive, *extreme.*
extinction, *extermination.*
hesitated, *wavered.*
hostility, *enmity.*
independent, *individual.*
indignities, *insults.*
intolerable, *insufferable.*
locality, *district.*
margin, *border.*
opportune, *timely.*
pilgrimage, *Journey.*
plundered, *pillaged.*
pronounced, *declared.*
reception, *entertaining.*
remainder, *residue.*
reputation, *character.*
settlement, *colony.*
simplicity, *plainness.*
spurring, *galloping.*
structure, *building.*
suffered, *permitted.*
undaunted, *intrepid.*
unprosperously, *unsuccessfully.*
well-reputed, *respectable.*

Questions

To what town did the Pilgrim Fathers originally belong? How were they prevented escaping to Holland on their first attempt? What happened next spring? How many years did the Pilgrims spend in Holland? How were they occupied? Why did they resolve to sail to

America? Where did they embark? In what year? Where did they meet the Mayflower? How many sailed from Plymouth? When did they land? Where? To what was their number reduced before spring? What did they erect on an eminence beside their town? Where had they framed their constitution? Who was appointed first governor? To what straits were they frequently subjected?

☆ ☆

诺丁汉郡的北部边境上屹立着一座叫斯克罗比的小城。大约在16世纪末的时候，那里出现了一些严肃而声名远扬的人，对于这些人而言，现有的宗教仪式是可耻的。这群人在某个绅士家中秘密会面，这名绅士名叫布鲁斯特尔。他们选了自己的牧师，牧师根据《圣经》的简明原则对他们训诫管理。牧师名叫罗宾逊，是个睿智而善良的人。他们的秘密集会被人告发之后，当局就开始对他们进行迫害，他们的日子也更难熬了。于是他们决定离开家乡，在陌生之地寻求在家乡找不到的自由。

他们带着自己的行李在荷兰登船。但当船起航的时候，突然来了一群士兵把他们抓起来，驱逐他们上岸。他们本想到波士顿的公共领地去，在那里新英格兰的祖先们忍受了难以想象的苦难和屈辱。在被关押了数个星期之后，他们不得不隐忍回到家乡。

第二年春天，他们再次想逃走。这次，登船的人很多，其他人则在等着小船回来接他们到大船上去。突然沙地里一下子跳出了骑兵，掌舵人拉起锚，带着大船上所有的乘客一同向海上驶去。剩下的人则被送进了监狱。过了一段时间，他们被释放了。这些人组成了一个个小队伍，向荷兰前进。罗宾逊先生和他的教众们重逢了，第一阶段的从旧英格兰到新世界的令人疲惫的移民之路，终于结束了。

他们在荷兰度过了平淡而硕果累累的十一年。新移民们辛勤而耐心地劳作于各行各业。不久他们就赢得了声誉，他们无论做什么都诚信而高效，因此有很多工作找上门。布鲁斯特先生创建了印刷社，他印刷的书籍都是关于自由的，因为他知道这样做可以极大地激怒愚昧的詹姆斯国王，这让他很高兴。这小小的殖民地不时会受到来自英格兰的欺压，慢慢地，这欺压变得越来越难以忍受了。

新移民心中关于独立的想法已经非常强烈。他们一想到自己的小殖民地和荷兰人搅和在一起，失去殖民地的独立性，就不能忍受。当时他们中的男男女女已经成立了要结束这一现状的联盟，开国者们认真考虑了很久，想着如何避免会遇到的危险，最后他们再次决定踏上移民之路。他们要在大西洋彼岸找到家园，在那里他们能独立生活，建立一个自由思想的国家。

1620年7月一个夏日的清晨，移民者跪在代尔夫特海文的海岸上，教士正为他们此次顺利航行祷告。在那波光粼粼的大海上，有一条小船在等待着他们。这艘船不能直接到达殖民地，上船的连100个人都不到。剩下的人则计划在情况允许的时候再追随前去。这一百多个人在泪水和祈祷中与亲友分别，并道了永别。罗宾逊先生用纯粹而高雅的、智慧的决策送走了他们，敦促他们用开放的心态来接纳新的真理。

他们的小船，即“史必得威尔”号，把他们带到了南安普顿，在那儿他们找到了“五月花”号，一艘为这次航行租来的船，上头有从伦敦而来的一小队移民。在朴茨茅斯，史必得威尔号因被认为不适合海上航行而被舍弃了，而“五月花”号则满载着所有人（102人）独自起航了。

“五月花”号载重160吨。海上暴风雨不断，天气寒冷，整个航行出乎意料得长。他们是在9月中旬的时候起航的，而一直到11月11日那天，“五月花”号才在鳕鱼角湾抛锚停泊。

他们面前是一片荒凉而毫无生气的海岸。眼前所见的只有低矮的山丘，一直延伸到大海的边缘，长得歪歪扭扭的树木覆盖在上面。新移民现在必须得找一个定居地。关于这一点，他们犹豫了良久，以至于船长威胁要把他们全部留在海岸上，弃他们而去。

他们几乎没进行什么探险活动。起初，因为找不到合适的居住地点，巨大的艰难险阻在等待他们。天气异常寒冷，他们的衣服上都结满了冰，于是便聚集在一件盔甲下取暖。最后，他们终于找到了一个栖身地。那儿的土地看起来不错，还有“味道甘美”的泉水遍布在各处。在12月23日这天，新移民们登陆了——他们在一个有巨大的圆形花岗岩的海岸上登陆了，那块大石到现在还被他们的后人满怀敬意地保留着。在这里，他们决心建立自己的居留地，他们一致决定把这个地方叫作新朴茨茅斯。

冬天是异常艰苦的，刚刚建立的殖民地几乎到了灭亡的边缘。他们在“五月花”号的甲板上勉强果腹，在登陆了一段时间之后，还没有足以遮风避雨的地方。疾病降临到疲惫不堪的新移民当中。每隔一天，冰冷的土地上就得挖掘一个新墓穴。春天来到的时候，只有五十个人幸存了下来，这些人憔悴不堪，精神萎靡。

但整个阴沉的冬天，新移民们都在从事繁重的劳动。他们需要照顾病人，掩埋死者，这些不幸都中断了他们的劳作。但他们建设小城镇的工作还在继续着。他们发现，建造19座房屋就足以容纳得下他们日渐减少的同伴。于是他们就建造了19座房屋。然后绕着这些房屋建造了一个栅栏。

他们在自己小城旁边的险要之地造了一个建筑，这个建筑有两个作用。首先，它是一个堡垒，他们可以在上面架上6门大炮；其次，这是他们的教堂。迄今为止，他们最恐惧的是印第安人，但印第安人从没伤害过他们，现在他们觉得安全了。的确，那里从未有过什么危险。最近的一场瘟疫，夺去了聚居在那里的印第安人大部分人的性命，而剩下的印第安人则不敢再挑起对那骇人的外来者的挑衅了。

新移民们很小心地建立起一个自治的政府。他们在“五月花”号的船舱上起草并签署文件，这份文件使他们成为一个政治体，承诺遵守为大部分人的利益而制定的所有法律。在这个宪法下，他们选定约翰·卡维尔作为他们的领袖。而出于义务，他们承认英国的詹姆斯国王，但同时，他们不承认詹姆斯国王的权威。从本质上来说，他们是一群自治的人。他们知道专制独裁的危害，于是他们非常相信民主无论怎样也沦落不到专制独裁的地步。

终于，宜人的春天来到了，“鸟儿在树林里欢快地歌唱”。殖民地的情况开始改观，但还有困难在等待着他们。夏天，他们收获了累累硕果。他们将印第安人丢弃的空地占为己有，轻而易举地实现了食物自足。秋天，来了一条载有新来移民的船只。这非常鼓舞人心，但不幸的是，船上并没有带来什么供应品，而殖民地的食物供给不足以应付这不期而至的新人。整整6个月的时间，每个人都只能有一半的食物分配。

在头两三年，这样的情况反复出现了多次。殖民地的人们知道早晨要少吃一点，否则就撑不到晚上了。有一两次幸运的情况，有船只到来，他们就免于挨饿了。他们经历了很多的艰难，但他们对于上帝的乐观信念和对于他们最终的胜利从未改变过。他们用无畏的心，面对处境中的困顿艰难。这小小的殖民地慢慢地坚定地生下了根，开始成长。

Lesson 17 THE PILGRIM FATHERS

第十七课 移民的先祖

The breaking waves dashed high on a stem and rock-bound coast,
And the woods against a stormy sky their giant branches tossed,
And the heavy night hung dark the hills and waters o'er,
When a band of exiles moored their bark on the wild New England shore.

Not as the conqueror comes, they, the true-hearted, came,—
Not with the roll of stirring drums, and the trumpet that sings of fame:
Not as the flying come, in silence and in fear,—
They shook the depths of the desert's gloom with their hymns of lofty cheer.

Amidst the storm they sang, and the stars heard and the sea!
And the sounding aisles of the dim wood rang to the anthers of the free:
The ocean-eagle soared from his nest by the white waves' foam,
And the rocking pines of the forest roared;—this was their welcome home!

There were men with hoary hair amidst that pilgrim band;
Why had they come to wither there, away from their childhood's land?
There was woman's fearless eye, lit by her deep love's truth;
There was manhood's brow, serenely high; and the fiery heart of youth.

What sought they thus afar? bright jewels of the mine?
The wealth of seas, the spoils of war?—They sought a faith's pure shrine!
Ay, call it holy ground, the soil where first they trod!
They have left unstained what there they found,—freedom to worship God!

—MRS. HEMANS (1793−1836)

Words

aisles, *passages*.
anthems, *hymns*.
conqueror, *victor*.
exiles, *refugees*.
fearless, *dauntless*.
hoary, *white*.
jewels, *riches*.
lofty, *exalted*.
serenely, *calmly*.
shrine, *temple*.
stir ring, *rousing*.
unstained, *spotless*.

☆ ☆

骇浪激起，高高拍打在船首和礁石丛生的海岸上，
暴风雨天气下，森林里巨大的枝条在摩摩挲挲，
深沉的夜晚将黑暗降临在群山上，笼罩在水域上，
一群流亡者划动着船到达了荒野般的新英格兰海岸。

他们不是作为征服者而来，而是怀着满心真挚，到来了，
没有滚滚的鼓声和吹动着胜利赞歌的号声：
他们不是逃亡而来，没有满怀恐惧，抑或沉默寡言，
他们用高贵的鼓舞的哼唱，撼动那沙漠一般的忧愁。

在暴风雨中他们歌唱，星星和大海都听到了他们的歌声！
那晦暗的森林中的，发出回声的小岛上，响动着对自由的高歌。
海鹰从它的巢穴一飞冲天，那巢穴旁边白浪涌动，
森林中摇曳的松树怒吼着——这是欢迎他们到来的家园！

移民的队伍中间有白发苍苍的人，
为什么他们来到了那里，远离儿时的故土？
女人那毫不惧怕的眸子，被她对真理深深的爱所点亮；
男人的额头，平静而高洁；还有年轻人炽热的心在搏动。

他们走了这么远为了找寻什么？是有光彩熠熠的珠宝的矿藏吗？
大海的财富、战争的破坏——他们找寻的是信念纯净的神殿！
啊，把它叫作神圣的土地吧，他们是第一次踏上这土地的人！
他们将找到的土地保留了本色——就是崇拜圣地的自由！

——赫曼斯夫人（1793–1836）

Lesson 18 LIVING STOVES

第十八课 有生命的火炉

[Animal heat is caused by the union of the oxygen of the air with the carbon derived from the food we eat. This carbon, taken in as a part of our food, and being used to form the tissues of the body, is dislodged, particle by particle, whenever we move a muscle, be it of the heart, lungs, or limbs, and whenever we think or feel; and it is then that the union with oxygen (that is, the combustion takes place.) The more intensely, therefore, we think, and act, and feel, the more carbon we burn, and the more repairs our bodies need. The condition of life is therefore death; and the faster we live the more rapidly are the particles of our bodies burning up—passing away. The following humorous article may help to fix some of these principles in our memories.]

We must be plain with our reader. It will not do to mince matters where questions of science are concerned. Dainty people will, no doubt, object to the proposition we are about to advance. Nevertheless we persist, and proceed to lay down the following assertion: We are all living stoves—walking fire-places—furnaces in the flesh.

Now we do not intend to say that any one can light a cigar, or boil an egg, or even ignite a lucifer-match at these human hearths. Still, we repeat, these bodies of ours are stoves—fire-places—furnaces, if these terms can be applied to any apparatus for the express production of heat. And is not heat produced in the human body by the union of oxygen with carbon, just the same as by the burning of wood in an open fire-place and does not this union take place in the capillaries of the blood-vessels?

But granting that our bodies are veritable stoves, the reader will desire to know where we procure our fuel. Fortunately, our coal and fire-wood are stored up in a very interesting form. They are laid before us in the shape of bread and butter, puddings and pies; rashers of bacon for the labourer, and haunches of venison or turtle-soup for the epicure. Instead of being brought up in scuttles, they are presented in tureens, dishes, or tumblers, or all of them, in pleasant succession.

In fact, whenever you send a person an invitation to dinner, you virtually request the honour of his company to take fuel; and when you see him enthusiastically employed on your dainties, you know that he is literally "shovelling" fuel into his corporeal stove. The ultimate form in which this fuel is burned in the capillaries is that of carbon, with a little hydrogen and sulphur; but we swallow it in the shape of fat, starch, sugar, alcohol, and other less inflam-matory compounds. By far the most heating of these substances is fat. Ten pounds of this material, imported into your stove, will do as much work—that is, will produce as much warmth—as twenty-five pounds of starch, twenty-five of sugar, or even twenty-six of spirits.

And a pleasant thing it is to observe how sagaciously the instinct of man has fastened upon the articles which will best supply him with the species of fuel he requires. The Esquimau is extremely partial to oily fare. He does not know why. He never heard of the doctrine of animal heat, but he feels intuitively that bear's grease and blubber are the things for him. Condemn him to live on potatoes or Indian corn, and the poor fellow would resent the cruelty as much as an alderman of the old school if sentenced to subsist on water-gruel alone.

And the savage would be perfectly light. Exposed as he is to the fierce cold of a northern sky, every object around him plundering him of his caloric incessantly, what he needs is plenty of oily food, because from that he can produce the greatest quantity of heat. On the other hand, the native of the tropics, equally ignorant of animal chemistry, eschews the fiery diet, which his climate renders inappropriate, and keeps himself cool on rice, or dates, or watery fruits.

Hence we see the reason why a very stout man, if deprived of food, can keep up his corporeal fires for a longer time than a slender one. Human fat is fuel laid away for use. It constitutes a hoard of combustible material upon which the owner may draw whenever his ordinary supplies are intercepted. Let all plump persons therefore rejoice. We offer them our hearty, perhaps somewhat envious, congratulations. They, at any rate, are prepared to stand a long siege from cold.

For the same reason, animals which hibernate, like the bear, jerboa, marmot, dormouse, bat, and others, generally grow plump before they retire into winter quarters. Upon their capital of fat they subsist during their lethargy, the respiration being lessened, the pulse reduced to a few beats per minute, and the temperature perhaps nearly to the freezing point. But when the season of torpor terminates, they issue from their caves and burrows meagre and ravenous, having burned up their stock of fuel; Bruin himself appearing to be anxious to defraud the perfumers of the unguent which is so precious in their eyes.

But perhaps the most striking feature in this warmth producing apparatus within us is the self-regulating power which it possesses. The fires on our domestic hearths decline at one moment, and augment at another. Sometimes the mistress of the house threatens to faint on account of excessive heat; sometimes the master endeavours to improve the temperature by a passionate use of the poker, with an occasional growl respecting the excessive cold.

Were such irregularities to prevail unchecked in our fleshy stoves, we should suffer considerable annoyance. After a meal of very inflammatory materials, or an hour went in extraordinary exertion, the gush of heat might throw the system into a state of high fever. How is this prevented? In some of our artificial stoves, little doors or slides are employed to control the admission of air; in furnaces connected with steam-engines we may have dampers, which will accomplish the same purpose by the ingenious workings of the machine itself.

But neither doors nor dampers, pokers nor stokers, can be employed in the bodily apparatus. If, on the one hand, our human fires should begin to flag from undue expenditure of heat, the appetite speaks out sharply and compels the owner to look around for fuel. Hunger rings the bell and orders up coal in the shape of savoury meats. Should the summons be neglected, the garnered fat, as we have seen, is thrown into the grate to keep the furnace in play.

If, on the other hand, the heat of the body should become unreasonably intense, a very cunning process of reduction is adopted. When a substance grows too hot, the simplest method of bringing it into a cooler frame is to sprinkle it with water. This is precisely what occurs in our human frames. For no sooner does our internal heat rise above its standard height than the perspiration tubes, with their six or seven millions of openings, indignant at the event, begin to pour out the fluid, so as to bathe the surface of the whole body. Whenever, therefore, a man becomes over-heated, by working, running, rowing, fighting, making furious speeches or other violent exertions, he invariably resorts to this method of quenching the heat, by "pouring on water."

What shall we say, then, good reader? Speaking seriously, and looking at the question from a mere human point of view, could any project appear more hopeless than one for burning fuel in a soft, delicate fabric, like the human body—a fabric composed for the most part of mere fluids—a fabric which might be easily scorched by excess of heat or damaged by excess of cold? Does it not seem strange that a stove should have flesh for its walls, veins for its flues, and skin for its covering? Yet here is an apparatus which, as if by magic, produces a steady stream of heat;—not trickling penuriously from its fountains, but flowing on day and night, winter and summer, without a moment's cessation, from January to December.

Carry this splendid machine to the coldest regions on the globe, set it up where the frosts are so crushing that nature seems to be trampled dead,—still it pours out its mysterious supplies with unabated profusion. It is an apparatus, too, which does its work unwatched, and in a great measure unaided. The very fuel, which is thrown into it in random heaps, is internally sifted and sorted, so that the true combustible elements are conveyed to their place and applied to their duty with unerring precision.

No hand is needed to trim its fires, to temper its glow, to remove its ashes. Smoke there is none, spark there is none, flame there is none. All is so delicately managed that the fairest skin is neither shrivelled nor blackened by the burning within. Is this apparatus placed in circumstances which rob it too fast of its heat? Then the appetite becomes clamorous for food, and in satisfying its demands the fleshy stove is silently replenished. Or, are we placed in peril from superabundant warmth? Then the tiny flood-gates of perspiration are flung open, and the surface is laid under water until the fires within are reduced to their wonted level.

Assailed on the one hand by heat, the body resists the attack, if resistance be possible, until the store of moisture is dissipated; assailed on the other by cold, it keeps the enemy at bay until the hoarded fuel is expended. Thus protected, thus provisioned, let us ask whether these human hearths are not entitled to rank among the standing marvels of creation; for is it not startling to find, that, let the climate be mild or rigorous, let the wind blow from the sultry desert or come loaded with polar sleet, let the fluctuations of temperature be as violent as they may without us, there shall still be a calm, unchanging, undying summer within us?

—GEORGE WILSON

Words

annoyance, *uneasiness.*
augment, *increase.*
constitutes, *forms.*
defraud, *cheat.*
dissipated, *dispersed.*
elements, *constituents.*
endeavors, *attempts.*
enthusiastically, *earnestly.*
eschews, *shuns.*
expenditure, *outlay.*
extraordinary, *unusual.*
extremely, *excessively.*
fabric, *frame.*
fluctuations, *changes.*
humorous, *amusing.*
inappropriate, *unfit.*
indignant, *angry.*
inflammatory, *exciting.*
ingenious, *skilful.*
intense, *severe.*
intensely, *earnestly.*
intercepted, *cut off.*
interesting, *pleasing.*
invariably, *uniformly.*
invitation, request.
irregularities, *disorders.*
mysterious, *hidden.*
particles, *atoms.*
penuriously, *stingily.*
perspiration, *sweat.*
preclusion, *accuracy.*
presented, *served up.*
procure, *obtain.*
production, *generation.*
profusion, *abundance.*
proposition, *assertion.*
quenching, *reducing.*
replenished, *refilled.*
resistance, *opposition.*
respiration, *breathing.*
rigorous, *severe.*
sagaciously, *shrewdly.*
contended, *condemned.*
subsist, *live.*
temperature, *degree of heat.*
terminates, *expires.*
ultimate, *final.*
veritable, *actual.*

Questions

How is animal heat produced? Where does the carbon come from? When does the combustion take place? To what may our bodies therefore be compared? W hat is their fuel? Which is the best fuel? In what countries is it the chief food? What does the native of the tropics prefer? Why can a stout man survive without food longer than a lean man? What are hibernating animals? Give examples. How are they sustained during winter? What is perhaps the most striking feature in our heat-producing apparatus? How does it intimate that more fuel is required? How is excessive heat reduced?

☆ ☆

【动物的热度是由空气中的氧气和我们吃的食物中的碳综合而产生的。这种碳，作为我们食物的一部分被摄取，用来形成我们的身体组织。当我们的肌肉运动的时候，无论是心脏的肌肉、肺部肌肉或是四肢的肌肉运动，或者我们思考或感觉的时候，它就会被一点儿一点儿地消耗掉；然后和氧气发生混合（也就是燃烧的过程）。我们思考，行动，感觉得越强烈，燃烧的碳就越多，我们身体所需的修复也就越多。因此生命最后的归宿就是死亡，而我们生活得越快，我们的身体燃烧得越快——死亡得越快。以下这篇幽默的文章或许可以帮助修订部分我们记忆中的这些原则。】

我们一定要谦虚对待自己的读者。只要涉及科学问题的时候，把事实说得琐碎并不可行。阳春白雪的人士，毫无疑问会反对我们的这个即将进行的提问。无论如何，我们还是坚持并主张以下观点：我们都是有生命的火炉——行走的壁炉——有血有肉的炉膛。

我们现在说的并不是任何人用自己的人肉灶台能点燃一根蜡烛，或是煮熟鸡蛋，甚至擦亮一根黄磷火柴。然而，我们仍重申，我们的身体是火炉——壁炉——炉膛，如果这些叫法能被应用到任何表示产生热的设备上的话，难道不是吗？人类身体产生热量是通过将氧气和碳混合，在血管当中的毛细血管中产生的，这和树林在开放式炉膛中燃烧不是一个道理吗？

姑且说我们的身体是名副其实的火炉，读者一定想知道我们是从哪里获得燃料的。幸运的是，我们燃烧用的煤和木柴是以非常奇妙的形式储藏起来的。它们以面包和黄油、布丁和派的形式呈现在我们面前，或者是给劳动者的薄片熏肉，摆放在老饕面前的鹿腰肉、甲鱼汤。它们不是一大筐一大筐地出现，而是盛放在盖碗、盘子、平底玻璃杯以及各种赏心悦目的碗碟器皿中呈现到我们面前的。

事实上，无论何时你给一个人送去晚餐的请柬的时候，你实质上是要求他赏光陪伴自己一起补充燃料；当你看到他在热情洋溢享用你的美食的时候，你知道其实他是在毫不掩饰地将燃料“铲进”他那血肉做成的火炉里。这种燃料最终在毛细血管中燃烧后，会变成碳，还有一点的氢气和硫；但是，我们吃进去的燃料却是以脂肪、淀粉、糖，酒精和其他燃烧性没那么好的化合物的形式存在的。迄今为止，脂肪在所有这些物质中产生的热量最多。十磅的脂肪，运进你的炉膛，就能产生相当于——也就是说，会产生相当于25磅淀粉、25磅糖，或者甚至是26磅的雪碧的热量。

观察一下这个现象，非常有趣：即当食物摆放在一个人面前的时候，他的本能是如何明智地锁定在能给他提供不同种类型的绝佳燃料上头的。爱斯基摩人对脂类食物青睐有加，虽然他并不知道其中的原因，也从没听说过动物产生热量的原理，但他本能地感觉到熊的油脂和鲸脂是他想要吃的食物。如果训诫他只吃西红柿或印第安玉米过活，这可怜人就会非常反感，就像从前学校里的校长被裁决只能吃清水糊糊一样，觉得这太残忍了。

这来自蛮荒地带的爱斯基摩人非常热爱脂类食物，因为如果把他放在北方那样严寒的环境下，他身边的每一样东西都不断地消耗着他的热量，那么他就需要大量的脂类食物，因为吃了这些食物，他能产生最大的热量。另外，热带地区的原住民，同样也对动物身上的化学反应一无所知，他们避免吃得油腻，因为油腻食物和他们的生活环境不符，为了保持凉爽，他们吃的食物有大米，枣子或是水分充足的水果。

因此我们知道了为什么一个身材壮硕的人，如果不给他吃东西的话，他活的时间要比一个身材羸弱的人长了。人类的脂肪是用来消耗的燃料。脂肪中包含了大量的可燃性物质，无论何时，只要人的日常饮食摄入中断，它就会被消耗。因此，那些身材丰满的人大可以高兴了。我们对他们送上最真挚的、在某种程度上又有些妒忌的祝贺。无论如何，他们的身体能承受长时间的寒冷的环境。

出于同样的原因，那些冬眠动物，如熊、跳鼠、土拨鼠、睡鼠、蝙蝠，等等，通常在进入到三个月的冬眠时间之前，变得很肥胖。他们在睡眠中，从体表的脂肪中汲取能量，他们的呼吸会减缓，脉搏降低到一分钟几次，体温可能接近零度的样子。但当睡眠的季节结束的时候，他们就会从洞穴和地洞中出来，一副饥肠辘辘的样子，他们已经把储存的燃料都燃烧殆尽了；熊则恨不得欺骗那些采集熊脂的人们，因为熊把自己的脂肪看的无比珍贵。

但我们产生热量的身体的一个最明显的特征，就是它拥有自我管理的能力。我们内部火炉的火焰在某个时刻会变弱，而在另一个时刻则会变旺。有时候，因为烧得过热，这火炉的主人都快要晕倒了；又有时候火炉的主人会通过热忱地挥动拨火棍来提高温度，并偶尔会发出对天气过于寒冷的抱怨。

如果在我们的血肉火炉中，这样的不规则变化未加约束地经常出现的话，我们会有无尽的麻烦。吃了一顿热量十足的饭菜之后，或者在经历了不同寻常的一小时之后，涌出的热量会把整个身体推到高烧状态。那如何避免这种情况呢？在我们这种人体火炉中，有通气门或者侧门用来控制空气的进入；而在壁炉中，和蒸汽机相连接的就是加湿器，这样可以保证机器自身的良好运转，两者是同样的道理。

但不管是通气口还是加湿器，拨火棍还是司炉，都不能被用在血肉之躯上。一方面来说，如果人类的火焰因得不到持续的热量而变弱，胃口就会大开，并敦促着人去觅得燃料。饥饿发出警告声，要求以可口的肉食为形式的“煤”的加入。如果这警告声被忽视的话，那么储存的脂肪，就如我们所知道的那样，会被扔到壁炉中，保持其燃烧顺畅。

从另一方面来说，如果身体的热度高得不合理，身体就会启用一种非常巧妙的降温过程。当一种物质变得太热，最简单的降温方式就是在它上面洒上水。而对于人体而言，也是同样的原理。我们的内部温度只要高于正常温度，排汗系统管道，也就是拥有六七百万毛孔的管道，愤愤不平于这种情况，马上就会开始排出体液，来浸湿整个体表。因此，只要一个人身体过热，无论是由工作、跑步、划船、打架、做言辞激烈的演说还是其他的剧烈活动所致，他一定会启用这种降温方法，也就是“泼水”。

那我们该说什么呢？亲爱的读者，严肃来说，从一个单纯的人的角度来看待这一问题的话，没有一个物体要比在柔软而较弱的组织做成的火炉中燃烧，更显得无助了；而这火炉就像人体一样——一个大部分仅由液体造就的组织——一个可能很容易因为过热被灼伤或因过度寒冷而受到损害的组织。难道这看起来不奇怪吗？一个火炉的炉壁是血肉做的，血管是它的烟道，皮肤是它的外壳，然而，这个设备，好像是具有魔力一般，产生持续的热流——不是吝啬地从它的热源中挤出一点点的热度，而是不分昼夜地流淌，无论春夏秋冬，没有一刻的停歇，从岁首到岁末。

将这个了不起的机器带至地球最寒冷的地带，让它运转在冰霜肆虐、大自然似乎无情到践踏死者的地方，它依旧能喷出不可思议而温度毫不降低的热气来。同时，它也是这样的机器，它不需要人看管就能运转，也几乎不需要别人的帮助。而那燃料，其实就是随意投入进去的堆料，在内部被筛选和分裂，这样，那些真正能燃烧的部分就能够被输送到相应地点，分毫无差地履行它们的职责了。

不需要用手去修剪它的火苗，或是掌控它的火光，抑或是清理它的烟灰。它既不会产生烟，也不会产生火花，更不会燃起火焰。一切都被妥善处理了，这样，光洁的皮肤既不会因为内部的燃烧而萎缩，也不会被熏黑了。这个机器要是被放置在一个消耗热量过快的环境中呢？那么，它的胃口就会大开，想大快朵颐一番，而一旦满足了它的需求之后，这血肉的火炉就不动声色地重新焕发光彩了。或者如果我们被放置在过热的危险环境中呢？那么，微小的排汗口就会张开，体表就会浸在一层水中，直到内部的火焰被降低到恰当的温度。

一方面，如果受到高温威胁，身体能抵御这种攻击，假设这种抵御是可能的话，而且这抵御会持续到人体储存的水分都使用殆尽；另一方面，如果受到寒冷的威胁，身体就会把敌人挡在外面，直到存储的燃料都使用完毕。这样身体就能受到保护，并得到供养，那我们有什么理由不把这人体火炉看成是造物主最精湛的创造的一部分呢？因为无论气候温和还是恶劣，无论风是来自干燥的沙漠，还是席卷着极地的冷空气，无论外部的气温怎样剧烈起伏，我们身体内仍有一个安静、恒温、永远的夏天存在，难道这不令人称奇吗？

Lesson 19 DAVID'S LAMENT FOR ABSALOM

第十九课　大卫王哀悼押沙龙

The pall was settled. He who slept beneath
Was straightened for the grave; and, as the folds
Sank to the still proportions, they betrayed
The matchless symmetry of Absalom.
His helm was at his feet: his banner, soiled
With trailing through Jerusalem, was laid
Reversed, beside him: and the jewelled hilt,
Whose diamonds lit the passage of his blade,
Rested, like mockery, on his covered brow.
The soldiers of the king trod to and fro,
Clad in the garb of battle; and their chief,
The mighty Joab, stood beside the bier,
And gazed upon the dark pall steadfastly,
As if he feared the slumberer might stir.
A slow step startled him. He grasped his blade,
As if a trumpet rang; but the bent form
Of David entered, and he gave command,
In a low tone, to his few followers,
And left him with his dead.—The king stood still
Till the last echo died; then, throwing off
The sackcloth from his brow, and laying back
The pall from the still features of his child,
He bowed his head upon him, and broke forth
In the resistless eloquence of woe:—

"Alas, my noble boy! that thou shouldst die!
　Thou, who wert made so beautifully fair;—
That Death should settle in thy glorious eye,
　And leave his stillness in this clustering hair!
How could he mark thee for the silent tomb,
　My proud boy, Absalom?

"Cold is thy brow, my son! and I am chill,
　As to my bosom I have tried to press thee!

How was I wont to feel my pulses thrill,
  Like a rich harp-string, yearning to caress thee,
And hear thy sweet *'My father!'* from those dumb
  And cold lips, Absalom!

"The grave hath won thee! I shall hear the gush
  Of music, and the voices of the young;
And life will pass me in the mantling blush,
  And the dark tresses to the soft winds flung;—
But thou no more with thy sweet voice shalt come
  To meet me, Absalom!

"And oh! when I am stricken, and my heart,
  Like a bruised reed, is waiting to be broken,
How will its love for thee, as I depart,
  Yearn for thine ear to drink its last deep token!
It were so sweet, amid death's gathering gloom,
  To see thee, Absalom!

"And now, farewell! 'Tis hard to give thee up,
  With death so like a gentle slumber on thee!—
And thy dark sin!—oh! I could drink the cup,
  If from this woe its bitterness had won thee.
May God have called thee, like a wanderer, home,
  My lost boy, Absalom!"

He covered up his face, and bowed himself
A moment on his child; then, giving him
A look of melting tenderness, he clasped
His hands convulsively, as if in prayer.
And, as if strength were given him of God,
He rose up calmly, and composed the pall
Firmly and decently,—and left him there,
As if his rest had been a breathing sleep.

—N. P. WILLIS

Words

bitterness, *sharpness*.
clustering, *gathering*.
decently, *becomingly*.
mantling, *flashing*.

matchless, *unequalled*.
mockery, *derision*.
resistless, *irresistible*.
reversed, *inverted*.
steadfastly, *fixedly*.
straightened, *laid out*.
stricken, *smitten*.
symmetry, *regularity*.
tenderness, *love*.
trailing, *dragging*.
yearning, *longing*.

☆ ☆

棺盖已落。沉睡在下面的他，
身子裹得笔挺，躺在墓穴中；而随着褶皱
落到一动不动的躯体上，它们就露出
了押沙龙无与伦比的俊美面容。
他的指挥棒落在他的脚边，他的战旗被
穿过耶路撒冷的泥浆弄脏，反着
躺在地上，就在他身边；还有那珠宝镶嵌的刀柄，
上头钻石的光彩照亮了整个刀刃，
那刀柄留在，就像讽刺一般，留在他被蒙着的额头上。
国王的士兵来来去去，
身穿战甲；而他们的统领，
权力至高的约押，站在棺材旁边，
一动不动地凝视着黑色的棺盖。
一阵缓慢的脚步声惊动了他。他抓紧佩刀，
好似听到号角吹响一样；但来的却是身形佝偻的
大卫王，他声音低沉地
下达命令，给身边的几个随从，
让他和死去的人单独待着。国王一动不动站着，
知道最后的声响消失了；然后，他掀起
押沙龙额头上盖的粗布，把棺盖从
他依然眉清目秀的孩子身上扶起，
他向着押沙龙低下头，发出
抑制不住的悲哀的苦嚎。

啊，我高贵的孩子！你竟然死了！

你，长得如此俊美；
死神竟然停留在你漂亮的眼中，
把他的静止留在了这浓重的长发中！
他怎么能把你送到沉默的墓穴中呢？
我骄傲的孩子，押沙龙。

你的额头冰冷，我的孩子！我在战栗，
我努力要把你拥抱进自己的怀中！
我怎么能习惯感觉到自己的脉搏战栗，
就像竖琴弦一样颤动，渴望能抚摸你，
听到你那甜甜的“我的父亲”的声音，
从这冰冷的双唇中发出，押沙龙！

墓穴已经得到了你！我将听到
音乐的喷涌，听到年轻人的声音；
地幔的红色，把生命传达到我身边，
黑暗的树木在轻柔的风中摇曳；
但你那甜美的声音不再和你一同到来
见我了，押沙龙！

“哦！当我听到噩耗的时候，我的心
就像受伤的芦苇，等待着被蹂躏，
它对你的爱怎么能，在我离开的时候，
渴望从你的耳朵能听到它最后的深沉象征！
它是如此的美好，在死亡聚集的晦暗当中，
来看看你，押沙龙！

“而现在，永别了！要放弃你太难了，
死亡好像在让你酣睡一般！
而你的黑暗的罪恶啊！哦！我能喝下这杯，
如果从这悲伤中它的苦楚能把你换回来。
愿上帝把你召唤，就像召唤流浪者一样，召唤你回家，
我迷失的孩子，押沙龙！”

他以手遮脸，向他的孩子
鞠了一会儿躬；然后，向他投去了
一种心碎的温柔眼神，
他痉挛地击打手掌，好像是在祷告。
然后，就像上帝给了他力量一样，
他平静地站起身来，把棺盖
坚定而有尊严地落下，把他留在了那儿。
好像他在长眠，在呼吸着沉睡一样。

——N.P.・威利斯

Lesson 20 SCENES IN CANTON

第二十课 广州景象

The recently arrived stranger naturally manifests surprise and incredulity on being told that the estimated population of Canton exceeds a million. When, however, he visits the close streets, with their dense population and busy wayfarers, huddled together in lanes from five to nine feet wide, where Europeans could scarcely inhale the breath of life, the greatness of the number no longer appears incredible. After the first feelings of novelty have passed away, disappointment, rather than admiration, occupies the mind. On leaving the open space before the factories, we behold an endless succession of narrow avenues, scarcely deserving the name of streets.

As the visitor pursues his course, narrow lanes still continue to succeed one another, and the conviction is gradually impressed on the mind that such is the general character of the streets of the city. Along these, busy traders, mechanics, barbers, venders, and porters, make their way; while occasionally the noisy abrupt tones of vociferating coolies remind the traveller that some materials of bulky dimensions are on their transit, and suggest the expediency of keeping at a distance, to avoid collision. Now and then the monotony of the scene is relieved by some portly mandarin, or merchant of the higher class, borne in a sedan chairs on the shoulders of two, or sometimes four men Yet, with all this hurry and din, there seldom occurs any accident or interruption of good nature.

On the river the same order and regularity prevail. Though there are probably not fewer than 200,000 denizens of the river, whose hereditary domains are the watery element that supports their little dwellings, yet harmony and good feeling are conspicuous in the accommodating manner with which they make way for each other. These aquatic tribes of the human species show a most philosophic spirit of equanimity, and contrive in this way to strip daily life of many of its little troubles; while the fortitude and patience with which the occasional injury or destruction of their boats is borne are remarkable.

SEDAN CHAIR

To return from the wide expanse

A STREET IN CANTON

of the river population to the streets in the suburbs, the same spirit of contented adaptation to external things is everywhere observable; and it is difficult which to regard with most surprise—the narrow abodes of the one, or the little boats which serve as family residences to the other.

There is something of romance in the effect of Chinese streets. On either aide are shops, decked out with native wares,—furniture and manufactures of various kinds.

These are adorned by pillar sign-boards, rising perpendicularly, and inscribed from top to bottom with the various kinds of saleable articles which may be had within. Native artists seem to have lavished their ingenuity on several of three inscriptions, in order to give, by their calligraphy, some idea of the superiority of the commodities for sale. Many of these sign-boards contain some fictitious emblem, adopted as the name of the shop—similar to the practice prevalent in London two centuries ago.

On entering, the proprietor, with his assistants or partners, welcomes a foreigner with sundry salutations; sometimes advancing to shake hands, and endeavouring to make the most of his scanty knowledge of English. They will show their goods with the utmost patience, and evince nothing of disappointment if, after gratifying his curiosity, he depart without purchasing.

At a distance from the factories, where the sight of a foreigner is a rarity, crowds of idlers, from fifty to a hundred, rapidly gather round the shop, and frequent embarrassment ensues, from an imperfect knowledge of their language. In these parts, the shopkeepers know no language but their own, are more moderate in their politeness, and, as a compensation, put a smaller price on their wares. To write one's name in Chinese characters is a sure method of securing their favour.

Sometimes no fewer than eight or ten blind beggars find their way into a shop, and there they remain, singing a melancholy, dirge-like strain, and most perseveringly beating together two pieces of wood. At length the weary shopman takes compassion on them, and provides for the quiet of his shop by giving a copper cash to each; on receiving which they depart, and repeat the same experiment elsewhere.

The streets abound with these blind beggars, who are seldom treated with indignity. A kindly indulgence is extended to them, and they enjoy a prescriptive right of levying a copper cash from every shop or house they enter. It is said that this furnishes a liberal means of livelihood to an immense number of blind persons, who in many instances are banded together in companies or societies, subject to a code of rules, on breach of which the transgressor is expelled the community.

In every little open space there are crowds of travelling doctors, haranguing the multitude on the wonderful power and healing virtues of the medicines which they expose for sale. Close by, some cunning fortune-teller may be seen, with crafty look, explaining to some awe-stricken simpleton his destiny in life, from a number of books arranged before him, and consulted with due solemnity. In another part some tame birds are exhibiting their clever feats, in singling out, from amongst a hundred others, a piece of paper enclosing a coin, and then receiving a grain of millet as a reward of their cleverness.

CHINESE FORTUEN–TELLER

At a little distance are some fruit-stalls, at which old and young are making purchases, casting lots for the quantity they are to receive. Near these, again, are noisy gangs of people, pursuing a less equivocal course of gambling, and evincing, by their excited looks and clamour, the intensity of their interest in the issue. In another part may be seen disposed the apparatus of some Chinese tensor, who is performing his skilful vocation on the crown of some fellow-countryman unable to command the attendance of the artist at a house of his own.

—ALBERT SMITH.

Words

avenues, *passages*.
clamour, *outcries*.
community, *society*.
compensation, *recompense*.
conspicuous, *prominent*.
conviction, *assurance*.
curiosity, *inquisitiveness*.
denizens, *inhabitants*.
destiny, *doom*.
disappointment, *dissatisfaction*.
ensues, *follows*,.
equanimity, *composure*.
estimated, *competed*.
evincing, *displaying*.
expediency, *propriety*.
gratifying, *Indulging*.
haranguing, *addressing*.
hereditary, *ancestral*.
incredulity, *disbelief*.
indignity, *dishonour*.
inhale, *draw in*.
intensity, *depth*.

interruption, *disturbance*.
lavished, *squandered*.
levying, *exacting*.
manifests, *exhibits*.
monotony, *sameness*.
perseveringly, *persistent*.
quantity, *amount*.
residences, *dwellings*.
salutations, *greetings*.
solemnity, *gravity*.
suburbs, *outskirts*.
transgressor, *offender*.
vocation, *calling*.
vociferating, *shouting*.

Questions

What is the estimated population of Canton? What is the general character of its streets? How many of the inhabitants live on the river? What spirit is generally observable among them? Describe the sign-boards of Chinese shops. How do the shopkeepers treat foreigners? How are poor blind persons supported in Canton? What people pursue their callings in the open air?

☆ ☆

如果听到广州的人口超过一百万的话，刚刚到达这里的陌生人会很自然地感到惊讶和难以置信。然而，当他去临近的街上走走，看到令欧洲人几乎喘不动气的场景：宽约五到九英尺的街上人头攒动，还有形迹匆匆的游客熙熙攘攘，他就不再觉得这巨大的人口有那么不可思议了。最初的新鲜感退去之后，接踵而来的不是羡慕，而是失望。在离开工厂前面的开阔空地的时候，我们看见绵延不尽的一排排的狭窄小路，它们根本就称不上是街道。

游客行走着，那狭窄的街道仍然继续一条连着一条，于是他们心中逐渐相信，这就是这座城市街道的了不起之处。顺着这些街道，繁忙的商人、技师、理发师、小贩以及搬运工各行其道；偶尔还会突然有苦力声嘶力竭的吆喝声，提醒着游客他们在运一些大件物品，让行人及时给自己让路，以免刮碰。这单一的场景时不时地用大声的普通话重现一番。有时候，上层阶级的商人，坐在由两个轿夫，有时候是四个轿夫抬着的轿子上走来。然而，尽管这一切都匆忙而嘈杂，很少会有意外或故意捣乱的情形发生。

河边也奉行同样的规矩。虽然河两岸的居民里，大约二十万人世代相传的营生是水上贸易，但他们彼此都很谦让融洽，和谐和友好的气氛非常明显。这些人类水边部落展示了一种最具有哲理性的平等精神，并据此精神来解决日常生活中的摩擦矛盾；因此对于他们船只的偶尔损伤，他们均以坚毅和耐心待之，这是了不起的。

从河边庞大的人口聚集区转向郊区的街道，对于身外物的达观精神也同样随处可见；而外人会很奇怪，因为在他们看来，一个人的狭窄居所或者小船，用来为大家服务，要做到这一点很难。

中国的街道有些浪漫主义成分。一边是商铺，摆出来当地的物产、家具或是各种各样的手工制品。

这些东西都被当成是招牌。招牌垂直悬挂着，上面从头到尾写着各式各样的店铺里头售卖的物品。当地的艺术家似乎把他们的才华浪费在了这些题词上，从他们的书法中可以看出，他们这么做为了能给出售的商品一点噱头。许多招牌上有一些杜撰的标志，是从店名衍化而来的，和两个世纪之前伦敦流行的做法如出一辙。

一进去，店主和他的伙计或同伴，就热情招呼外国客人；有时候他们还会握个手，努力地把他知道的一点英语用上。他们会极其耐心地展示自己的货品，而如果在满足了客人的好奇心之后，客人未买东西而去，他也不会失望。

离着工厂不远的地方，偶尔出现个外国人，就会有五十到一百个闲人，很快聚集到商店旁，但这经常会引起尴尬，因为他们不怎么会说外语。这里，店主只会说他们自己的语言，他们的礼节更周到，而作为补偿会要价低一些。用汉语来写一个人的名字绝对是取悦外国人的方法。

有时候，会有不少于八个或十个失明的乞丐走到店里头，他们停留在那儿，哼唱着，说着一串吉祥话儿，不间断地拍打着两块木板。最后，店里头听腻了的人对他们心生同情，为了店铺能恢复宁静，便给他们每人一个铜板；一拿到铜板，这群乞丐就离开了，去别的地方重复这一套动作。

街上这样的失明乞丐很多，他们通常都不会感到欺辱。他们养成了一种嗜好，很享受他们走进每家的店铺和房子里要得一个铜板的愉悦。据说，这在盲人中间催生了一个自由的营生行当，在很多故事中，他们都聚集在一起，组成社团，遵守着某些规矩，如果有人违反规矩的话，就会被驱逐出社团。

在每个空地上，都会有游医聚集，他们向老百姓吹嘘着自己的药粉和创伤药的神奇功效，向人们兜售。再走近些，会看见一些精明的算命先生，他们一脸狡黠，根据一些摆放在他面前的书，算着那些对他们敬畏不已而头脑简单的人的命运，摆出严肃的神态来给人们解疑。在别的地方，则会有驯养的鸟儿展示它们的聪明技巧，它们能从一百多张的纸中抽出包了铜子儿的那张来，然后它们会得到一把谷子作为对它们聪明的奖励。

再走远一点儿，就是水果摊了，旁边老老少少都在买水果，挑来拣去买足自己需要的数量。在水果摊旁边，聚集着些聒噪的人，他们在进行赌博这算不得营生的营生，从他们激动的表情和喧闹声中可以看出他们对于赌博的兴致很高。在别的地方则会看到有一些中国壮汉，他们在那些不能照看自家庭院的乡绅家的屋顶上，娴熟地做着自己的工作。

Lesson 21 THE RAINBOW

第二十一课 彩虹

[All transparent bodies have the power of decomposing the light which falls on them. A soap-bubble, for example, exhibits a beautiful play of colours on its surface; and so is it with that most beautiful of all the phenomena of the atmosphere, the rainbow. The drops of rain act as a prism, and separate the white light of the solar rays into the even prismatic colours of which sunlight is composed—namely, violet, indigo, blue, green, yellow, orange, and red; the dark cloud behind the falling shower acting as a screen, on which the brilliant arch is made visible to the spectator.]

【所有透明体都能够在光照到它们身上的时候发生反射。例如，肥皂泡的表面有绚丽的五颜六色；同样，作为大气层中最美丽的现象之一的彩虹也是如此。雨滴作为棱镜，能将阳光中的白色光线分离出来，使之变成均匀的棱柱光——也就是，赤橙黄绿青蓝紫；而大雨之后的乌云则起到背景的作用，在它的映衬下，绚丽的弧形就变得肉眼可见了。】

Triumphal arch, that fill'st the sky	胜利的弧形，在暴风雨即将离去的时候，
When storms prepare to part!	擎在天穹！
I ask not proud philosophy	我问那傲慢的哲学，
To teach me what thou art;	问他为何这么绚烂。
Still seem, as to my childhood's sight,	在我孩童一样的眼中，依然看起来
A midway station given	这给予人们
For happy spirits to alight	欢愉的驿站
Betwixt the earth and heaven.	就存在于这天和地之间。
Can all that optics teach unfold	光学全部的知识把你
Thy form to please me so,	的形成清晰阐述，这令我高兴吗？
As when I dreamt of gems and gold	当我梦到在你那绚烂的弧形下，
Hid in thy radiant bow?	藏着的是宝石和黄金。
When science from Creation's face	科学揭开造物主脸上
Enchantment's veil withdraws,	神秘的面纱的时候，
What lovely visions yield their place	那美丽的景象因为冷冰冰的物质定律，
To cold material laws!	变得毫无生气！
And yet, fair bow,	然而，美丽的彩虹，
no fabling dreams,	不是那些寓言般的梦，
But Words of the Most High,	而是那些关于神仙的传说，
Have told why first thy robe of beams	告诉我你那天穹中的第一缕
Was woven in the sky.	光彩是如何织就。
When o'er the green undeluged earth	从天庭的神殿上，
Heaven's cov'nant thou didst shine,	洒落在油绿无垠的大地上，你没有抱怨，
How came the world's gray fathers forth	要不然那些世间白发苍苍的老人们怎么
To watch thy sacred sign!	能来看到你神圣的光彩！
And when its yellow lustre smiled	当它金黄色的光彩笑着
O'er mountains yet untrod,	照在未被攀越过的群山上，

Each mother held aloft her child, 每一位母亲都高高地抱住自己的孩子，
To bless the bow of God. 感恩上帝的弓箭。

Methinks thy jubilee to keep, 我想，你的快乐让
The first-made anthem rang 大地上，第一首国歌在唱响，
On earth, delivered from the deep, 从那深沉的地方而来，
And the first poet sang. 是那首位诗人在吟唱。

Nor ever shall the Muse's eye 缪斯女神的欣喜眸子也不曾
Unraptured greet thy beam: 能和你的闪耀相媲美：
Theme of primeval prophecy, 远古预言的主题，
Be still the poet's theme. 依然是诗人的主旋律。

The Earth to thee her incense yields, 大地向你焚香膜拜，
The lark thy welcome sings, 云雀向你歌唱欢迎，
When, glittering in the freshened fields, 但雪白的蘑菇如雨后春笋一般冒出，
The snowy mushroom springs. 你闪耀在新鲜的田野上。

How glorious is the girdle, cast 多么美丽的条带啊，飘扬
O'er mountain, tower, and town; 在群山上头，高塔顶上，城镇上空；
Or mirrored in the ocean vast, 或者映射在万丈之下的
A thousand fathoms down! 广袤的海面上。

As fresh in yon horizon dark, 如同从黑暗的地平线刚刚升起，
As young thy beauties seem, 你的美是如此青春，
As when the eagle from the ark 如同从方舟中飞出的鹰，
First sported in thy beam. 第一次展翅就落在你的光辉里。

For, faithful to its sacred page, 忠于自己神圣的职责，
Heaven still rebuilds thy span, 天庭会重建你的弧线，
Nor lets the type grow pale with age 它不会容许你因为时间逝去而变得苍白，
That first spoke peace to man. 因为你是和人类讲和的首位使者。

—Thomas Campbell ——托马斯·坎贝尔

Words

decomposing, *resolving.*
delivered, *released.*
enchantment, *magic.*
faithful, *constant.*
girdle, *bell.*
glorious, *magnificent.*
horizon, *sky-line.*
incense, *offerings.*
lustre, *brightness.*
material, *physical.*
mirrored, *reflected.*
phenomena, *appearances.*
philosophy, *science.*
radiant, *shining.*
sported, *played.*
theme, *subject.*
transparent, *clear.*
undeluged, *freed from the Flood.*
unfold, *explain.*

Lesson 22 GREENLAND (I)

第二十二课 格陵兰岛(一)

Greenland is a vast island, or cluster of islands perpetually joined together by ice, forming a continent about seven times as large as the British Isles; but its exact extent is not known, as its northern limit, which lies far within the Arctic Ocean, has never been explored.

The American expeditions of 1853, under the command of the celebrated Dr. Kane, reached a point on the western coast of Greenland farther north than had previously been attained. It was within six hundred miles of the North Pole. Here they discovered an immense glacier, since named the Humboldt Glacier, which, as described by Dr. Kane, rose like a solid glassy wall, three hundred feet above the level of the water! He considers this great glacier to be the northern termination of a vast ice ocean, which occupies the interior of nearly the whole of Greenland.

Attempts were made by one of Dr. Kane's sledge parties to climb the glacier; but, though provided with apparatus, they failed in all their efforts to scale the stupendous mass. Another party, pushing northward and keeping parallel to the glacier, at a distance of about six miles from it, came in sight of a vast open sea, extending as far as the eye could reach. This sea abounded with seals, bears, and all kinds of Arctic birds. It would thus seem as if the limit of the icy barrier had been reached, and that probably round the pole itself there exists an open sea, in which animal life is abundant.

ESQUIMAN HOUSER

The native inhabitants of Greenland are true Esquimaux; and from them, indeed, our earliest knowledge of the Esquimau race was obtained. The habits of these people have been made familiar to us by the accounts given to the world by Danish colonists and missionaries hundreds of years ago; and, in later times, by the Arctic explorers and whale fishers who have visited the frozen regions of the North.

They inhabit a vast territory,

extending from Greenland to the shores of the Pacific; and yet the whole Esquimau race is supposed to number only about fifty thousand, or not much more than the population of such a town as Carlisle. The average stature of the Esquimaux is far below that of European nations. The common height is little more than five feet, and an Esquimau of six feet would be a giant among his people.

The northern Esquimaux live in houses built of snow or ice; but the huts in the south of Greenland are made of stone or wood, and covered with brush, turf, and earth. In the summer they live in tents made of skins. It is not uncommon to find several families crowded together in the smallest possible space, where they eat, drink, and sleep, with fish and flesh lying all around, and dogs reposing on every side.

The food of the Esquimaux includes almost every animal found within their region, but the seal and the walrus are their principal support for nine months of the year. Their improvidence often reduces them to terrible Straits. Captain Parry speaks of meeting with some who had no food, and who, to keep themselves from starvation, were devouring the very skins which composed their clothes!

The children are carried about by the mother very carefully on her back, in a fur hood, until they are two or three years of age, and then the take care of themselves, being expected to imitate what they see their elders do. A boy very early has a bow and arrows put into his hands, that he may practice shooting at a mark. Towards his tenth year his father provides him with a kayak, that he may initiate him in the arts of rowing, rising, oversetting and coming up again, fowling, fishing, and all those dexterous feats in which he is himself skilled. In his sixteenth year he is expected to accompany his father in seal-catching; and his first seal is made the occasion of great festivity. The girls at fourteen years of age are required to sew, cook, and dress leather; and two or three years later they must learn to row the woman's boat, and build houses!

The traffic of the Greenlanders is, of course, limited to a very small number of articles. They not unfrequently! load their sledges and boats with various commodities, and start off with their families on a trading expedition. They often stay away for a year or more, during which time they build a house in the neighbourhood of some settlement.

They rarely cheat, much less rob, each other; but they think it fair, and even to the credit of their shrewdness, to cheat Europeans, or steal from them all they can! The blubber and skins which they sell to them are in exchange for almost any article manufactured from iron or steel. They are ignorant of the value of gold, which they do not prize more than tin or brass; but iron, in any shape, is invaluable to them.

The Esquimaux are not without their festivities. The chief of these is called the Sun Feast, at the winter solstice, to celebrate the reappearance of the sun, and the renewal of hunting and fishing opportunities. Throughout the country they assemble together in companies, and do their best in the way of entertainment.

The perfection to which the Esquimaux carry such work as they attempt is quite wonderful, when we consider the scarcity of material and the want of emulation and of any division of labour among them. Their houses are built with mathematical regularity, and are well adapted for securing warmth and protection against the encroachments of the weather.

Words

abundant, *plentiful.*
accompany, *go with.*
average, *medium.*
celebrated, *distinguished.*
commodities, *wares.*
considers, *believes.*
emulation, *rivalry.*
encroachments, *ravages.*
explored, *examined.*
extending, *stretching.*
festivities, *entertainments.*
festivity, *rejoicing.*
imitate, *copy.*
improvidence, *thoughtlessness.*
includes, *embraces.*
invaluable, *precious.*
obtained, *derived.*
perpetually, *continually.*
previously, *before.*
provided, *furnished.*
reposing, *resting.*
scarcity, *rarity.*
shrewdness, *cleverness.*
stature, *height.*
Straits, *hardships.*
stupendous, *amazing.*
supposed, *believed.*
termination, *limit.*
territory, *region.*
uncommon, *unusual.*

Questions

What is Greenland? Who reached the most northerly point in it that has ever been attained? When? What did they discover? What did a party going still further north discover? Who are the natives of Greenland? How many do the Esquimaux number in all? Of what are their houses built? What does their food include? At what age are their boys taught to manage a boat? What is their man's boat called? For what purpose do the Esquimaux often go on distant expeditions? What metals do they prise most highly? What is their chief festivity?

☆ ☆

格陵兰岛是个面积巨大的岛屿，或者说它是由一些被冰雪永久连接在一起的岛屿组成的。格陵兰岛形成了一个相当不列颠群岛面积七倍大的陆地，但实际上它真正的面积却无人知晓，因为它的北端深深地伸入北冰洋中，还没有人勘探过。

1853年，一支美国探险队在声名远扬的凯恩博士的带领下，到达了格陵兰岛远北端的西海岸，之前曾有人到达过那里。它位于离北极点不到六百英里的地方。在那儿，他们发现了一座巨大的冰川，就像一个巨大的玻璃墙一样矗立着，离海面居然有300英尺之高！凯恩博士认为这座巨大的冰川是一个巨大的冰洋的北部终点，而这个冰洋则覆盖了整个格陵兰岛的土地。

凯恩博士的雪橇队做了攀登这座冰川的尝试，他们虽然有相应装备，也尽了全力，但还是没能够测量出这巨大的冰川的高度。另外一队人，则向北行进，他们到达的地方和冰川所在的纬度相同，距离冰川约六英里。他们到达了一片开阔的海域，眼睛望不到尽头。这片海域中有许多的海豹、北极熊以及其他各种的北冰洋鸟类。这看起来就像到达了冰地的边缘，在北极周围存在一片开阔的海域，那里有很多动物。

格陵兰岛真正的原住民是爱斯基摩人。从他们那里，我们最早了解到关于爱斯基摩人的资料。这些人的生活习惯得以流传于世，为我们所知晓，是源自于数百年前的丹麦殖民者和传教士；在之后的岁月中，则是来自于光顾过这北部冰雪覆盖的土地的北极探险者和捕鲸者。

爱斯基摩人生活的范围很广，从格陵兰岛一直延伸到太平洋海岸；然而，据估计，整个爱斯基摩人的数目不过仅仅5万，也就是相当于英国卡莱尔城的居民的数目。爱斯基摩人的平均身高大大低于欧洲国家的居民。他们的平均身高不过5英尺，而一个6英尺高的爱斯基摩人在他族人当中可以算是巨人了。

北方的爱斯基摩人生活在雪或冰堆成的屋子内，而在南部的格陵兰岛他们的屋舍则是由石头或木材建造的，上头还铺上了毛、兽皮和泥土。夏天的时候，他们就生活在兽皮做的帐篷里。经常有的一个场景是，几个家庭蜷缩在一个小得不能再小的空间内，在里头吃饭、喝水、睡觉，到处都是鱼和肉散在地上，狗则在各个角落睡觉。

爱斯基摩人的食物几乎涵盖了所有他们生活区域的动物，但他们的主食是海豹和海象，它们能支撑爱斯基摩人度过一年中的9个月。爱斯基摩人目光短浅，这使得他们经常会面临糟糕的境遇。帕里上校就说起过见到几个没有食物的爱斯基摩人，他们为了不饿死，居然拿那些作为衣服的动物毛皮吃！

爱斯基摩人的孩子由其母亲用皮毛斗篷包着，非常小心地背在背上，直到他们到两三岁能照顾自己，能够模仿长辈做事的时候才放他们自己走。男孩子在很小的时候就有弓和箭，这样他就能练习射击了。等到他长到十岁的时候，父亲就会给他一只皮艇，这样他就能学着划船，逆流而上，顺流直下，再划到上游，捕鸟、打渔以及做一些其他擅长技艺。男孩子到16岁的时候，就能和他父亲一同去捕海豹了；他捕到第一头海豹时会有盛大的庆祝仪式。女孩子到14岁的时候，就要会缝补衣物，会做饭以及裁制皮衣了；两三年之后，他们必须学会划女子的小船，并且会建造房屋！

格陵兰岛人的交通工具当然是局限在几样工具上。他们经常在雪橇和小船上装满各式各样的东西，一家人一起去做买卖。他们经常会离家一年甚至更长的时间，在这段时间里，他们会在某个定居点附近建造一座房屋。

他们几乎不会欺诈彼此，更不要说从彼此那里抢夺物品了；但他们觉得如果是欺诈欧洲人或是从他们那里偷盗东西的话，则是天经地义的，而且也很符合他们的狡黠个性。他们向欧洲人出卖鲸脂和毛皮，以换取几乎所有铁制或钢制的物品。他们对于金子的价值一无所知，觉得它和锡或铜差不多；但铁，无论是什么样的铁，对于他们来说都是宝贵的。

爱斯基摩人常有庆祝活动。其中最主要的活动是太阳节。太阳节在冬至那一天，目的是庆祝太阳的再次出现。那时候他们全族的人都会聚集在一起，尽情地庆祝、娱乐。

想想爱斯基摩人匮乏的物资和短缺的劳动力，他们能把自己想到的事情，做到如此完美的地步，这是相当了不起的。从数学上来看，他们的房屋建造得很规整，并能够很好地保温，为他们提供保护，抵御严寒的天气。

Lesson 23 GREENLAND (II)

第二十三课 格陵兰岛(二)

The kayak, or man's boat, has a canoe-shaped frame work, from eighteen to twenty feet in length, tapering to a point at the head and stern, so that it is shaped like a weaver's shuttle. The breadth at the centre is from one foot and a half to two feet, and the depth about one foot. The interior of the vessel is hollowed just enough to allow a person to sit with his feet extended on the bottom; and as each man is his own boat-builder, it is always constructed with a nice adaptation to his particular size and weight. When completed, the whole weight of the vessel is not more than sixty pounds, and it can be easily carried on the head without the assistance of the hands.

KAYAK

In front of the kayaker lies his line, rolled up on a little raised seat made for it; and behind him rests his seal-skin bladder—an air-tight sack, which is always kept inflated and fastened to the sealing-line. This is said to answer the double purpose of a buoy and a brake or drag to retard the motion of the prey after it has been struck. The double-bladed oar or paddle is about seven feet in length. It is made of solid red deal, if that can be procured, with inlaid bone at the sides. The kayak is covered with new seal-skin once a year, and is so expeditious and convenient that the Danish authorities of Greenland use this kind of boat as an express for communication between different posts.

The oomiak, or woman's boat, is usually about twenty feet long, five feet broad, and three feet deep. It is sometimes built so as to accommodate twenty persons. It is made of slender laths, fastened with whalebone, and covered with dressed scal-skin. These boats are generally managed by three or four women together; and in fair weather they row them very rapidly. In any danger, a man with his kayak keeps them in sight, to aid them if required.

The next object of importance to the Esquimau is the sledge, which finds occupation during at least three-fourths of the year. A native who possesses both a kayak and a sledgc is considered a person of property.

The best sledges have their runners made of the jaw-bones of the whale; the upper part consisting of bones, pieces of wood, or deer horns lashed across. Sledge-runners are sometimes made of frozen walrus skin. By an ingenious contrivance they are also formed out of seal-skin. Cases of this skin are filled with earth and moss, a little water is added, and the whole soon becomes frozen into a solid piece. The length of a bone sledge is from four to fourteen feet, and the breadth about twenty inches.

Scarcely any coasts in the world teem more abundantly with animal life than the sterile and ice-bound shores of the Arctic regions. From Greenland westward, along the northern coasts of America, thousands of bears, seals, walruses, foxes, dogs, and other Arctic mammals, and millions of gulls, geese, auks, and other far-flying aquatic birds, are continually passing to and fro, some through the air, and others upon vast fields of ice, either fixed or moving.

The animals found in these frozen regions have a double interest to the voyager; for besides supplying him with nourishing food, they interrupt the intense solitude of that vast and silent land. Vegetable life grows more scant and stunted as he advances north; but animal life is larger and more abundant in development, although seen in less variety. The Arctic animals show less beauty of colouring than those of warmer climates; white and different shades of brown principally supplying the place of the more brilliant tints.

There is nothing more wonderful than the adaptation of the clothing of creatures to their natural condition. In warm latitudes the quadrupeds have thin and short hair, but those of the polar regions are supplied with the thickest furs. The aquatic birds, also, are protected by a coat of oily feathers, so that they can plunge securely into the icy waters.

Almost all Arctic animals are beasts and birds of prey; and they derive their sustenance mainly from the sea, the land furnishing very scanty means of supporting life. The ultimate source from which the food of all these animals comes—and which, from its abundance, is the cause of life being so extremely prolific in all those regions—is to be found in the vast number of *medusoe* or jelly-fishes with which the seas in those latitudes are filled.

Some of the species have a sort of fringe of hairs, like little snakes, which hang from the margin of the cup-shaped disc that is formed by their bodies, and float writhing and twisting in the water as the cup, by alternate expansions and contractions, forces its way along. It is from this circumstance that they have received their name of medusoe—Medusa having been a fabled monster of ancient times whose head was adorned with snakes instead of hair.

Many of the medusoe are phosphorescent: and these luminous species are sometimes so numerous that the whole surface of the ocean glows with them at night, as if the waves were undulations of liquid fire.

The different species vary extremely, both in form and in size.Some are so minute as not to be seen by the naked eye; in consequence of which it often happens that curious persons, seeing the whole surface of the sea glowing with the light which they produce, are surprised to find nothing visible in the water when they draw up a bucketful of it to the deck of the ship in order to ascertain the cause.

Others of the medusae are of great size and strength. They sometimes seize and devour fishes of considerable magnitude; and yet their bodies contain so little substance, that when drawn up on the beach, they look like a mere mass of jelly. On being exposed for a short time to the sun and air, they almost entirely dry up and disappear, leaving nothing behind them but a thin filmy web.

Animals of this class swarm in countless millions in all the northern seas. So dense are the shoals sometimes, that the whole colour of the sea for hundreds of miles ii changed by them! They furnish, of course, immense quantities of food for whales and other cetaceous animals, and also for fishes of all kinds; which in their turn give sustenance to bears, seals, walruses, and multitudes of other animals.

Words

accommodate, *contain.*
adaptation, *suitableness.*
alternate, *by turns.*
aquatic, *water.*
ascertain, *determine.*
circumstance, *fact.*
communication, *intercourse.*
constructed, *made.*
contraction, *narrowing.*
contrivance, *device.*
countless, *numberless.*
development, *growth.*
expansion, *widening.*
expeditious, *speedy.*
extended, *stretched.*
filmy, *cob-web-like.*
inflated, *distended.*
ingenious, *clever.*
interior, *inside.*
luminous, *shining.*
magnitude, *greatness.*
managed, *guided.*
multitudes, *hosts.*
nourishing, *wholesome.*
occupation, *employment.*
prolific, *productive.*
quadrupeds, *four-footed animals.*
solitude, *loneliness.*
sterile, *unfruitful.*
surprised, *astonished.*
sustenance, *nourishment.*
tapering, *diminishing.*
undulations, *waves.*
writhing, *twisting.*

Questions

What is the usual length of a kayak? And its weight? With what is it propelled? What is the length of the oomiak? Of what are the best sledges made? With what do the Arctic regions abound? What difference is noticed between Arctic animals and those of warmer regions? Mention instances of the adaptation of the clothing of animals to their condition? What is the chief source of food for animal life in the Arctic regions? What is the origin of the name? What is the cause of the luminous appearance which of them give the sea?

☆ ☆

卡亚克或者叫男子的小船，有独木舟一样的外形，从中间向船头和船尾逐渐变尖，这样划起来就像是织布的梭子。船中间的宽度从一英尺到两英尺半不等，船深则差不多有一英尺。船中间挖空，刚好够一个人双脚伸开踩到船底部；每个人的船都是自己造的，因此船和他自己的身高和体重都极其相配。船造好的时候，它的毛重不会超过六十磅，能够轻易地顶在头上，不需要双手的支撑。

划卡亚克的人前面放着卷起来的、放在比自己座位稍高一点的位置上的线；身后则放着海豹皮做的袋子——它是一个隔绝空气的袋子，总是被放空了气，紧紧系在线上。据说这么做有两个目的，一是可以做漂浮物，二是可以制动或者在捕到猎物的时候拉住它减缓它的挣扎。双面桨或橹长约七英尺，由红洋杉做成的，如果能得到这种材料的话。船两边则是内嵌的骨头。卡亚克的外部是由每年更换一次的海豹皮做的，它划行速度很快，用起来很方便，因此格陵兰岛的丹麦政府把这种船作为不同区域之间的交通工具。

而乌米亚克，或者叫女子的船，则通常有二十英尺长，五英尺宽，三英尺深。有时候，它造得能容纳下二十个人。它是由窄板条和鲸鱼骨钉成的，外部是处理好的海豹皮。这些船一般由三到四个女子划动；天气好的时候，她们划的速度非常快。为防止危险，会有一个划卡亚克的男子跟随她们，如果她们需要帮助，这名男子就会给予援手。

对于爱斯基摩人来说第二重要的东西就是雪橇了。他们一年中有四分之三的时间都要用到它。一个爱斯基摩人，如果他同时拥有卡亚克和雪橇两样东西，就会被看成是个富有的人。

最好的雪橇的撬体是由鲸鱼的颌骨做的，雪橇上部装有一些骨头、木块或者鹿角。雪橇上的滑行板有时是用冻结的海象皮做的，它通过一个灵巧的装置完成滑行。爱斯基摩人会在动物皮中填上泥土和苔藓，也会加上一点儿水，这样这张皮就会马上被冻得结结实实了。一个骨头做的雪橇长度从四英尺到十四英尺不等，而宽度仅仅有二十英寸。

世界上几乎没有什么海岸能和贫瘠并被冰雪覆盖的北极地区的海岸一样，拥有这么丰富的动物资源。从格陵兰岛往西，顺着美洲的北部海岸线，有数以千计的熊类、海豹、海象、狐狸，和其他生活在北极的哺乳动物，还有数以百万计的海鸥、野雁、海雀和其他能进行长途飞行的水鸟，它们陆陆续续地来来去去，无论是定居动物还是迁徙动物，他们有些是从空中来回，有的则取道广袤的冰地。

对于爱斯基摩人而言，在这些冰冻地区找到动物是一件双重的美事；因为这些动物一方面给他们提供了有营养的食物，另一方面打破了那广袤而沉寂的土地上的沉默孤独。越往北走，会发现植物越来越少，也越来越稀疏；但发现的动物个头却越来越大，数量也越来越多，不过动物的种类却越来越单一。北极地区动物的颜色比不上气候温暖地区的动物颜色艳丽；白色和不同色度的棕色是那片美丽的冰冻世界的动物主色调。

再也没有比这更棒的了，即用自然环境中的动物的毛皮直接做衣服。在温暖地带，四肢动物毛发稀疏而短小，但极地地区的动物则生有厚厚的毛皮。水鸟也有一层油脂丰厚的羽毛，这样它们在冲向冰一样的水面时就不会被冻伤了。

几乎所有的北极动物，不论兽类还是鸟类，都是食肉的；它们的食物主要来自大海，因为贫瘠的土地提供不了足够的食物。所有这些动物的食物最终来自于——从它的宏大的数量这一点来看，是让这些地区生命如此繁盛的原因——一种大量发现的、被叫作美杜莎或水母的生物，它们在这一纬度大量繁殖。

水母有一种像刘海一样的发丝，就像小蛇一样，从杯子状的圆盘上垂落下来，而这圆盘就是水母的躯干。通过躯干不断交替的舒张和收缩，发丝纠缠在水中和躯干一起漂游，向前行进。正是因为如此，水母才获得了美杜莎这个名字——美杜莎是古代神话中的怪物，她头上不是头发而是满头的蛇。

许多美杜莎都会发光，这些发光的生物有时候数量巨大，以至于整片海域在夜晚的时候也会发光，好像海洋是起伏着的液体火焰一般。

不同种类的水母在形态和大小上都很不一样。有的非常微小，以至于肉眼都看不到。经常会发生这样的情况，一些好奇的人看见海面泛起水母发出的光，就舀了一杯水到船上看看是怎么回事，结果却很惊讶地发现水里头什么也没有。

还有的美杜莎个头非常庞大，力量惊人。它们有时会抓住并吞掉数量惊人的鱼；然而它们的身体其实并没那么强大，当它们被冲上海滩的时候，看起来不过就是一堆的胶状物罢了。只要在太阳和空气中暴露很短的时间，水母几乎就会完全干透而消失，只留下薄薄的薄膜状的网。

这一纲目的动物在所有的北部海区数量不计其数。有时候，它们数量庞大，整片数百英里的海域颜色都会随着它们而改变。当然，它们为鲸鱼和其他的白垩纪动物提供了大量的食物；而这些动物又供养了熊类、海豹、海象以及其他数之不尽的动物。

Lesson 24 ICELAND, AND THE GEYSERS

第二十四课 冰岛和间歇泉

Iceland is an island somewhat larger than Ireland. It is situated in the Atlantic Ocean, on the confines of the Arctic Circle, amid regions of ice and snow; yet it gives abundant evidence of the volcanic fires which are slum bering beneath its surface.

Among its most remarkable features are its hot springs, which in some places throw up a column of water to the height of a hundred feet. These springs abound on many parts of the coast, as well as in the interior of the island; and in some cases the waters of the ocean are sensibly heated by their action.

The most celebrated of these hot springs are the Geysers, situated in the north of the island, where, within the space of a few acres, more than fifty of them may be seen.

The Great Geyser rises from a mound of flinty earth, deposited by the water, about thirty feet in height, and extending about two hundred feet across. On the top of this mound is a basin sixty feet wide and seven feet deep, in the centre of which is the opening through which the water rises.

A visit to the Geysers is thus described by Lord Dufferin in his book entitled "Letters from High Latitudes," giving an account of a voyage and visit to Iceland:—

"As the baggage-horses with our tents and beds had net yet arrived, we sat quietly down to coffee brewed in Geysers' water, when suddenly it seemed as if, beneath our very feet, a number of cannon were going off under ground. The whole earth shook. We set off at full speed toward the Great Geyser, expecting to see the grand water explosion. By the time we reached its brim, however, the noise had ceased, and all we could see was a slight trembling movement in the centre.

"Irritated by this false alarm, we determined to avenge ourselves by going and tormenting the Strokr. Strokr, or *the churn*, you must know, is an unfortunate Geyser, with so little command over his temper and his stomach that you can get a rise out of him whenever you like. All that is necessary is to collect a quantity of sods, and throw them down his funnel. As he has no basin to protect himself from these liberties, you can approach to the very edge of the pipe, about five feet in diameter, and look down at the water, which is perpetually boiling at the bottom.

"In a few minutes the dose of turf you have just administered begins to disagree with him. He works himself up into an awful passion. Tormented by the qualms of sickness, he groans, and hisses, and boils up, and spits at you with malicious vehemence, until at last, with a roar of mingled pain and rage, he throws up into the air a column of water forty feet high, which carries with it all the sods that have been

cast in, and scatters them scalded and half digested at your feet.

"So irritated has the poor thing's stomach become by the discipline it has undergone, that even long after all foreign matter has been thrown off, it goes on retching and sputtering, until at last nature is exhausted, when, sobbing and sighing to itself, it sinks back into the bottom of its den.

"As the Great Geyser explodes only once in forty hours or more, it was, of course, necessary that we should wait his pleasure—in fact, our movements entirely depended on his. For the next two or three days, therefore, like pilgrims round an ancient shrine, we patiently kept watch; but he scarcely deigned to favour us with the slightest manifestation of his latent energies. Two or three times the cannonading we had heard immediately after our arrival recommenced, and once an eruption to the height of about ten feet occurred; but so brief was its duration, that by the time we were on the spot, although the tent was not eighty yards distant, all was over.

"At length, after three days' watching in languid expectation of the eruption, our desire was gratified. A cry from the guides made us start to our feet and rush toward the basin. The usual underground thunders had already commenced; a violent agitation was disturbing the centre of the pool. Suddenly a dome of water lifted itself to the height of eight or ten feet, then burst and fell; immediately after which a shining liquid column, or rather a sheaf of columns, wreathed in robes of vapour, sprang about seventy feet into the air, and, in a succession of jerking leaps, each higher than the former, flung their silvery crests against the sky. For a few minutes the fountain held its own, then all at once it seemed to lose its ascending energy. The unstable waters faltered, drooped, fell, 'like a broken purpose,' back upon themselves, and were immediately sucked down into the recesses from which they had sprung."

Words

administered, *supplied.*
agitation, *commotion.*
celebrated, *famous.*
column, *pillar.*
confines, *borders.*
deposited, *laid down.*
diameter, *measurement across.*
discipline, *treatment.*

energies, *powers*.
evidence, *proof*.
exhausted, *tired out*.
expectation, *anticipation*.
expecting, *hoping*.
explosion, *eruption*.
extending, *measuring*.
irritated, *enraged*.
malicious, *mischievous*.
manifestation, *indication*.
occurred, *happened*.
pilgrims, *wanderers*.
recesses, *cavities*.
sensibly, *perceptibly*.
situated, *placed*.
succession, *series*.
tormenting, *harassing*.
trembling, *vibrating*.
underground, *subterranean*.
vehemence, *violence*.
wreathed, *enveloped*.

Questions

Where is Iceland situated? What slumber beneath its surface? What are the most celebrated of the hot springs called? What is the peculiarity of the *Strokr*? What does the name mean? How often does the Great Geyser explode? How high does it send its column of water?

☆ ☆

冰岛是一个差不多和爱尔兰岛一样大的岛屿。它位于大西洋，在北极圈上，冰雪地带之间；然而这座岛上却有许多火山，这些火山的岩浆都在地表下缓缓流动。

冰岛上最奇妙的景观要数温泉了，有的地方温泉会喷起高达一百英尺的水柱。这些喷泉位于海岸线上很多地方，在冰岛中部也有；在某些情况下，海水会很明显地因为温泉活动而温度升高。

温泉中最著名的就是间歇泉，它们位于冰岛的北部，在那里，数英亩的土地上可能会有超过五十个间歇泉。

巨大的间歇泉会从一个燧石土堆中一涌而起，喷射出水，喷射的水柱高达30英尺，范围达到200英尺。土堆的顶部是一个宽60英尺深7英尺左右的水洼，水洼的中间有一个开口，水就是从那里喷涌而出的。

杜福林阁下在他那本《来自高纬度地区的信》中描述了他有一次造访间歇泉的情形，书中还描写了他的冰岛之行的情景：

“当载有我们帐篷和旅行床的马匹还没有到达的时候，我们静静地坐在地上喝着间歇泉的水冲的咖啡，突然间，我们脚下好像有许多大炮在地底下轰鸣。整个大地晃动起来。我们全速向着大间歇泉跑去，想看看这巨大温泉的爆炸。但当我们快到那里的时候，噪声消失了，我们所能看到的只是中间稍稍颤动的水的运动。

“因为被骗，我们很恼怒，因而决定通过折磨一下这斯托克尔或者叫作查姆的间歇泉来报复一番。要知道，斯托克尔是喜怒无常的间歇泉，它对自己的脾气和胃没一点儿控制力，只要你愿意，你能让它在任何时候喷涌。所需的就是有足够数量的草皮，然后把它们扔到它的漏斗中去。鉴于它没有水洼来保护它免受这些草皮的叨扰，你可以靠近到它的管道的边缘处。管道直径大约有五英尺，从上往下看，能看到下面与底部垂直的水在沸腾。”

“不出几分钟，你刚刚扔进去的草皮就和间歇泉不对付了。它开始激烈地反应起来。受到不适的折磨，它发出呻吟声，嘶嘶叫着，沸腾起来，恶意而猛烈地发出疼痛和仇恨交织的怒吼，最后向空中喷涌出四十英尺高的水柱，连同之前扔进去的草皮一块喷涌了出来，把它们体无完肤地散落在你脚下。”

“可怜的间歇泉的肚子因为刚刚的遭遇而变得恼怒不堪，即使外来物都给喷涌个干净，它还继续反胃呕吐着，直到最后累了，重新陷入它洞穴的底部，自己抽抽搭搭、叹着气。”

“鉴于大间歇泉每隔40个小时或更长的时间才喷涌一次，当然我们等待它发作也就有必要了。实际上，我们的行程完全取决于它的行动。因此，在接下来的两到三天里，我们就像朝圣者围在古代神殿周围一样，耐心地等着瞧着，但它并不常常屈尊给予我们观看它潜藏的能量爆发的场景的喜悦。有两三次，我们刚到就马上听到轰隆声开始了，还有一次看到喷涌出十英尺那么高的水柱；但它持续的时间都很短暂，以至于我们到那里的时候，虽然帐篷就在八码开外的地方，一切就结束了。”

“最后，在一连三天疲惫地观看我们梦寐以求的间歇泉爆发之后，我们心满意足了。那次，导游突然大叫一声，于是我们立马跑着冲向水洼。那通常听到的地下雷声已经轰鸣开来；一阵剧烈的躁动围绕着水池的中心。突然水呈穹形飞到8或10英尺的高度，然后就炸开落在地上；其后紧接着是闪亮的水柱，或者不如说是水束，被水蒸气围成的圈子所包裹着，跳跃到了空中70英尺的高度，然后是一串跳跃的水柱，一束高于前一束，直把它们那银色的水冠甩入天空。就这样持续了几分钟，突然间，这喷泉像是失去了向上的力量一样。不稳定的水流晃晃悠悠，萎靡下泄，跌落下来，就好像被打碎了一样，落到自己身上，然后马上被吸回到它们喷涌而出的隐蔽之处了。”

Lesson 25 LADY CLARE

第二十五课 克莱尔小姐

It was the time when lilies blow,
And clouds are highest up in air,
Lord Ronald brought a lily-white doe
To give his cousin, Lady Clare.

I trow they did not part in scorn;
Lovers long betrothed were they:
They two will wed the morrow morn;
God's blessing on the day.

"He does not love me for my birth,
Nor for my lands, so broad and fair;
He loves me for my own true worth,
And that is well," said Lady Clare.

In there came old Alice the nurse;
Said, "Who was this that went from thee?"—
"It was my cousin," said Lady Clare;
"To-morrow he weds with me."

"O God be thanked!" said Alice the nurse,
"That all comes round so just and fair;—
Lord Ronald is heir of all your lands,
And you are not the Lady Clare."

"Are ye out of your mind, my nurse, my nurse,
Said Lady Clare, "that ye speak so wild?"—
"As God's above," said Alice the nurse,
"I speak the truth—you are my child.

"The old Earl's daughter died at my breast—
I speak the truth, as I live by bread!
I buried her like my own sweet child,
And put my child in her stead."

"Falsely, falsely have ye done,
O mother," she said, "if this be true;
To keep the best man under the sun
So many years from his due."

"Nay, now, my child," said Alice the nurse;
"But keep the secret for your life,
And all you have will be Lord Ronald's
When you are man and wife."

"If I'm a beggar born," she «aid,
"I will speak out, for dare not lie;—
Pull off, pull off the brooch of gold,
And fling the diamond necklace by!"

"Nay, now, my child," said Alice the nurse;
"But keep the secret all ye can."—
She said, "Not so; but I will know
If there be any faith in man."

"Nay, now, what faith?" said Alice the nurse;
"The man will cleave unto his right."—
"And he shall have it," the lady replied,
"Though I should die, to-night!"

"Yet give one kiss to your mother dear!
Alas, my child, I sinned for thee."—
"O mother, mother, mother," she said,
"So strange it seems to me.

"Yet here's a kiss for my mother dear,—
My mother dear, if this be so;
And lay your hand upon my head,
And bless me, mother, ere I go."

She clad herself in a russet gown;
She was no longer Lady Clare:
She went by dale, and she went by down,
With a single rose in her hair.

The lily-white doe Lord Ronald had brought,

Leapt up from where she lay,
Dropt her head in the maiden's hand,
And followed her all the way.

Down stept Lord Ronald from his tower:
"O Lady Clare, you shame your worth!
Why come you drest like a village maid,
That are the flower of the earth?"

"If I come drest like a village maid,
I am but as my fortunes are;
I am a beggar born," she said,
"And not the Lady Clare."

"Flay me no tricks," said Lord Ronald,
"For I am yours m word and deed;—
Play me no tricks," said Lord Ronald;
"Your riddle is hard to read."

O, and proudly stood she up!
Her heart within her did not fail;
She looked into Lord Ronald's eyes,
And told him all her nurse's tale.

He laughed a laugh of merry scorn;
He turned and kissed her where she stood:
"If you are not the heiress born,
And I," said he, "the next in blood—

"If you are not the heiress born,
And I," said he, "the lawful heir,
We two will wed to-morrow mom,
And you shall still be Lady Clare."

—ALFRED TENNYSON

Words

betrothed, *affianced.*
blessing, *benediction.*
brooch, *ornament.*
burled, *Interred.*
cleave, *adhere.*
diamond, *precious stone.*

faith, *sincerity*.
falsely, *wrongly*.
fortunes, *fate*.
heiress, *a female heir*.
lawful, *rightful*.
lilies, *flowers*.
merry, *jovial*.
necklace, *string of gems*.
proudly, *nobly*.
replied , *answered*.
riddle, *puzzle*.
scorn, *contempt*.
secret, *mystery*.
Stead, *place*.
Strange, *inexplicable*.

☆ ☆

那是百合花绽放的时节，
云朵高高飘扬在天空，
罗纳德大人带来了一头百合花一样洁白的雌鹿，
送给他的表妹——克莱尔小姐。

我想象他们这样相爱的情人，
一定不会在龃龉中别离。
他们俩会在明天早晨结婚；
上帝的祝福降临在那一天。

“他爱的不是我的出身，
也不是我那宽广而美丽的土地；
他爱的是我这个人，
这真好，”克莱尔小姐说。

年老的保姆爱丽丝来了，
她问，“刚才离去的是哪一位？”
“是我的表兄，”克莱尔小姐说，
“明天他就会和我结婚。”

“哦，感谢上帝！”保姆爱丽丝说，
“这一切的到来都这么公正而美好，
罗纳德大人是你土地的继承人，
而你并不是克莱尔小姐。”

“你是不是糊涂了，我的保姆，我的保姆，
克莱尔小姐说，“你怎么胡言乱语？”
“上帝在上，”保姆爱丽丝说，
“我说的是事实——你是我的孩子。”

“老伯爵的女儿死在我的怀里——
我说的是事实，就像我吃面包这样的事实一样！
我埋葬了她，就像埋葬自己亲爱的孩子一样，
然后让自己的孩子充当她的位置。”

“假的，你说的是假的，
哦，姆妈，”她说，“如果这一切是真的话，
这世界上最好的人，在光天化日之下，
这么多年不能得到他应得的东西。”

“不，现在，我的孩子，”保姆爱丽丝说道，
“你一生都要保留这个秘密，
当你和罗纳德大人成亲的时候，
你的一切也就成为他的。”

“如果我生来是个穷人，”她说，
“我会把真相说出来，因为我不想说谎。
褪下来，把这金镯子褪下来，
把这钻石项链也扔到一旁！”

“不，现在，我的孩子，”保姆爱丽丝说，
“尽可能地保住这个秘密。”
她说，“不能这样；如此我便会知道，
人间尚有信念。”

“不，现在，什么信念？”保姆爱丽丝说，
“他会得到他的权利。”

“他会的，”小姐回答道，
“只不过我今晚就要死去了！”

“那给你妈妈一个吻吧！
啊，我的孩子，我对不起你。”
“哦，妈妈，妈妈，妈妈，”她说，
“这看起来太不可思议。”

“这是给我亲爱的妈妈的吻，
我亲爱的妈妈，如果这是真的的话；
把你的手放在我的额头上，
祝福我吧，妈妈，我去了。”

她身着赤褐色的袍子，
不再是克莱尔小姐了；
她走在河谷，走在乡村，
发间别了一支玫瑰。

是罗纳德大人带来的百合花一样的玫瑰，
从生长的土地上萌芽，
在少女的手中枯萎，
一路上追随着她。

罗纳德大人从他的塔楼上走下，
“哦，克莱尔小姐，你怎能如此羞辱你自己！
为什么你穿得像个村姑，
好似那乡间的花朵？”

“如果我穿得像村姑一样，
那是因为这就是我的命运；
我生来就是穷人，”她说，
“不是什么克莱尔小姐。”

“不要逗我玩儿，”罗纳德大人说，
“我全身心爱着你，
不要和我开玩笑，”罗纳德大人说；
“你打的哑谜太难猜透。”

哦，她骄傲地站立起身子！
身体里的那颗心并没有沉下去；
她看着罗纳德大人的双眼，
告诉了他保姆跟她说的一切。

他笑了起来，笑声中透着快乐的不屑；
他转身向她去，吻了她：
“如果你不是出身高贵的话，
那么我，”他说，“也并非贵族血脉。”

“如果你不是贵族出身的话，
那么我，”他说，“则是法定继承人，
我们明天早晨结婚，
这样你依然还是克莱尔小姐。”

——阿尔弗雷德·丁尼生

Lesson 26 THE BATTLE OF THE NILE

第二十六课 尼罗河河口海战

'Tis an old story now, that Battle of the Nile; but a brave story can never die of age.

The Bay is wide, but dangerous from shoals: the line of deep blue water, and the old castle of Aboukir, map out the position of the French fleet on the 1st of August 1798. Having landed Buonaparte and his army, the French Admiral moored his fleet in the form of a crescent close along the shore. His vastly superior force, and the strength of his position (protected towards the north by dangerous shoals, and towards the west by the castle and batteries), made him consider that position impregnable; and on the strength of this conviction he wrote to Paris that Nelson had purposely avoided him.

Was he undeceived when Hood, in the *Zealous*, made signal that the enemy was in sight, and a cheer of triumph burst from every ship in the British fleet—that fleet which had been sweeping the seas with bursting sails for six long weeks in search of its formidable foe, and which now bore down upon him with fearless exultation. The soundings of that dangerous bay were unknown to Nelson; but he knew that where there was room for a French ship to swing, there must be room for an Englishman to anchor at either side of him,—and the closer the better!

As his proud and fearless fleet came on, he hailed Hood, to ask whether the action should commence that night; then receiving the answer he longed for, the signal for "close battle" flew from his mast-head. The delay thus caused to the *Zealous* gave Foley the lead. He showed the example of leading *inside* the enemy's lines, and anchored by the stern alongside the second ship; thus leaving to Hood the first. The latter, putting his own generous construction on an accident, exclaimed, "Thank God, he has nobly left to his old friend still to lead the van!"

Slowly and majestically, as the evening fell, the remainder of the fleet came on beneath a cloud of sails, receiving the fire of the castle and the batteries in portentous silence, only broken by the crash of spars, or the boatswain's whistle; each ship furling her sails calmly, as a sea-bird might fold its wings, and gliding tranquilly onward till she found her destined foe. Then the anchor dropped astern, and the fire burst from her blood-stained decks with a vigour that showed how sternly it had been repressed till then.

The leading ships passed between the enemy and the shore; but when the Admiral came up, he led the remainder of the fleet along the seaward side, thus doubling on the Frenchman's line, and placing it in a defile of fire.

The sun went down soon after Nelson anchored; and his rearward ships were guided through the darkness and the dangers of that formidable bay only by the

Frenchman's fire flashing fierce welcome, as each enemy arrived and went hovering along the lines. He coolly scrutinized how he might draw most of that fire upon himself. The *Bellerophon*, with reckless gallantry, fastened on the gigantic *Orient*, by whose terrible artillery she was soon crushed, and scorched into a wreck. Then she drifted helplessly to leeward. But she had already done her work,—the *Orient* was on fire, and through the terrible roar of battle a whisper went for a moment that paralyzed every eager heart and hand. During that dread pause the fight was suspended; the very wounded ceased to groan: yet the burning ship still continued to fire broadsides from her flaming decks; her gallant crew alone unawed by their approaching fate, and shouting their own death-song.

At length the terrible explosion came; and the column of flame, that shot upwards into the very sky, for a moment rendered visible the whole surrounding scene, from the red flags aloft to the reddened decks below; the wide shore with all its swarthy crowds, and the far-off glittering seas with the torn and dismantled fleets. Then darkness and silence came again, broken only by the shower of blazing fragments in which that brave ship fell upon the waters.

Till that moment, Nelson was ignorant how the battle went. He knew that every man was doing his duty, but he knew not how successfully. He had been wounded in the forehead, but had found his way unnoticed to the deck in the suspense of the coming explosion. Its light was a fitting lamp for eyes like his to read by. He saw his own proud flag still floating everywhere; and at the same moment his crew recognized their wounded chief. Their cheer of welcome was only drowned in the renewed roar of their artillery, which continued until it no longer found an answer, and Silence had confessed Destruction.

Morning rose up on an altered scene. The sun had set upon as proud a fleet as ever sailed from the gay shores on France. Now only torn and blackened hulls marked the position they had then occupied; and where their Admiral's ship had been, the blank sea sparkled in the sunshine. Two ships of the line and two frigates escaped, only to be captured soon afterwards; but within the bay the tricolour was flying on only one ship. As the *Theseus* approached to attack her, attempting to capitulate she hoisted a flag of truce. "Your battle-flag or none!" was the stern reply, as her enemy rounded to, and the matches glimmered over her line of guns. Slowly and reluctantly, like an expiring hope, that pale flag fluttered down from her lofty spars, and the next that floated was that of England.

And now the battle was over—India was saved upon the shores of Egypt—the career of Buonaparte was checked, and his navy annihilated. Seven years later that navy was revived, to perish utterly at Trafalgar—a fitting hecatomb for the obsequies of Nelson, whose life, it seemed, terminated as his mission was accomplished.

—WARBURTON

Words

annihilated, *demolished.*
approaching, *coming.*
artillery, *cannon.*
capitulate, *surrender.*
captured, *secured.*
consider, *deem.*
contraction, *interpretation.*
conviction, *belief.*
crescent, *semi-circle.*
dangerous, *perilous.*
destined, *appointed.*
destruction, *demolition.*
dismantled, *destroyed.*
explosion, *bursting.*
exultation, *delight.*
formidable, *terrible.*
generous, *liberal.*
gigantic, *tremendous.*
impregnable, *invincible.*
majestically, *grandly.*
paralyzed, *unnerved.*
portentous, *ominous.*
recognized, *discovered.*
reluctantly, *unwillingly.*
repressed, *restrained.*
scrutinized, *calculated.*
suspense, *anxiety.*
terminated, *closed.*
undeceived, *enlightened.*

Questions

When was the Battle of the Nile fought? What account of Nelson's doings had the French Admiral sent to Paris? What had Nelson really been doing for six weeks? Who showed the example of leading inside the enemy's lines? In what position was the French fleet placed when Nelson came up? What was the turning-point of the battle? How many ships carried the French flag next morning? What were the results of the victory?

☆ ☆

"现在说起来，这是个老故事了；但一个大无畏的故事是不会老到无趣的。"

"那是一个开阔的海湾，但是因为浅滩丛生，那里潜藏着危险：蓝色深水线和阿布吉尔的古老城堡标识出1798年8月1日的法国舰队的位置。在拿破仑和他的军团登陆后，法国海军上将把他的舰队呈新月形停泊在海岸沿线。他无与伦比的火力装备和有利的位置（北部有危险浅滩的保护，西部则有城堡和关隘为屏障），让他觉得这个地方固若金汤。在这种想法的驱使下，他写信给巴黎，说尼尔森故意躲避他。

当热忱号上的胡德发出信号说看到敌人，并听到英国舰队的每一条船都爆发出胜利的欢呼的时候，他是不是醒悟了呢？英国舰队已经在海上乘风破浪地巡游了整整六个星期，为的是找到它可怕的敌人，而现在它步步向其逼近，无所畏惧而又欣喜若狂。尼尔森并不了解危险的海湾附近环境，但他知道只要有地方容得下法国军舰游弋施展，就一定有英国军舰在其左右抛锚的空间，而且是离得越近越好！

当他骄傲而无畏的军舰聚集上来时，他向胡德大声喊话，问他是否应该当晚发动进攻，然后他得到了自己梦寐以求的答复，“血战”的信号从热忱号的桅杆上飘扬起来。热忱号上的拖沓让弗雷能够领先。他展示了如何在敌人阵线内部指挥若定的智慧，在贴近第二艘船右舷侧抛锚，这样胡德就领先了。而胡德，把这小小意外看成是上帝的恩泽，喊道：“感谢上帝，他高贵地留在了他的老朋友身边，依然引领群舰！”

夜幕降临，舰队中剩余的船只，扬着帆缓慢而威严地驶进着，在不详的沉寂中即将受到来自城堡和大炮的火力攻击，当桅杆断裂或者船员发出哨声的时候，这种沉寂才被打破。每条船都镇定地收起帆，如同雄鸟把自己的羽翼收拢一般，然后静静地前进，直到找到自己的宿敌。锚在船尾被抛下，从血迹斑斑的船舱喷射出猛烈的火焰，似乎是压抑了良久之后的大爆发。

领头的船只从敌船和海岸中间穿梭而过；但当海军上将出现的时候，他领导剩余的舰队船只沿海岸行驶，以此来加强法国人的战线，同时形成纵队火力。

尼尔森的船一抛锚，太阳就下山了。其后的船只在指引下穿越了黑暗的夜色和法国人猛烈的火力进攻的危险，每一只法国战船都已经各就各位，在其防线游弋。尼尔森冷静而仔细地判断出他可能会吸引到部分的火力到自己这条船——柏勒洛丰号上。于是，他以大无畏的勇猛精神，加紧向那巨大的东方号驶进，在后者的骇人火力攻击下，它不久就被击中并烧着了。接着，它无助地往下风向漂去。但它已经完成了自己的使命——东方号着火了，从这可怕的战争的咆哮声中，暂时出现了一阵低语似的每一颗渴望的心脏和手都痉挛了。在这可怕的停顿中，战斗终止了，那些受伤的人不再发出呻吟声。然而燃烧的战船继续从它火光闪耀的船舱胡乱地开火，只有它勇猛的船员被即将到来的命运威慑住了，喊出死亡的绝响。

最后就是可怕的爆炸了。火柱一飞冲天，在一段时间里整片邻近的船只都被照亮了，从飘扬着的红色战旗到漆成红色的下面的船舱都看得一清二楚；开阔的海岸线联着聚集着的人群，远处波光粼粼的海面和上面毁坏的战舰也都清晰可见。然后黑暗和寂静再次降临，仅仅能听到从船只掉落到水面上的燃烧的碎片的声音。

直到那时，尼尔森还是不知道战事的进展情况。他只知道每个人都各司其职，但不知道他们究竟做得有多好。他的额头受了伤，但在即将到来爆炸的间歇中，他去船舱时发现没有人发现自己。船上的火光就好像一盏为他点燃的，刚好够他看清东西的灯一样。他瞧见自己那骄傲的战旗依然在各处飘扬；同时，他的手下也认出了他们受伤的将军。他们欢迎的欢呼声湮没在新一轮开始的火力攻击中，这番火力攻击不断持续，直到听不到敌船地回击了，沉默表明了其灭亡。

早晨的到来唤醒的是另外一番场景。太阳高高升起，那骄傲的法国舰队从法国的灰白色海岸驶进。他们曾经占领的地方如今只剩下破败和熏黑的船壳，他们海军上将的战船去哪儿了，眼前只有空阔的大海在阳光下闪动着。舰队中有两只战船和两只护卫舰逃走了，之后不久才被捉到，但整个海湾上，只有一条船上还飘扬着三色国旗。当时西斯号靠近，攻击那条船，想让它屈服，升起休战的旗帜。“撤下你的战旗或什么旗都不挂！”当对方的船舰包围它时，严厉地喊话道，接着它上头就闪动着攻击的火光。于是就像抓住最后的救命稻草一样，它缓慢而不情愿地将那白色的旗子从高高的桅杆上降落下来，转而升起了英国的战旗。

现在海战结束了——印度因为埃及海岸的战役而获救——波拿巴的事业受到遏制，他的海军被歼灭了。7年之后，这支舰队才得以重建，并最终在特拉法加被消灭。特拉法加歼灭战是对尼尔森之死再也合适不过的祭礼，尼尔森的一生似乎就在自己使命完成时终止了。

——沃尔波顿

Lesson 27 THE AURORA

第二十七课 极 光

One of the most mysterious and beautiful of Nature's manifestations is the Aurora. In our own latitudes strikingly beautiful auroral displays may sometimes be witnessed; but it is in the Arctic and Antarctic regions that the phenomenon appears in its fullest beauty. The following description may be taken as an example of what is often seen in the Polar regions—the true home of the aurora:—

Darkness broods over the Polar world. Even the outlines of the mighty hills can scarcely be distinguished. No object can be seen moving over the wide expanse of frozen sea.

Suddenly from east to west appears a beautiful arch of living gold! The lights dart to and fro, their colours rivalling those of the rainbow. Beyond the arch, a stream of golden rays shoots up far above all the rest, and the stars are obscured as the "merrie dancers" sweep along in waves of light.

There is something surpassingly beautiful in the appearance of the true "auroral curtain." Fringed with coloured streamers, it waves to and fro, as if shaken by some unseen hand. Then, from end to end, there passes a succession of undulations, and the curtain seems to wave in a series of graceful curves.

Suddenly, and as it were by magic, there succeeds a perfect stillness; as if the unseen power, which had been displaying the varied beauties of the auroral curtain, were resting for a moment. But even while the motion of the curtain is stilled, we see the alternate waxing and waning of its mysterious light.

While we gaze, fresh waves of disturbance traverse the magic canopy. Startling coruscations add splendour to the scene; and the noble span of the auroral arch, from which the waving curtain seems to hang, gives a grandeur to the spectacle which no words can adequately describe.

THE AURORA IN THE POLAR REGIONS

At length the luminous zone breaks up. The scene of the display becomes covered with scattered streaks and patches of ashen gray light, which hang like clouds over the heavens. Then these in turn disappear, and nothing remains of the brilliant spectacle but a dark smoke-like cloud on the horizon.

Words

adequately, *fitly*.
coruscations, flashes, *or gleams of light*.
description, *account*.
displaying, *unfolding*.
grandeur, *splendour*.
luminous, *full of light*.
manifestations, *exhibitions*.
rivalling, *emulating*.
spectacle, *sight*.
surpassingly, *exceedingly*.
traverse, *cross*.
undulations, *vibrations*.

☆ ☆

最神秘最美的大自然景象之一就是极光现象。我们生活的纬度有时候能看见美轮美奂的极光现象，但只有在北极和南极地区，极光之美才会完全绽放。以下可以被看作是经常在极地地区——也就是极光真正的原生地——出现极光的描写范例：

黑暗沉浸了极地世界，甚至高大的山峦轮廓都几乎分辨不出了。看不到任何物体在这冰冻的广袤海上的移动。

突然自东向西出现了一道闪亮的美丽金色弧光！其光线左右跳跃，颜色绮丽无比，可以和彩虹媲美。在弧光之外，有一帘金色的光束像从高远的天空中抛出一般，这“快乐的舞者”在光的起伏中一扫而过的时候，星星都隐匿不见了。

真正的“极光帘”的景象有着非同寻常的美。其边缘是彩色的光束，来回波动，好像有一只看不见的手在抖动着它一样。然后从一端到另一端，出现了连绵的起伏，而整个极光帘看起来就像是一系列优美的弧线在此起彼伏着。

突然间，似乎有魔法在驱使它，它紧接着一动不动了，好像那向我们展示极光帘多姿多彩美得看不见的力量。有时候它会停下来休息一会儿，但即使极光帘静止了，我们还是能看到它神秘的光或盛或衰。

我们凝望它的时候，会有新的干扰性光波横穿过这魔幻般的华盖，赋予了极光帘光彩和绚烂；而那似乎垂落下的起伏帘子的美好极光弧线，给这景象增添了一份语言无法传达的伟大。

最后，发光地带消失了，整个景象变成零零散散的光带和灰色光点，如同云朵一样悬在天空之中。之后连光带和光点也消失不见了，那绮丽的景象什么也没留下，只有那如烟的黯黑云朵出现在地平线上。

Lesson 28 THE BATTLE OF THE BALTIC

第二十八课 波罗的海之战

(A.D. 1801)

Of Nelson and the North
Sing the glorious day's renown,
When to battle fierce came forth
All the might of Denmark's crown,
And her arms along the deep proudly shone;
By each gun the lighted brand
In a bold determined hand,
And the Prince of all the land
Led them on.

Like leviathans afloat,
Lay their bulwarks on the brine;
While the sign of battle flew
On the lofty British line;
It was ten of April morn by the chime:
As they drifted on their path,
There was silence deep as death;
And the boldest held his breath
For a time.

But the might of England flushed
To anticipate the scene;
And her van the fleeter rushed
O'er the deadly space between.
"Hearts of oak!" our captains cried, when each gun
From its adamantine lips
Spread a death-shade round the ships,
Like the hurricane eclipse
Of the sun!

Again! again! again!
And the havoc did not slack,
Till a feeble cheer the Dane

To our cheering sent us back.
Their shots along the deep slowly boom;—
Then cease—and all is wail,
As they strike the shattered sail;
Or, in conflagration pale,
Light the gloom!

Out spoke the Victor then,
As he hailed them o'er the wave:
"Ye are brothers! ye are men!
And we conquer but to save!
So peace, instead of death, let us bring;—
But yield, proud foe, thy fleet,
With the crews, at England's feet,
And make submission meet
To our King."

Then Denmark blessed our Chief,
That he gave her wounds repose;
And the sounds of joy and grief
From her people wildly rose,
As Death withdrew his shades from the day.
While the Sun looked smiling bright
O'er a wide and woful sight,
Where the fires of funeral light
Died away!

Now joy, Old England, raise!
For the tidings of thy might,
By the festal cities' blaze,
While the wine-cup shines in light;—
And yet, amidst that joy and uproar,
Let us think of them that sleep,
Full many a fathom deep,
By thy wild and stormy steep,
Elsinore!

Brave hearts! to Britain's pride
Once so faithful and so true,
On the deck of fame that died,
With the gallant, good Riou!
Soft sigh the winds of heaven o'er their grave!

While the billow mournful rolls,
And the mermaid's song condoles,
Singing glory to the souls
Of the brave!

—THOMAS CAMPBELL

Words

anticipate, *forestall*.
condoles, *sympathizes*.
conflagration, *flame*.
determined, *resolute*.
eclipse, *obscuration*.
gallant, *brave*.
havoc, *devastation*.
hurricane, *tempestuous*.
leviathans, *monsters*.
renown , *fame*.
shattered, *shivered*.
submission, *surrender*.

☆ ☆

（公元1801年）

歌唱着那些关于尼尔森和北方之战的
广为人知的辉煌岁月，
丹麦王室的全部权势
和装备熠熠闪光，
都投入到激烈的战争中；
每把枪上都系着飘带，
它们被握在无畏的视死如归的人手中，
而这个国家的王子
引领他们前进。

就像海上巨兽一样漂流，
将它们的防波堤建在海水之上；
然后战争的信号飞扬在了
高远的大不列颠海岸线上；
和谐的歌声奏响，刚刚是4月10日的早晨，
它们在航线上前进，

沉寂如同死亡一般深沉；
最勇猛的人在那段时间里，
屏住了呼吸。

但英国的权贵们激动不已，
因为他们已经预测到这情形的到来；
于是他们派出战舰冲锋在那生死危急的空隙。
“橡树之心！”我们的长官喊着，
每把枪从它坚定不移的嘴唇间
将死亡阴影传播开来，使之萦绕整个船队，
如同飓风来临，
遮蔽太阳一般！

再一次！再一次！再一次！
破坏与蹂躏直到
听见丹麦人发出羸弱的欢呼
我们才撤退。
他们在深海一带的射击渐渐安静开来，
停止了——所有人都在悲号，
当他们驶动那满目疮痍的帆船；
或者，那苍白的大火，
点亮了那片晦暗！

胜者开始发言，
他乘风破浪驾着船：
“你们是我的兄弟！你们是我的子民！
我们的征服是为了解救你们！
所以，让我们带来和平吧，不要带来死亡；
骄傲的敌人啊，你们的舰队投降吧，
带你们的追随者一起投诚在英格兰脚下吧，
以顺从之心来谒见
我们的国王。”

丹麦祝福了我们的指挥官，
使他有时间疗养伤口；
然后从它的人民当中突然响起热烈的
喜悦和悲伤的声音，
好像死神把它的阴影从这一天当中撤离一般。
太阳看起来微笑着闪耀光彩，
照耀在广泛存在而悲伤的目光中，
那目光中葬礼的火焰终于
消失不见！

现在欢呼吧，英格兰，举手欢庆吧！
因为你强大力量的浪涛，
在那些欢庆城市的火焰之畔，
酒杯在这火光中闪亮；
然而，在那欢庆和骚动之间，
我们不妨想一想那些沉睡的人们，
有太多人陷入深深的沉睡中，
就在那荒野而多暴风雨的陡峭的
艾尔西诺之畔！

勇敢的心啊！大不列颠的骄傲，
曾如此忠贞如此真诚，
在争名夺利的甲板上死去了，
随那勇敢而善良的里乌一起去了！
天堂的柔风轻抚过他们的墓室！
当哀悼的巨浪翻滚的时候，
当美人鱼的歌声来慰藉的时候，
请唱响胜利的歌谣来慰藉
勇敢的英灵吧！

——托马斯·坎贝尔

Lesson 29
TRIUMPHS OF THE ENGLISH LANGUAGE
第二十九课　英语的胜利

Now gather all our Saxon bards, let harps and heart be strung,
To celebrate the triumphs of our own good Saxon tongue;
For stronger far than hosts that march with battle-flags unfurled,
It goes with FREEDOM, THOUGHT, and TRUTH, to rouse and rule the world.

Stout Albion learns its household lays on every surf-worn shore,
And Scotland hears its echoing far as Orkney's breakers roar—
From Jura's crags and Mona's hills it floats on every gale,
And warms with eloquence and song the homes of Innisfail.

On many a wide and swarming deck it scales the rough wave's crest,
Seeking its peerless heritage—the fresh and fruitful West:
It climbs New England's rocky steeps as victor mounts a throne;
Niagara knows and greets the voice, still mightier than its own.

It spreads where Winter piles deep snows on bleak Canadian plains,
And where on Essequibo's banks eternal Summer reigns:
It glads Acadia's misty coasts, Jamaica's glowing isle,
And bides where, gay with early flowers, green Texan prairies smile:
It tracks the loud swift Oregon through sunset valleys rolled,
And soars where Californian brooks wash down their sands of gold.

It sounds in Borneo's camphor groves, on seas of fierce Malay,
In fields that curb old Ganges' flood, and towers of proud Bombay;
It wakes up Aden's flashing eyes, dusk brows, and swarthy limbs;
The dark Liberian soothes her child with English cradle hymns.

Tasmania's maids are wooed and won in gentle Saxon speech;
Australian boys read Crusoe's life by Sydney's sheltered beach;
It dwells where Afric's southmost capes meet oceans broad and blue,
And Nieuveld's rugged mountains gird the wide and waste karroo.

It kindles realms so far apart, that, while its praise you sing,
These may be clad with Autumn's fruits, and those with flower of Spring;

It quickens Lands whose meteor lights flame in an Arctic sky,
And lands for which the Southern Cross hangs its orbed fires on high.

It goes with all that prophets told, and righteous kings desired,—
With all that great apostles taught, and glorious Greeks admired,—
With Shakespeare's deep and wondrous verse, and Milton's loftier mind,—
With Alfred's laws, and Newton's lore,—to cheer and bless mankind.

Mark, as it spreads, how deserts bloom, and error flies away,
As vanishes the mist of night before the star of day!
But grand as are the victories whose monuments we see,
These are but as the dawn, which speaks of noontide yet to be

Take heed, then, heirs of Saxon fame! take heed, nor once disgrace,
With deadly pen or spoiling sword, our noble tongue and race.
Go forth prepared in every clime to love and help each other,
And judge that they who counsel strife would bid you smite—a brother.

Go forth, and jointly speed the time, by good men prayed for long,
When Christian States, grown just and wise, will scorn revenge and wrong;
When Earth's oppressed and savage tribes shall cease to pine or roam,
All taught to prize these English Words—FAITH, FREEDOM, HEAVEN,
and HOME.

—J. G. LYONS

Words

cerebrate, *commemorate.*
counsel, *advise.*
disgrace, *debase.*
eloquence, *oratory.*
heritage, *inheritance.*
household, *familiar.*
kindles, *excite.*
meteor, *flashing.*
monuments, *memorials.*
peerless, *unequalled.*
prepared, *equipped.*
quickens, *enlivens.*
revenge, *retaliation.*
righteous, *upright.*
sheltered, *protected.*
swarthy, *dusky.*
triumphs, *victories.*
unfurled, *unrolled.*
vanishes, *disappears.*
wondrous, *marvelous.*

现在把我们所有撒克逊的吟游诗人都聚集起来吧，让竖琴拨响，心儿跳动吧，
来庆祝我们伟大的撒克逊语言的胜利。
因为它比那战旗飘扬的外来者更加强大，
同自由、思想与真理一同唤醒并统治世界。

雄壮的埃尔比恩在每一个被海浪侵蚀的海岸上歌唱家喻户晓的音律，
苏格兰则从遥远的奥克尼侵入者的嚎叫中听到它的回声。
它随着从侏罗山脉的峭壁上，和着蒙娜的群山上吹动的风而飘荡，
用雄辩和歌声温暖着位于因尼斯费尔的家乡。

在众多的宽阔而拥挤的甲板之上，它把最汹涌巨浪的浪头测量，
找寻它那无与伦比的传承——那新鲜而多产的西方。
它攀登上新英格兰陡峭的山峰，如同胜利者坐上王座一样，
尼亚加拉大瀑布知道它的声音并欢迎它的到来，而这声音比它自身更有力量。

它在冬天聚集起厚厚的大雪的荒凉的加拿大平原上做弥散，
在爱斯基摩的河岸上统治那永恒的夏天。
它为阿卡迪亚迷雾重重的海岸线而欣喜，为牙买加闪耀的岛屿而高兴，
为早早绽放的花儿而欢乐，看到葱郁的德克萨斯的大草原而微笑。
它追踪大声而迅疾的俄勒冈，穿越了日落的峡谷，在里头翻滚，
在加利福尼亚的溪流之上高飞，洗涤水中的泥沙淘出金子。

它在婆罗洲的樟脑树上响动，在马来西亚汹涌的大海上声响，
回响在拦截了古老的恒河大水的田地里，和那骄傲的孟买高塔上。
它唤醒了亚丁湾闪动的双眼，浓黑的眉毛和有力的臂膀，
黝黑的利比亚人用英文摇篮歌谣安抚着自己的孩子。

塔斯马尼亚岛上的女仆在求爱，并用彬彬有礼的撒克逊语言赢得了爱情；
澳大利亚男孩在悉尼树荫遮蔽的沙滩上读着《鲁滨孙漂流记》。
它在法国最南端的海角栖身，遇到广袤而湛蓝的海洋，
捏瓦尔德的崎岖山峦将荒野而干燥的南非台地草原隔开。

它所点亮的疆土彼此相距如此之远，以至于当你唱起它的赞歌的时候，

这里还是金果累累的秋天，那里就是百花盛开的春日。
它加快着那些点亮北极天空的流星的脉搏，
还有那些南十字星座，将它星球的火焰高高挂在天际的国度。

和所有的预言所预测的一样，和所有正直的国王所希冀的无差，
它教授最伟大的信徒，为光辉的希腊人所羡慕。
它拥有莎士比亚深沉而奇妙的诗行，和弥尔顿高远的思想，
以及艾尔弗莱德的准则，牛顿的学问，来为人类欢呼雀跃。

在它扩散的时候，请记住，沙漠是如何开花，错误是如何消失的，
如同雾霭沉沉的夜晚消失在白日的星光下！
我们看到的那些丰功伟绩的碑石如此伟岸，
但它们不过就如同黄昏，诉说着正午即将到来。

那么谨慎些吧，光荣的撒克森人的继承者们！谨慎些吧，不要再有耻辱之事发生，
谨慎使用那致命的笔伐，或是令人扫兴的宝剑，我们高贵的语言，伟大的民族。
在任何的时候都准备好怜爱彼此，帮助彼此吧，
从那些助纣为虐的人身上，从那些会重重击打你的人身上判断出谁是你的兄弟。

来吧，和善良的人一起慢慢祈祷吧，祈祷时间加快脚步，
在基督的国度中，生长出公正和智慧，蔑视复仇和屈枉。
当人间的压迫和野蛮部落的抢掠停止，消失的时候，
所有人都学会了珍视这些英文词语——信念、自由、天堂和家园。

——J. G. · 里昂

Lesson 30 YOUNG LOCHINVAR

第三十课 年轻的列奇瓦尔

Oh, young Lochinvar is come out of the west;
Through all the wide Border his steed was the best:
And save his good broad-sword he weapons had none;
He rode all unarmed, and he rode all alone.
So faithful in love, and so dauntless in war,
There never was knight like the young Lochinvar.

He stayed not for brake, and he stopped not for stone,
He swam the Esk river where ford there was none;
But, ere he alighted at Netherby gate,
The bride had consented—the gallant came late:
For a laggard in love and a dastard in war
Was to wed the fair Ellen of brave Lochinvar.

So boldly he entered the Netherby hall,
Among bridesmen, and kinsmen, and brothers and all
Then spoke the bride's father, his hand on his sword,
(For the poor craven bridegroom said never a word),
"Come ye in peace here, or come ye in war,
Or to dance at our bridal, young Lord Lochinvar."

"I long wooed your daughter, my suit you denied;—
Love swells like the Solway, but ebbs like its tide—
And now am I come, with this lost love of mine
To lead but one measure, drink one cup of wine.
There are maidens in Scotland, more lovely by far,
That would gladly be bride to the young Lochinvar."

The bride kissed the goblet; the knight took it up,
He quaffed off the wine, and he threw down the cup;
She looked down to blush, and she looked up to sigh,
With a smile on her lips and a tear in her eye.
He took her soft hand, ere her mother could bar,—
"Now tread we a measure!" said young Lochinvar.

So stately his form, and so lovely her face,
That never a hall such a galliard did grace;
While her mother did fret, and her father did fume,
And the bridegroom stood dangling his bonnet and plume;
And the bride-maidens whispered, "'Twere better by far
To have matched our fair cousin with young Lochinvar."

One touch to her hand, and one word in her ear,
When they reached the hall door, and the charger stood near,
So light to the croupe the fair lady he swung,
So light to the saddle before her he sprung!—
"She is won! we are gone, over bank, bush, and scaur!
They'll have fleet steeds that follow!" quoth young Lochinvar.

There was mounting 'mong Graemes of the Netherby clan;
Forsters, Fenwicks, and Musgraves, they rode and they ran;
There was racing and chasing on Cannobie lee,
But the lost bride of Netherby ne'er did they see!
So daring in love and so dauntless in war,
Have ye e'er heard of gallant like young Lochinvar?

—SIR WALTER SCOTT (1771–1882)

Words

bridal, *wedding.*
charger, *steed.*
consented, *agreed.*
craven, *cowardly.*
dangling, *swinging.*
daring, *bold.*
dauntless, *fearless.*
gallant, *lover.*
goblet, *cup.*
kinsmen, *relatives.*
matched, *married.*
quaffed, *drank.*
Stately, *dignified.*
whispered, *hinted.*
weapons, *arms.*

☆ ☆

哦，年轻的列奇瓦尔从西方而来，
所有开阔的边境线上，他的骏马最棒；
除了他那无可比拟的不做兵器的宝剑之外，
他不带武器独自一人骑马而来；

他对爱情如此忠贞，对战争如此无畏，
从未有一位像年轻的列奇瓦尔一样的骑士。

他不为阻碍所羁绊，不为绊脚石而停歇，
当不见浅滩的时候，他就溯游过艾斯克河；
然后，他到达了内瑟比的城门，
新娘已经同意出嫁——英勇的骑士来迟了；
因为爱情而来迟，因为战争而拖沓，
美丽的艾琳和勇敢的列奇瓦尔不能结合了。

他无畏地走进内瑟比的大厅，
里面都是男傧相，亲朋好友，兄弟姐妹。
之后新娘的父亲开口说话了，他的手放在宝剑上，
（而可怜的胆怯的新郎则一言不发），
“你悄悄地走过来，要不然我们就搏斗，
你也可以在婚礼上跳舞，年轻的列奇瓦尔。”

“我已经追求您的女儿很久了，而您拒绝了我的提亲，
爱就像索尔韦湾的潮水一样来得汹涌，退得也快；
现在我来这里，带着我逝去的爱情而来；
只有一个请求，想品尝一下第一杯美酒。
苏格兰有许多美丽的少女，
她们会很高兴做年轻的列奇瓦尔的新娘。”

新娘亲吻了一下高脚杯，骑士将杯子举起，
他一饮而尽，把酒杯扔在一旁；
她看着地上的碎屑，抬起头叹了口气，
她嘴角在微笑，眼中却含着泪水。
他握住她柔软的手，她母亲企图阻止，
“现在让我们来跳支舞吧。”年轻的列奇瓦尔说道。

他的身材是那么伟岸，她的脸庞是如此清秀，
从未有一个大厅这样蓬荜生辉过；

她母亲则在一旁生气愤怒，她父亲则雷霆万钧，
而那新郎则站在那里摆弄着帽子和羽毛；
伴娘们窃窃私语着，“到现在为止，最能够配得上
我们美丽表妹的，就是年轻的列奇瓦尔了。”

他碰了碰她的手，在她耳畔说了一句话，
当他们到大厅门口的时候，那坐骑就在眼前，
他以迅雷不及掩耳之势把新娘抱到马上，
接着如电闪雷鸣一样飞身上马！
她成功了！我们走了，越过了河岸，草地和裂谷，
他们将会派来骏马追赶我们！”年轻的列奇瓦尔说。

内瑟比家族登上哥乐美找寻，
福斯特、冯伟奇，还有姆斯格雷夫家族都在找寻，他们骑马，他们追赶，
在坎诺比上追赶，
但内瑟比那失踪的新娘却没有找见！
对爱情如此忠贞，对战争如此无畏，
你曾听过像年轻的列奇瓦尔这样的骑士吗？

——沃尔特·司各特爵士（1771–1882）

Lesson 31
THE TIDAL BORE OF THE TSIEN-TANG
第三十一课　钱塘江大潮

In the open expanse of the Southern Ocean, as well as over a large portion of the Pacific, the tidal wave rarely exceeds five or six feet in height, and in the Indian and Atlantic Oceans perhaps eight or ten. In bays and gulfs, however, opening broadly to its course, and narrowing towards their interior recesses—such as the Bay of Bengal, the Bristol Channel, and the Bay of Fundy in America—it may rise to twenty, thirty, or, under favourable circumstances o! wind and season, even to fifty or sixty feet in height! And where such seas terminate in river-estuaries, the wave, still converging, forms a high head or wall of water, termed a *Bore*, which ascends the river with sudden and destructive force.

Tidal bores of considerable magnitude occur in many rivers, such as the Severn, Garonne, Amazon, and Hoogly; but that of the Tsien-tang in China appears to excel them all in grandeur, especially at spring-tides and during strong easterly gales. Dr. Macgowan gives the following graphic account of it in the *Transactions of the Royal Asiatic Society*:—

"Between the river and the city walls, which are a mile distant, dense suburbs extend for several miles along the banks. As the hour of flood-tide approached, crowds gathered in the streets running at right angles with the Tsien-tang, but at safe distances. My position was a terrace in front of the *Tri-wave* Temple, which afforded a good view of the entire scene.

"On a sudden all traffic in the thronged mart was suspended; porters cleared the front street of every description of merchandise, boatmen ceased lading and unlading their vessels, and put out into the middle of the stream, so that a few minutes sufficed to give a deserted appearance to the busiest part of one of the busiest cities of Asia. The centre of the river teemed with craft, from small boats to large barges, including the gay 'flower-boats.'

"Loud shouting from the fleet announced the appearance of the flood, which seemed like a glistening white cable stretched athwart the river at its mouth, as far down as the eye could reach. Its noise, compared by Chinese poets to that of thunder, speedily drowned that of the boatmen; and as it advanced with great rapidity—at the rate, I should judge, of twenty-five miles an hour—it assumed the appearance of an alabaster wall, or rather of a cataract four or five miles across, and about thirty feet high, moving bodily onward! Soon it reached the advanced guard of the immense assemblage of vessels awaiting its approach.

"Knowing that the Bore of the Hoogly—which scarcely deserves mention in connection with the one before me—invariably overturned boats which were not skilfully managed, I could not but feel apprehensive for the lives of the floating multitude. As the foaming wall of water dashed furiously onward they were silenced, all being intently occupied in keeping their prows towards the wave, which threatened to submerge everything afloat; but they all vaulted, as it were, to the summit with perfect safety.

"The spectacle was of greatest interest when the Bore had passed about half way among the craft. On one side they were quietly reposing on the surface of the unruflled stream, while those on the lower portion were pitching and heaving on the flood: others were scaling, with the agility of salmon, the formidable cascade.

"This grand and exciting scene was of but a moment's duration,—it passed up the river in an instant; but, from this point, with gradually diminishing force, size, and velocity, until it ceased to perceptible, at a distance, say the Chinese accounts, of eighty miles from the city. The change from ebb- to flood-tide was almost instantaneous. A slight flood continued after the passage of the wave, but it soon began to ebb.

THE TIDAL BORE OF THE TSIEN–TANG

"A very short period elapsed between the passage of the Bore and the resumption of traffic. The vessels were soon attached to the shore again, and women and children were occupied in gathering articles which the careless or unskilful had lost in the confusion. The streets were drenched with spray, and a considerable volume of water splashed over the banks into the head of the Grand Canal, a few feet distant."

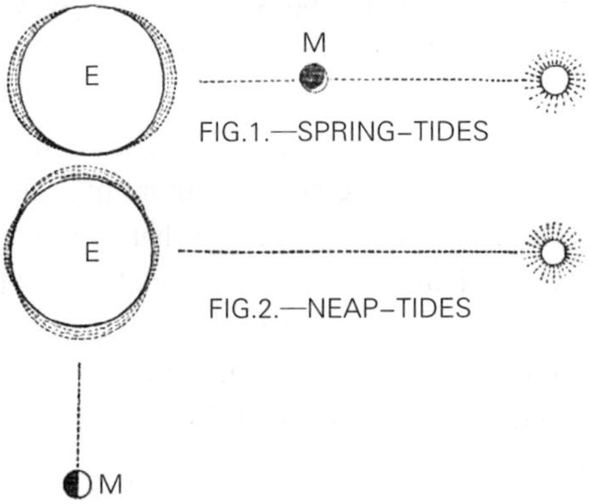

FIG.1.—SPRING–TIDES

FIG.2.—NEAP–TIDES

Tidal wave.—Tides are periodical swells in the ocean, produced by the attraction of the (sun and the moon. The influence of the moon in producing the tides is seven times as great as that of the sun, owing to its nearness to the Earth. A great protuberance of water, forming a tidal wave, follows the moon round the Earth; and its crest marks flood-tide, or high-water, wherever it happens to be.

This would account for one tide

each day; but there are two tides in twenty-four hours,—or rather in twenty-four hours fifty minutes, the length of the lunar day; i.e., the time that elapses between moon-rise and moon-rise at the same place. The two tidal waves are always at opposite sides of the globe, and as it were chase one another round the Earth.

The reason of this is, that while the moon draws the waters from the Earth on the side nearest to it, it also draws the solid Earth away from the waters on the opposite side, and causes a corresponding protuberance there.

When the sun and the moon exert their influence in the same direction the tides are highest, and are called *spring*-tides. (See fig. 1.) When they operate at right angles to each other, the force of the sun neutralizes to some extent that of the moon, and the tides are lowest; then called *neap-tides*. (See fig. 2.)

Words:

afforded, *gave.*
announced, *intimated.*
apprehensive, *anxious.*
approached, drew *near.*
assemblage, *collection.*
cascade, *waterfall.*
circumstances, *conditions.*
confusion, *turmoil.*
converging, *narrowing.*
description, *kind.*
elapsed, *passed.*
especially, *particularly.*
expanse, *space.*
glistening, *shining.*
graphic, *vivid.*
instantaneous, *momentary.*
intently, *eagerly.*
magnitude, *size.*
merchandise, *commodities.*
recesses, *bays.*
resumption, *reopening.*
submerge, *overflow.*
sufficed, *were enough.*
suspended, *stopped.*
terminate, *finish.*
unruffled, *smooth.*
vaulted, *sprang.*
velocity, *speed.*

Questions

What is the usual height of the tidal wave in the open sea? Where does it rise to a much greater height? What is it termed in narrow estuaries? Where do tidal bores occur? Which is the most remarkable? What change did its approach make on the streets? What did the boatmen do? At what rate did it advance? What appearance did it assume? When was the spectacle of greatest interest? How long did the scene last?

☆ ☆

在开阔的南海海域，也就是太平洋的一片广阔的海域上，潮汐高度超过五英尺或六英尺的情况鲜有发生，而在印度洋和大西洋上，潮汐的最高高度会达到八或十英尺之高。然而在海湾地带，越往内部越开阔，但通往它内部的通道却是越来越狭窄的地带——例如孟加拉海湾，布里斯托尔海峡以及美洲的芬迪湾——潮汐可能会达到二十英尺，三十英尺，或者在具有天时地利的季风季节中，甚至会达到五十或六十英尺的高度！当这些海域到达入河口的时候，这些大潮却依然在汇聚，形成高高的浪头或水墙，术语叫作汐，它会突然发力，以一种毁灭性的巨大力量抬高河流。

许多河流中都有具有巨大能量潮汐出现，例如塞汶河、加仑河、亚马孙河以及胡格里河，但中国的钱塘江大潮却在气势规模上超越了所有的这些潮汐，特别是春天刮着强劲东风时候的大潮。麦克格文博士曾在《皇家亚洲社会的交易》一书中形象地记录了钱塘江大潮的景象：

“在钱塘江和城墙之间，那城墙自一英里远处的人口密集的郊区延伸而来，沿河岸绵延了数英里。当快要出现大潮的时候，万人空巷，他们站在和钱塘江呈直角的位置，并保持了安全距离。而我是在三浪庙前面的一个平房里，里头的视野良好，能俯瞰整个大潮景观。”

“突然，人头攒动的集市上交通中断了，搬运工把街上所有种类的商品都清理完毕，船工们则不再载客接客，而是渡到河流中间，这样，亚洲最繁忙的城市中最繁忙的一隅就在几分钟的时间内变得荒凉了。江中间满满的都是船，小船，大船应有尽有，还有花船。”

“船上传来的大声喊叫，预示了潮水开始涌动，那潮水就像白色的闪亮的缆线一样，把河流缚住吞进口中，甩到眼睛能看到的最远处。它发出的噪响，被中国诗人比喻成雷声，以迅雷不及掩耳之势把船工的喊叫声湮没了；潮水急速向前——据我判断，它的速度能达到每小时二十五英里——涌起了一道雪花一样的浪墙，或者不如说是一道宽四五英里的瀑布，高度达到三十英尺，扭捏着身躯向前挺进！一会儿工夫，它就到达了等待着它的巨大船队前面。”

“我心里知道，胡格利河的潮汐——根本和眼前的这个大潮不能相提并论——无疑会将驾驶不娴熟的船只掀翻，于是我对那些船上人的性命担忧起来。当翻滚着白沫的水墙猛烈地向前砸去的时候，船上的人一言不发，他们一心忙着要把船头向那威胁着要吞噬江上一切船舶的大浪的方向调转；然后他们好像撑竿跳了起来一样，到达了浪顶部，安然无恙。”

“当潮汐大约有一半进入船队中间的时候，那景象是最有趣的。他们一边在静静的江面上休息，稍下游的人则在大浪的顶峰上，剩下的人则像三文鱼一样灵巧地攀附着这骇人的水瀑。”

“这伟大而激动人心的景观仅仅持续了一会儿——霎时间，它就越过了江面，然而，从那一刻起，它的力量不断衰减，规模和速度也在减小，直到在远处，根据中国人的说法，也就是在离着城区八十英里的地方偃旗息鼓了。从退潮到涨潮的变化几乎就在一瞬间，在大浪推进的过程中，会有稍小一点的浪紧随其后，但不一会儿就开始退潮了。”

“大潮的持续时间很短，人流车流如故。船只不一会儿就回到江岸了，女人和孩子们则忙着收拾那些无意或不小心在混乱中丢失的物品。街上到处都是水洼，几英尺开外的地方，还有不少水都溅到江的两岸，一直到大运河的河首。”

潮汐——潮汐是海洋中由于太阳和月球的引力，周期性发生的涨落现象。（月球的引力所产生的潮汐会比太阳的引力所产生的大六倍，因为月球是距离地球最近的天体）。大量涨起的水，会形成潮流，跟随着绕地球的月亮；潮汐的顶部就形成了潮流或高浪，无论在什么地方发生都是如此。

这可以作为每天都会发生的潮汐的解释，但一天二十四小时中有两次潮汐，或者不如说在二十四小时五十分钟里，就是在一个太阴日里，也就是两次月亮升起在同一个地方的时间间隔。两次潮汐总是出现在地球的相反面，就好像它们在彼此绕地球追逐一样。

发生这种现象的原因，是月亮从邻近它一面的地球上吸引起潮水来，同时在相反面上吸引地球远离那一面的潮水，这样就在那里产生了相应的潮汐了。

当太阳和月球的引力发生在同一方向的时候，潮汐是最宏大的，它也被称作大潮。当太阳和月球呈直角的时候，太阳的引力在某种程度上会中和月球的引力，这样的潮汐就是最小的，因此被称作小潮。

Lesson 32 THE SAXON AND THE GAEL

第三十二课 撒克逊人和盖尔人

The Chief in silence strode before,
And reached that torrent's sounding shore,
Which, daughter of three mighty lakes,
From Vennachar in silver breaks,
Sweeps through the plain, and ceaseless mines
On Bochastle the mouldering lines,
Where Rome, the empress of the world,
Of yore her eagle-wings unfurled.
And here his course the Chieftain stayed,
Threw down his target and his plaid,
And to the Lowland warrior said:
"Bold Saxon! to his promise just,
Vich-Alpine has discharged his trust
This murderous Chief, this ruthless man,
This head of a rebellious clan,
Hath led thee safe through watch and ward,
Far past Clan-Alpine's outmost guard.
Now, man to man, and steel to steel,
A Chieftain's vengeance thou shalt feel!
See here, all vantageless I stand,
Armed, like thyself, with single brand:
For this is Coilantogle ford,
And thou must keep thee with thy sword."
The Saxon paused:—"I ne'er delayed,
When foeman bade me draw my blade;

Nay, more, brave Chief, I vowed thy death;
Yet sure thy fair and generous faith,
And my deep debt for life preserved,
A better meed have well deserved:
Can nought but blood our feud atone?
Are there no means—?" "No, Stranger, none?
And hear,—to fire thy flagging zeal,—
The Saxon cause rests on thy steel;

For thus spoke Fate, by prophet bred
Between the living and the dead:
'Who spills the foremost foeman's life,
His party conquers in the strife.'"—
"Then, by my word," the Saxon said,
"The riddle is already read
Seek yonder brake beneath the cliff,—
There lies Red Murdoch, stark and stiff
Thus Fate has solved her prophecy;
Then yield to Fate, and not to me.
To James, at Stirling, let us go;
When, if thou wilt be still his foe,
Or if the King shall not agree
To grant thee grace and favour free,
I plight mine honour, oath, and word,
That, to thy native strengths restored,
With each advantage shalt thou stand
That aids thee now to guard thy land."—

Dark lightning flashed from Roderick's eye
"Soars thy presumption, then, so high,
Because a wretched kern ye slew,
Homage to name to Roderick Dhu?
He yields not, he, to man nor Fate!
Thou add'st but fuel to my hate:—
My clansman's blood demands revenge.—
Not yet prepared! Nay, then, I change
My thought, and hold thy valour light
As that of some vain carpet knight,
Who ill deserved my courteous care,
And whose best boast is but to wear
A braid of his fair lady's hair."—
"I thank thee, Roderick, for the word!
It nerves my heart, it steels my sword;
For I have sworn this braid to stain
In the best blood that warms thy vein.
Now, truce farewell! and ruth begone!—
Yet think not that by thee alone,
Proud Chief! can courtesy be shown;
Though not from copse, or heath, or cairn,
Start at my whistle clansmen stern,
Of this small horn one feeble blast

Would fearful odds against thee cast.
But fear not—doubt not—which thou wilt—
We try this quarrel hilt to hilt."

Then each at once his falchion drew;
Each on the ground his scabbard threw;
Each looked to sun, and stream, and plain,
As what he ne'er might see again;—
Then foot, and point, and eye opposed,
In dubious strife they darkly closed.—
I'll fared it then with Roderick Dhu
That on the field his targe he threw,
Whose brazen studs and tough bull-hide
Had death so often dashed aside;
For, trained abroad his arms to wield,
Fitz-James's blade was sword and shield.
He practised every pass and ward,
To thrust, to strike, to feint, to guard;
While, less expert, though stronger far,
The Gael maintained unequal war.
Three times in closing strife they stood,
And thrice the Saxon blade drank blood;
No stinted draught, no scanty tide—
The gushing flood the tartans dyed.
Fierce Roderick felt the fatal drain,
And showered his blows like wintry rain;
And as firm rock, or castle-roof,
Against the winter shower is proof,
The foe, invulnerable still,
Foiled his wild rage by steady skill;
Till, at advantage ta'en, his brand
Forced Roderick's weapon from his hand,
And backward borne upon the lea,
Brought the proud Chieftain to his knee!—

"Now yield thee, or by vows oft made
Thy very heart's blood dyes my blade!"—
"Thy threats, thy mercy, I defy!
Let recreant yield, who fears to die."—
Like adder darting from his coil,
Like wolf that dashes through the toil,
Like mountain-cat who guards her young,

Full at Fitz-James's throat he sprung;
Received, but recked not of a wound,
And locked his arms his foeman round!—
Now, gallant Saxon, hold thine own!
No maiden's hand is round thee thrown!
That desperate grasp thy frame might feel
Through bars of brass and triple steel!—
They tug, they strain!—down, down they go
The Gael above, Fitz-James below!
The Chieftain's gripe his throat compressed.
His knee was planted on his breast;
His clotted locks he backward threw,
Across his brow his hand he drew,
From blood and mist to clear his sight,
Then gleamed aloft his dagger bright!—
But hate and fury ill supplied
The stream of life's exhausted tide,
And all too late the advantage came
To turn the odds of deadly game;
For, while the dagger gleamed on high,
Reeled soul and sense, reeled brain and eye.
Down came the blow, but in the heath
The erring blade found bloodless sheath!
The struggling foe may now unclasp
The fainting Chief's relaxing grasp;—
Unwounded from the dreadful close,
But breathless all, Fitz-James arose.

—SIR WALTER SCOTT (1771–1832)

Words

Ceaseless, *continually*.
compressed, *squeezed*.
conquers, *triumphs*.
courteous, *obliging*.
demands, *calls for*.
deserved, *merited*.
desperate, *violent*.
discharged, *fulfilled*.
dubious, *doubtful*.
exhausted, *drained*.
falchion, *sword*.
feint, *make a mock attack*.
invulnerable, *invincible*.
maintained, *supported*.
mouldering, *decaying*.
plight, *pledge*.
presumption, *arrogance*.
prophecy, *prediction*.

quarrel, *dispute*.
recreant, *coward*.
relaxing, *loosening*.
restored, *returned*.
ruthless, *pitiless*.
scabbard, *sheath*.
stinted, *limited*.
struggling, *straining*.
supplied, *compensated*.
torrent, *river*.
vantageless, *without advantage*.
weapon, *sword*.

☆ ☆

一言不发的首领之前曾大步走在
并到达湍流响动的海岸上，
那海岸，三个伟大湖泊的女儿，
从那银色的岩层间出现的维纳查尔，
从平原上一扫而过，还有那不停歇的
位于渐趋破败的博洽斯特尔的矿藏，
在那里，作为远古世界的鹰隼
一样的罗马帝国伸展开羽翼。
而在这里，首领等待在自己的道路上，
他把靶子和花呢布放下，
对低地上的战士说道：
“大胆的撒克森人！
维奇·阿尔比尼违背了他刚刚许下的诺言，
这个杀人犯首领，这个铁面无情的人，
这叛逆族人的领袖，
曾经带领你安全穿过了戒备森严的地方，
远离阿尔比尼家族驻守最远的守卫。
现在，男人对男人，剑对剑，
让你尝一尝首领复仇的滋味！
看看现在，我优势全无，
和你一样，仅仅只有一剑在手：
因为这是科尔兰托格尔浅滩，
而你必须身带佩剑。”
撒克逊人停顿了一下：“我从不怠慢，
当我的敌人命令我拔出佩剑。”

“我不会再发誓誓死效忠，勇敢的首领；
但我终生所深深歉疚的
是你的高贵而慷慨的信念，
这是更好的奖赏，更值得获取：
是不是除了鲜血就没有东西可以来解除我们的仇恨了？
难道没有办法了吗？没有了，陌生人，没有了吗？
听吧，点燃你那昂扬的热忱吧，
撒克逊人会在你的剑下长眠；
因为你说了宿命，这是预言中说到的，
不是你死就是我亡：
“‘能把最厉害敌人的生命夺走的人，
他一定能在战斗中获胜。’”
“那么，依我而言，”撒克逊人说道，
“这个谜语已经给出谜底了，
是在悬崖下找到勒马之处，
那里有红默多克山，荒凉而僵硬
这样命运就能实现她的预言了；
然后向命运屈服，而不是向我，
向在斯特灵的詹姆斯国王臣服，并放我们离开；
届时，如果你还愿意与他为敌的话，
或者如果国王不同意赦免你，
给你自由和地位的话，
我会以我自己的荣耀，誓言和承诺为赌注，
来恢复你的权势，
这样无论如何你都占有有利形势了，
这样就能帮助你来守卫自己的疆土。”

罗德里克的眼中闪过黑色的闪电，
“你把自己的许诺说得比天高，
因为你已经走投无路，无力回天了，
仅仅来表现对罗德里克德鲁的敬意罢了？
罗德里克不会投降，不向任何人也不向命运屈服！
你说了这么多，只是让我仇恨之火更旺：

不必再准备了！不，那是，我改变了
自己的想法，坚定勇敢的光芒，
就好像那是某种徒劳的骑士的品质一样，
那骑士不值得我全心全意的爱戴，
而他的最好的夸口不过是给
他美丽的小姐发间系上一条穗带。”
“感谢你，罗德里克，你能说这些话！
它们拨动了我的心弦，坚固了我的宝剑；
因为我曾经起过誓言，这根穗带如果被玷污，
只能是玷污上你温暖的血。
现在，休战不再！不必手下留情！
你并不是只想到你自己，
骄傲的首领！展示出礼节来吧；
虽然不是从树丛、荒野和石塚中，
开始我们族人开战的庄严哨声，
吹响这一只羸弱的号角，
你投下了可怕的阴影。
但不要害怕——亦不要怀疑——而你还是会如此，
我们尽量公正地解决这次争端吧。”

然后他一次次地拔出刀来，
他一次次把剑鞘扔到地上；
每一次都抬头看看太阳，看看溪流，看看平原，
好像他从未见过一样；
然后那些对峙着的脚步，剑尖和眼睛，
在这值得怀疑的冲突中他们紧闭上双眼。
我一定要坚持到和罗德里克·德鲁对峙的时刻，
等到他把圆盾丢在战场上的时候，
那圆盾是黄铜和坚硬的牛皮制成
曾无数次死里逃生；
因为他能训练有素地挥动起
菲兹詹姆斯的剑和盾牌。
他每天早晚都操练，

练习打，练习劈，练习进攻，练习防守；
然而，虽然身体要强壮得多，但没有同样的水准，
因此盖尔人处在了战事的下风。
有三次他们在战斗即将结束时挺了过来，
有三次撒克逊人的剑吮吸到了他们的血；
没有严重的旱情，潮水汹涌，
苏格兰人被大水吞噬。
勇猛的罗德里克感觉到了致命的大水，
如同冬天的大雨一般浇在他身上击打着他；
像坚硬的岩石或者顶棚一样，
扑面砸来的倾盆大雨，
敌人还是坚定地一动不动站立着，
用娴熟的技巧控制自己狂野的怒火，
直到优势渐显，他的刀剑
迫使罗德里克的兵器脱手，
向草地撤退，
使得那骄傲的首领跪了下来！

“现在投降吧，或者就像我经常的誓言一样
我的刀剑会让你的心脏染血！”
“我蔑视你的威胁，蔑视你的怜悯！
让那些害怕死亡的懦夫投降吧。”
好像蝰蛇从蜷曲的形态突然跃起，
如同野狼在疲惫挣扎时候突然冲出，
好像山猫守卫自己的后代一般，
他以最快速度扑向了菲兹詹姆斯的咽喉；
他身上没有受一处伤，
而是双臂紧紧锁住他的仇敌！
现在，勇敢的撒克逊人，站好了！
抱住你把你摔倒的可不是姑娘的手臂！
你可能会感觉到我的绝望挣扎，
用那黄铜块和三齿叉！
他们拉呀，扯呀！——向下去，他们倒下了，

盖尔人在上头，菲兹詹姆斯在底下！
首领紧紧地压住自己的喉咙。
他的膝盖顶到胸膛；
他猛地向后一松手，
手交叉着从他眉毛两端收回，
他把血迹擦干，透过雾气看清，
他的匕首在高高地闪耀。
但仇恨和愤怒不能够满足
精疲力竭的生命潮水的逝去，
而扭转这致命对决的
乾坤之势来得为时过晚；
因为，当匕首在高处闪闪发光的时候，
灵魂和知觉已经弥散，大脑和眼睛已经眩晕。
下面的人发出一击，但是石塚中，
错误的刀剑上终于找到没有血迹的剑鞘！
挣扎的敌人现在可以松手了，
快要昏迷的首领也可以放松角力了；
虽然气喘吁吁，菲兹詹姆斯还是
从这场势均力敌的搏斗中毫发无损地站起身来。

——沃尔特·司各特爵士（1771–1832）

Lesson 33 THE WELL OF ST. KEYNE

第三十三课 圣凯恩井

A well there is in the west country,
  And a clearer one never was seen;
There is not a wife in the west country
  But has heard of the Well of St. Keyne.

An oak and an elm tree stand beside,
  And behind does an ash tree grow;
And a willow from the bank above
  Droops to the water below.

A traveller came to the Well of St. Keyne,
  Joyfully he drew nigh;
For from cock-crow he had been travelling,
  And there was not a cloud in the sky.

He drank of the water so cool and clear,
  For hot and thirsty was he;
And he sat down upon the bank,
  Under the willow tree.

There came a man from the neighbouring town,
  At the Well to fill his pail;
By the well-side he rested it,
  And he bade the stranger hail.

"Now, art thou a bachelor, stranger?" quoth he,
  "For an if thou hast a wife,
The happiest draught thou hast drunk this day
  That ever thou didst in thy life.

"Or has thy good woman, if one thou hast,
  Ever here in Cornwall been?
For an if she have I'll venture my life
  She has drunk of the Well of St. Keyne."

"I have left a good woman who never was here,"
 The stranger he made reply;
"But that my draught should be better for that,
 I pray you answer me why."

"St Keyne," quoth the Cornishman, "many a time
 Drank of this crystal Well;
And before the angel summoned her
 She laid on the water a spell;—

"If the husband, of this gifted
 Well Shall drink before his wife,
A happy man henceforth is he,
 For he shall be master for life.

"But if the wife should drink of it first,
 Woe be to the husband then!"—
The stranger stooped to the Well of St Keyne,
 And drank of the water again.

"You drank of the Well, I warrant, betimes,"
 He to the Cornishman said;
But the Cornishman smiled as the stranger spake,
 And sheepishly shook his head.

"I hastened as soon as the wedding was done,
 And left my wife in the porch;
But in truth she had been wiser than I,
 For she took a bottle to church!"

—ROBERT SOUTHEY

Words

bachelor, *unmarried man.*
clearer, *draught.*
drinking, *gifted.*
potent, *hastened.*
hurried, *joyfully.*
gladly, *master.*
superior, *neighbouring.*
adjoining, *reply.*
sheepishly, *bashfully.*
summoned, *called.*
venture, *stake.*
warrant, *engage.*

在西方国家有一口井，
从没有人见过如此清澈的井水；
西方国家没有一个妻子，
没听说过圣凯恩井的。

井旁有一棵橡树还有一棵榆树，
井后则生长了一棵白蜡树；
井沿上生长了一棵柳树，
枝条一直垂落到井水水面。

有位旅行者来到圣凯恩井，
高兴地取水喝；
因为从鸡鸣开始，他就开始旅行，
天空中没有一片云朵。

他喝了一口又清凉又清澈的井水，
因为他又热又渴；
然后他坐在井沿上的柳树下。

从邻近的城镇里来了一个人，
他打了满满一桶井水；
然后在井旁歇息，
和这个陌生人打招呼。

“现在，陌生人，你是单身吗？”他问道，
“因为如果你有妻子的话，
你今天喝到的，
一定是你这辈子喝过的最好的水。”

“如果你有个好女人，你拥有了她的话，
会在科恩沃尔这儿出现吗？
因为一旦她来了，我会赌上自己的姓名，
让她喝一口圣凯恩的井水。”

“我曾经离开了一个好女人，她不生活在这儿，”
陌生人如此回答道，
“但我喝过的水比这还要甘甜，
我求你告诉我这是为什么。”

“圣凯恩，”科恩人回答道，“有很多次
从这口水晶一样的井里汲水喝；
在天使召唤她之前，
她给这口井下了一个咒语。”

“如果有一位丈夫，从这口有灵性的
井中汲水并在他妻子面前喝下的话，
那么他从此之后就会成为一个幸福的人，
因为他能够主宰自己的人生。”

“但如果他的妻子先喝到的话，
那么他就会成为不幸的丈夫！”
陌生人再一次弯下腰到圣凯恩井处，
喝下一口井水。

“我敢说，你经常喝圣凯恩井的井水。”
他对科恩人说道。
但科恩人在跟陌生人说话的时候只是笑笑，
然后不好意思地摇了摇头。

“我在婚礼结束之后就匆匆忙忙赶过来了，
把我的妻子留在了家里；
但事实上，她要比我聪明得多，
因为上教堂的时候，她就带上了一瓶井水！”

——罗比特·索契

Lesson 34 CAPTURING THE WILD HORSE

第三十四课 捕野马记

We left the buffalo camp about eight o'clock, and had a toilsome and harassing march of two hours, over ridges of hills covered with a ragged forest of scrub oaks and broken by deep gullies.

About ten o'clock in the morning we came to where this line of rugged hills swept down into a valley, through which flowed the north fork of Red River. A beautiful meadow, about half a mile wide, enamelled with yellow autumnal flowers, stretched for two or three miles along the foot of the hills.

The meadow was finely diversified by groves and clump of trees, so happily disposed that they seemed as if set out by the hand of Art. As we cast our eyes over this fresh and delightful valley, we beheld a troop of wild horses, quietly grazing on a green lawn about a mile distant, to our right; while to our left, at nearly the same distance, were several buffaloes, some feeding, others reposing and ruminating, among the high, rich herbage, under the shade of a clump of cotton-wood trees. The whole had the appearance of a broad beautiful tract of pasture-land on the highly ornamental estate of some gentleman farmer, with his cattle grazing about the lawns and meadows.

A council of war was now held, and it was determined to profit by the present favourable opportunity, and try our hand at the grand hunting manoeuvre, which is called "ringing the wild horse." This requires a large party of horsemen, well mounted. They extend themselves in every direction, at certain distances apart, and gradually form a ring of two or three miles in circumference, so as to surround the game. This must be done with extreme care, for the wild horse is the most readily alarmed inhabitant of the prairie, and can scent a hunter at a great distance, if to windward.

The ring being formed, two or three ride toward the horses, which start off in the opposite direction. Whenever they approach the bounds of the ring, however, a huntsman presents himself, and turns them from their course. In this way they are checked and driven back at every point, and kept galloping round and round this magic circle, until, being completely tired down, it is easy for hunters to ride up to them and throw the lariat over their heads. The prime horses, however, of the most speed, courage, and strength, are apt to break through and escape; so that, in general, it is the second-rate horses that are taken.

Preparations were now made for a hunt of this kind. The pack horses were taken into the woods, and firmly tied to trees, lest, in a rush of wild horses, they should break away. Twenty-five men were then sent, under the command of a lieutenant, to steal along the edge of the valley, within the strip of wood that skirted the hills. They were to station themselves about fifty yards apart, within the edge of the woods, and not to advance or show themselves until the horses dashed in that direction. Twenty-five men were also sent across the valley, to steal in like manner along the river bank that bordered the opposite side, and to station themselves among the trees.

A third party, of about the same number, was to form a line stretching across the lower part of the valley, so as to connect the two wings. Beatte and our other half-breed, Antoine, together with the ever-officious Tonish, were to make a circuit through the woods, so as to get to the upper part of the valley, in the rear of the horses, and drive them forward into the kind of sack that we had formed, while the two wings should join behind them, and make a complete circle.

The flanking parties were quietly extending themselves out of sight on each side of the valley, and the residue were stretching themselves like the links of a chain across it, when the wild horses gave signs that they scented an enemy,—snuffing the air, snorting, and looking about. At length they pranced off slowly toward the river, and disappeared behind a green bank.

Here, had the regulations of the chase been observed, they would have been quietly checked and turned back by the advance of a hunter from among the trees; unluckily, however, we had our wild-fire, Jack-o'-lantern, little Frenchman to deal with. Instead of keeping quietly up the right side of the valley, to get above the horses, the moment he saw them move toward the river he broke out of the covert of woods, and dashed furiously across the plain in pursuit of them. This put an end to all system. The half-breeds and half a score of rangers joined in the chase.

Away they all went over the green bank. In a moment or two the wild horses reappeared, and came thundering down the valley, with Frenchman, half-breeds, and rangers galloping and bellowing behind them. It was in vain that the line drawn across the valley attempted to check and turn back the fugitives—they were too hotly pressed by their pursuers; in their panic they dashed through the line, and clattered down the plain.

The whole troop joined in the headlong chase; some of the rangers without hats or caps, their hair flying about their ears; and others with handkerchiefs tied round their heads. The buffaloes, which had been calmly ruminating among the herbage, heaved up their huge forms, gazed for a moment at the tempest that came scouring down the meadow, then turned and took to heavy rolling flight. They were soon overtaken. The promiscuous masses were pressed together by the contracting sides of the valley, and away they went, pell-mell, hurry skurry, wild buffalo, wild horse, wild huntsman, with clang and clatter, and whoop and halloo, that made the forests ring.

At length the buffaloes turned into a green brake on the river bank, while the horses dashed up a narrow defile of the hills, with their pursuers close at their heels. Beatte passed several of them, having fixed his eye upon a fine Pawnee horse, that had his ears slit and saddle-marks upon his hack. He pressed him gallantly, but lost him in the woods.

Among the wild horses was a fine black mare, which, in scrambling up the defile, tripped and fell. A young ranger sprang from his horse and seized her by the mane and muzzle. Another ranger dismounted, and came to his assistance. The mare struggled fiercely, kicking and biting, and striking with her fore feet; but a noose was slipped over her head, and her struggles were in vain.

It was some time, however, before she gave over rearing and plunging and lashing out with her feet on every side. The two rangers then led her along the valley by two strong lariats, which enabled them to keep at a sufficient distance on each side to be out of the reach of her hoofs; and whenever she struck out in one direction, she was jerked in the other. In this way her spirit was gradually subdued.

As to Tonish, who had marred the whole scheme by his precipitancy, he had been more successful than he deserved, having managed to catch a beautiful cream-coloured colt, about seven months old, that had not had strength to keep up with its companions. The mercurial little Frenchman was beside himself with exultation. It was amusing to see him with his prize. The colt would rear and kick, and struggle to get free, when Tonish would take it round the neck, wrestle with it, jump on its back, and cut as many antics as a monkey with a kitten.

Nothing surprised me more, however, than to witness how soon these poor animals, thus taken from the unbounded freedom of the prairie, yielded to the dominion of man. In the course of two or three days the mare and colt went with the lead horses, and became quite docile.

—WASHINGTON IRVING

Words

antics, *capers.*
assistance, *help.*
bellowing, *roaring.*
buffaloes, *wild oxen.*
circuit, *round-about route.*
circumference, *measurement around.*
clattered, *rattled.*
companions, *fellows.*
completely, *utterly.*
defile, *ravine.*
direction, *way; line.*
disposed, *arranged.*

diversified, *varied.*
docile, *tractable.*
dominion, *rule.*
enamelled, *inlaid.*
exultation, *delight.*
flanking, *tide.*
furiously, *violently.*
gallantly, *bravely.*
gradually, *by degrees.*
inhabitant, *denizen.*
lieutenant, *officer below captain.*
managed, *contrived.*
manoeuvre, *tactics.*
opportunity, *occasion.*
ornamental, *embellished.*
precipitancy, *rashness.*
preparations, *arrangement.*
prime, *first rate.*
promiscuous, *mixed.*
pursuit, *chase.*
reposing, *resting.*
residue, *remainder.*
scented, *smelled.*
scrambling, *strugglingly.*
toilsome, *laborious.*
unluckily, *unfortunate.*

Questions

How is the manoeuvre of "ringing the wild horse" performed? Why did the plan fail on this occasion? By what were the wild horses joined in their flight? Where did the buffaloes turn aside? Where did the horses go? How was the black mare captured? How was she led along the valley? What had the Frenchman captured? What was the most surprising thing in the ease of the captives?

☆ ☆

我们大约8点钟的时候离开了水牛营地，然后跌跌撞撞地行进了两个小时，穿过了深沟纵横和长满胭脂栎的高低不平的森林的山脊。

上午10点钟左右，我们就到达了崎岖的山脊，下面是一片山谷，山谷的那边是红河的北麓。有一片大约半英里宽的美丽草地，上面点缀着黄色的秋天的滑索，沿着山脚下绵延了两到三英里的长度。

草地上一丛丛一堆堆的树木起了很好的分隔作用，不会显得单调，它们的分布非常合理，就好像是艺术家的双手把他们布置成那样似的。我们极目远眺这片清新而宜人的山谷的时候，看见了一群野马，静静地在我们右面一英里开外的草坪上觅着食；而在我们左面也差不多一英里的位置上，则是数头水牛，有几头在那又高又茂密的草丛中进食，另有几头则在那木棉树的潮湿的树荫下歇息反刍。整片山谷看起来就像一个开阔而美丽的农场一样，大有在景色宜人的土地上，有绅士在摇着扇子，而他的牲畜在草坪和草地上吃着草的景象。

捕野马的会议召开了，会议决定要利用眼前的这个有利时机，通过我们安排的围捕行动，也就是叫作“围野马”的行动来进行。这个行动需要大量骑马的人身手敏捷。他们需要分散在各个方向，彼此之间保持一定距离，然后慢慢地形成一个方圆两三英里的圈子，这样就可以围捕野马了。而一切都必须进行的谨慎而小心，因为野马是大草原上警惕性较高的动物，如果它在下风向，它在很远的距离就能嗅到猎人的气味。

围捕的圈子形成了，有两三个人骑马靠近野马群，于是马群马上向着相反的方向跑去。只要它们快要跑出围捕的圈子，就会有一位骑马的人出来，打乱它们的逃跑路线。如此这般，它们就被控制住了，而且总是在被来回驱赶，来来回回地在这个神奇的圈子里蹿来蹿去。直到它们精疲力竭了，猎人们就很容易地追赶上它们，把套马的绳子抛出去绕在它们的脑袋上。最好的野马速度最快，最有胆识和魄力，因而它们很容易就挣脱掉逃跑了，因此，大体而言，能捕到的都是二等货色的野马。

要完成这样的围捕，需要做好准备。马群要带到森林里去，结实地拴在树上，以防止野马冲撞起来会挣脱掉。然后要派二十五个人在一位指挥官的带领下，沿着山谷的边沿行走在点缀山头的森林深处。他们彼此之间要相距五十码的距离，但不能出森林，也不能在野马向一个方向飞驰之前出现或现身。另外还要派二十五个人，横穿山谷，以同样的方式沿着河岸推进，也就是守在相反方向的边缘，在树丛中静候。

然后还有第三批人，大约也有二十五人，他们形成一道横亘于山谷地势较低部分的防线，这样就能和两翼的人相照应了。贝蒂和我们的另外一个混血儿安东尼，连同那总是颐指气使的托尼史，一起在森林里绕道而行，以这样的方式到达山谷较高地势的那一部分，也就是紧随马群其后，把它们向我们事先设好的圈套里驱赶，然后两翼的力量也向着它们而去，这样就形成了一个完整的围捕圈。

当野马发出嗅到敌人信号的时候，也就是嗅闻空气，吸鼻子，四处张望，两翼的力量静悄悄而不被察觉地散布在山谷的两边，剩下的则像一条锁链的链扣一样分布。最后，他们慢慢地靠近了河流，消失在翠绿的河岸之后了。

这时，如果说围捕当中有什么规矩可讲的话，那这些规则一定是在悄悄地践行着，不能因树丛中的狩猎者的一跃而起打破了；然而，不幸的是，我们当中有个脾气火爆的杰克·奥兰登，一个小个子法国人。他没有悄悄地从山谷的右翼跟上野马群的脚步，而是一看到它们向河边而去，就马上从掩护的树丛中跳出来，然后猛地在草原上追逐马群。这样我们整个围捕计划就都打乱了。那些混血儿和一半的突击队员都加入了追逐野马的行列。

然后他们都跑上了翠绿的河岸。有一两分钟的时间，野马群重新出现了，并以雷霆之势冲下山谷，然后是法国人，混血儿还有突击队员快马加鞭追随其后。在山谷中部形成的控制和让野马群掉头的防线一点儿也没有起到作用。它们后面的追捕者追捕得太过紧迫，于是它们在惊慌之下就冲过了防线，分散着跑到了草原上。

整个围捕队都加入了猛烈的追击之中；有些突击队员头上的帽子都不见了，头发在耳边飞扬着，其他的人则用手帕系在头上。在草丛中本来安心反刍着的水牛，巨大的身体突然站立起来，盯着这暴风雨一样倾泻到草地上的马群看了一会儿，然后就调转身子，沉重地飞奔开来。不久它们就被超越了。这混乱的一大群被越来越收紧的山谷给挤压得越来越紧凑，野水牛、野马、野马围捕者，它们夸张而手忙脚乱地一边跑着，一边发出叮叮当当的喧嚣的声音，还有那奔跑声和喘息声混杂其间，整个森林都轰鸣了。

最后，水牛群冲进了位于河岸边的一片绿林中，而野马群则冲进了一个山中的狭窄的峡谷里，而它们的追逐者则紧随其后穷追不舍。贝蒂超过了几头野马之后，把目光锁定在一匹俊美的伯尼马身上，它的耳朵有撕裂，背上还有马鞍的印子。他勇敢地追逐它，但追到树林里的时候把它追丢了。

野马群中有一匹黑骏的母马，它在向着峡谷挺进的时候摔了一跤，倒在地上。一个年轻的突击队员从自己的马上一跃而起，紧紧抓住这母马的鬃毛和马嘴。另外一个突击队员则翻身下马，去帮他。母马猛烈地挣扎，又踢又咬，不断踢打着自己的前蹄，但有一个套索套住了它的脑袋，它的挣扎也就没用了。

然而，在它放弃用蹄子向各个方向又踢又打又冲之前，还是过了一段时间。两个突击队员就用两个很结实的套索，牵着它向前走，这样他们就和母马的蹄子之间保持了足够的距离；无论它向哪个方向踢打，它就会被向另外一个方向拽去。这样它的气势就渐渐消减了。

对托尼史来说，因为他的鲁莽而毁了整个计划，所以他最后的成功就比他实际应该得到的成功要多，他勉强捉到了一只漂亮的奶白色的小马，大约七个月大小，尚没有力量能赶得上它的同伴。那皮肤苍白的小个子法国人则兴冲冲地在他身边。看到他和自己的战利品，实在是一件有意思的事。小马又是暴跳又是踢腿，挣扎着要逃跑，而托尼史则捉住它的脖子，和它扭打，跳到它的背上，那滑稽的样子就好像一只猴子在和小猫扭打一样。

然而没有什么比看到这些可怜的动物那么快从在草原上无拘无束的自由状态变成被人驯服的牲畜，更让我惊讶的了。在接下来的两三天的时间里，那匹母马和小马和它们领头的马一起走着，变得非常温顺了。

——华盛顿·欧文

Lesson 35 THE SIEGE OF QUEBEC

第三十五课 围城魁北克

(A.D. 1759)

The closing scene of French dominion in Canada was marked by circumstances of deep and peculiar interest. The pages of romance can furnish no more striking episode than the Battle of Quebec. The skill and daring of the plan which brought on the combat, and the success and fortune of its execution, are unparalleled. A broad, open plain, offering no advantages to either party, was the field of fight. The contending armies were nearly equal in military strength, if not in numbers. The chiefs of both were men already of honourable fame. France trusted firmly in the wise and chivalrous Montcalm: England trusted hopefully in the young and heroic Wolfe. The magnificent stronghold which was staked upon the issue of the strife stood close at hand. For miles and miles around, the prospect extended over as fair a land as ever rejoiced the sight of man—mountain and valley, forest and waters, city and solitude, grouped together in forms of almost ideal beauty.

Quebec stands on the slope of a lofty eminence on the left bank of the St. Lawrence. A table-land extends westward from the citadel for about nine miles. The portion of the heights nearest the town on the west is called the Plains of Abraham. Wolfe had discovered a narrow path winding up the side of the steep precipice from the river. For miles on either side there was no other possible access to the heights. Up this narrow path Wolfe decided to lead secretly his whole army, and make the plains his battle-ground!

The extraordinary daring of the enterprise was its safety. The wise and cautious Montcalm had guarded against all the probable chances of war; but he was not prepared against an attempt for which the pages of romance can scarcely furnish a parallel.

Great preparations were made throughout the fleet and the army for the decisive

QUEBEC

movement; but the plans were still kept secret. A wise caution was observed in this respect; for the treachery of a single deserter might have imperilled the success of the expedition had its exact object been known. At nine o'clock at night, on the 13th of September, 1759, the first division of the army, 1600 strong, silently removed into flat-bottomed boats. The soldiers were in high spirits: Wolfe led in person. About an hour before day-light, the flotilla dropt down with the ebb-tide. "Weather favourable; a star light night."

Silently and swiftly, unchallenged by the French sentries, Wolfe's flotilla dropped down the stream in the shade of the overhanging cliffs. The rowers scarcely stirred the waters with their oars; the soldiers sat motionless. Not a word was spoken, save by the young general. He, as a midshipman on board of his boat afterwards related, repeated, in a low voice, to the officers by his side, Gray's "Elegy in a Country Churchyard;" and as he concluded the beautiful verses, he said, " Now, gentlemen, I would rather be the author of that poem than take Quebec!"

But while Wolfe thus in the poet's Words gave vent to the intensity of his feelings, his eye was constantly bent upon the dark outline of the heights under which he was hurrying. He recognised at length the appointed spot (now called Wolfe's Cove), and leaped ashore. Some of the leading boats, conveying the light company of the 78th Highlanders, had, in the meantime, been carried about two hundred yards lower down by the strength of the tide. These Highlanders, under Captain Donald MacDonald, were the first to land. Immediately over their heads hung a woody precipice, without path or track upon its rocky face. On the summit, a French sentinel marched to and fro, still unconscious of their presence.

Without a moment's hesitation, MacDonald and his men dashed at the height. They scrambled up, holding on by rocks and branches of trees, guided only by the stars that shone over the top of the cliff. Half the ascent was already won, when, for the first time, "*Qui vive*?" broke the silence of the night. "*La France*" answered the Highland captain, with ready self-possession, and the sentry shouldered his musket and pursued his round.

In a few minutes, however, the rustling of the trees close at hand alarmed the French guard. They hastily turned out, fired one irregular volley down the precipice, and fled in panic. The captain, M. de Vergor, alone, though wounded, stood his ground. When summoned to surrender, he fired at one of the leading assailant, but was instantly overpowered. In the meantime, nearly five hundred men landed and made their way up the height. Those who had first reached the summit then took possession of the intrenched post at the top of the path which Wolfe had selected for the ascent of his army.

Wolfe, Monckton, and Murray landed with the first division. As fast as each boat was cleared, it put back for reinforcements to the ships, which had now also floated down with the tide to a point nearly opposite that of disembarkation. The battalions formed on the narrow beach at the foot of the winding path; and as soon as completed, each ascended the cliff, when they again formed upon the plains above.

The boats plied busily; company after company was quickly landed; and as soon as the men touched the shore, they swarmed up the steep ascent with ready alacrity. When morning broke, the whole disposable force of Wolfe's army stood in firm array upon the table-land above the cove. Only one gun, however, could be carried up the hill; and even that was not got into position without incredible difficulty.

Montcalm was already worsted as a general: it was still, however, left him to fight as a soldier. His order of battle was steadily and promptly made. He commanded the centre column in person. His total force engaged was 7620, besides Indians. Wolfe showed only a force of 4828 of all ranks; but every man was a trained soldier.

The French attacked. After a spirited advance made by a swarm of skirmishers, their main body, in long unbroken lines, was seen approaching Wolfe's position. Soon a murderous and incessant fire began. The British troops fell fast. Wolfe, at the head of the 28th, was struck in the wrist, but was not disabled. Wrapping a handkerchief round the wound, he hastened from one rank to another, exhorting the men to be steady and to reserve their fire. No English soldier pulled a trigger: with matchless endurance they sustained the trial. Not a company wavered: their arms shouldered as if on parade, and motionless, save when they closed up the ghastly gaps, they waited the word of command.

When the head of the French attack had reached within forty yards, Wolfe gave the order to "fire." At once the long row of muskets was levelled, and a volley, distinct as a single shot, flashed from the British line. For a moment the advancing columns still pressed on, shivering like pennons in the fatal storm; but a few paces told how terrible had been the force of the long-suspended blow.

Montcalm commanded the attack in person. Not fifteen minutes had elapsed since he had first moved on his line of battle, and already all was lost! But the gallant Frenchman, though ruined, was not dismayed. He rode through the broken ranks, cheered them with his voice, encouraged them by his dauntless bearing, and, aided by a small redoubt, even succeeded in once again presenting a front to his enemy.

Meanwhile Wolfe's troops had reloaded. He seized the opportunity of the hesitation in the hostile ranks, and ordered the whole British line to advance. At first they moved forward with majestic regularity, receiving and paying back with deadly interest the volleys of the French; but soon the ardour of the soldiers broke through the restraints of discipline—they increased their pace to a run, rushing over the dying and the dead, and sweeping the living enemy off their path.

THE DEATH OF WOLFE

Wolfe was then wounded in the body; but he concealed his suffering, for his duty was not yet accomplished. Again a ball from the redoubt struck him on the breast. He reeled on one side; but at the moment that was not generally observed. "Support me," said he to a grenadier officer who was close at hand, "that my brave fellows may not see me fall." In a few seconds, however, he sank, and was borne a little to the rear.

The brief struggle fell heavily upon the British, but was ruinous to the French. They wavered under the carnage the columns which death had disordered were soon broken and scattered. Montcalm, with a courage that rose above the wreck of hope, galloped through the groups of his stubborn veterans, who still made head against the enemy, and strove to show a front of battle. His efforts were vain. The head of every formation was swept away before that terrible musketry. In a few minutes the French gave way in all directions. Just then their gallant general fell with a mortal wound: from that time all was utter rout.

While the British troops were carrying all before them, their young general's life was ebbing fast away. From time to time he tried, with his faint hand, to clear away the death-mist that gathered on his sight, but the efforts seemed vain, for presently he lay back, and gave no signs of life beyond a heavy breathing and an occasional groan.

Meantime the French had given way, and were flying in all directions. A grenadier officer seeing this, called out to those around him, "See! they run!" The Words caught the ear of the dying man. He raised himself, like one aroused from sleep, and asked eagerly, "Who run?" "The enemy, sir," answered the officer; "they give way everywhere." "Go, one of you, to Colonel Burton," said Wolfe: "tell him to march Webbe's (the 48th) regiment with all speed down to the St. Charles river, to cut off the retreat." His voice grew faint as he spoke, and he turned on his side, as if seeking an easier position. When he had given this last order, his eyes closed in death.

When the news reached England, triumph and lamentation were strangely intermingled. Astonishment and admiration at the splendid victory, with sorrow for the loss of the gallant victor, filled every breast. Throughout all the land were illuminations and public rejoicings, except in the little Kentish village of Westerham, where Wolfe had been born, and where his widowed mother now mourned her only child.

Wolfe's body was embalmed, and borne to the river for conveyance to England. The army escorted it in solemn state to the beach. They mourned their young general's death as sincerely as they had followed him in battle bravely. His remains were landed at Plymouth with the highest honours: minute-guns were fired, flags were hoisted half-mast high, and an escort with arms reversed received the coffin on the shore. They were then conveyed to Greenwich, and buried beside those of his father, who had died hut a few months before.

After further successes of the British in other parts of Canada, under Generals Amherst, Haviland, and Sit William Johnson, the French cause became utterly hopeless. On the 8th of September, 1760, a British force of 16,000 men assembled before Montreal; and on the same day a capitulation was signed which severed Canada from France for ever.

One of the most momentous political questions that have ever moved the human race was decided in this struggle. When a few English and French emigrants first landed among the Virginian and Canadian forests it began: when the British flag was hoisted on the citadel of Quebec it was decided. From that day Providence pointed out to the Anglo-Saxon race that to them was henceforth intrusted the destiny of the New World.

—WARBURTON

Words

alacrity, *liveliness.*
ardour, *eagerness.*
aroused, *awakened.*
assailants, *enemies.*
capitulation, *surrender.*
chivalrous, *heroic.*
commanded, *headed.*
concealed, *hid.*
conveyance, *carriage.*
decisive, *final.*
disembarkation, *landing.*
dismayed, *disheartened.*
disposable, *available.*
dominion, *supremacy.*
eminence, *height.*
escorted, *accompanied.*
exhorting, *encouraging.*
extraordinary, *uncommon.*
hesitation, *delay.*
imperiled, *endangered.*
incessant, *ceaseless.*
incredible, *not to be believed.*
intensity, *high strain.*
intermingled, *mixed.*
intrenched, *fortified.*
intrusted, *committed.*
irregular, *indiscriminate.*
lamentation, *sorrow.*
momentous, *Important.*
musketry, *fire.*
peculiar, *strange.*
precipice, *cliff.*
regularity, *order.*
reinforcements, *fresh troops.*
repeated, *recited.*
romance, *fiction.*
ruinous, *destructive.*
surrender, *yield.*
sustained, *bore.*
unchallenged, *unquestioned.*
unconscious, *ignorant.*
unparalleled, *unequalled.*

Questions

Where does Quebec stand? When are the Plains of Abraham? What plan did Wolfe form for reaching them? How did the safety of the plan depend upon its daring? At what time did the expedition start? What poem did Wolfe repeat as they floated down? What is the place where he leaped ashore now called? Where were the 78th Highlanders carried? How did their captain deceive the sentry? What did the soldiers who first reached the summit do? By what time had Wolfe his army marshalled on the table-land? How strong was it? How many were in the French army? Who commanded the latter? Which began the attack? What order did Wolfe give which tried the endurance of his men? What was the result of this plan? What order did Wolfe give when the French wavered? What happened to him soon after? What did Montcalm do when the French ranks were broken? What happened to Montcalm? What was Wolfe's last order? How was the news received in England? Where was Wolfe buried?

☆ ☆

（公元 1759年）

法国在加拿大的领地边境标志非常深刻显眼，也特别有趣。所有的征战中，没有比魁北克之战更激动人心的了。该战争中所体现出来计划的技巧和胆识，实施的成功和幸运，都是无与伦比的。一片广袤而宽阔的草原，对于交战双方而言都没有什么优势，魁北克之战就在草原上打响了。交战的双方虽然在士兵数量上有所出入，但整个作战实力基本相当。双方的统领都已经是享誉盛名。法国人对他们睿智而勇敢的蒙塔卡姆笃信不移，而英格兰人则把希望都寄托在了年轻而有英雄气概的沃尔夫身上。那处在本次争端风口浪尖的伟大要塞近在眼前，周围数英里之内，景色宜人，映入眼帘的景象让人目不暇接、心旷神怡——山峦和山谷，森林和湖泊，城市和乡村，都以一种几乎完美的状态共同呈现。

魁北克位于圣劳伦斯河左岸一个非常有名的高坡上。如同一张长桌一样的土地，从大本营向西伸展了大约九英里。其中有一处高地，离着魁北克城的西翼最近，被称作亚布拉罕高原。沃尔夫发现了一条蜿蜒而狭仄的小路，从河边一直延伸到陡峭的悬崖。河两岸数英里的距离之内，没有其他可能的通道能登上高地。沃尔夫决定秘密带领他的整支部队顺着这条小路向上走，在高原上进行战斗！

这是非同寻常的险招，但这么做很安全。蒙特卡姆本人睿智而谨慎，他已经把可能开战的可能性降到最低；但他并没有做好准备，抵御一次征战史上鲜有比拟的奇兵险招了。

整个舰队和军队都做好了万全准备，进行着决定意义的行动；但鉴于行动计划还是秘密，于是部队做了明智的预防措施。因为只要有一个人出卖了计划，整个计划内容就曝光了，而整个行动的成功就会受到威胁。1759年9月13日夜里9点钟的时候，第一批由一千六百名精兵猛将组成的先行部队悄悄乘坐上平底船。这些士兵全都士气高涨，他们由沃尔夫亲自率领。黎明前一个钟头的时候，这支分队就随着退潮上岸了，“我们有天时地利，夜空中群星闪耀。”

他们悄悄行动，迅速麻利，不惊动法国哨兵。沃尔夫的小舰队在悬崖的荫庇阴影交错的溪流中停泊。划船的人几乎没有用船桨惊动到水面，士兵静静坐着。没有人说话，除了年轻的将军给出指令。他在甲板中部给身边的军官低声讲述着，重复着格雷的那首《乡村目的挽歌》；在他诵完这优美诗歌的最后一句诗行的时候，他总结道，“现在，先生们，我宁愿成为这首诗的作者也不愿意夺取魁北克！”

当沃尔夫通过朗诵诗歌宣泄自己内心强烈感受的时候，他目不转睛地盯着他前进的高地在黑暗中的轮廓。他终于认出了锁定的地点（也就是现在被称作“沃尔夫角”的地方），然后纵身跳上了岸。一些先行的船只同时输送来了第七十八高地战队，他们因为浪太大，被冲在较低的二百码开外的地方。这些高地战队队员在多纳德·麦克多纳德上校的带领下，最先登陆。他们的头顶就是林木悬生的山崖，石质的外表上没有路径或者通道。悬崖顶部，有法国哨兵在走来走去放哨，完全不知道底下有人。

麦克多纳德和他的手下，没有丝毫犹豫就冲向高地。他们向上攀爬，抓住石头和树枝，紧紧靠着悬崖顶闪烁的星星的光芒来引路。已经有一半的士兵攀爬成功，这时，一句“是谁？”，打破了夜的宁静。“自己人”，高地战队的上校回答道，他气定神闲，而哨兵则扛着火枪到别处巡逻了。

然而，几分钟过后，近处的树中间传出窸窸窣窣的声影，惊动了法国守卫。他们马上行动，冲着悬崖下一通乱射，然后就惊慌而逃了。麦·德威格尔上校虽然负伤，但还是一个人坚守阵地。有人招降他的时候，他冲着领头的敌人射了一枪，但很快被敌人强大的火力盖过了。同时，大约有五百人登陆，并向高地攀爬。那些已经登顶的人，占领了位于沃尔夫选定作为军队制高点的小路顶端的战壕。

沃尔夫、蒙克顿和穆雷以及第一分队登陆。船上的人都登陆之后，船就驶回舰队，以求增援。那会儿，舰队也已经跟着大潮漂流到一个几乎和此次登陆相反方向的一个地方。整个营队汇合在狭窄的沙滩上，在蜿蜒的山路脚下，一切准备就绪之后，每个人都开始攀爬悬崖，之后再次在上面的高地上汇合。

船只快速行进，一拨又一拨的士兵很快登陆了。士兵一登陆，他们就动作敏捷地涌向陡峭的悬崖。破晓的时候，沃尔夫部队中的敢死队员们队形整齐地站在海湾之上的高地上。然而，只有一支枪能带到山上，但即使是这样，要带上去也不是容易的事。

蒙特卡姆作为指挥将领已经是心力交瘁了，然而，他还需要像个士兵一样战斗。他沉稳而迅捷地下达战斗命令。他亲自指挥中间部队。他的整个总站部队有7 620个人，包括印第安人。沃尔夫带领的所有的士兵只有4 828人，但每个人都训练有素。

法国人发动进攻。冲锋的战士们士气高昂地向前挺进了一段距离之后，主力部队排着长而坚不可摧的队形，向着沃尔夫的位置挺进。不久之后杀戮和不间断的火力开始了，英国军队很快落了下风。沃尔夫在带领第二十八小队的时候，手腕受了伤，但并没有致残。他用手帕包住伤口，就匆忙地从一支部队赶往另一支，劝告士兵要沉稳，保持火力。没有一个英国士兵开枪，他们用无与伦比的忍耐力，经受这次考验。每个人都意志坚定。他们把武器扛在肩头，就好像是在参加游行一样，除了要靠近那可怕的战地，他们一动不动，等待着指挥官的命令。

当法国人的首轮攻击达到四十码的覆盖范围的时候，沃尔夫下命“开火”。马上一长排火枪火力齐发，火炮鹤立鸡群一般从英国人的阵地发射。有一段时间，前进的纵队依然向前挺进，就如同在猛烈的暴风雨中的鸟翼一样战栗；走了几步之后，他们知道长久等待的攻击的力量是多么可怕。

蒙特卡姆亲自指挥进攻。仅仅过了十五分钟，他就首先冲进战队中，但一切都失去了！但这位英勇的法国人，虽然身心俱疲，但并没有沮丧。他从受创的军队中穿过，和他们说话打气，用自己无畏的品质鼓励他们，在防御障碍物的掩护下，他再一次成功地在敌人面前筑起了防线。

沃尔夫当时身体负伤了，但他隐藏了自己受伤的事实，因为他还没有完成自己的职责。防御碉堡中的火力再次击中他的胸口，他向一边翻滚，但并没有什么人发现。“扶住我，”他对一个靠近自己的掷弹兵喊道，“不能让我勇敢的士兵看到我倒下了。”但过了几秒钟之后，他就倒下了，然后被运到了部队的后面。

整个战斗的压力都落在了英国人身上，但他们对法国人还是造成了毁灭性的打击。在大屠杀的威胁下，他们放弃了充满死亡气息的纵队，不久之后就被击溃而四处逃散了。蒙特卡姆从溃败中燃起了希望，鼓足勇气，快马加鞭穿越过他坚定的士兵，也就是那些依然向着敌军挺进的士兵。但他的努力是徒劳的。每支小队的统领都倒在可怕的火力下。过了几分钟之后，法国人在各个方向上撤退。就在那时，他们勇敢的将军负了致命伤：从那一刻起，一切尘埃落定。

而英国军队则背着所有倒下去的同胞，他们年轻的将军的生命则在快速流逝。他时不时地努力支撑起羸弱的手臂，想要把眼前遮盖视线的灰尘给抹去，但这些努力都是徒劳的，因为他马上就躺回去了，除了沉重的喘息声和偶尔发出的呻吟声外，看不出生命的迹象。

同时法国人已经撤退了，他们向四处逃散。一名掷弹兵看到这种情况，就把周围的人召集来，“快看！他们逃了！”这句话传到了快要死的将军耳中。他支撑起来，就像从睡梦中醒来一样，急切地问道，“谁逃了？”“敌人，先生，”掷弹兵回答说，“他们从各个方向都撤退了。”“你们中一个人到波顿上校那儿去，”沃尔夫说，“告诉他向着韦伯（第48小队）打，要他全速下山开拔到圣查尔斯河，截断敌人的退路。”他说话的时候，声音越来越弱，他侧过身子，好像在找个更舒服的睡姿。当最后一个命令下达完之后，他双目紧闭，死去了。

当消息传到英格兰的时候，胜利和悼念奇怪地交织在一起。每一个人都对这起了不起的胜利惊奇而钦佩，但他们很难过失去勇敢的将军。整个国家都在庆祝，除了位于韦斯特海姆的小肯迪斯村，那是沃尔夫出生的地方，在那里他寡居的母亲在悼念着自己唯一的孩子。

沃尔夫的遗体经过防腐处理后，运到了河上以运回英格兰。军队转眼把他护送到了河滩。他们真心为年轻将军的死而难过，因为他们都曾经追随将军英勇地战斗过。他的遗体在朴茨茅斯登陆，并受到最高的礼遇：发射礼炮，降半旗，还有将棺材抬上岸的护送队。之后他被运往了格林尼治，并埋葬在他父亲的墓旁，他父亲刚刚在数月前去世。

在阿穆赫尔斯特将军、哈维兰德以及威廉·约翰逊爵士的带领下，英国在加拿大取得另外的几次胜利后，法国人的殖民事业彻底泡汤了。1760年9月8日这一天，一支由1.6万人组成的英国军队在蒙特利尔集合；同一天，加拿大永久脱离法国统治的条约签订了。

曾经改变了整个人类进程的一个具有重大政治意义的问题，在这次战斗中决定了。当一些英国和法国移民首次在弗吉尼亚和加拿大的森林登陆的时候，这个问题就开始了：当英国的旗帜飘扬在魁北克碉堡的城墙上空的时候，这个问题就决定了。从那天开始，上帝就像安格鲁·萨克逊民族指出，自此之后新世界的命运就交托在他们手上了。

——沃尔波恩顿

Lesson 36 THE DESERTED VILLAGE

第三十六课 废弃的村庄

Sweet Auburn! loveliest village of the plain,
Where health and plenty cheered the labouring swain;
Where smiling Spring in earliest visit paid,
And parting Summer' lingering blooms delayed;
Dear lovely bowers of innocence and ease,
Seats of ray youth, when every sport could please;
How often have I loitered o'er thy green,
Where humble happiness endeared each scene!
How often have I paused on every charm;—
The sheltered cot, the cultivated farm,
The never-failing brook, the busy mill,
The decent church that topped the neighbouring hill;
The hawthorn bush, with seats beneath the shade.
For talking age and whispering lovers made!
How often have I blessed the coming day,
When toil, remitting, lent its turn to play;
And all the village train, from labour free,
Led up their sports beneath the spreading tree;
While many a pastime circled in the shade,
The young contending, as the old surveyed;
And many a gambol frolicked o'er the ground,
And sleigh to of art and feats of strength went round,
And still, as each repeated pleasure tired,
Succeeding sports the mirthful band inspired:—
The dancing pair, that simply sought renown
By holding out to tire each other down;
The swain, mistrustless of his smutted face,
While secret laughter tittered round the place;
The bashful virgin's sidelong looks of love;
The matron's glance that would those looks reprove
These were thy charms, sweet village! sports like these
With sweet succession, taught e'en toil to please.

Sweet was the sound, when oft, at evening's close,
Up yonder hill the village murmur rose;

There as I passed, with careless steps and slow,
The mingling notes came softened from below:—
The swain, responsive as the milk-maid sung;
The sober herd, that lowed to meet their young;
The noisy geese, that gabbled o'er the pool;
The playful children, just let loose from school;
The watch-dog's voice, that bayed the whispering wind;
And the loud laugh, that spoke the vacant mind;—
These all, in sweet confusion, sought the shade,
And filled each pause the nightingale had made.

—OLIVER GOLDSMITH

Words

bashful, *retiring*.
contending, *striving*.
endeared, *made dear*.
gambol, *frolic*.
inspired, *excited*.
labouring, *hard-working*.
lingering, *loitering*.
remitting, *ceasing*.
reprove, *rebuke*.
responsive, *answering*.
surveyed, *looked on*.
vacant, *empty*.

☆ ☆

亲爱的奥伯恩！这片平原上最可爱的村庄，
那里有幸福安康和许多劳作的乡村小伙；
那里微笑的春天早早来到，
而邻近的夏日的绽放则姗姗来迟；
亲爱的凉亭啊，你是那么纯真闲暇，
坐满了年轻的人儿，什么游戏都能让他们心满意足；
我曾有多少次在你的葱绿中徜徉，
那里谦逊的幸福恩泽到每一个角落；
我曾经有多少次停留在每一方美景中；
那庇护的小屋，精心耕耘的农场，
奔流不息的小河，还有忙忙碌碌的磨坊
以及矗立在附近山上庄重的教堂；
大家端坐在山楂树的树荫下
都是一群爱闲聊的年轻人和窃窃私语的恋人！

我曾有多少次祝福第二天的来临，
届时劳作和辛苦就要让位于嬉戏玩耍；
所有村里的人，都不用再劳动了，
而是在枝繁叶茂的树荫下玩着游戏；
在这树荫下有许多的闲暇时光这样度过，
年轻人在争辩，年老的人则当调停人；
在这片土地上有许多的游戏如此玩耍，
有艺术的高下和力量的角逐
以及当每一项重复的兴致变得厌烦，
就会产生新的趣味横生的游戏：
双人舞，也就是大家知道的简单地
抱住彼此跳到大家筋疲力尽的舞蹈；
小伙子们，觉察不到自己的脸脏了，
而周围人却偷偷地讥笑他；
还有腼腆少女的侧脸流露出的爱意；
主妇的一瞥，证实了少女的爱意流露；
这些都是你的魅力所在啊，亲爱的村落！像你这样的
有趣而连续的游戏，让劳顿的人们有机会放松一番。
经常在夜晚来临的时候，会有甜美的声响
在那边的山头响起，就是村庄的呢喃声；
我从那里经过的时候，踏着不经意的脚步，缓慢前行，
从脚下，交织的音符开始变得温柔，
小伙子们，和着挤奶女工的歌谣；
清醒的牛群，低头摩挲着自己的小牛；
叫个不停的家鹅，在水塘边七嘴八舌；
嬉戏玩耍的孩童，刚刚放学；
看门狗的吠声，随着微风吹拂到了整个村落；
还有爽朗的笑声，把它简单的思想显露无余；
所有的一切，甜蜜地交织在一起，寻找着阴凉处，
把夜莺停顿的留白填充完整。

——奥利弗·戈尔德史密斯

Lesson 37 HUDSON BAY TERRITORY

第三十七课 哈德逊海湾的领地

One of the boldest and most successful of early navigators was the celebrated Henry Hudson, discoverer of that vast inland sea now known by the name of Hudson Bay.

He first distinguished himself by making three attempts to reach China by the Arctic seas to the north of Europe; but on each occasion the solid ice arrested his progress, and at last he was convinced that a north-eastern passage did not exist. The correctness of this judgment has been established by the more accurate knowledge of these dreary regions which we now possess. Baffled in that direction, Hudson resolved to pursue his explorations in another quarter, and crossed the Atlantic to America, where, with most insignificant means, his skill and daring were destined to achieve the greatest results.

He sailed along the coast of North America, and at length was rewarded for his toils by the discovery of the bay on which New York stands, and of the magnificent river which, as he was the first to explore it, has since borne his name—the Hudson.

Soon afterwards he returned to England, and obtained the command of a vessel of fifty-five tons burden, manned by twenty-three men, and victualled for six months. In this humble craft he set sail in 1610 on what proved to be his last voyage. After touching at the Orkney Islands, and at Iceland,—where he saw Mount Hecla in violent eruption in the midst of perpetual snows,—Hudson passed the south of Greenland and reached the strait which now bears his name. Here, in addition to the ordinary difficulties and dangers of navigation among the ice, he had to struggle against a mutiny among his crew; but, in spite of all, this intrepid explorer boldly pushed on till his vessel ploughed the waters of that great inland sea now known as Hudson Bay.

He did not know for a long time that it was a bay, but indulged the hope that he had discovered what he had so long sought—a passage by the north-west to China. Indeed the extent of its surface amply justified this expectation, since, with the exception of the Mediterranean, it is the largest inland sea in the world.

Here he was obliged to pass the winter. It is impossible to describe the hardships which the men endured. Notwithstanding all the birds, fishes, and animals serviceable for food which they could succeed in catching, they were always in dread of starvation.

When the ice broke up, Hudson prepared for the homeward voyage. The last ration of bread was dealt out to the crew on the day of their setting sail. A report that their commander had concealed a quantity of bread for his own use was readily believed by his famishing men, and a mutiny broke out.

Having put their captain, together with the sick and the frost-maimed, into the shallop, the crew cast the boat adrift with its hapless freight, and stood out to sea. Doubtless, Hudson and his miserable companions found a grave in the great inland sea which he had discovered; for the boat was never seen or heard of more.

Two days after the mutineers had sailed, they encountered a violent storm, and for fourteen days were in the greatest danger from the ice. That storm was probably fatal to their intrepid commander and his forlorn party, who may thus have escaped a still more terrible death from want and exposure. Just retribution overtook the guilty mutineers. Not one of the ringleaders lived to reach the land; and the rest gained the shore only after suffering the most awful extremities of famine. None of them were ever brought to trial for their misdeeds;—probably because those who were deepest in guilt had already paid the penalty of their crime.

Sixty years after the death of Hudson, a Company wag formed in London, under the direction of Prince Rupert, for the purpose of prosecuting the fur trade in the region surrounding Hudson Bay.

The first fort established by the Company was near the head of James Bay. Soon afterwards several others were built, in different parts of the country; and before long the Company spread and grew wealthy, and eventually extended their trade far beyond the chartered limits.

Imagine an immense extent of country, many hundred miles broad and many hundred miles long, covered with dense forests, expanded lakes, broad rivers, wide prairies, dreary swamps, and mighty mountains; and all in a stats of primeval simplicity—undefaced by the axe of civilized man, and untenanted by aught save a few roving hordes of Red Indians and myriads of wild animals. Imagine amid this wilderness a number of small squares, each enclosing half-a-dozen wooden houses and about a dozen men, and between each of these establishments a space of forest varying from fifty to three hundred miles in length; and you will have a pretty correct idea of the Hudson Bay Territory, and of the number of its forts, and the distance between them. If Great Britain were converted into a wilderness and placed in the middle of Rupert's Land, three forts would be built in it—one at the Land's End, one in Wales, and one in the Highlands; so that in Britain there would be but three hamlets, with a population of some thirty men, half-a-dozen women, and a few children! The Company's posts extended, with these intervals between them, from the Atlantic to the Pacific Ocean, and from within the Arctic Circle to the northern boundaries of the United States.

The country was divided into four large departments; again divided into districts, each under the direction of an influential officer; and these were subdivided into numerous establishments, forts, posts, and outposts.

The name of *fort* was given to all the posts in the country, but the only two that are real, *bond fide* forts, are Fort Garry and the Stone Fort, in the colony of Red River, which are surrounded by stone walls with bastions at the comers. The others are

A FORT IN HUDSON BAY TERRITOEY

merely defended by wooden pickets or stockades; and a few, where the Indians are quiet and harmless, are entirely destitute of defence of any kind. Some of the chief posts have a complement of about thirty or forty men; but most of them have only ten, five, four, or even *two*, besides the gentleman in charge.

The trade carried on in this desolate region is in peltries of all sorts: oil, dried and salted fish, feathers, quills, and ivory.

The most valuable of the furs which it produces is that of the *black fox*. This beautiful animal resembles in shape the common fox of England, but it is much larger, and jet black, with the exception of one or two white hairs along the back bone and a pure white tuft on the end of the tail.A single skin sometimes brings from twenty-five to thirty pounds in the British market! but—they are very scarce.

Beaver, in days of yore, was the staple fur of the Territory; but, alas! the silk hat has given it its death-blow. The most profitable fur in the country is that of the marten. It somewhat resembles the Russian sable, and generally maintains a steady price. These animals, moreover, are very numerous, particularly in the region of Mackenzie River, whence great numbers of skins are annually sent to England.

Trade is carried on with the natives by means of a standard valuation, called in some parts of the country a *castor*. This is to obviate the necessity of circulating money, of which there is little or none, excepting in the colony of Red River. Probably a trader tells an Indian, after looking over his furs, that he has got fifty or sixty castors; at the same time he hands to him fifty or sixty little bits of wood in lieu of cash, so that the latter may know, by returning these in payment of the goods for which he really exchanges his skins, how fast his funds decrease. Having selected the blankets, knives, and other articles which he wishes to purchase, to the extent that his wooden money will admit of, he packs up his goods, and departs to show his treasures to his wife. The value of a castor is from one to two shillings. The natives generally visit the trading establishments twice a year;—once in October, when they bring in the produce of their autumn hunts; and again in March, when they come in with that of the great winter hunt.

The number of castors that an Indian makes in a winter hunt varies from fifty to two hundred, according to his perseverance and activity, and the part of the country in which he hunts. The largest amount I ever heard of made by one man, was two hundred and sixty castors. The poor fellow was soon afterwards poisoned by his relatives, who were jealous of his superior abilities as a hunter, and envious of the favour shown him by the white men.

After the furs are collected in spring at all the different out-posts, they are packed in conveniently-sized bales, and forwarded, by means of boats and canoes, to the depots on the sea-coast, whence they are transported to England. The whole country in summer is, consequently, in commotion with the passing and repassing of brigades of boats laden with bales of merchandise and furs; the still waters of the lakes and rivers are rippled by the paddle and the oar; and the long silent echoes, which have slumbered in the icy embrace of a dreary winter, are now once more awakened by the merry voice and tuneful song of the hardy *voyageur*.

—R. M. BALLANTINE

Words

abilities, *skill.*
arrested, *checked.*
baffled, *frustrated.*
bastions, *fortifications.*
brigades, *squadrons.*
commotion, *stir.*
converted, *transformed.*
departments, *divisions.*
destitute, *devoid.*
embrace, *clasp.*
encountered, *met with.*
establishments, *settlements.*
eventually, *ultimately.*
famishing, *starving.*
indulged, *cherished.*
influential, *important.*
insignificant, *inconsiderable.*
intervals, *spaces.*
intrepid, *fearless.*
jealous, *envious.*
justified, *warranted.*
lieu, *place.*
magnificent, *splendid.*
miserable, *wretched.*
mutiny, *insurrection.*
myriads, *immense numbers.*
navigators, *explorers by sea.*
numerous, *plentiful.*
Obviate, *prevent.*
peltries, *furry skins.*
perseverance, *application.*
prairies, *meadows.*
primeval, *pristine.*
prosecuting, *carrying on.*
purchase, *buy.*
retribution, *punishment.*
selected, *chosen.*
serviceable, *available.*

staple, *standard.*
transported, *conveyed.*
victualled, *provisioned.*

Questions

From whom is Hudson Bay named? How did Hudson first distinguish himself? In what year did he set out on his last voyage? What places did he touch at on his way to America? What did he suppose Hudson Bay to be? From what did his crew suffer during the winter? What did they do on the homeward voyage? Why were not the survivors brought to trial? When was the Hudson's Bay Company established? Where was their first fort built? How many stations would be built in an area equal to Great Britain? In what articles did the Company trade? Which is the most valuable fur? Which used to be the staple? Why has it gone down? Which is the most profitable fur? What is a castor? How many castors does an Indian usually make in a winter hunt?

☆ ☆

最具有胆识也最成功的一位早期航行家，是负有盛名的亨利·哈德逊，也就是发现了现在我们称作哈德逊湾大内陆海的人。

哈德逊以自己做的从北极海域到达欧洲北部从而最终到达中国的三次尝试而闻名；但每一次尝试都因为遇到坚固的冰层而无法继续，最终他确信从北然后再向东行进的航线其实并不存在。对于这个判断的纠正是由后来我们掌握的关于这些最荒凉地区更精确的知识而来的。在此航线上做了无谓的挣扎之后，哈德逊下定决心从另外一条路继续自己的探险，横渡过大西洋到达美洲。在那里，由于装备设施极其简陋，哈德逊要想达成他了不起的目标，就得靠自己的技艺和胆识了。

他沿着北美洲的海岸线航行，最终他的劳苦得到回报，发现了纽约所在的一片海湾以及一条河流，鉴于他是第一个发现这里的人，海湾就以他的名字命名为——哈德逊湾。

不久之后他就返回英格兰，并获得了一艘载重55吨的船只的指挥权。船上有23名船员，上头的食物可以消耗6个月。1610年他驾这艘不起眼的船起航了，事后这成了他最后一次的航行经历。在遇到奥克内群岛和冰岛之后，在那里他看到赫克拉火山猛烈爆发，岩浆流向永久积雪之中，哈德逊绕过格陵兰岛的南部，到达了如今以他的名字命名的海峡。在这里，除了遇到平时在结冰海域的艰难险阻和航行危险之外，哈德逊还要应付船员的暴乱，但尽管有这么多的困难，这位勇敢的探险家还是无畏地向前行进，乘风破浪，直到船到达了伟大的内海，也就是现在所知的哈德逊海湾。

有很长时间，他都不知道这是个海湾，而是还沉浸在发现了长久以来一直找寻的通往中国的西北航线的希望中。的确，从海湾的表面来说，看起来很像海洋，鉴于它是除了地中海之外世界上最大的内海。

他不得不在这里过冬。他们遇到了难以描述的艰难情形。尽管他们捉到鸟类、鱼类还有动物可以做食物，但依然处于可怕的饥饿的边缘。

冰破开的时候，哈德逊准备向家乡驶去。最后配给船员的定额面包在起锚那天就分完了。有人传言，说他们的长官私藏了大量的面包供自己享用，而饥肠辘辘的船员对此则深信不疑，暴动终于爆发了。

他们把船长、病人和由于霜冻而残疾的人弄上小船。船员把小船扔到水面上，让其自生自灭，小船只能孤零零在海上漂流。毫无疑问，这成为哈德逊和他可怜的同伴在他们自己发现的伟大的内海上的坟墓，因为人们再也没有看到或听说过这只小船。

暴动的船员行驶了两天之后，遇上了猛烈的冒风雨，他们都遭遇的冰冻致命危险则有十四天之久。那场暴风雨对于他们受伤的指挥官和被遗弃的同伴而言，很可能是致命的，但他们也可能因此而逃脱了因为食物短缺和烈日炎炎的更可怕的死亡煎熬。报应降临到罪孽的暴动者身上，暴动首领中没有一个人活着到达陆地，剩下的人则在经历了极端的饥饿煎熬之后才勉强到达海岸。没有一个人因他们的不耻行为接受审判，可能因为那些罪孽深重的人为自己的罪行付出过生命的代价了。

在哈德逊死去60年后，伦敦成立了一家公司，董事为罗伯特亲王，这家公司成立的目的是从事哈德逊湾周围地区的皮货生意。

该公司建立的第一座城堡位于詹姆斯海湾的北端。不久之后其他的城堡也建立起来，它们位于这个国家的各个地区，之后不久，该公司迅速扩张，变得非常富有，最终他们的生意扩展到地图上最北端的地方。

试想，一片广袤的国土，长度和宽度都各自绵延了数百英里，那里有茂密的森林覆盖，还有开阔的湖泊，宽广的河流，原生的大草原，潮湿的沼泽以及巍峨的群山；而一切都处在一种原始的简单状态——没有被文明人的斧子砍伐破坏过，除了红种印第安人的游牧部落和各种各样的野生动物外，也没有人居住过。可以想象，在这片荒野中，有许多片小广场，每一片都由六座木屋围成，这里一共生活了12个人，而两个小广场之间的间隔，则是长度从50到300英里不等的森林。这样，你就能对哈德逊湾的领地有相当正确的认识了，对于它据点的数量以及彼此之间的距离，可以打个比方：如果大不列颠王国是一片荒野，放置在罗伯特亲王的领地中间的话，那么这里只能建造三个村落——一座在这片土地的最末端，一座在威尔士，还有一座在苏格兰，这样英国就只能有三座村落了，每一个村里头住着差不多三十个男人，六个女人，还有一些孩子。村落的范围在扩展，这是依照村落之间的间距产生的，也就是从大西洋到太平洋，从北极圈内部一直到美国的北部边界。

这个地区被分成了四个大的单位，然后又进一步分成了地区，每一个地区都由一个有影响力的地方官领导，而这些地区再次被分成了许多的建筑群、据点和村落。

据点的名称可以用在这里所有的村落上，但只有两处可以称得上是真正的据点，或名副其实的据点，它们是盖里据点和斯通据点，均位于红河殖民地。他们被石墙包围，四角都是堡垒，其他的据点则仅仅是用木质的尖木桩或栅栏保护。在印第安人不侵犯的许多据点，完全没有任何的防卫措施。一些大的村落有大约四十到五十个成年人，但大部分的村落仅仅有十个人，五个人，四个人，甚至只有两个人，如果把指挥官算在内的话。

在这片荒凉的地区，生意的范围涵盖了动物的各种产品：有油脂、干鱼、咸鱼、羽毛、翎毛以及象牙。

所有皮毛中最珍贵的就是黑狐的皮毛。这种美丽的动物外形和英国普通的狐狸很相像，只不过个头更大，除了黑色的脊背上有一两撮白毛，或者尾端是纯白色的毛之外，皮毛乌黑油亮。有时候一张狐狸皮能在英国卖到二十五到三十英镑的价钱！但这样的皮毛非常罕见。

那个年代的海狸是领地主要的皮毛来源，但，唉！那里的海狸因为过度捕杀而灭绝了。领地里利润最高的皮毛是貂皮。貂长得有点像俄罗斯黑貂，通常价格非常稳定。而这些动物，数量非常多，特别是在麦肯锡河流域，那里大量的动物毛皮每年都运往英格兰。

生意是和土著人通过标准等价兑换的形式进行的。这种兑换形式在有的地区叫作卡斯托。这样就省去了钱币流通的麻烦，因为除了在红河流域之外，还没有钱币流通。在看了毛皮之后，贩卖毛皮的人会告诉印第安人，说他愿意出价五十或六十卡斯托，同时他就递给印第安人五十或六十片木块来代替钱币，这样印第安人就会知道这些木块是他的皮毛交换来的，知道他的财富贬值的快慢。在选定了毯子、刀具，还有其他要购买的东西之后，他就离开了，把自己的财物向妻子展示。一卡斯托的价值可以从一先令到两先令不等。土著人通常一年两次去这些交易地点，一次是在10月，他们带上秋季的猎物；还有一次是在三月，他们满载着冬天的猎物而来。

印第安人给冬天猎物定的卡斯托价格，从五十到两百不等，这要根据他保存的程度和获得猎物的难度以及他是在哪个地区获得的而定。我曾听说过的一个人定过的最高价格，是两百六十卡斯托。这个可怜人后来被他的亲戚毒死了，因为他们嫉妒他是个能力出众的狩猎者，同时还嫉妒他受到白人的青睐。

春天从各个边区村落收集完皮毛之后，它们就被打包成各种方便携带的包裹，通过船只或筏子运往海边口岸，在那里他们会被运往英格兰。整个领地在夏天的时候，会有很多满载着各种商品和皮毛包裹的船只络绎不绝；湖泊和河流的水面因为桨和橹的滑动而荡漾，那在枯燥而被寒冷拥抱的冬季中沉睡了的、长长而静谧的回声，再一次被欢声笑语和辛勤的旅客们唤醒了。

——R.M.·巴兰廷

Lesson 38 THE FOUR ERAS

第三十八课 四只耳朵

The lark has sung his carol in the sky;
The bees have hummed their noontide harmony;
Still in the vale the village bells ring round,
Still in Llewellyn Hall the jests resound:
For now the candle-cup is circling there;
Now, glad at heart, the gossips breathe their prayer,
And, crowding, stop the cradle to admire
The babe, the sleeping image of his sire.
　A few short years, and then these sounds shall had
The day again, and gladness fill the vale;
So soon the child a youth, the youth a man,
Eager to run the race his fathers ran.
Then the huge or shall yield the broad sirloin;
The ale, new-brewed, in floods of amber shine;
And, basking in the chimney's ample blaze,
'Mid many a tale told of his boyish days,
The nurse shall cry, of all her ills beguiled,
"'Twas on these knees he sate so oft, and smiled.
　And soon again shall music swell the breeze;
Soon, issuing forth, shall glitter through the trees
Vestures of nuptial white; and hymns be sung,
And violets scattered round; and old and young,
In every cottage porch, with garlands green,
Stand still to gaze, and, gazing, bless the scene;
While, her dark eyes declining, by his side
Moves in her virgin-veil the gentle bride.
　And once, alas! nor in a distant hour,
Another voice shall come from yonder tower;
When in dim chambers long black weeds are seen,
And weepings heard where only joy has been;
When by his children borne, and from his door
Slowly departing, to return no more,
He rests in holy earth with them that went before.

—SAMUEL ROGERS

Words

Basking, *luxuriating*.
beguiled , *deprived*.
carol, *song*.
chambers, *rooms*.
declining, *casting down*.
departing, *withdrawing*.
distant, *remote*.
garlands, *wreaths*.
harmony, *music*.
image, *picture*.
nuptial, *wedding*.
resound , *echo*.
scattered, *sprinkled*.
sirloin, *loin of beef*.
vestures, *garments*.

☆ ☆

天空中云雀唱着颂歌，
蜜蜂哼唱着他们和谐的正午曲调；
而溪谷的村庄中铃儿响彻，
利文大厅里，笑声再次响起。
此时此刻，酒杯在轮转，
现在，心花怒放，祈祷声中窃窃私语着，
人群，拦下摇篮去瞧瞧，
那熟睡中和他父亲一个模样的婴儿。
过了几年，曾经的那些声音即将响起。
又是那一天，欣喜之情溢满溪谷，
转眼工夫那孩子就长成一个少年，又从少年长成一个男人，
迫不及待地想要开始狩猎，就像他父亲当年那般。
然后用巨大的斧头砍下了厚实的牛脊梁肉；
新酿的麦芽酒，咕咕流淌闪动着琥珀色的光芒，
照耀在烟囱的明亮的火光中。
在他小时候听到过的许多故事中有一个
是保姆听了会哭泣的，她所有的缺点都不见了，
他经常坐在她的膝头，微笑着。
不久之后，音乐再次吹拂在微风里，
又过了一会儿，乐声就会越过树林，
在苍茫的夜色中探险，然后哼唱起小调来，

紫罗兰到处散落，无论是年轻人还是老人，
在每一个村舍之中，戴着绿色的花环，
静静站立凝望着、凝望着，祝福这番景象；
而当她黑色的眸子垂下，
这温柔的新娘在他身边掀起她少女的面纱。
再一次，啊！不再是遥远的未来，
那声音会再一次从那边的塔楼传来；
在昏暗的屋子里，能看到又长又黑的杂草，
在本该只有欢声笑语的地方听到了哭泣；
到他的孩子出生的时候，从他家门
缓慢离去，不再回来，
他在那神圣的曾经生活过的土地上长眠了。

——塞缪尔·罗杰斯

Lesson 39
THE SKATER AND THE WOLVES
第三十九课　滑冰者和狼

[The following remarkable account of an escape from wolves in America, during the winter of 1844, is related by Mr. Whitehead.]

I had left my friend's house one evening just before dusk, with the intention of skating a short distance up the noble river which glided directly before the door. The night was beautifully clear. A peerless moon rode through an occasional fleecy cloud, and stars twinkled from the sky and from every frost-covered tree in millions. Light also came glinting from ice, and snow-wreath, and encrusted branches as the eye followed for miles the broad gleam of the river, that like a jewelled zone swept between the mighty forests on its banks. And yet all was still. The cold seemed to have frozen tree, and air, and water, and every living thing. Even the ringing of my skates echoed back from the hill with a startling clearness; and the crackle of the ice, as I passed over it in my course, seemed to follow the tide of the river with lightning speed.

I had gone up the river nearly two miles, when, coming to a little stream which empties into the larger, I turned into it to explore its course. Fir and hemlock of a century's growth met overhead, and formed an archway radiant with frost-work. All was dark within; but I was young and fearless, and as I peered into an unbroken forest that reared itself on the borders of the stream, I laughed with very joyousness.

My wild hurrah rang through the silent woods, and stood listening to the echo that reverberated again and again, until all was hushed. Suddenly a sound arose—it seemed to me to come from beneath the ice; it was low and tremulous at first, but it ended in one long wild yell I was appalled. Never before had such a noise met my ears. Presently I heard the brushwood on shore crash, as though from the tread of some animal. The blood rushed to my forehead—my energies returned, and I looked around me for some means of escape.

The moon shone through the opening at the mouth of the creek by which I had entered the forest, and, considering this the best means of escape, I darted toward it like an arrow. It was hardly a hundred yards distant, and the swallow could scarcely have excelled me in flight; yet, as I turned my head to the shore, I could see several dark objects dashing through the brushwood at a pace nearly double in speed to my own. By their great speed, and the short yells which they occasionally gave, I knew at once that these were the much dreaded gray wolves.

The bushes that skirted the shore flew past with the velocity of lightning as I dashed on in my flight to pass the narrow opening. The outlet was nearly gained—a few seconds more and I would be comparatively safe; but in a moment my pursuers appeared on the bank above me, which here rose to the height of ten feet. There was no time for thought—I bent my head and dashed madly forward. The wolves sprang, but, miscalculating my speed, fell behind, while their intended prey glided out upon the river!

Nature turned me toward home. The light flakes of snow spun from the iron of my skates, and I was some distance from my pursuers, when their fierce howl told me I was still their fugitive. I did not look back; I did not feel afraid, or sorry, or glad; one thought of home, of the bright faces awaiting my return, and of their tears if they never should see me,—and then all the energies of body and mind were exerted for escape.

SKATER CHASED BY WOLVES

I was perfectly at home on the ice. Many were the days that I had spent on my good skates, never thinking that they would thus prove my only means of safety. Every half minute a furious yelp from my fierce attendants made me but too certain that they were in close pursuit. Nearer and nearer they came,—at last I heard their feet pattering on the ice—I even felt their very breath and heard their snuffing scent! Every nerve and muscle in my frame was stretched to the utmost tension.

The trees along the shore seemed to dance in an uncertain light, and my brain turned with my own breathless speed; yet still my pursuers seemed to hiss forth their breath with a sound truly horrible, when an involuntary motion on my part turned me out of my course. The wolves, close behind, unable to stop, and as unable to turn on the smooth ice, slipped and fell, still going on far ahead Their tongues were lolling out; their white tusks wert gleaming from their bloody mouths; their dark shaggy breasts were fleeced with foam; and as they passed me their eyes glared, and they howled with fury. The thought flashed on my mind that by this means I could avoid them,—namely, by turning aside whenever they came too near; for, by the formation of their feet, they are unable to run on ice except in a straight line.

I immediately acted upon this plan. The wolves having regained their feet, sprang directly towards me. The race was renewed for twenty yards up the stream; they were already close at my back, when I glided round and dashed directly past them. A fierce yell greeted my evolution,and the wolves, slipping on their haunches, sailed onward, presenting a perfect picture of helplessness and baffled rage. Thus I gained nearly a hundred yards at each turning. This was repeated two or three times, the animals becoming more excited and baffled every moment.

At one time, by delaying my turning too long, my sanguinary antagonists came so near that they threw their white foam over my dress as they sprang to seize me, and their teeth clashed together like the spring of a fox-trap! Had my skates failed for one instant,—had I tripped on a stick, or had my foot been caught in a fissure of the ice,—the story I am now telling would never have been told.

I thought over all the chances. I knew where they would first seize me if I fell. I thought how long it would be before I died; and then of the search for my body, that would already have had its tomb; for oh! how fast man's mind traces out all the dread colours of death's picture, only those who have been near the grim original can tell.

At last I came opposite the house, and my hounds—I knew their deep voices—roused by the noise, bayed furiously from their kennels. I heard their chains rattle; how I wished they would break them!—then I should have had protector to match the fiercest denizens of the forest. The wolves, taking the hint conveyed by the dogs, stopped in their mad career, and after a few moments turned and fled.

I watched them until their forms disappeared over a neighbourmg hill; then, taking off my skates, I wended my way to the house, with feelings which may be better imagined than described. But even yet I never see a broad sheet of ice by moonlight without thinking of that snuffing breath, and those fearful things that followed me so closely down that frozen river.

Such is the strange tale of escape from the winter wolves of America. In Russia they are no less dreaded; and the traveller, even when flying over the snow in his swift sledge, often finds the speed of his horses barely sufficient to rescue him from the hungry pack. On such occasions their merciless rapacity often proves his means of escape; for no sooner does he shoot down one of the foremost, than the whole pack crowd round it and tear it to pieces! By such means time is gained, and the affrighted horses, fleeing at their utmost speed, at length dash with the sledge into the shelter of the long wished-for station.

Words

affrighted, *terrified.*
antagonists, *foes.*
appalled, *dismayed.*
attendants, *pursuers.*
comparatively, *relatively.*
considering, *deeming.*
denizens, *inhabitants.*
dreaded, *feared.*
encrusted, *coated with frost.*
energies, *powers.*
excelled, *surpassed.*
exerted, *put forth.*
formation, *construction.*
fugitive, *object pursued.*

furiously, *wildly.*
helplessness, *feebleness.*
imagined, *fancied.*
intention, *purpose.*
involuntary, *unintentional.*
joyousness, *gladness.*
miscalculating, *not allowing for.*
original, *reality.*
protectors, *guardians.*
radiant, *lustrous.*
rapacity, *greediness.*
regained, *recovered.*
rescue, *deliver.*
sanguinary, *bloodthirsty.*
startling, *surprising.*
tremulous, *quivering.*
twinkled, *glittered.*
uncertain, *wavering.*
velocity, *swiftness.*

Questions

Where did this incident occur? At what time? How far the river had the skater gone when he turned into the forest? Of what kind were the wolves that pursued him? Why did they miss him when they sprang from the bank? By what plan did he at last escape from them? What made them atop and return to the forest? By what means do travellers often escapes from Russian wolf-packs?

☆ ☆

【以下这段惊心动魄的故事，是关于一次在美洲的狼群中死里逃生的经历，发生在1844年冬天，故事由怀特·海德先生讲述。】

傍晚天还没擦黑的时候，我就离开了朋友家，心想顺着直接蜿蜒到门前的圣河，往北滑一会儿冰。那天晚上当真是美极了，夜空澄澈。偶尔天空中会出现快速流走的云朵，那无与伦比的月亮冒出来，星星在夜空中和数以百万的被霜冻覆盖的枝头闪烁。顺着宽阔的河面极目眺望，冰面上、雪堆上，结了霜的枝条也都闪动着亮光，而那河面就像从大森林到它的两岸间扫除了一片宝石般的地方似的。一切都静悄悄的，寒冷似乎已经把树都冻僵了，空气、水，还有所有的生物也都被冻在其中了。我滑冰时转动的回声从山谷中传来，清晰得吓人；而我滑过之后的冰面上的划痕，就像用风驰电掣一样的速度把河流的浪潮做上页码一般。

我顺着河向上游滑了大约两英里的路，然后到了一条注入更大河流的小溪上，我滑到小溪上顺着它的流向滑动。百年树龄的冷杉和铁杉在我的头顶摩挲，并在前方形成了拱形通道，闪动着冰晶。通道里黑不见五指，可我当时初生牛犊不怕虎，因此就滑向一片位于溪流后面，而且横亘在溪流两岸的原始森林，我欣喜若狂，大笑起来。

我不羁的笑声在静谧的森林中回响，我站立着静静听着那一波又一波的回声，直到一切又静寂了下来。突然间，我听到一声叫声，我觉得它似乎是从冰面下传来的。起初，这声音低沉而震颤，最后它伴以一声长长狂野的嚎叫。我害怕了，我从来没听到过这样的声音。接着我听到灌木丛中传来窸窸窣窣的响动，就好像有什么动物从上面踏过一样。血液一下子涌到了脑门，我的身体又有了力量，我向四周看看，看应该怎样逃跑才好。

月亮照耀在河流入口，而我正是从河边进到森林里，我心想河流是最好的逃生之路，像箭一般飞奔向它。我离着它不到一百码的距离，飞燕都不能超过我滑动的速度，然而，当我转过头看河岸的时候，我能看见几个黑东西从草丛中箭一般冲了出来，速度相当于我的两倍。从它们飞快的速度和时不时发出的越来越近的叫声，我马上知道，它们是最可怕的灰狼。

我通过狭窄的河口飞快划去的时候，沿河岸生长的灌木丛以闪电般的速度向后隐去。我几乎快要到达河口了——只需几秒钟，我就能相对安全了。但那时，追逐我的狼群出现在高高的河岸上，比我站的地方高十英尺。没时间思考了，我低下头，疯了一样地向前划去。当它们要追到的猎物在河面上滑动的时候，狼群跳起来，但因为他们错估了我的速度，落在了后面。

大自然送我向家划去。轻盈的雪花从我的冰刀旁飞溅而出，我离着追逐的狼群有一段距离了，但它们激烈的叫声告诉我，我依然是它们追逐的对象。我没有向后看，也没有感觉到害怕或遗憾，或者高兴。我心里头只有一个念头，就是回家，想到家里等候我回去的一张张期盼的脸，而如果他们再也见不到我的话，他们会哭泣，于是身体所有的能量和所有的心思都放到了逃生上。

到了冰上我就特别安心了。因为我滑冰由来已久，不曾想滑冰会成为我安然无恙的唯一手段。每半分钟，那猛烈的追击者就会发出愤怒的吼叫，因此我特别确定，他们距离我特别近。它们距离我越来越近，最后我听到他们的爪子快速拍打在冰面上——我甚至能感觉到它们的呼吸，听到它们嗅闻的声音！我身上的每根神经，每块肌肉都紧张到极点。

岸边的树看起来就像在不确定的光线中跳舞，我脑子里则合着我屏住呼吸的速度打着拍子，然而我的追逐者们似乎伴随着发出的嘶嘶声，发出非常可怕的叫声，突然我不小心一下子滑偏了方向，而紧随其后的狼群，没能及时停住，因为它们不能在光滑的冰面上转弯，滑倒了，然后它们继续向前追赶。它们吐着舌头，白色尖牙在血红的大嘴里发光；它们深色而蓬松的胸部沾满了白沫，从我身边经过的时候，它们眼神狰狞，怒声嚎叫着。我头脑中马上闪现出一个念头，我能够躲过它们，也就是说，只要它们离我太近了，我就向旁边转弯；因为它们脚的结构，在冰面上只能走直线。

于是我马上实施这个计划。狼群重新站起来，向我身上扑来。新的追逐在距溪流二十码的上游位置开始了，它们离着我的后背已经很近了，这时我滑了个圈，直接从它们中间滑过去。一声尖利的叫声提醒它们我转变了方向，然后狼群，用后腿滑动，继续向前，不能刹住向前的脚步，那无可奈何的样子和受挫的愤怒的样子可笑极了。因此，我每转向一次就赢得了差不多一百码的时间。这样重复了两三次以后，狼群变得越来越亢奋，也越来越受挫。

有一次，我因为转弯前耽搁的时间太长了，我那残暴的对手们距离我特别近，近到它们扑过来抓我的时候，嘴里的白沫都喷到了我的衣服上，它们的利齿咬合在一处，就好像捕狐狸的陷阱夹子一下子闭合了一样。要是我哪怕有一瞬间滑动不稳的话，要是我被枝条绊倒的话，或者要是我的脚陷在冰缝中的话，我也就不可能在这里给诸位讲这个故事了。

我仔细权衡了一下所有的可能性。我知道，如果我跌倒了，它们会马上抓住我。我想自己在死之前还有多长时间，而一旦它们抓住我的话，无疑这里就是我的葬身之所了。因为，唉！人类的思想能多快逃脱出死亡的可怕色彩绘就的图画呢，只有那些曾在死亡边缘挣扎过的人们才能告诉你答案。

最后，我到了我家门前，而我家的狗——我辨识得出它们低沉的叫声——它们听到动静，从它们的窝里极其大声地吠着。我听到它们的铁链咣咣作响，心想要是它们能挣脱锁链该多好啊，这样我就有能和森林的凶残的狼群相匹敌的保护者了。狼群，听到狗传达出的警告，停止了它们疯狂的追逐，过了一会儿之后，它们就转身逃走了。

我看着它们，知道它们的身影消失在临近的山丘上，才脱下冰刀鞋，走进家去，心里头百感交集，只可意会不可言传。但从那时起，只要我看到月夜下的冰面，就必定会想起那嗅闻的喘息声，还有那些可怕的动物紧追不舍地在结冰的河面上追着我的场景。

这就是我从冬季的美洲狼群口中死里逃生的故事。在俄国，狼同样可怕；旅行者们即使是坐在飞速前进的雪橇上在雪地里行进，也经常会发现马匹的速度不足以使他从饥饿的狼群口中逃生。在这样的情况下，他只有狠下心来快速采取行动，才是逃生之法，因为如果他不快点击毙领头的那只狼的话，整个狼群就会包围雪橇，把人撕成碎片，而受惊的马匹，就以最快的速度飞驰着拉着雪橇，最终到达一直期盼的地点。

Lesson 40 THE VILLAGE PREACHER

第四十课 乡村牧师

Near yonder copse, where once the garden smiled,
And still where many a garden flower grows wild,
There, where a few torn shrubs the place disclose,
The village preacher's modest mansion rose.
A man he was to all the country dear,
And passing rich with forty pounds a year;
Remote from towns he ran his godly race,
Nor e'er had changed, nor wished to change, his place.
Unskilful he to fawn, or seek for power,
By doctrines fashioned to the varying hour;
Far other aims his heart had learned to prize,
More bent to raise the wretched than to rise.
His house was known to all the vagrant train;
He chid their wanderings, but relieved their pain.
The long-remembered beggar was his guest,
Whose beard descending swept his aged breast;
The ruined spendthrift, now no longer proud,
Claimed kindred there, and had his claim allowed;
The broken soldier, kindly bade to stay,
Sat by his fire and talked the night away,
Wept o'er his wounds, or, tales of sorrow done,
Shouldered his crutch, and showed how fields were won.
Pleased with his guests, the good man learned to glow,
And quite forgot their vices, in their woe;
Careless their merits or their faults to scan,
His pity gave, ere charity began.
Thus to relieve the wretched was his pride,
And even his failings leaned to virtue's side;
But, in his duty prompt at every call,
He watched and wept, he prayed and felt for all:
And, as a bird each fond endearment tries
To tempt her new-fledged offspring to the skies,
He tried each art, reproved each dull delay,
Allured to brighter worlds, and led the way.

Beside the bed where parting life was laid,
And sorrow, guilt, and pain, by turns dismayed,
The reverend champion stood. At his control,
Despair and anguish fled the struggling soul;
Comfort came down the trembling wretch to raise,
And his last faltering accents whispered praise.
  At church, with meek and unaffected grace,
His looks adorned the venerable place;
Truth from his lips prevailed with double sway;
And fools, who came to scoff, remained to pray.
The service past, around the pious man,
With ready zeal, each honest rustic ran;
Even children followed with endearing wile,
And plucked his gown, to share the good man's smile
His ready smile a parent's warmth expressed,
Their welfare pleased him, and their cares distressed
To them his heart, his love, his griefs were given,
But all his serious thoughts had rest in heaven:
As some tall cliff, that lifts its awful form,
Swells from the vale, and midway leaves the storm;
Though round its breast the rolling clouds are spread.
Eternal sunshine settles on its head.

—OLIVER GOLDSMITH

Words

allowed, *acknowledged.*
allured, *enticed.*
anguish, *torment.*
charity, *Alms-giving.*
descending, *flowing down.*
disclose, *reveal.*
distressed, *grieved.*
endearment, *caress.*
failings, *frailties.*
faltering, *Inarticulate.*
fashioned, *adapted.*
mansion, *dwelling.*
relieved, *alleviated.*
unaffected, *natural.*
unskilful, *unqualified.*
vagrant, *begging.*
venerable, *sacred.*
wile, *sly artifice.*

☆ ☆

在那边的树丛中，花园里的花绽放着，
曾经有许多的花朵无拘无束地生长，

在那儿，花园映衬下是几处破败的灌木丛，
那里就是乡村牧师低调的住所。
他是一位全村上下都敬仰的人物，
过着每年四十英镑的富足生活；
他骑着骏马从遥远的城镇而来，
他从没有改变过，也从来不希望改变自己的住所。
他不善逢迎，也不追逐权势，
每时每刻都践行着信条，
对于其他的目标，他心无旁骛，
对于穷困的人们，他奉行授人以鱼不如授人以渔。
所有流浪无家的人们都知道他的居所；
他训斥他们的流浪行为，但减轻他们的痛苦。
长久的乞丐是他的座上客，
乞丐的胡子拖到他年老的胸膛上；
声名狼藉的吝啬鬼，如今不再高高在上，
说如果自己的条件允许的话，许诺在那里施舍；
断腿的士兵，态度友善，留宿在此，
坐在他的火堆旁和他彻夜长谈，
他啜泣自己的伤口，讲着那些悲伤的故事，
他扛起拐杖，给别人看战争是怎样取胜的。
他很高兴有这样一群客人，这好心人红光满面，
听着他们的悲伤而彻底忘记了他们的声音；
他把怜悯给了
他们无心之失或品质优劣而造成的失误，然后开始施舍。
解救受苦之人是他的骄傲，
甚至他徒劳的努力都是美德所使；
但对每一次的请求，他都马上履行自己的职责，
他看着所有人，为他们抽泣着，祈祷着，同他们感同身受。
然而，就像每一只钟爱的鸟儿，
哄得羽翼刚丰的小鸟飞向蓝天一样，
他尝试了各种方法，责骂他们故意拖延，
诱使他们去更光明的世界，引领他们前行。
在那曾经无数人儿躺过的床的旁边，

悲伤、愧疚和痛苦轮番交错，
那受人尊敬的牧师站立着。在他的掌控下，
绝望和忧伤从这些挣扎的灵魂中走掉；
安抚那些战栗着的穷困人儿，
最后他支支吾吾地给了他们慰藉的表扬。
教堂里，他神色恭顺而自持，
他的神情使这受人尊崇之地生辉；
他唇间吐露的真理在是非摇摆之间传播；
嗤之以鼻的愚蠢人，只知道祈祷。
仪式结束后，周围都是虔诚的人们，
他们满怀热情，有着乡村人的朴实；
甚至孩子们都在嬉戏顽皮，
揪揪他的袍子，惹得那好心人笑一笑。
他开心地笑着，饱含着一个家长的温情，
他们的好生活让他满足，他也忧心于
他们忧心的地方，他付出了爱，为他们所哀伤，
但他所有的严肃想法都可以在天堂歇息了：
某个深邃的悬崖，形态陡峭，
巍峨在山谷之上，暴风雪在其半山腰肆虐；
虽然翻滚的云朵在它胸际弥散，
它头顶上是永恒的阳光在照耀。

——奥利弗·戈尔德史密斯

Lesson 41 AN INDIAN'S TRAPS

第四十一课 印第安人的陷阱

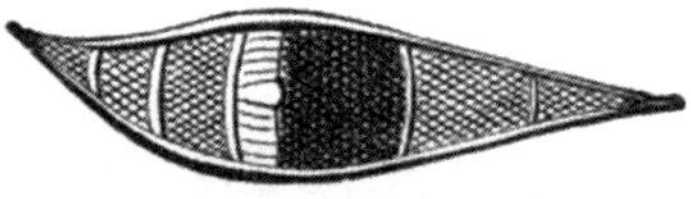

SNOW-SHON

Suppose yourself, gentle reader, standing at the gate of one of the forts in Hudson Bay, watching a savage arranging his snow-shoes, preparatory to entering the gloomy forest. Let us walk with this Indian on a visit to his traps.

The night is very dark, as the moon is hid by thick clouds; yet it occasionally breaks out sufficiently to illumine our path to the Indian's wigwam, and to throw the shadows of the neighbouring trees upon the pale snow, which, owing to the intense cold, crunches under our feet as we advance. The tent, at which we soon arrive, is pitched at the foot of an immense tree, which stands in a little hollow where the willows and pines are luxuriant enough to afford a shelter from the north wind. Suddenly the deer-skin robe that covers the entrance to the wigwam is raised, and a bright stream of warm light gushes out, tipping the dark green points of the opposite trees, and mingling strangely with the paler light of the moon—and the Indian stands erect in front of his solitary home.

MOCCASIN

He is in his usual hunting costume. A large leathern coat, very much overlapped in front, and fastened round his waist with a scarlet belt, protects his body from the cold. A small rat-skin cap covers his head, and his legs are cased in the ordinary blue cloth leggins. Large moccasins, with two or three pairs of blanket socks, clothe his feet; and fingerless mittens, made of deer-skin, complete his costume.

After a few minutes passed in contemplation of the heavens, the Indian prepares himself for the walk. First he sticks a small axe in his belt, serving as a counterpoise to a large hunting-knife and fire-bags which depend from the other side. He then slips his feet through the cords is of his snow-shoes, and throws the line of a small hand-sledge over his shoulder. Having attached the sledge to his back, he stoops to receive his gun from his faithful squaw, who has been watching his operations through a hole in the tent; and throwing it on his shoulder, strides off, without uttering a word, across the moonlit space in front of the tent, turns into a narrow track that leads down the dark ravine, and disappears in the shades of the forest.

The forest is now almost dark, the foliage overhead having become so dense that the moon penetrates through it only in a few places, rendering the surrounding masses darker by contrast. The outline of an old snow-shoe track, at first faintly seen, is soon no longer visible; but still the Indian moves forward with rapid, noiseless step, as sure of his way as if a broad beaten track lay before him. In this manner he moves on for nearly two miles, sometimes stooping to examine closely the newly-made track of some wild animal, and occasionally giving a glance at the sky through the openings in the leafy canopy above him. Suddenly a faint sound in the bushes ahead brings him to a full stop.

He listens attentively, and a noise, like the rattling of a chain, is heard proceeding from the recesses of a dark, wild-looking hollow, a few paces in front. Another moment, and the rattle is again distinctly heard. A slight smile of satisfaction crosses the Indian's dark visage; for one of his traps is set in that place, and he knows that something has been caught. Quickly descending the slope, he enters the bushes whence the sound proceeds, and pauses when within a yard or two of his trap, to peer through the gloom.

A cloud passes off the moon, and a faint ray reveals, it may be, a beautiful black fox caught in the snare. A slight blow on the snout from the Indian's axe-shaft kills the unfortunate animal; in ten minutes more it is tied on his sledge, the trap is re-set and again covered over with snow, so that it is almost impossible to tell that anything is there; and the Indian pursues his way.

The steel-trap used by the Indians is very similar to the ordinary rat-trap of England, with this difference, that it is a little larger, is destitute of teeth, and has two springs in place of one.A chain is attached to one of the springs, for the purpose of fixing a weight to the trap, so that the animal caught may not be able to drag it far from the place where it has been set. The track in the snow enables the hunter to find his trap again. It is generally so set that the jaws, when spread out flat, are exactly on a level with the snow.

The chain and weight are both hid, and a thin layer of snow is spread on the top of the trap. The bait (which generally consists of chips of a frozen partridge, rabbit, or fish) is then scattered around in every direction; and, with the exception of this, nothing distinguishes the spot.

A TRAP

Foxes, beavers, wolves, lynxes, and other animals, are caught in this way, sometimes by a fore-leg, sometimes by a hind-leg, sometimes by two legs at once, and occasionally by the nose. Of all these ways the Indians prefer catching by two legs, as there is then not the slightest possibility of the animal escaping.

When foxes are caught by one leg, they often eat it off close to the trap, and escape on the other three! I have frequently seen this happen; and I once saw a fox caught which had evidently escaped in this way, as one of its legs was gone and the stump healed up and covered again with hair. When they are caught by the nose they are almost sure to escape, unless taken out of the trap very soon, as their snouts are so sharp or wedge-like that they can pull them from between the jaws of the trap without much difficulty.

Having described this machine, we shall now rejoin the Indian, whom we left on his way to his next trap. There he goes, moving swiftly over the snow, mile after mile, as if he could not feel fatigue; turning aside now and then to visit a trap, and giving a short grunt when nothing is in it; or killing the animal when caught, and tying it on the sledge.

Toward midnight, however, he begins to walk more cautiously, examines the priming of his gun, and moves the axe in his belt, as if he expected to meet some enemy suddenly. The fact is, that close to where he now stands are two traps which he set in the morning close to each other, for the purpose of catching one of the formidable coast wolves.

These animals are so sagacious that they will scrape all round a trap, let it be ever so well set, and, after eating all the bait, walk away unhurt. Indians, consequently, endeavour in every possible way to catch them, and, among others, by setting two traps close together; so that while the wolf scrapes at one, he may perhaps put his foot in the other. It is in this way that our Indian friend's traps are set, and he now proceeds cautiously towards them, his gun in the hollow of his left arm.

Slowly he advances, peering through the bushes; but nothing is visible. Suddenly a branch crashes under his snow-shoe, and with a savage growl a large wolf bounds toward him, landing almost at his feet! A single glance, however, shows the Indian that both traps are on its legs, and that the chains prevent its further advance. He places his gun against a tree, draws the axe from his belt, and advances to kill the animal.

It is, however, an undertaking of some difficulty. The fierce brute, which is larger than a Newfoundland dog, strains every nerve and sinew to break its chains, while its eyes glisten in the uncertain light, and foam curls from its blood-red mouth. Now it retreats as the Indian advances, grinning horribly the while; and anon, as the chains check its further retreat, it springs with fearful growl toward the Indian, who slightly wounds it with his axe, as he jumps backward just in time to save himself from the infuriated animal, which catches in its fangs the flap of his leggin, and tears it from his limb. Again the Indian advances, and the wolf retreats and again springs on him, but with out success.

At last, as the wolf glances for a moment to one side—apparently to see if there is any way of escape—quick as lightning the axe flashes in the air, and descends with stunning violence on its head; another blow follows, and in five minutes more the animal is bound to the sledge.

—R. M. BALLANTYNE

Words

attached, *fastened*.
attentively, *Intently*.
cautiously, *warily*.
contemplation, *study*.
costume, *dress*.
counterpoise, *offset*.
difference, *exception*.
distinguishes, *marks*.
endeavour, *strive*.
evidently, *apparently*.
examine, *inspect*.
fatigue, *weariness*.
frequently, *often*.
illumine, *light*.
infuriated, *enraged*.
luxuriant, *exuberant*.
occasionally, *sometimes*.
operations, *proceedings*.
ordinary, *common*.
penetrates, *pierces*.
possibility, *chance*.
preparatory, *Introductory*.
proceeds, *advances*.
ravine, *pass*.
recesses, *depths*.
retreats, *retires*.
sagacious, *shrewd*.
satisfaction, *pleasure*.
slightly, *triflingly*.
solitary, *lonely*.
undertaking, *work*.
unfortunate, *luckless*.
uttering, *speaking*.
violence, *force*.

Questions

Where had the Indian pitched his tent? Why there? What covered the entrance to the hut? How was the Indian dressed? How was he armed? What brought him to a full stop in his round? What did the sound resemble? What did it tell the Indian? How did he kill the animal? What difference is there between the Indian's steel-trap and an English rat-trap? With what is it baited? What do foxes often do, when caught by one leg? Why had the Indian set two traps close together in one place? What was the result? What risk did he run, in attempting to kill the wolf? What moment did he seize for striking it with his axe?

☆ ☆

亲爱的读者，请设想一下你自己站在哈德逊湾其中一个据点的门口，看着一个野蛮人穿上雪地靴，准备好要大步走进昏暗的森林。我们不妨就同这个印第安人一起走到他设下的陷阱那儿看看。

夜色很深，月亮隐藏在厚厚的云层之后，然而它会偶尔探出头来，其亮光足够能照亮我们去往印第安人栅屋的道路，把邻近树木的影子映在苍白的雪上，而由于强烈的寒冷，我们一边走，脚下的积雪一边吱吱作响。我们不久之后到达的帐篷，是在一棵巨大的树底下搭建起来的，大树生长在一个小空洞中，那里北风吹过柳树和松树就能够形成一个庇护之地了。突然间，覆盖在通往通光口的入口的鹿皮袍子被掀起来，一束温暖的光束涌出，在对面的树木上照射出深绿色的点，并和苍白的月光奇怪地糅合在一起——印第安人在自己孤零零的房子面前站直了身子。

他身着平常的狩猎装束。那是一个宽大的皮质大衣，在身前交叠得很厉害，在腰部用一根深红色的腰带束紧，可以保护他的身体免受寒冷的侵害。他头戴一顶小巧的鼠皮帽，腿上包裹着平常的蓝布护腿裤。巨大的麂皮鞋，还有两三双毛织袜，包裹着他的脚；他手上戴着鹿皮做的连指手套，这就是他一身的行头。

在几分钟思索了天穹之后，印第安人准备好上路了。首先，他把一把小斧头别在自己的腰带上，腰带是用来固定一些大的狩猎刀具和火袋的，这些东西分别挂在两边。然后他穿着雪靴一路滑过对面，把一个小的手持雪橇的绳子扛在自己肩头。雪橇贴在背部之后，他就弯下腰从他忠贞的妻子手中接过猎枪，妻子一直透过帐篷上的小孔观察着他的行动；然后他把猎枪扛在肩头，一语不发大步流星地走过帐篷前月光照耀的空地，转而走上一段狭窄并通往下面黑暗山涧的小路，之后消失在森林的阴影之中了。

现在，森林里几乎一片黑暗，头顶上交叠着的枝叶变得非常浓密，以至于月亮仅仅通过有限的几处才能将光亮渗透进去。对比之下，周围显得愈加黑暗了。踏过的雪靴的轮廓，一开始还能隐隐瞧见，之后不久就看不见了；然而印第安人还是继续快速前行，踏着没有噪声的步伐，好像对前路信心满满，就像前路是一条已经踏出的康庄大道似的。就这样，他向前走了约两英里的路程，又弯下腰仔细看看被野生动物新踏出的路，偶尔会透过树叶交织的缝隙瞧一眼头顶的天空。突然间，前方灌木丛中传来一声微弱的声响，他马上停下脚步。

他听得很仔细，而那噪声就像链条的当当声一样，能听出来是从晦暗而原始的空洞庇荫处，也就是前方几步路的地方传来的。过了一会儿，那当当声又清晰了。印第安人黝黑的脸上展露出满意的微笑；因为他其中一个陷阱就设在那个地方，而他知道一定是有东西被捉住了。于是他快速下了山坡，走进发出声响的灌木丛里，在离着他设下的陷阱一两码远的地方停住，向那晦暗处瞧去。

一朵云彩遮住了月亮，从微弱的光线中可以看出，可能是一只漂亮的黑狐掉入陷阱了。印第安人轻轻挥动斧头砍向狐狸头部，就结束了这只不走运动物的生命；十分钟之后，狐狸就挂在他的雪橇上了，然后陷阱被重新设好，上面再次覆盖上雪，这样就几乎看不出来是不是有什么东西在那儿了；之后印第安人继续赶路。

印第安人使用的钢质陷阱和平常的英格兰的老鼠夹子非常相像，两者只有一个不同，即印第安人的稍微大一点，钢齿更为稀疏，而且有两个弹簧而不是一个。有一根链条链接在其中一根弹簧上，目的是为了链接上一块重物，这样被捉住的猎物就不能拖着陷阱架子跑得离着原来陷阱的地方太远。通常陷阱在设定的时候，锯齿展开平放的时候，和雪的高度要精确地保持一致。

链条和重物都被隐藏起来，陷阱上头撒上一层薄薄的雪。之后，诱饵（通常是一些冷冻的鹧鸪肉，兔肉或鱼肉）会被均匀地洒在各个方向；除了这点之外，其他地方并没有不同。

捕捉狐狸、水獭、狼、山猫以及其他动物都会用这种方式，有时是捉前腿，有时是捉后腿，有时两条腿会同时被捉住，偶尔还会被捉住鼻子。在所有的这些捕捉方法中，印第安人更喜欢捉住动物的两条腿，因为这样的话，动物逃跑的可能性就非常小了。

当狐狸被捉住一条腿的时候，它们经常会在靠近陷阱的地方把腿咬断，用剩下的三条腿逃跑。我经常见到这样的事情发生；而且我有一次看见一只被捉住的狐狸，很明显它就曾用这样的方法逃跑的，因为它丢了一条腿，而腿根部愈合了还长出了毛遮盖着。当它们被捉住鼻子的时候，几乎可以确定它们一定能逃走，除非它们很快被从陷阱中捉走，否则鉴于他们的口鼻部非常尖利，或者很像楔子，它们就能不费很大力气从陷阱的锯齿中间挣脱了。

在描述了这个装置之后，我们现在不妨来和印第安人汇合，他一个人去挖他下一个陷阱了。他在路上走着，飞快地走在雪地上，走了一英里又一英里的路，好像感觉不到疲劳似的；他时不时地从路上岔过去看看陷阱，当看到一无所获的时候会简单抱怨几句；而当发现有动物被捉住的时候就杀掉它，把它系在自己的雪橇上。

然而临近子夜的时候，他开始走得越来越小心，仔细检查枪里的火药，把斧头移到腰带上，好像盼着突然遇上什么敌人似的。事实上，邻近他站立的地方有两个他早晨设下的陷阱，两个陷阱彼此靠得很近，目的是为了能捉住一只可怕的海岸狼。

狼这种动物非常聪明，它们会在陷阱周围剐剐蹭蹭，即使是设立得再好的陷阱，它们也能够在吃完所有诱饵之后，安然无恙地离去。印第安人因此用各种可能的方法努力捉到他们，而在所有的方法中，把两个陷阱紧紧设在一起是最常用的；这样当狼犬在一个陷阱处刮擦的时候，它就肯定能把脚爪伸进另一个陷阱中。我们印第安朋友的陷阱就这样设定了，现在他小心翼翼地向着它们走去，他的枪就夹在他的左腋下。

他慢慢向前走着，朝灌木丛瞧着；但什么也看不到。突然他脚下踩断了一根枝条，一只身形高大的狼发出野性的吼叫之后，就向他扑去，差点就扑到他身上！然而，只看一眼，印第安人就知道两个陷阱都夹在狼的腿上，而链条则阻止了狼进一步向前。他把枪靠在一棵树上，从腰带中拽出斧子来，挥动斧头杀死了这只动物。

然而，做这件事需要费些功夫。凶残的狼，身形要比新大陆的狗大些，每根神经紧绷，撕咬着要把链条咬断，亮眼在忽明忽暗的光线中闪闪发光，白沫从它的血红的嘴里喷出来。现在，印第安人在步步向前，而它则步步后退，可怕的龇牙咧嘴；而当链条绷紧到狼只能后退的最远地方的时候，它发出骇人的吼叫，扑向印第安人，印第安人及时向后跳去以免被这穷凶极恶的动物伤到的时候，用斧头砍伤了狼，而狼的尖牙则咬在他的护腿裤上，把裤子撕咬了下来。印第安人再次往前走，狼再次后退，然后再次扑向他，但这一次没有成功。

最后，当狼向一边看了一眼的时候——很明显它是在看是不是有逃生的办法——斧头如同闪电一样快速在空中挥动，以惊人的力道重重落在狼头上；接着又是一击，五分多钟后，这只动物就被拴在雪橇上了。

——R. M. 巴兰蒂涅

Lesson 42 VIRGINIA

第四十二课 弗吉尼亚

Sir Walter Raleigh spent a large fortune in attempting to colonize Virginia. He succeeded in directing the attention of his countrymen to the region which had kindled his own enthusiasm. But his colonies never prospered. Sometimes the colonists returned home disgusted by the hardships of the wilderness. Once they were massacred by the Indians. When help came from England, the infant settlement was in ruins. The bones of unburied men lay about the fields; wild deer strayed among the untenanted houses. Once a colony wholly disappeared. To this day its fate is unknown.

Sir Walter was enduring his long captivity in the Tower, writing his "History of the World," and moaning piteously over the havoc which prison-damps had wrought upon his handsome frame. The time had now come, and his labours were about to bear fruit. The history of Virginia was about to open. It opened with meagre promise. In 1606 A.D. a charter from the King established a Company whose function was to colonize—whose privilege was to trade.

The Company sent out an expedition, which sailed in three small vessels. It consisted of one hundred and five men. Of these, one half were gentlemen of broken fortune. Some were tradesmen; others were footmen. Only a very few were farmers, or mechanics, or persons in any way fitted for the life they sought. Morally, the aspect of the expedition was even more discouraging. "An hundred dissolute persons" were on board the ships. The respect able portion of the expedition must have gone into very little space.

But, happily for Virginia, there sailed with these reprobate founders of a new empire a man whom Providence had highly gifted with fitness to govern his fellow-men. His name was John Smith. No writer of romance would have given his hero this name. But, in spite of his name, the man was truly heroic. He was still under thirty, a strong-limbed, deep-cheated, massively-built man. From boyhood he had been a soldier—roaming over the world in each of adventures, wherever hard blows were being exchanged.

Returning to England when the passion for colonizing was at its height, he caught at once the prevailing impulse. He joined the Virginian expedition. Ultimately he became its chief. His fitness was so manifest, that no reluctance on his own part, no jealousies on that of his companions, could bar him from the highest place. Men became kings of old by the same process which now made Smith a chief.

The "dissolute persons" sailed in their ships up the James river. Landing there, they proceeded to construct a little town, which they named Jamestown, in honour of the

King. This was the first colony which struck its roots in American soil. The colonists were charmed with the climate, and with the luxuriant beauty of the wilderness on whose confines they had settled.

But as yet it was only a wilderness. The forest had to be cleared that food might be grown. The exiled gentlemen laboured manfully, but under grievous discouragements. "The axes so oft blistered their tender finger that many times every third blow had a loud oath to drown the echo." Smith was a man upon whose soul there lay a becoming reverence for sacred things. He devised how to have every man's oaths numbered; "and at night, for every oath, to have a can of water poured down his sleeve." Under this treatment the evil assuaged.

The emigrants had landed in early spring. Summer came with its burning heat. Supplies of food ran low. "Had we been as free from all sins as from gluttony and drunkenness," Smith wrote, "we might have been canonized as saints." The colonists sickened and died. From those poor blistered fingers dropped for ever the unaccustomed axe. Before autumn every second man had died. But the hot Virginian sun, which proved so deadly to the settlers, ripened the wheat they had sowed in the spring, and freed the survivors from the pressure of want. Winter brought them a healthier temperature and abundant supplies of wild-fowl and game.

When the welfare of the colony was in some measure secured, Smith set forth with a few companions to explore the interior of the country. He and his followers were captured by the Indians. The followers were summarily butchered. Smith's composure did not fail him in the worst extremity. He produced his pocket- compass, and interested the savages by explaining its properties. He wrote a letter in their sight—to their infinite wonder. They spared him, and made a show of him in all the settlements round about. He was to them an unfathomable mystery. He was plainly superhuman. Whether his power would bring to them good or evil, they were not able to determine.

After much hesitation they chose the course which prudence seemed to counsel. They resolved to extinguish powers so formidable, regarding whose use they could obtain no guarantee. Smith was bound and stretched upon the earth, his head resting upon a great stone. The mighty club was uplifted to dash out his brains. But Smith was a man who won golden opinions from all. The Indian chief had a daughter, Pocahontas, a child of ten or twelve years. She could not bear to see the pleasing Englishman destroyed. As Smith lay waiting the fatal stroke, she seized him in her arms and interposed herself between him and the club. Her intercession prevailed, and Smith was set free.

Five years later, "an honest and discreet" young Englishman called John Rolfe loved this young Indian girl. He had a sore mental struggle about uniting himself with "one of barbarous breeding and of a cursed race." But love triumphed. He laboured for her conversion, and had the happiness of seeing her baptized in the little church of Jamestown. Then he married her.

After a time he took her home to England. Her appearance was pleasing; her mind was acute; her piety was sincere; her manners bore picturesque evidence of hex forest upbringing. The English King and Court regarded her with lively interest as the first-fruits of the wilderness. Great hopes were founded on this union of the two races. She is the brightest picture—this young Virginian wife and mother—which the history of the doomed native races presents to us. But she did not live to revisit her native land. Death parted her very early from her husband and her child.

When Smith returned from captivity the colony was on the verge of extinction. Only thirty-eight persons were left, and they were preparing to depart. With Smith hope returned to the despairing settlers. They resumed their work, confident in the resources of their chief. Fresh arrivals from England cheered them.

The character of these reinforcements was no improvement upon that of their predecessors. "Vagabond gentlemen" formed still a large majority of the settlers—many of them, we are told, "packed off to escape worse destinies at home." The colony, thus composed, had already warned a very had reputation: so bad, that some, rather than be sent there, "chose to be hanged, and were"

Over these most undesirable subjects Smith ruled with an authority which no man dared or desired to question. But he was severely injured by an accidental explosion of gunpowder. Surgical aid was not in the colony. Smith required to go to England, and once more hungry ruin settled down upon Virginia. In six months the five hundred men whom Smith had left had dwindled to sixty. These were already embarked and departing when they were met by Lord Delaware, the new governor. Once more the colony was saved.

Years of quiet growth succeeded. Emigrants—not wholly now of the dissolute sort-flowed steadily in. In 1688 the population of Virginia had increased to 50,000; and within a few years of the settlement, the Virginians had a written Constitution, according to which they were ruled.

—ROBERT MACKENZIE

Words

abundant, *plentiful.*
adventures, *enterprises.*
assuaged, *diminished.*
barbarous, *savage.*
canonized, *enrolled.*
cleared, *freed of trees.*
colonize, *make settlement.*
companions, *associates.*
composure, *self-possession.*
confident, *trustful.*
confines, *borders.*
construct, *build.*
departing, *leaving.*
destinies, *fates.*
discouraging, *dispiriting.*
dissolute, *vicious.*
dwindled, *fallen.*
enthusiasm, *ardent zeal.*
exchanged, *given and taken.*
explaining, *describing.*
extinction, *annihilation.*
extinguish, *quench.*

function, *duty*.
Separate, *security*.
intercession, *mediation*.
massacred, *murdered*.
meagre, *scanty*.
picturesque, *quaint*.
piteously, *grievously*.
predecessors, *precursors*.
prevailing, *predominant*.
privilege, *right*.
properties, *peculiarities*.
reluctance, *backwardness*.
reprobate, *profligate*.
reputation, *character*.
resources, *powers of contrivance*.
respectable, *moral*.
reverence, *veneration*.
succeeded, *followed*.
summarily, *quickly*.
unfathomable, *incomprehensible*.
untenanted, *uninhabited*.
wilderness, *forest*.

Questions

Who first attempted to colonize Virginia? With what success? When was a company chartered to colonize it? What was the character of the emigrants? Who became the chief of the expedition? What was the first English town in America? How did Smith put down the vice of swearing? From what did the settlers suffer in their first summer? How many died before autumn? What brought them relief? What befell Smith when exploring the interior? How was his life saved? What subsequently became of Pocahontas? In what state was the colony when Smith returned from captivity? Why was he compelled to return to England? Whom did Lord Delaware meet on his arrival? What was the population of Virginia in 1688?

☆ ☆

沃尔特·拉雷夫爵士投入了大量资金用在殖民弗吉尼亚州上。他成功地引起了一些地区同胞的注意，那些人点燃了去往弗吉尼亚的热情。但他的殖民地从来没有富足过。有时候，那些从殖民地回国的人对那里荒野而艰苦的环境诉苦不已。有一次，他们遭遇了印第安人的大屠杀。当英格兰的支援到达时，他们发现刚刚建立起的殖民地已经被破坏殆尽了。人们的尸骨到处散落在地上，野鹿占据了无人居住的房屋。还有一次，整个殖民地的人都消失了，直到今天他们的命运还是无从知晓。

沃尔特爵士在高塔中被长期囚禁的时候，完成了《世界史》一书，为潮湿的牢狱对他俊朗外表的蹂躏而怜惜地呻吟。时机到来，他的努力就要有结果了。弗吉尼亚的史篇即将开启，但它的前途渺茫。公元1606年，国王签署了一个委任状，上面说建立一个商号，其作用就是进行殖民，而其特权是贸易经营。

商号派出了一支探险队，探险队乘坐三艘小船起航，共有105个人。这些人之中，有一半是破产的绅士。有一些人从事商贸，另一些则从事脚力工作。仅仅有非常少数的农民，或者技师，或者是能够适应他们寻求的生活的人。从道德的角度来说，这次探险活动的实质让人更加失去信心。“一百个筚路蓝缕的人”登上了船，相应地，探险队中有能力的人数量就很有限了。

但值得为弗吉尼亚州高兴的是，随船航行的那些备受诟病的新帝国建国者中有一个人，他拥有上帝赋予的领导群众的非凡魄力。他叫约翰·史密斯。没有一个探险小说作者会让小说主人公叫这个名字。他不到30岁，四肢发达，身体结实，身形魁梧。从孩提时代起，他就是一名士兵了——他游走在每一次的重拳出击的冒险活动中。

当他回到英格兰的时候，人们对殖民的向往已经白热化，他马上捕捉到这举国上下的冲动情绪，于是加入了弗吉尼亚的探险队。最终他成为探险队的领袖。他的魄力是非凡的，即使是他自己的不情愿或者同伴的嫉妒情绪，都不能阻止他登上领袖的位子。国王的产生和现在史密斯是如何当上领袖的是同一个道理。

“筚路蓝缕的人们”顺着詹姆斯河溯游而上。在那里登陆之后，他们建立起了一个小城镇，并命名为詹姆斯敦，以表示对国王的尊崇，这是第一个在美洲的土地上生根的殖民地。殖民者们很喜欢它的气候，而野外的美不胜收的景色也让他们愿意留下来定居。

然而它还是一片荒野之地。森林必须清空，这样才有地方种植作物。虽然条件艰苦，被放逐的绅士们却勇敢地劳作着。“斧头经常把他们的手指磨出水泡，以至于他们每挥动三下斧头，就发出呻吟声，把挥动斧头的声音都淹没了。”史密斯是一个对待神圣事物很敬仰的人，他想到怎样来保护每个人，“到了夜晚的时候，每个人都要装一罐水浇在自己的衣袖上，这样的话就不会被邪恶入侵了。”

移民们在早春时节登陆。夏天热浪袭人，食物供给不够。“如果我们能摆脱贪食和贪喝之罪，”史密斯写道，“那我们就能够加入圣徒的行列了。”殖民者生病死去了，从这些可怜的生水泡的手指间，那未使用娴熟的斧头就永远脱落了。秋季之前，有一半的人都死去了。然而那炽热的弗吉尼亚的太阳，对于先民们来说曾是致命的，但却催熟了他们春天剥下的种子，让幸存者们免于饥荒之灾。冬天的温度更适宜他们生存，给他们提供了大量的禽类和猎物。

当殖民地的温饱在一定程度上有所保证之后，史密斯就派出了一些人开拓这片疆土的内陆。他和同伴们被印第安人俘虏，大部分的同伴都被杀了。史密斯镇定自若，因而度过了这最可怕的险境。他拿出口袋里的指南针，解释它的功用，引起了那些野蛮人的兴趣。当着他们的面写了一封信——这让他们惊奇不已。他们放了他，还在周围左右的聚居地让他表演了一圈。对印第安人而言，他是个解不开的谜。他简直就是超人，至于他的能力是会给他们带来好处还是厄运，他们却决定不了。

他们在犹豫良久之后，选择了一条有待谨慎协商的路。他们决定摧毁这如此强大的力量，因为他们不能保证这种力量会落到谁的手中。史密斯被绑着，躺在地上，他的头靠在一块大石头上。巨大的棍棒高高升起，一落下就能把他的脑浆给敲出来。但所有人都对史密斯印象很好。印第安酋长有个女儿，叫普卡宏塔斯，是个十岁或十二岁的孩子。她不忍心看到这个有意思的英国人被杀掉。当史密斯躺在那里等待致命一击的时候，她一把抱住他，横在史密斯和大棒之间。她的阻挡成功了，史密斯自由了。

五年之后，“一位诚实而谨慎”名叫约翰·拉尔夫的年轻英国人爱上了这位年轻的印第安姑娘。他心里头做了很久的挣扎，因为这样就会把自己和“最野蛮最受诅咒的一个民族”联系在一块了。但爱情战胜了一切。他劝说她皈依，然后很高兴地看着她在詹姆士敦的一个小教堂里进行了洗礼。之后，他就娶了她。

过了一段时间之后，他就把她带回英格兰。她长得很可爱，心思敏捷，态度虔诚，举止则透露出自己是在森林中成长的。英国国王和宫廷对她很感兴趣，就好像对野外的新鲜水果的兴趣盎然一样。在这两个民族结合的婚姻上，人们寄托了很高的希望。她——这位年轻的弗吉尼亚人的妻子和母亲——提供了灭顶之灾的土著民族的活生生的历史。可惜她没能活到重访故土。她很年轻就离开自己的丈夫和孩子，撒手人寰了。

当史密斯从被俘之地回来的时候，殖民地挣扎在死亡线上。只剩下38个人了，而他们正准备要离开这里。随着史密斯的回归，希望也回到了绝望的先民中间。他们重新开始工作，对他们首领的能力笃信不疑。而从英格兰来的新移民则让他们受到鼓舞。

这些巩固措施，相比之前的殖民地水平并没有很大提高。“穷困的绅士”依然还是先民中的主流——据说，他们中许多人，“打了个包就来了，以逃避在家的穷困潦倒”。这样，殖民地的名声就很不好了，不好到有些人宁愿选择被绞死，都不愿意被送到殖民地去。

对于这些最不想遇到的遭遇，史密斯用一种无人敢质问也无人想质问的权威来应对。但他在一次火药爆炸意外中严重负伤。殖民地没有手术救助。史密斯不得不被送往英格兰，而弗吉尼亚则再一次受到更严重的饥饿的袭击。六个月之后，史密斯留下的500人已经缩减成了60人。当受到德拉威尔阁下，也就是新长官接见的时候，他们都已经登船准备要离开了。殖民地再一次被拯救了。

多年的静静成长终于成功了。移民们——现在不全是筚路蓝缕的人了——大批涌进。到1688年，弗吉尼亚的人数增长到5万人；而在殖民地数年的时间里，弗吉尼亚人根据他们的管辖原则，完成了宪法的制定。

——罗伯特·麦肯锡

Lesson 43 WATERLOO

第四十三课 滑铁卢

There was a sound of revelry by night,
And Belgium's capital had gathered then
Her beauty and her chivalry, and bright
The lamps shone o'er fair women and brave men:
A thousand hearts beat happily; and when
Music arose with its voluptuous swell,
Soft eyes looked love to eyes which spake again,
And all went merry as a marriage bell;
But hush! hark! a deep sound strikes like a rising knell.

Did ye not hear it?—No; 'twas but the wind,
Or the car rattling o'er the stony street;
On with the dance! let joy be unconfined;
No sleep till morn, when youth and pleasure meet,
To chase the glowing hours with flying feet:—
But hark! that heavy sound breaks in once more,
As if the clouds its echo would repeat;
And nearer, clearer, deadlier than before!—
Arm! arm! it is—it is—the cannon's opening roar!

Within a windowed niche of that high hall Sate
Brunswick's fated chieftain: he did hear
That sound the first amidst the festival,
And caught its tone with death's prophetic ear;
And when they smiled because he deemed it near,
His heart more truly knew that peal too well
Which stretched his father on a bloody bier,
And roused the vengeance blood alone could quell:
He rushed into the field, and foremost fighting fell.

Ah! then and there was hurrying to and fro,
And gathering tears, and tremblings of distress,
And cheeks all pale, which but an hour ago
Blushed at the praise of their own loveliness;

And there were sudden partings, such as press
The life from out young hearts; and choking sighs
Which ne'er might be repeated;—who could guess
If ever more should meet those mutual eyes?
Since upon night so sweet such awful morn could rise.

And there was mounting in hot haste: the steed,
The mustering squadron, and the clattering car
Went pouring forward with impetuous speed,
And swiftly forming in the ranks of war;
And the deep thunder, peal on peal afar;
And near, the beat of the alarming drum
Roused up the soldier ere the morning star;
While thronged the citizens with terror dumb,
Or whispering, with white lips—"The foe! They come I they come!"

And wild and high the "Camerons' gathering"rose!
The war-note of Lochiel, which Albyn's hills
Have heard—and heard, too, have her Saxon foes.
How in the noon of night that pibroch thrills,
Savage and shrill! but with the breath which fills
Their mountain-pipe, so fill the mountaineers
With the fierce native daring which instils
The stirring memory of a thousand years:
And Evan's, Donald's fame, rings in each clansman's ears

And Ardennes waves above them her green leaves,
Dewy with Nature's tear-drops, as they pass,
Grieving, if aught inanimate e'er grieves,
Over the unreturning brave—alas!
Ere evening to be trodden like the grass,
Which now beneath them, but above shall grow
In its next verdure, when this fiery mass
Of living valour, rolliug on the foe,
And burning with high hope, shall moulder cold and low.

Last noon beheld them full of lusty life;
Last eve in beauty's circle proudly gay;
The midnight brought the signal-sound of strife;
The morn, the marshalling in arms; the day,
Battle's magnificently stern array!
The thunder-clouds close o'er it, which, when rent,

The Earth is covered thick with other clay,
Which her own clay shall cover,—heaped and pent,
Rider and horse, friend, foe, in one red burial blent!

—LORD BYRON (1788–1824)

Words

alarming, *warning*.
blent, *mingled*.
festival, *banquet*.
impetuous, *furious*.
inanimate, *lifeless*.
instils, *pours in*.
knell, *death-signal*.
loveliness, *beauty*.
marshalling, *arraying*.
memory, *recollection*.
mountaineers, *highlanders*.
mustering, *assembling*.
prophetic, *portentous*.
repeat, *return*.
revelry, *festivity*.
unconfined, *unbounded*.
valour, *courage*.
vengeance, *revengefulness*.
voluptuous, *delicious*.

☆ ☆

夜晚一片狂欢之音，火树银花，
比利时首府把当时
它的美人和勇士聚集一处；
灯光照耀在美人脸上，照亮了勇士的脸庞，
一千个人心儿幸福荡漾；而当
音乐声想起它奢靡的旋律，
温柔的眼睛爱意浓浓，眼神闪亮，
一切如同婚礼钟声敲响一样欢愉；
但嘘！听！有一声深沉的声音，如同丧钟敲响。

你没听到吗？没有，不过是风声罢了，
或者是车在石头路上颠簸的声响；
继续跳舞吧！让欢乐无拘无束，
通宵达旦，直到年轻和欢愉相会，
用轻快的舞步来追逐快乐时光吧；
但是，听！那沉重的声音再次响起，

好像云层传来它的回音；
它比之前越来越近，越来越清晰，越来越骇人！
啊！啊！是——是——是炮火的咆哮声！

坐在高高的宫殿窗户边的
是布伦瑞克那厄运已定的首领，他确实听到了
掺杂在节日声中的第一声炮响，
用自己能预言死亡的耳朵听到它的声响。

他的心更真切地感受到那轰隆声，
就是那声音把他父亲拖进了染满鲜血的棺材；
只有那激起复仇的鲜血能够平息，
他冲上战场，在最激烈的战斗中倒下了。

啊！人们形迹匆匆来来去去，
眼泪汇集，因困顿而发抖，
脸颊苍白，而仅仅一小时之前
还脸颊通红夸赞着彼此的惹人怜爱。
生离死别突然降临，诸如
把生命从年轻人的心中挤压出去，哽咽地叹气声，
以后再也不会被重复，有谁能猜得到，
这些芸芸众生的眼睛还会见到怎样的情形？
昨夜如此美妙，噩耗一般的早晨却如此来到。

一切越来越紧迫，骏马、
召集的小分队，还有发出嗒嗒声的汽车，
以奔腾的速度呼啸着向前而去，
飞快地融入战争的行列之中；
还有那深沉的雷声，在远处轰鸣着，轰鸣着，
近处是震天彻地的鼓声阵阵，
把早晨繁星下的士兵叫醒；
人们一队队行进向前，惊吓之余变得麻木，
他们嘴唇惨白，窃窃私语：“敌人！他们来了，他们来了！”

苏格兰人的队伍狂野而高傲地来到了！
洛奇儿的战争纪实中记载了在爱尔柏恩山上，
听到的——也能听到的，撒克逊敌人的声音。
子夜时分，风笛声在栗叫，
野蛮人来袭，恐惧连连！但其中尚有喘息的空间，
填充了他们的风笛，用强烈的原始的胆识，
填充在攀登者的心中，而那胆识已经
灌输在激动不已的记忆中有一千年；
而伊万的名声，多纳德的声名，在每一个家族成员的耳畔流连。

阿登高地在上面用自己翠绿的枝叶向他们招手，
上面的露珠连连，是大自然的眼泪，当他们经过的时候，
心里难过，如果任何没有生命的事物也值得难过的话，
为那不曾归返的英雄而难过——啊！
夜晚就像野草被踏过一样，
现在就在他们脚下，但在下一次青春来临的时候，
又会生长如故，当这炽热的
包蕴着活生生的英勇气概的一切，滚滚而去向着敌人而去的时候，
高高的希望燃起，将会击退寒冷和低落。

最后一个中午见证了他们的精力充沛；
最后一个晚上他们排成美丽的队伍，骄傲而欢快；
子夜来临，战斗的信号打响；
到了早晨，军队全副武装；白日时分，
战斗进行得如火如荼！
乌云滚滚，逐渐压近，当云层撤去，
大地上覆盖了一层厚厚的泥土，
那是它本身的泥土在覆盖，不断积聚，
骑士和战马，朋友和宿敌，都掩埋进了一片赤红，不分彼此！

——拜伦勋爵（1788–1824）

Lesson 44 THE SLAVE'S DREAM

第四十四课 奴隶的梦

Beside the ungathered rice he lay, his sickle in his hand;
His breast was bare, his matted hair was buried in the sand.
Again, in the mist and shadow of sleep, he saw his native land.

Wide through the landscape of his dreams the lordly Niger flowed;
Beneath the palm-trees on the plain once more a king he strode,
And heard the tinkling caravans descend the mountain-road.

He saw once more his dark-eyed queen among her children stand;
They clasped his neck, they kissed his cheeks, they held him by the hand!—
A tear burst from the sleeper's lids, and fell into the sand.

And then at furious speed he rode along the Niger's bank;
His bridle-reins were golden chains, and, with a martial clank,
At each leap he could feel his scabbard of steel smiting his stallion's flank.

Before him, like a blood-red flag, the bright flamingoes flew;
From morn till night he followed their flight, o'er plains where
the tamarind grew,
Till he saw the roofs of Caffre huts, and the ocean rose to view.

At night he heard the lion roar, and the hyena scream stream
And the river-horse, as he crushed the reeds beside some bidden stream
And it passed, like a glorious roll of drums, through the triumph of his dream.

The formats, with their myriad tongues, shouted of liberty;
And the blast of the desert cried aloud, with a voice so wild and free,
That he started in his sleep and smiled at their tempestuous glee.

He did not feel the driver's whip, nor the burning heat of day,
For death had illumined the land of sleep, and his lifeless body lay
A worn-out fetter that the soul had broken and thrown away.

—LONGFELLOW

Words

caravans, *companies of travelers.*
fetter, *chain.*
furious, *wild.*
glorious, *grand.*
illumined, *lighted.*
landscape, *scene.*
liberty, *freedom.*
martial, *warlike.*
matted, *tangled.*
scabbard, *sheath.*
stallion, *horse.*
tempestuous, *boisterous.*

Questions

Where was the slave lying? What had he once been? What did he dream? How did the dream end?

☆ ☆

他躺在没有收割的稻田旁，手里拿着镰刀；
胸膛赤裸着，蓬乱的头发埋在沙地里。
在梦境中飘忽的薄雾和阴影中，他再一次看到了自己的故土。

梦中那片宽广的土地上，威严的尼日尔河在奔淌；
地上的棕榈树下，他大步流星，宛若国王，
耳中是从山路上往下行驶的大篷车叮叮当当的声响。

他再一次看到了他黑色眸子的王后站在她的孩子中间；
他们抱住他的颈部，亲吻他的脸颊，拉住他的手！
睡梦中的人儿眼中流出了泪水，滚落到沙地上。

之后他突然愤怒地沿着尼日尔的河岸驰骋；
他的缰绳是鎏金的锁链，发出勇猛的铿锵声，
每腾跃一步，他都能感觉到青钢刀鞘连连撞击到他坐骑的腹部。

在他面前，如同一面旗帜飘扬，鲜血一样艳红，那是鲜艳的火烈鸟在翱翔；
从清晨到夜晚他都跟随着它们，驰骋在那

罗望子生长的草原，
直到他看见卡莱村的屋顶，看到奔腾浩瀚的海洋。

黑夜，他耳畔是雄狮的吼叫，土狼的嘶喊，
而那河边的骏马，当他踏过幽暗的溪流旁的芦苇丛时，
它纵身一跃，如同阵阵激越的鼓声，
击响了他梦中的胜利之音。

树林说着各自不同的语言，呐喊自由；
而滚滚沙漠，则狂野而不羁地大声怒吼，
他猛地从睡梦中惊醒，对于他们暴风骤雨般的欢乐微笑以对。

他感觉不到工头的鞭笞，也感觉不到烈日的烘烤，
因为死亡照亮了这片梦境中的国度，而他没有生命的身体躺着，
被破败的锁链束缚着，灵魂粉碎出窍！

——朗费罗

Lesson 45
THE SIEGE OF TORQUILSTONE (I)
第四十五课　围城陶其史东（一）

The noise within the castle, occasioned by the defensive preparations, which had been considerable for some time, now increased into tenfold bustle and clamour. The heavy yet hasty step of the men-at-arms traversed the battlements, or resounded on the narrow and winding passages and stairs which led to the various bartisans and points of defence. The voices of the knights were heard animating their followers, or directing means of defence, while their commands were often drowned in the clashing of armour, or the clamorous shouts of those whom they addressed.

Tremendous as these sounds were, and yet more terrible from the awful event which they presaged, there was a sublimity mixed with them which Rebecca's high-toned mind could feel even in that moment of terror. Her eye kindled, although the blood fled from her cheeks; and there was a strong mixture of fear with a thrilling sense of the sublime as she repeated, half whispering to herself, half speaking to her companion, the sacred text—"The quiver rattleth—the glittering spear and the shield—the noise of the captains and the shouting!"

But Ivanhoe was, like the war-horse of that sublime passage, glowing with impatience at his own inactivity, and with an ardent desire to mingle in the affray of which these sounds were the introduction. "If I could but drag myself," he said, " to yonder window, that I might see how this brave game is like to go;—if I had but bow to shoot a shaft, or battle-axe to strike were it but a single blow for our deliverance! It is in vain—it is in vain; I am alike nerveless and weaponless!"

"Fret not thyself, noble knight," answered Rebecca; "the sounds have ceased of a sudden—it may be they join not battle."

"Thou knowest naught of it," said Wilfred impatiently. "This dead pause only shows that the men are at their posts on the walls, and expecting an instant attack. What we have heard was but the distant muttering of the storm—it will burst anon in all its fury. Could I but reach yonder window!"

"Thou wilt but injure thyself by the attempt, noble knight," replied his attendant. Observing his extreme solicitude, she firmly added, "I myself will stand at the lattice, and describe to thee as I can what passes without."

"You must not—you shall not!" exclaimed Ivanhoe. "Each lattice, each aperture, will be soon a mark for the archers; some random shaft—"

"It shall be welcome," murmured Rebecca, as with firm pace she ascended two or three steps which led to the window of which they spoke.

"Rebecca! dear Rebecca!" exclaimed Ivanhoe, this is no maiden's pastime—do not expose thyself to wounds and death, and render me for ever miserable for having given occasion; at least cover thyself with yonder ancient buckler, and show as little of thy person at the lattice as may be."

Following with wonderful promptitude the directions of Ivanhoe, and availing herself of the protection of the large ancient shield, which she placed against the lower part of the window, Rebecca, with tolerable security to herself, could witness part of what was passing without the castle, and report to Ivanhoe the preparations which the assailants were making for the storm. Indeed the situation which she thus obtained was peculiarly favourable for this purpose; because, being placed on an angle of the main building, Rebecca could not only see what passed beyond the precincts of the castle, but could also command a view of the outwork likely to be the first object of the meditated assault.

It was an exterior fortification of no great height or strength, intended to protect the postern gate, through which Cedric had been recently dismissed by Front-de-Boeuf. The castle moat divided this species of barbicans from the rest of the fortress; so that, in case of its being taken, it was easy to cut off the communication with the main building by withdrawing the temporary bridge. In the outwork was a sally-port, corresponding to the postern of the castle; and the whole was surrounded by a strong palisade. Rebecca could observe, from the number of men placed for the defence of this post, that the besieged entertained apprehensions for its safety; and from the mustering of the assailants in a direction nearly opposite to the outwork, it seemed no less plain that it had been selected as a vulnerable point of attack.

These appearances she hastily communicated to Ivanhoe and added, "The skirts of the wood seem lined with archers, although only a few are advanced from its dark shadow."

"Under what banner?" asked Ivanhoe.

"Under no ensign of war which I can observe," answered Rebecca.

"A singular novelty," muttered the knight, "to advance to storm such a castle without pennon or banner displayed .—Seest thou who they be who act as leaders?"

"A knight clad in sable armour is the most conspicuous," said the Jewess. "He alone is armed from head to heel, and seems to assume the direction of all around him."

"What device does he bear on his shield" replied Ivanhoe.

"Something resembling a bar of iron and a padlock, painted blue on the black shield."

"A fetterlock and shacklebolt azure," said Ivanhoe. "I know not who may bear the device, but well I ween it might now be mine own. Canst thou not see the motto?"

"Scarce the device itself at this distance," replied Rebecca; "but when the sun glances fair upon his shield, it shows as I tell you."

"Seem there; no other leaders?" exclaimed the anxious inquirer.

"None of mark and distinction that I can behold from this station," said Rebecca;

"but, doubtless, the other side of the castle is also assailed. They appear even now preparing to advance......What a dreadful sight! Those who advance first bear huge shields, and defences made of plank; the others follow, bending their bows as they come on. They raise their bows!"......

Her description was here suddenly interrupted by the signal for assault, which was given by the blast of a shrill bugle, and at once answered by a flourish of the Norman trumpets from the battlements, which, mingled with the deep and hollow clang of the nakers (a species of kettledrum), retorted in notes of defiance the challenge of the enemy. The shouts of both parties augmented the fearful din, the assailants crying, "St. George for merry England!" and the Normans answering them with their battle-cries.

It was not, however, by clamour that the contest was to be decided, and the desperate efforts of the assailants were met by an equally vigorous defence on the part of the besieged. The archers, trained by their woodland pastimes to the most effective use of the long-bow, shot—to use the appropriate phrase of the time—so "wholly together," that no point at which a defender could show the least part of his person escaped their cloth-yard shafts.

By this heavy discharge, which continued as thick and sharp as hail, while, notwithstanding every arrow had its individual aim, they flew by scores together against each embrasure and opening in the parapet, as well as at every window where a defender either occasionally had post or might be suspected to be stationed—by this sustained discharge two or three of the garrison were slain, and several others wounded.

"And I must lie here like a bed-ridden monk!" exclaimed Ivanhoe, " while the game that gives me freedom or death is played out by the hands of others. Look from the window once again, kind maiden; but beware that you are not marked by the archers beneath. Look out once more, and tell me if they yet advance to the storm."

Words

animating, *encouraging.*
anxious, *eager.*
aperture *opening.*
apprehensions, *fears.*
appropriate, *proper.*
assailed, *attacked.*
augmented, *Increased.*
buckler, *shield.*
glamorous, *noisy.*
communication, *connection.*
conspicuous, *prominent.*
deliverance, *freedom.*
desperate, *stupendous.*
device, *emblem.*
distinction, *particularity.*
ensign, *standard.*
impatience, *fretfulness.*
instant, *immediate.*
interrupted, *broken off.*
meditated, *intended.*
novelty, new *custom.*
occasioned, *caused.*
peculiarly, *singularly.*
precincts, *boundaries.*

presaged, *foretold*.
promptitude, *readiness*.
random, *chance*.
resembling, *like*.
retorted, *answered*.
security, *safety*.
traversed, *crossed*.
tremendous, *terrific*.
vigorous, *energetic*.
vulnerable, *weak*.
solicitude, *anxiety*.
sublimity, *grandeur*.
suspected, *supposed*.
temporary, *provisional*.

Questions

Why was Ivanhoe unable to witness the assault? Who was tending him in prison? How was he made aware of what went on? What point was expected to be attacked first? What separated the barbican from the fortress? Who was the most conspicuous of the besiegers?

☆ ☆

城堡内时不时发出的为防守准备的噪声，响动很大地持续了一段时间，现在变成了较之前十倍的喧嚣和嘈杂了。携带武器的人踏着沉重而匆忙的脚步穿过战场，脚步声在狭窄而蜿蜒的通道和楼梯上回响，那些通道和楼梯通往不同的战区和防御点。能够听见骑士们鼓舞士兵的声音以及他们指挥防御作战的声音，而他们下达命令的声音经常淹没在盔甲的碰撞声或者那些人们的喧闹喊叫声中了。

这些声音惊天动地，然而在这些声音出现之前，有更加可怕的声音，那是同它们混杂在一起的一种崇高的声音，甚至吕蓓卡惊魂未定的心在那个可怕的一刻都能感觉到。她的眼睛闪亮，虽然鲜血从她脸颊上流了下来；当她在一边低声私语对着自己重复，一边和她同伴朗读着那神圣的文本的时候，她脸上有一种强烈的恐惧并混杂着一种崇高的战栗感：“箭袋响动——闪亮的矛戈和盾牌——上校们的呼喊和嚎叫声！”

但伊凡赫，就像那段神圣的篇章中的战马一样，虽然一动不动，却显得躁动不安，他有一种要加入那些声音产生的骚乱当中的强烈愿望。“如果我能自己起身，”他说道，“去那边的床边，我就能看到这勇敢的游戏是如何进行的；如果我能射出一支箭去，或者为我们的救赎而用战斧出击，劈上一下！但这是徒劳的——这是徒劳的；我内心脆弱，手无寸铁！”

“不要折磨你自己，高贵的骑士，”吕蓓卡回答道。突然那些声音都沉寂下来——可能是他们不再参与战争了。”

“您不知道，”威尔弗莱德急躁地说道，“这死寂的停顿紧紧表明人们已经兵临城下，期望给出快速攻击。我们能听到的仅仅是远处暴风雨的轰隆声——暴风雨将会以雷霆之势爆发。要是我能到达那边的窗户就好了！”

“你这样做只会伤害到自己，高贵的骑士，”他的随从回答道。在发现他极端的孤独之后，她坚定地补充道：“我自己会站在窗户上，向您描述我旁边发生的一切。”

“你不能这么做——你不准这样做！”伊凡赫喊道。“每一个窗户，每一个孔隙，都很快会成为弓箭手的目标，还有那些乱箭——”

“让它们来好了，”吕蓓卡喃喃道，她踏着坚毅的步伐走上两三个台阶，那台阶通到他们提到的那个窗户。

“吕蓓卡！亲爱的吕蓓卡！”伊凡赫喊道，“这不是姑娘们可以闹着玩的——不要把自己置于受伤和死亡的境地中，不要让我终生抱憾曾有过这样的疏忽；至少你用古代的圆盾来掩护自己，尽可能少地把自己暴露在窗户前。”

跟随着伊凡赫卓越而反应迅速的指挥，吕蓓卡用巨大的古代圆盾作掩护，她把圆盾倚在窗户下方，算是勉强能够保证自己的安全，她能够看到一点城堡外面正在发生的事情，然后向伊凡赫报告攻城者们在为攻击所做的准备。的确，她现在占据的位置非常有利于观测，因为在这样一个主楼的一角，吕蓓卡不仅能看到远处城堡周围的情况，而且能够俯瞰可能会成为酝酿已久的首个攻击对象的面貌。

那是外围的一处防御措施，不是很高，也不是很坚固，本来是用来保护后门的，通过后门锡德里克最先被先头部队击溃了。城堡的护城河把外堡同城堡的其他部分隔开，这样，万一城堡被占领，还能够通过收起这座临时吊桥，轻易地切断主楼同城堡的联系。城外是突围口，根据城堡后门而建，它整个都被坚固的栅栏包围着。吕蓓卡能够看到，从安排到防御这个据点的人的数目来看，被围困的城堡的安危甚为堪忧；而从在城外突围口相反方向聚集而来的攻城敌人动向，则能清楚看出这个据点已经被选定为攻击的薄弱点。

她马上和伊凡赫反映了这些事态，并补充道：“森林边缘地带似乎潜伏着弓箭手，虽然只有几个人从黑暗的阴影中走了出来。”

“他们挂的什么旗？”伊凡赫问道。

“据我观察，没有战旗，”吕蓓卡回答道。

“好新奇的一件事，”骑士喃喃自语道，“向这样的城堡发出进攻却没有悬挂任何的旗帜或战旗。你看看，他们是什么人，谁是他们的首领？”

“其中一个身穿黑貂盔甲的骑士最引人注目，”犹太女人说道，“只有他自己从头到脚全副武装，而且似乎在指挥周围的人。”

“他的盾牌上有什么标志吗？”伊凡赫说道。

“有个好像铁块和挂锁的东西，漆成蓝色，嵌在黑色的盾牌上。”

“是镣铐锁和螺栓形状的蔚蓝标识，”伊凡赫说道，“我不知道有谁会带有这样的标识，但我现在想，可能是自己人。你能不能看见上面的字？”

“这样的距离看不清楚上面的字，”吕蓓卡回答道，“但当太阳光清晰地照耀在他的盾牌上的时候，我会告诉您它上头的字。”

“看起来，是不是没有别的首领了？”焦急的询问者问道。

“从这个地方，我看不到什么标志或显著特征，”吕蓓卡说道，“毫无疑问，城堡的另一边也遭到攻击。他们现在甚至看起来准备进攻了……多么可怕的场景啊！那些首先进攻的人被巨大的盾牌挡在外面，承受着木条的攻击；其他人紧随其后，拉紧弓箭向前行进。他们举起弓箭了！”……

突然间，她的描述被攻击的信号打断了，信号是一声尖利的军号的巨大声响，随后就听到一大群从各处战场传来的诺曼军号嘶鸣的回声，而这军号声同低沉而空旷的光皮鼓（一种半球形鼓）的响声混在一起，用轻蔑的音符来反驳着敌人的挑衅。双方的嘶喊声加大了可怕的喧闹声响，进攻者喊道：“圣乔治为了快乐的英格兰！”而诺曼人则以他们的战场上的嚎叫声进行回击。

然而，双方的胜负并不是通过喧闹声的大小来决定的，而攻城者发动的背水一搏的努力都遭到了被围困一方同样猛烈的回击。那些通过在树林里消遣习得的技艺的弓箭手们以最高效的效率使用长弓，发射出——为了能使用符合那个时代的措辞——如此“箭无虚发”的箭发射到守城者那里，以至于守城者找不到能从那箭下死里逃生的人。

在这强大的攻势下，也就是如同冰雹一样致密而尖利的攻势下，尽管每一支箭都瞄准各自的目标，因为是同时射出，所以彼此之间稍有摩擦，向着矮护墙的开口处飞去，同时也飞往每一扇守城者要么偶尔站起身来的，要么可能是潜伏在旁边的窗子，在这样持久的攻势下，有两三个士兵牺牲了，其他不少人受了伤。

“我得像个卧床不起的僧侣一样躺在这儿不动！”伊凡赫喊道，“而我能否在战争中获得自由或者被杀掉，都掌握在别人手中。再次从窗子那里望一次吧，好心的少女，但要小心，你不要被底下的弓箭手瞄准。再一次向外张望一下，然后告诉我他们是不是发动进攻了。”

Lesson 46
THE SIEGE OF TORQUILSTONE (II)
第四十六课　围城陶其史东（二）

With patient courage, strengthened by the interval which she had employed in mental devotion, Rebecca again took post at the lattice; sheltering herself, however, so as not to be visible from beneath.

"What dost thou see, Rebecca?" again demanded the wounded knight.

"Nothing but the cloud of arrows flying so thick as to dazzle mine eyes, and to hide the bowmen who shoot them."

"That cannot endure," said Ivanhoe. "If they press not right on to carry the castle by pure force of arms, the archery may avail but little against stone walls and bulwarks. Look for the Knight of the Fetterlock, fair Rebecca, and see how he bears himself; for as the leader is, so will his followers be."

"I see him not," said Rebecca.

"Foul craven!" exclaimed Ivanhoe; "does he blench from the helm when the wind blows highest?"

"He blenches not! he blenches not!" said Rebecca; "I see him now. He leads a body of men close under the outer barrier of the barbican. They pull down the piles and palisades; they hew down the barriers with axes. His high black plume floats abroad over the throng, like a raven over the field of the slain. They have made a breach in the barriers—they rush in—they are thrust back! Front-de-Breuf heads the defenders; I see his gigantic form above the press. They throng again to the breach, and the pass is disputed hand to hand, and man to man. It is like the meeting of two fierce tides—the conflict of two oceans moved by adverse winds!"

She turned her head from the lattice, as if unable longer to endure a sight so terrible.

"Look forth again, Rebecca," said Ivanhoe, mistaking the cause of her retiring; "the archery must in some degree have ceased, since they are now fighting hand to hand. Look again; there is now less danger."

Rebecca again looked forth, and almost immediately exclaimed, "Ah! Front-de-Bceuf and the Black Knight fight hand to hand in the breach, amid the roar of their followers, who watch the progress of the strife—Heaven strike with the cause of the oppressed and of the captive!" She then uttered a loud shriek, and exclaimed, "He is down!—he is down!"

"Who is down?" cried Ivanhoe; "tell me which has fallen."

"The Black Knight," answered Rebecca, faintly; then instantly shouted, with joyful eagerness—"But no!—but no!—he is on foot again, and fights as if there were twenty men's strength in his single arm. His sword is broken!—he snatches an axe from a yeoman—he presses Front-de-Boeuf with blow on blow. The giant stoops and totters like an oak under the steel of the woodman—he falls!—he falls!"

"Front-de-Boeuf?" exclaimed Ivanhoe.

"Front-de-Bceuf!" answered the Jewess. "His men rush to the rescue, headed by the haughty Templar—their united force compels the champion to pause—they drag Front-de-Boeuf within the walls."

"The assailants have won the barriers, have they not?" said Ivanhoe.

"They have!—they have!" exclaimed Rebecca; "and they press the besieged hard upon the outer wall. Some plant ladders, some swarm like bees, and endeavour to ascend on the shoulders of each other. Down go stones, beams, and trunks of trees upon their heads; and as fast as they boar the wounded to the rear, fresh men supply their places in the assault. Great God hast thou given men thine own image that it should be thus cruelly defaced by the hands of their brethren?"

"Think not of that," said Ivanhoe; "this is no time for such thoughts. Who yield?—who push their way?"

"The ladders are thrown down," replied Rebecca, shuddering; "the soldiers lie grovelling under them like crushed reptiles—the besieged have the better."

"Ah!" exclaimed the knight; "do the false yeomen give way?"

"No!" exclaimed Rebecca; " they bear themselves right yeomanly. The Black Knight approaches the postern with his huge axe; the thundering blows which he deals,—you may hear them above all the din and shouts of the battle. Stones and beams are hailed down on the bold champion—he regards them no more than if they were thistle-down or feathers!"

"Ha!" said Ivanhoe, raising himself joyfully on his couch, "methought there was but one man in England that might do such a deed!"

"The postern gateshakes," continued Rebecca; "it crashes—it is splintered by his blows—they rush in—the outwork is won! O God!—they hurl the defenders from the battlements—they throw them into the moat. O men, if ye be indeed men, spare them that can resist no longer!"

"The bridge—the bridge which communicates with the castle—have they won that pass?" exclaimed Ivanhoe.

"No," replied Rebecca; "the Templar has destroyed the plank on which they crossed. A few of the defenders have escaped with him into the castle—the shrieks and cries which you hear tell the fate of the others. Alas! I see it is even more difficult to look upon victory than upon battle."

"What do they now, maiden?" said Ivanhoe; "look forth yet again—this is no time to faint at bloodshed."

"It is over for the time," answered Rebecca. "Out friends strengthen themselves within the outwork which they have mastered; and it affords them so good a shelter from the foemen's shot, that the garrison only bestow a few bolts on it from time to time, as if rather to disquiet than effectually to injure them."

"Our friends," said Wilfred, "will surely not abandon an enterprise so gloriously begun and so happily attained. Oh, no! I will put my faith in the good knight whose axe hath rent heart-of-oak and bars of iron. Singular," he again muttered to himself, "if there be two who can do a deed of such *deeringdo*! A fetter lock and shackle-bolt on a field-sable—what may that mean? Seest thou naught else, Rebecca, by which the Black Knight may be distinguished?"

"Nothing," said the Jewess; "all about him is black as the wing of the night raven. Nothing can I spy that can mark him further;—but having once seen him put forth his strength in battle, methinks I could know him again among a thousand warriors. He rushes to the fray as ii he were summoned to a banquet. There is more than mere strength,—there seems as if the whole soul and spirit of the champion were given to every blow which he deals upon his enemies. God forgive him the sin of bloodshed!—it is fearful, yet magnificent, to behold how the arm and heart of one man can triumph over hundreds."

—SIB WALTER SCOTT

Words

abandon, *give up*.
ad verse, *contrary*.
barrier, *fence*.
bestow, *deliver*.
bulwark, *ramparts*.
champion, *hero*.
defaced, *disfigured*.
destroyed, *broken down*.
difficult, *trying*.
disputed, *contested*.
disquiet, *disturb*.
distinguished, *recognized*.
eagerness, *alacrity*.
effectually, *seriously*.
endure, *last*.
enterprise, *adventure*.
gigantic, *giant-like*.
grovelling, *prostrate*.
joyfully, *gladly*.
magnificent, *splendid*.
mistaking, *misunderstanding*.
oppressed, *afflicted*.
sheltering, *protecting*.
shuddering, *trembling*.
splintered, *shattered*.
strengthen, *fortify*.
summoned, *called*.
yeomanly, *bravely*.

Questions

With whom did the Black Knight tight hand to hand In the breach made in the palisade? With what result? What advance did the besiegers then make? Who beat down the postern gate? What did Ivanhoe say when he hears of his valour? To whom did he refer? Why did not the besiegers reach the fortress? But what had they gained?

吕蓓卡凭借自己耐心的勇气和坚定的意志，再一次来到窗边，掩护好自己，不被下面的人瞧见。

“你看到什么了，吕蓓卡？”负伤的骑士再次问道。

“看不到什么，除了像密云一样的箭乌压压地飞来，简直晃得我的眼睛都睁不开了，我不得不避开那些弓箭手们。”

“要坚持不下去了，”伊凡赫说道，“如果他们单纯依靠兵器的力量来夺取城堡，这并不是上上策，因为箭虽能伤到城墙和堡垒，但损伤极小。找一找有没有骑马的骑士吧，高尚的吕蓓卡，看看他站在哪一边；因为只要统领坚持，他的手下便会追随。”

“我看不到他。”吕蓓卡说道。

“可恶！”伊凡赫喊道，“战事正紧急的时候，难道他悄悄躲起来了吗？”

“他没有！他没有！”吕蓓卡说道，“我现在看见他了，他带领的人马正好就在外堡的防御之外。他们推倒了桩尖和围栏；他们用斧头砍掉了障碍物。他那高耸的黑色羽毛在人群中飘扬着，就像一只屠杀场上的乌鸦一样。他们已经在防御线上打开了缺口——他们冲进来了——他们被击退了！是先头兵率领守城者们将他们击退的，我看到他明显高于别人的身影。他们再次涌向缺口，而守城的士兵则和他们一对一地对抗，进行肉搏。就好像两支劲旅相遇一样——冲突的两个海洋逆风而动！”

她把头从窗子那边转过来，好像不能忍受再看一眼这么可怕的场景似的。

“再向前看看，吕蓓卡，”伊凡赫说道，他不明白她从窗子那里转头的原因，“弓箭攻击在某种程度上已经停止了，因为他们现在正进行肉搏战。再看一次吧；现在已经不那么危险了。”

吕蓓卡再次向前望去，她几乎马上喊起来，“啊！先头兵和黑色骑士在他们各自追随者的喧嚣声中，在缺口处一对一地决斗，而追随者们则在一旁观看他们决斗的进展——老天啊，这是压迫者和被俘者之间的决斗啊！”然后她发出一声尖利的叫声，大喊道，“他倒下了！他倒下了！”

“谁倒下了？”伊凡赫喊道，“告诉我谁倒下了。”

“黑骑士倒下了。”吕蓓卡低声回答道，然后马上兴高采烈地喊道：“但不！但不！他再次站起来了，而且他每只胳膊都像积聚了20个人的力量一样。他的剑断了，他从一个仆人那里夺了一把斧头，一下一下地向着先头兵砸去。那个身形巨大的先头兵踉踉跄跄就像在伐木工的钢斧下的橡树一样，他倒下了！他倒下了！”

“先头兵吗？”伊凡赫喊道。

“是先头兵！”犹太女人回答道，“他的手下冲着去救他，他们由高大的坦普勒率领——他们统一的力量使得获胜的黑骑士停顿了下来——他们把先头兵拖进了城墙内。”

“攻城的人占领了防御线，是不是？”伊凡赫问道。

“是的！是的！”吕蓓卡叫道，“他们步步逼近被围困的城堡的外墙。有些开始搭建梯子，有些则像蜜蜂一样蜂拥而来，他们奋力地站在彼此的肩头。石块、横木和树干向下砸去，砸在他们头上；他们以最快的速度把受伤的人撤回后方，新的士兵不断加入到他们进攻的行列中去。伟大的上帝给了人类自己的形象，而这个形象竟然被自己兄弟的双手残忍地玷污了。”

“不要想这些，”伊凡赫说道，“现在不是想这些事情的时候。谁挥动了武器？谁把他们推开？”

“梯子掉下了，”吕蓓卡回答道，她战栗地说；“士兵们就像被压垮的爬行动物一样在下面爬行——守城者占了上风。”

“啊！”骑士叫道，“是不是敌人撤退了？”

“不是，”吕蓓卡喊道，“他们士气高昂。黑骑士手拿巨大的斧头向着后门靠近；他以雷霆之势劈砍，你可以从整个城堡上头听到他们的声音，和战场上的嘶嚎。石块和木块像冰雹一样砸向黑骑士。他对它们不屑一顾，好像它们就像蓟或羽毛一样！”

“哈！”伊凡赫说，他兴奋地从榻上站起来，“我以为英格兰只有一个人有能耐做到这些！”

“后门晃动了，”吕蓓卡继续说道，“后门撞垮了，被他的斧头劈裂了，他们涌了进来，攻城的人获胜了！哦，上帝啊，他们把守城者从战场上拽走，把他们扔进护城河。哦，天啊，如果他们还是人的话，让他们免于受这样的遭遇吧，他们坚持不下去了！”

“桥——连着城堡的桥，他们也过去了！”伊凡赫问道。

“没有，”吕蓓卡回答道，“坦普勒已经把他们桥的木板捣毁了。有一些守城者跟随着坦普勒逃入城堡，从那些尖叫声和哭喊声中，你就能知道其他人的命运了。唉！比起之前战场上的惨烈景象，我现在更不忍看眼前的胜利场景了。”

“他们现在在做什么，女孩？”伊凡赫说，“再次向前看吧，现在不是晕血的时候。”

“现在一切都结束了，”吕蓓卡回答道，“我们朋友的力量在外围积聚，而外围就是他们掌控的地方；那里给他们提供了一个绝佳的庇护所来防御敌人的炮火，这样士兵只需要时不时地发射炮火就好了，好像这么做与其说是为了伤害敌人，还不如说是为了让敌人自乱阵脚。”

“我们的朋友，”伊凡赫说道，“是绝对不会放弃这样一个有着光辉开始并如此快乐，达到现在的状况的城池的。哦，不！我愿意相信那了不起的骑士，他的斧头让他有了橡树之心和铁块一样的力量。就一个人，”他开始喃喃自语道，“如果有两个人能有这样的功绩，能做到这个盾牌上铸有锁链之锁和链带标志的人这样——那将意味着什么？你向那边看，吕蓓卡，有没有什么突出黑色骑士的？”

“没有，”犹太女人说道，“他全身都是黑色，就像黑夜中的乌鸦一样。我看不到什么能进一步显示出他的特征，不过我曾经看见过他有一次在战场上积聚全力拼杀，我觉得我能把他从一千个战士中辨别出来。他向前冲着，好像是被召唤着去参加一个宴会一样。不仅仅是他的力量，似乎是他的整个灵魂和斗志都击打在他的敌人身上。上帝原谅他杀戮的罪孽吧。这太可怕了，然而又很了不起，能看到一个人的力量和斗志胜过千百个人的力量和斗志。”

——沃尔特·司各特爵士

Lesson 47 PENNSYLVANIA

第四十七课 宾夕法尼亚

It was not till the year 1682 that the uneventful but quietly prosperous career of Pennsylvania began. The Stuarts were again upon the throne of England. They had learned nothing from their exile; and now, with the hour of their final rejection at hand, they were as wickedly despotic as ever.

William Penn was the son of an admirals who had gained victories for England, and enjoyed the favour of the royal family as well as of the eminent statesmen of his time. The highest honours of the State would in due time have come within the young man's reach, and the brightest hopes of his future were reasonably entertained by his. friends.

To the dismay of all, Penn became a Quaker. It was an unspeakable humiliation to the well-connected admiral. He turned his son out of doors, trusting that hunger would subdue his intractable spirit. After a time, however, he relented, and the youthful heretic was restored to favour. His father's influence could not shield him from persecution. Penn had suffered fine, and had lain in the Tower for his opinions.

Ere long the admiral died, and Penn succeeded to his possessions. It deeply grieved him that his brethren in the faith should endure such wrongs as were continually inflicted upon them. He could do nothing at home to mitigate the severities under which they groaned. Therefore he formed the great design of leading them forth to a new world. King Charles II. had owed to the admiral a sum of £16,000 of arrears, and this doubtful investment had descended from the father to the son. Penn offered to take payment in land, and the king readily bestowed upon him a vast region stretching westward from the river Delaware.

Here Penn proposed to found a State free and self-governing. It was his noble ambition "to show men as free and as happy as they can be." He proclaimed to the people already settled in his new dominions that they should be governed by laws of their own making. "Whatever sober and free men can reasonably desire," he told them, "for the security and improvement of their own happiness, I shall heartily comply with." He was as good as his word. The people appointed representatives, by whom a Constitution was framed. Penn confirmed the arrangements which the people chose to adopt.

Penn dealt justly and kindly with the Indians, and they requited him with a reverential love such as they evinced to no other Englishman. The neighbouring colonies waged bloody wars with the Indians who lived around them—now inflicting defeats which were almost ex terminating—now sustaining hideous massacres. Penn's

Indians were his children and most loyal subjects. No drop of Quaker blood was ever shed by Indian hand in the Pennsylvanian territory.

Soon after Penn's arrival, he invited the chief men of the Indian tribes to a conference. The meeting took place beneath a huge elm-tree. The pathless forest has long ago given way to the houses and streets of Philadelphia, but a marble monument points out to strangers the scene of this memorable interview. Penn, with a few companions, unarmed, and dressed according to the simple fashion of their sect, met the crowd of formidable savages.

They met, he assured them, as brothers "on the broad pathway of good faith and good will." No advantage was to be taken on either side. All was to be "openness and love." And Penn meant what he said. Strong in the power of truth and kindness, he bent the fierce savages of the Delaware to his will. They vowed "to live in love with William Penn and his children as long as the moon and the sun shall endure." They kept their vow. Long years after, they were known to recount to strangers, with deep emotion, the words which Penn had spoken to them under the old elm-tree.

The fame of Penn's settlement went abroad in all lands. Men wearied with the vulgar tyranny of kings heard gladly that the reign of freedom and tranquility was established on the banks of the Delaware. An asylum was opened "for the good and oppressed of every nation." Of these there was no lack. Pennsylvania had nothing to attract such "dissolute persons" as had laid the foundations of Virginia. But grave and God-fearing men from all the Protestant countries sought a home where they might live conscience taught them.

The new colony grew apace. Its natural advantages were tempting. Penn reported it as "a good land, with plentiful springs, the air clear and fresh, and an immense quantity of wild-fowl and fish;—what Abraham, Isaac, and Jacob would be well contented with." During the first year, twenty-two vessels arrived, bringing two thousand persons. In three years Philadelphia was a town of six hundred houses. It was half a century from its foundation before New York attained equal dimensions.

When Penn, after a few years, revisited England, he was able truly to relate that "things went on sweetly with Friends in Pennsylvania; that they increased finely in outward things and in wisdom."

—ROBERT MACKENZIE

Words

asylum, *refuge*.
conference, *interview*.
contented, *satisfied*.
despotic, *tyrannical*.
dimensions, *proportions*.
dominions, *territory*.
eminent, *distinguished*.
exterminating, *annihilating*.
formidable, *terrible*.
hideous, *dreadful*.

humiliation, *mortification*.
improvement, *advancement*.
inflicted, *imposed*.
intractable, *perverse*.
investment, *outlay*.
memorable, *celebrated*.
mitigate, *reduce*.
proclaimed, *announced*.
prosperous, *successful*.
reasonably, *warrantably*.
recount, *repeat*.
requited, *rewarded*.
tempting, *attractive*.
tranquility, *peace*.
uneventful, *uniform*.

Questions

In what year was Pennsylvania founded? Who was its founder? Why did his father quarrel with Penn? How did he get the land on which hit State was founded? What did he proclaim to the people already settled there? How did he deal with the Indians? Where did he hold an interview with their chiefs? What did the latter tow? For whom was Pennsylvania an asylum? How many vessels arrived during the first year? How many personas? How soon did Philadelphia become a town of six handled houses? How long was it before New York attained equal dimensions?

☆ ☆

直到1682年，宾夕法尼亚那平静却又不平静中蓬勃而起的命运开始了。斯图尔特家族再次登上英格兰的王座。他们没有从上次的放逐中吸取任何教训，现在将要到来的第二次驱逐，他们变得变本加厉的专制。

威廉·宾是一位为英格兰赢得了许多辉煌战绩的海军上将之子，他享有皇室的优厚待遇，同时在他生活的时代也很受人们尊崇。所有至高荣誉都会在恰当的时机落到这位年轻人的身上，因而，他的大好前程自然就成为朋友们的谈资。

但让所有人大跌眼镜的是，宾居然成了贵格会教徒。而这对身处上流社会的海军上将而言，是极大的耻辱。他把自己的儿子逐出家门，因为他认定饥饿能让宾打消自己的想法。然而过了一段时间，他态度变温和了，年轻的英雄再次获得了他父亲的青睐。父亲的权势也没能够保护他逃脱迫害。于是宾受到处罚，并被锁在塔楼里悔过自新。

海军上将死后不久，宾就继承了父亲的财产。让他非常难受的是，那些和他有同样信仰的人，还需要继续忍受降临到他们身上的不公正待遇。他在家什么也做不了，一点儿也帮不上那些在逆境中挣扎的人们。因此，他想到了一个带领他们建立一个新世界的计划。查理二世国王欠海军准将16 000英镑的债款，而这笔让人怀疑的投资已经从宾的父亲身上转移到他这里了。宾提出，国王可以用土地来偿还，国王欣然同意，给了他一块从德拉瓦尔河向西延伸的广大土地。

在这里，宾提出要建立一个自由自治的国家。他崇高的抱负就是为了给大家建立一个尽可能自由而幸福的国度。他对那些已经在他的新国度居住的人们说，他们应该根据自己制定的法律生活。“无论理性而自由的你们希望如何生活，以确保并提高自身的幸福，我都将全身心地服从你们的决定。”他言出必行。人民选定了代表，然后建立起宪法的框架。宾确保人们能依据宪法行事。

宾公允而友好地对待印第安人，而印第安人对他也报以尊敬和爱戴，这在其他英国人那里是没有的事情。邻近的殖民地则和生活在附近的印第安人进行血战——现在印第安人被打败，因而几乎就被灭族了——他们在实行惨无人道的大屠杀。宾对印第安人则像他的孩子一样，都对他很忠诚。在宾夕法尼亚州的土地上，没有一个贵格人死在印第安人手上。

在宾到达不久，他就邀请了印第安部落的酋长参加会议。会议在一棵巨大的榆树下举行。没有路径的森林在很久之前就已经成为宾夕法尼亚的房屋和街道所在了，而现在大理石的纪念碑则向陌生人表明了这场有纪念意义的见面的情景。宾和几个随从，没有带武器，根据印第安人的要求身上穿着最简单的服饰，会见了最让人敬畏的蛮夷人。

他向他们保证，他们的会面是像兄弟一样，是在高尚的信念和良好的意愿下进行的。没有一方能够占得先机。一切都是开诚布公和心存爱意的。然后宾言出必行。他非常坚信真理和友善，所以他能让特拉华州最凶残的蛮夷人归于他的麾下。他们起誓，“只要太阳还会升起，月亮依然出现在天空，就和威廉·宾以及他的孩子一起相亲相爱地生活在一起。”他们实现了自己的誓言。过了许多年，陌生人从他们感情深沉的转述中，知道了宾在那颗老榆树底下对他们说过的话。

宾州作为居住地的盛名在所有地区都传播开来。那些对混沌的暴君统治忍无可忍的人们，听说在特拉华河河畔建立起了这样一个自由而平静的国度，都欣喜不已。避难所建立起来了，收留所有国家的善良而受到压迫的人们。而这样的人有很多。宾夕法尼亚州对于那些已经在弗吉尼亚州生活的“放荡不羁的人”没什么吸引力，但对那些对上帝敬畏的清教徒而言，这是他们能够找到的乐土。他们能根据自己学到的道德准则生活。

新殖民地急速成长，它优越的自然环境非常有吸引力。宾把它描述成“一片乐土、温暖如春、空气清新，还有数量庞大的野禽和鱼；要是亚伯拉罕-伊塞克和约伯看见了，也会心满意足的。”第一年，有22艘船到来，带来了2 000个人。宾夕法尼亚在三年的时间里，就发展成有600余所房屋的城镇。而纽约直到建成半个世纪之后，才追上宾夕法尼亚的水平。

当若干年后，宾重访英格兰的时候，他终于可以真心地说那句话，“我们在宾夕法尼亚的朋友一切都好，他们不仅物资渐丰，而且智慧渐长。”

——罗伯特·麦肯锡

Lesson 48 THE SKY-LARK

第四十八课 云 雀

Bird of the wilderness,	荒野之地的鸟儿，
Blithesome and cumberless,	无忧无虑，不计其数，
Sweet be thy matin o'er moorland and lea!	你在沼泽和草地上空唱着甜美的晨歌！
Emblem of happiness,	快乐的象征，
Blest is thy dwelling-place—	幸福降临在你的栖身之所——
O to abide in the desert with thee!	哦，如果能和你一同在沙漠中生活！
Wild is thy lay and loud,	你自由自在地在天际大声歌唱，
Far in the downy cloud;	歌声在氤氲的云朵间传播；
Love gives it energy, love gave it birth.	爱给了它力量，爱让它萌生。
Where, on thy dewy wing,	何方，挥动你缀露的翅膀，
Where art thou journeying?	你要去往何方？
Thy lay is in heaven,	你的归宿在天堂，
thy love is on earth.	你的爱却给了大地。
O'er fell and fountain sheen,	你所飞过之处，瀑布如注，喷泉涌动，
O'er moor and mountain green,	你所拂过之地，沼泽青翠，山峦葱绿，
O'er the red streamer that heralds the day;	你飞越在预示一天到来的朝霞之上，
Over the cloudlet dim,	翱翔在云际，
Over the rainbow's rim,	飞翔在彩虹边缘，
Musical cherub, soar, singing, away!	音乐的天使，歌唱，歌唱，飞去！
Then, when the gloaming comes,	然后，当黄昏来临，
Low in the heather blooms	地上石楠萌发，
Sweet will thy welcome and bed of love be!	你还会用甜美和爱来欢唱！
Emblem of happiness,	快乐的象征，
Blest is thy dwelling-place—	幸福降临在你的栖身之所——

O to abide in the desert with thee! 哦，如果能和你一同在沙漠中生活！

—JAMES HOGG ——詹姆斯·豪格

Words

blithesome, *sprightly*.
cherub, *angel*.
cloudlet, *little cloud*.
cumberless, *free from care*.
emblem, *token*.
energy, *strength*.
fell, *rocky hill*.
gloaming, *twilight*.
heralds, *announces*.
journeying, *travelling*.
lea, *meadow*.
matin, *morning song*.
moorland, *marshy ground*.
sheen, *bright*.
wilderness, *desert*.

Lesson 49 WEATHERING CAPE HORN

第四十九课 横渡合恩角

The first introduction of my reader to the good ship Wales, whereby we pass to the Pacific, is as she is lying at the islands called Foul Weather Group, or the Falkland Islands. Cape Horn weather here begins, and the ship and her company put on their Cape Horn suit. This group of islands is so near the gate of the Pacific, though belonging to the Atlantic side, that an account of a ramble over the moss-covered rocks and penguin roosts of the uninhabited land off which we now lie is no inappropriate introduction to the island world we are just entering.

CAPS HORN

Selecting a small indentation or bight in the cliff as a landing-place, what was our surprise to find what we had thought a facing of white stone to be innumerable penguins, standing erect, in the rank and file of battle array, upon the declivity of the rocks, and occupying at least two acres, in dense columns, away back to the moss and grass!......

To those who have never seen a picture of the penguin, it would be impossible to convey an idea by description of this odd amphibious creature. It has the head, bill, and two web-feet of a bird, and stands erect on land, sometimes two and a half or three feet in height. Penguins have no wings, nor proper feathers, but a covering intermediate between fur and feather, and two fins or flippers like the seal. Their motion on land is by successive hops, in the most awkward manner conceivable. When going down a declivity, the centre of gravity is often thrown too far forward, and away they tumble, and scramble, and roll, till they get to the sea, in which they dive and swim with great celerity.

They are often seen singly, or two or three together, far out at sea. Their cry or bark is like the inarticulate human voice and when all is clear and calm, and no object can be seen around the horizon, it will sometimes startle and appal one, sounding as it does, from the surface of the ocean, like the cry of a man in distress. Near the penguin quarter of this island were thousands of ducks sit ting upon their eggs, which sailors and passengers destroyed with remorseless cruelty, shooting and knocking down the birds by hundreds in barbarous sport......

A month from the Falkland Islands, and this is the first day of smooth sea and warm sun we have enjoyed during all that time! Long and cold have been the days we have spent battling with the rough winds and mountainous seam off Cape Horn. Between south-west and south-east gales on the one side of the Cape, and north-west on the other, our course has been zig-zag and slow. Happily we have escaped injury, except the loss of a jib-boom, and our ship remains tight in spite of all the straining.

PENGUINS

We congratulate ourselves on having weathered the Cape in less time than it often takes, though it was more than is sometimes the fortune of the Cape Horn navigator. One of our seamen had twice before tried the passage, but without success; and after fifty-four days of most fatiguing warfare with contrary winds, his brig opened at the bow, and the crew were compelled to put about and run for Rio Janeiro, where the damaged vessel and cargo were sold for the benefit of the underwriters, and the voyage was abandoned.

A frigate was once fifty days off the Cape; yet it is not uncommon for vessels to make the Cape once, and after four or five weeks' sailing, to make it again. Hope is predominant that our tempestuous weather is over, and that a fortnight at the utmost will bring us to port. While the inmates of the cabin, like birds after a storm, are gunning themselves on deck, let those of my readers who purpose traversing with me the ISLAND WORLD take a leisurely survey of our first fortnight in the Pacific.

We little thought that doubling Cape Horn in summer would be so full of difficulty. Now we doubt whether it would be worse in mid-winter. It would seem as if the genii of storms ruled the realm. The ancients, had they known it, would have located the cave of AEolus at the end of Tierra del Fuego, in the side of one of those burning mountains. Auster and Eurus, and Boreas and Euroclydon, and all the intermediate winds of the thirty-two points of the compass, seem to have arranged their forces so as most advantageously to dispute every inch of the way with the bold navigator.

Four other ships, which we caught sight of at different times, were contesting the passage in like manner with ourselves, through cold, and sleet, and opposing seas. All of us, we argued, cannot be baffled, and our own chance is as good as any. Patience held out with most. At every abatement of the gale, and interval of sunshine, the sailors would cheerfully hang up their sea-soaked clothes, joke over the perils of the storm, and equip themselves anew for reefing and tacking.

It was truly pitiable, sometimes, at the hours for changing watches, to see the top of a sea break over the bow or quarter, and wet them all while pulling at the ropes; so that the watch just called must stay wet during their four hours of duty, and the watch going below must turn in dripping. A landsman could hardly help trembling for their safety, when they were ordered aloft to furl, while the ship was rolling so violently, and the wind blowing in such gusts of fury, that it seemed almost impossible for the topmasts and yards to sustain the shocks.

For several days we were reduced to close-reefed fore and main topsails, the ship meantime rolling so tremendously that a man incurred no small risk of broken bones who should attempt to cross the deck, or stand for a moment anywhere without being firmly braced, or having a rope to hold by.

We did not get sight of the redoubtable Cape, but were driven off to the parallel of 60°, near the South Shetlands, and afterwards made the land of Capo Desolation, on the western side of Tierra del Fuego. Discoverers have rightly named it, for we thought land had never seemed so bleak and desolate, snow lying between the hills and in the hollows of the mountains in this July of the South.

—Cheever

Words

abandoned, *given up.*
abatement, *mitigation.*
argued, *reasoned.*
arranged, *disposed.*
awkward, *clumsy.*
baffled, *defeated.*
celerity, *quickness.*
Company, *passengers.*
conceivable, *imaginable.*
congratulate, *compliment.*
creature, *animal.*
declivity, *slope.*
desolate, *lonely.*
doubling, *sailing round.*
fatiguing, *exhausting.*
horizon, *sky-line.*
inappropriate, *unsuitable.*
inarticulate, *indistinct.*
incurred, *ran.*
indentation, *bay.*
innumerable, *numberless.*
intermediate, *intervening.*
leisurely, *deliberate.*
located, *placed.*
mountainous, *billowy.*
predominant, *in the asscendant.*
ramie, *excursion.*
redoubtable, *formidable.*
reefing, *taking in sail.*
remorseless, *relentless.*
tempestuous, *stormy.*
tremendously, *frightsfully.*

Questions

What birds are found in large numbers on the Falkland Islands? On what element are penguins most at home? How do they move on land! What does their cry resemble?

首先要向我的读者介绍的是，我们要乘一艘很好的船——威尔士号去太平洋的时候，这艘船正停泊在坏天气群岛或者叫作福克兰群岛的附近。在这里，天气就变成合恩角的天气了。威尔士号和它的同行船只武装上了去合恩角的装备。这个群岛虽然实际上属于南极洲的边界，但它离太平洋的入口非常近，因此，如果我们对这片靠近苔藓覆盖的石岛和企鹅林立的无人之地漫谈一番的话，并不算是对我们即将要踏上的岛上世界的不合时宜的介绍。

我们选定了悬崖上一个小小的拗口或者海湾作为登陆的地点，让我们惊奇的是，原来我们认为的白色石头居然是由无数的企鹅组成的，它们直立站着，排列成战队，密密麻麻地在岩石坡上占据了整整两英亩的地方，向着有苔藓和草的地方走去……

对于那些从未见过企鹅的人来说，要想象出这种奇怪的两栖生物的模样可能有些困难。它长着鸟的头、喙和两个蹼爪，能直立站在陆地上，有时候会达到两英尺或三英尺的高度。企鹅没有翅膀，也没有什么像样的羽毛，但在皮和羽毛之间有一层过渡的覆盖物，还有两只像海豹一样的鳍或短翼。它们在陆地上是通过不断跳跃行动的，姿势极其滑稽可笑。当它们下坡的时候，会因为重心太过向前而东倒西歪，跌倒滚落，直到它们到达了大海，才能挥洒自如地潜水游泳。

企鹅经常单只出现，有时也会三三两两地在一起。它们的喊声或叫声很像咿咿呀呀的人在说话，当周围的一切清晰安静，地平线附近看不到什么东西的时候，企鹅有时就会发出一声惊叫或骇声，这声音从海面上传来，就像一个沮丧的人在哭泣一样。岛上企鹅圈附近是成千上万的正在孵蛋的鸭子，水手和过往的人会毫不留情地摧毁它们的蛋，成百上千地猎杀它们，把它们踢倒，非常野蛮……

我们在福克兰群岛待了一个月的时间，这么长时间里我们还是第一次看到平静的大海，享受到温暖的太阳！我们和合恩角上的劲风和山峦一样的罅隙斗争了好几个又长又寒冷的日子。合恩角的一边，西南风和东南风交替吹动，另一边则吹着西北风，因此我们的行程很辗转，很缓慢。不过值得庆幸的是，除了丢失了起重杆，我们没有受伤，船只虽然历经磨难也没有散架。

与通常渡过合恩角的时间相比，我们为自己花费的较短的时间而暗暗庆贺，虽然这更应该归功于领航员的好运气。我们其中有一位海员曾两次想渡过合恩角，都没有成功，在经历了和逆风斗争了疲惫不堪的45天的航程后，他小船的船头开裂，船上的人不得不跳水逃到里约热内卢去，在那里受损的船只和船上的货物出于对担保人利益的保护而被卖掉了，航程也就终止了。

护卫舰曾有50天的时间远离合恩角，然而船只做出渡合恩角的努力并不罕见，在航行了四五个星期之后，又会做再次的尝试。当恶劣的天气过去的时候，人人心中充满了希望，而在持续两个星期的希望满怀之后，我们就靠岸了。船舱的人就像经历了暴风雨的鸟儿一样都冲向甲板，这样和我一起横渡这岛屿所在的海域的读者们也能歇一歇，看看我们在太平洋上的首个14天是如何渡过的了。

我们几乎没想到夏天渡过合恩角居然有这么多艰险。现在我们怀疑，到深冬时节情况是不是会更糟，好像这片海域被暴风雪之神占领了似的。如果古人知道有风神存在的话，一定会把风神的洞府放置在火地岛的南端，也就是那些燃烧的火山的一端。东南西北风以及罗盘上所有32个方向的偏向风似乎都早已养精蓄锐完毕，猛烈地呼啸，方寸必争地争夺无畏的领航者。

其余的四条船，我们不时能看见它们的身影，就像我们的领航舰一样被风弄得左摇右晃，穿越这片寒冷、冰冻、恶劣的海域。我们认为，所有的人要打起精神来的话，我们还是有不错的机会能渡过去的。大家都很耐心，在每一次和大风的对弈中，在每一次出现间歇性阳光的时候，水手们都会亢奋地把自己被海水浸透的衣服高高举起，对暴风雨中遇到的危险情景一笑了之，然后再次整装待发，迎接暗礁和飓风的挑战。

我们有时候会觉得很心疼，因为在瞭望员换岗的时候，看到浪头涌得高过船头或船舷，把仍然拉着绳子的瞭望员打得浑身湿透；执勤的瞭望员在他们四小时的瞭望过程中身上一直都是湿的，而下面的瞭望员则浑身都滴着水。一个不出海的人，看到船猛烈颠簸，风狂吼呼啸，而且看着那桅杆顶部和杆子几乎撑不住了那样的颠簸晃动，他们则奉命爬上桅杆去收帆的时候，一定会情不自禁因为担忧他们的安全而瑟瑟发抖。

在几天的时间里，我们都将帆降到最低，减速行进，但船却剧烈地颠簸着，以至于如果有人想要穿过甲板，就会有折断骨头的不小风险，或者如果他不是被紧紧地固定在一个地方或手里抓着绳子的话，可能一刻都站不住脚。

我们看不见让我们再次疑惑的合恩角了，我们被冲向了南纬60度的位置，靠近南设德兰群岛，最后又到达了位于火地岛西海岸的荒芜角。发现荒芜角的人给它起的这个名字很贴切，因为我们从未见过如此荒芜而贫瘠的土地，在南半球的7月里，在山脉之中的山峦和峡谷之间，只有皑皑白雪。

——奇契尔

Lesson 50
ON THE DOWNFALL OF POLAND
第五十课　波兰的衰亡

Oh, sacred Truth! thy triumph ceased a while,
And Hope, thy sister, ceased with thee to smile,
When leagued Oppressions poured to Northern wars
Her whiskered pandoors and her fierce hussars;
Waved her dread standard to the breeze of morn
Pealed her loud drum, and twanged her trumpet born:
Tumultuous Horror brooded o'er her van;
Presaging wrath to Poland—and to man!

Warsaw's last champion from her height surveyed
Wide o'er the fields a waste of ruin laid:
"O Heaven!" he cried, "my bleeding country save!
Is there no hand on high to shield the brave?
Yet, though Destruction sweep those lovely plains,
Rise, fellow-men! our country yet remains!
By that dread name we wave the sword on high!
And swear for her to live!—with her to die!"

He said; and on the rampart-heights arrayed
His trusty warriors,—few, but undismayed;
Firm-paced, and slow, a horrid front they form,
Still as the breeze, but dreadful as the storm;
Low, murmuring sounds along their banners fly,
"Revenge or death!"—the watchword and reply;
Then pealed the notes, omnipotent to charm,
And the loud tocsins tolled their last alarm!

In vain, alas!—in vain, ye gallant few!
From rank to rank your volleyed thunder flew:—
Oh, bloodiest picture in the book of Time!
Sarmatia fell, unwept, without a crime!
Found not a generous friend, a pitying foe,
Strength in her arms, nor mercy in her woe!

Dropped from her nerveless grasp the shattered spear,
Closed her bright eye, and curbed her high career:
Hope, for a season, bade the world farewell,
And Freedom shrieked—as KOSCIUSKO fell!

The sun went down, nor ceased the carnage there,—
Tumultuous Murder shook the midnight air;
On Prague's proud arch the fires of Ruin glow,
His blood-dyed waters murmuring below;
The storm prevails—the rampart yields a way—
Bursts the wild cry of horror and dismay!
Hark as the smouldering piles with thunder fall,
A thousand shrieks for hopeless mercy call!
Earth shook! red meteors flashed along the sky!
And conscious Nature shuddered at the cry!

Departed spirits of the mighty dead!
Ye that at Marathons and Leuctra bled!
Friends of the world! restore your swords to man.
Fight in his sacred cause, and lead the van!
Yet for Sarmatia's tears of blood atone,
And make her arm puissant as your own!
Oh! once again to Freedom's cause return
The patriot TELL—the BRUCE of Bannockburn!

—THOMAS CAMPBELL

Words

Atone, *make amends.*
carnage, *slaughter.*
generous, *kind.*
hussars, *cavalry.*
leagued, *confederated.*
murmuring, *whispering.*
nerveless, *feeble.*
omnipotent, *all-powerful.*
patriot, *lover of country.*
pitying, *compassionate.*
puissant, *powerful.*
remains, *abides.*
restore, *return.*
shrieked, *screamed.*
shuddered, *trembled.*
smouldering, *slowly burning.*
surveyed, *observed.*
tumultuous, *turbulent.*
undismayed, *fearless.*

哦，神圣的真理啊！你的胜利停歇了一会儿，
你的妹妹希望和你一同停下来去微笑，
而那时联盟的压迫涌向北方战事，
她那些长着络腮胡的凶残士兵和凶猛的骑兵；
挥动着她可怕的旗帜，迎着清晨的微风，
击打着响亮的大鼓，吹动着号角，
狂躁的恐惧在她的车子上方沉思；
预示着那雷霆万钧会降临到波兰——和人民头上！

华沙最后的冠军从她的高地上，
俯瞰到的是一片断壁残垣：
“哦，天哪！”他哭泣道，“救救我流血的祖国吧！”
难道天上没有营救之手来为勇敢的人们保驾护航吗？
然而，虽然毁灭夷平了这些美丽的平原，
站起来吧，同胞们！我们的国家尚存！
对着那可怕的名字，我们在天堂挥动着刀剑！
并发下誓言，愿为国家而生！但求为国而死！

他说道；在堡垒高地上布列着
他那忠诚的战士，人数无几，但士气高昂，
步伐坚定，节奏稳重，他们形成一支可怕的先头兵，
依然如同微风一般无声无息，但却有暴风雨的骤然之势头；
他们的战旗在地空中飒飒然飘动着，
“复仇或死亡！”这是士兵们的口号和回答；
然后他们吹动号角，那无处不在的音符极富魅力，
那声响轰鸣的警钟则敲响了他们最后一次警报！

呜呼，一切都是徒劳！都是徒劳啊，少数的勇敢的人儿！
你们一排又一排地发射雷鸣一般的火炮，
哦，那是有史以来最血腥的场面！
萨尔玛提雅倒下了，没有哭泣，没有作下什么孽事！
找到的不是一位慷慨的朋友，而是一个有怜悯之心的敌人，
她的手臂尚有气力，没有同情她的遭遇！

从她麻木而紧握的手中掉落的是断裂的矛戟，
她闭上明亮的眼睛，停下了高贵的事业，
希望，在这个季节和世界道了永别，
而自由则尖叫起来——因为可修斯克倒下了！

太阳落下去了，大屠杀也没有停止，
狂暴的杀戮撼动了子夜的空气；
我们的布拉格骄傲的拱桥上闪动着毁灭之火的光芒，
他那血红色的水流在桥下喃喃不已；
暴风雨肆虐，堡垒向后退缩，
那因恐惧和沮丧而发出的狂野的呼号迸发了！
听那雷声一起如同硝烟滚滚消失，
千声请求怜悯的绝望呼唤在尖叫！
大地晃动！天际滑过红色的流星，
清醒的大自然则对着这喊叫声不寒而栗！

伟大的死者灵魂已逝！
他们在马拉松和留克特拉流血！
世界的朋友啊！重新把刀剑还给人类吧，
为他神圣的事业而战，引领战车！
然而为萨马提亚的血泪而赎罪，
使得她的臂膀像你的一样强大，
哦！再一次重返自由的事业吧，
爱国者说道——班诺克本的布鲁斯！

——托马斯·坎贝尔

Lesson 51 THE EYE (I)

第五十一课 眼 睛(一)

It is one of the prerogatives of man to have eyes. Many living creatures have none. The eyes which others—for example, the star-fishes—have, are mere sensitive points, dimly conscious of light and darkness, but not perceiving colours or distinguishing forms. The eyes of flies are hard horny lanterns, which cannot be moved about like our restless eyes, but look always in the same direction; whilst spiders, having many more things to look after than one pair of such lanterns will suffice for, have eyes stuck all over their heads, and can watch a trapped gnat with one eye, and peer through a hole in their webs with another.

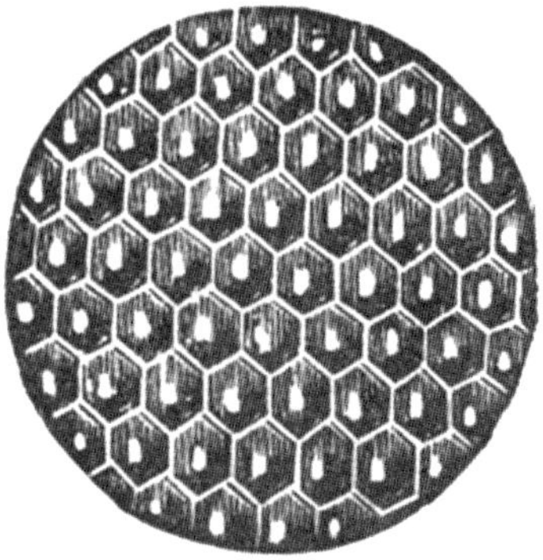

A FLY' S EYE (MAGNIFIED)

We are much better provided for than any of these creatures, although we have but two small orbs to see with. Think, first, how beautiful the human eye is, excelling in beauty the eye of every creature. The eyes of many of the lower animals are doubtless very beautiful. You must have admired the bold, fierce, bright eye of the eagle; the large, gentle, brown eye of the ox; the treacherous green eye of the cat, waxing and waning like the moon, as the sun shines upon it or deserts it; the pert eye of the sparrow; the sly eye of the fox; the peering little bead of black enamel in the mouse's head; the gem-like eye which redeems the toad from ugliness; and the intelligent, affectionate expression which looks out from the humanlike eye of the horse and the dog.

There are these and the eyes of many other animals full of beauty; there are none, indeed, which are not beautiful; but there is a glory which excellent in the eye of man. We realize this fully only when we gaze into the faces of those we love. It is their eyes we look at when we are near them, and recall when we are far away. The face is a blank without the eye; and the eye seems to concentrate every feature in itself. It is the eye that smiles, not the lips; it is the eye that listens, not the ear; it that frowns, not the brow; it that mourns, not the voice. Every sense and every faculty seems to flow towards it, and find expression through it—nay, to be lost in it: for all must at times have felt as if the eye of another were not his, but he; as if it had not merely a life, but also a personality of its own; as if it were not only a living thing, but also a thinking being.

But apart from this source of beauty, in which man's eye must excel that of all other creatures as much as his spirit excels in endowments theirs; it is in itself, even

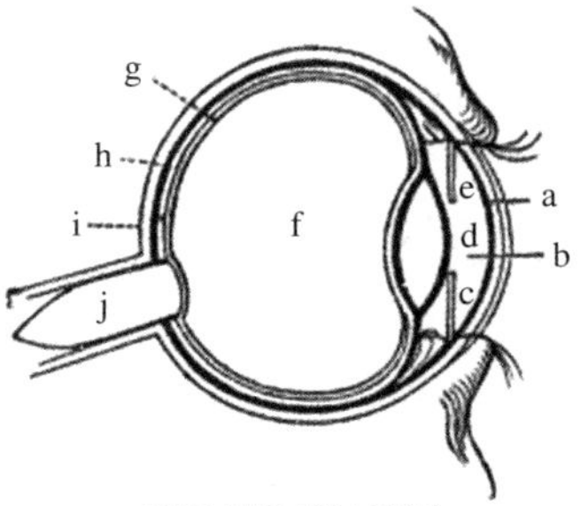

THE HUMAN EYE

a. Cornea.
b. Aqueous humour.
c. Iris.
d. Pupil.
e. Crystalline lens.
f. Vitreous humour.
g. Retina.
h. Choroid.
i. Sclerotic coat.
j. Optic nerve.

when life has departed from it, and the soul no longer looks through its window, a beautiful and a very wonderful thing. Its beauty is, perhaps, most apparent in the eye of an infant, which, if you please, we shall suppose not dead, but only asleep with its eyes wide open. How large and round they are; how pure and pearly the white is, with but one blue vein or two marbling its surface; how beautiful the rainbow ring, opening its mottled circle wide to the light!

How sharply defined the pupil, so black and yet so clear, that you look into it as into some deep, dark well, and see a little face look back at you, which you forget is your own, whilst you rejoice that the days are not yet come for those infant eyes when "they that look out of the windows shall be darkened"! And then, the soft pink curtains which we call eyelids, with their long silken fringes of eyelashes, and the unshed tears bathing and brightening all! How exquisite the whole! How precious in the sight of God must those little orbs be, when he has bestowed upon them so much beauty!

But apart altogether from that beauty which delights the painter, the human eye is a wondrous construction. Let us glance for a moment at its wonderfulness.

It is essentially a hollow globe, or small spherical chamber. There is no human chamber like it in form, unless we include among human dwelling-places the great hollow balls which surmount the Cathedral or Basilica Domes of St. Peter's and St. Paul's.

The eye is such a ball. The larger part of it, which we do not see when we look in each other's faces, forms the white of the eye, and consists of a strong, thick, tough membrane, something like parchment, but more pliable. This forms the outer wall, as it were, of the chamber of the eye. It may be compared to the cup of an acorn; or to a still more familiar thing, an egg-cup; or to a round wine-glass with a narrow stem. It is strong, so that it cannot easily be injured; thick, so that light cannot pass through it; and round, so that it can be moved about in every direction, and let us see much better on all sides with a single pair of eyes than the spider can with its host of them.

In the front of the eye is a clear, transparent window, exactly like the glass of a watch. If you look at a face sideways, you see it projecting with a bent surface like a bow window, and may observe its perfect transparency. The eyelids, which I formerly described as curtains, may perhaps be better compared to a pair of outside shutters for this window, which are put up when we go to sleep, and taken down when we awake.

But these shutters are not useless, or merely ornamental, during the day. Every moment they are rising and falling; or, as we say, winking. We do this so unceasingly, that we forget that we do it at all. But the object of this unconscious winking is a very important one. An outside window soon gets soiled and dirty; and a careful shopkeeper cleans his windows every morning. But our eye-windows must never have so much as a speck or spot upon them; and the winking eyelid is the busy apprentice who, not once a day, but all the day, keeps the living glass clean: so that, after all, we are nearly as well off as the fishes, who bathe their eyes and wash their faces every moment.

Behind this ever-clean window, and at some distance from it, hangs that beautiful circular curtain which forms the coloured part of the eye, and in the centre of which is the pupil. It is named the iris, which is only another name for the rainbow; for though we speak of eyes of simply blue, or gray, or black, because they have one prevailing tint, we cannot fail to notice that the ring of the eye is always variously mottled, and flecked or streaked with colours as the rainbow is.

This rainbow curtain, or iris, answers the same purpose which a Venetian blind does. Like it, it can be opened and closed at intervals; and like it, it never is closed altogether. But it is a much more wonderful piece of mechanism than a Venetian blind, and it opens and closes in a different way.

There is nothing this iris so much resembles, both in shape and in mode of action, as that much-loved flower, the daisy. The name signifies literally day's eye; the flower which opens its eye to the day, or when the day dawns. Shakespeare, who saw all analogies, referring to the similar action of the marigold, in the morning song in Cymbeline, tells how

"Winking Mary-buds begin.
To ope their golden eyes."

The daisy and the iris agree in this, that their opening and closing are determined by their exposure to light or darkness: but they differ in this, that the daisy opens widest when the sun is at its height, and shuts altogether when the sun goes down; whilst the iris opens widest in utter darkness, and closes so as to make the pupil a mere black point when sunshine falls upon it.

If we wish to observe this in our own eyes, we need only close them for a little while before a looking-glass, so that the dropped eyelids may shut out the day, when, like shy night-birds, the living circles will stretch outwards; and the pupil of the eye, like a hole which the sun is melting in the ice, will quickly widen into a deep clear pool. If now we open our eyes, we see the rainbow-rings contract as the light falls upon them, and the dark pupil rapidly narrow, like the well-head of a spring almost sealed by the frost.

But probably all have seen the movement I am describing in the eyes of a cat, where the change is more conspicuous than in our own eyes; and have noticed the broad iris spread out in twilight, till the look, usually so suspicious, softened into a mild glance; whilst when pussy is basking in the sun, as she dearly loves to do, she shows between her frequent windings only a narrow slit for a pupil, like the chink of a shutter, or the space between the spars of a lattice-blind.

The endless motions of this living curtain, which, like the nesting sea, is ever changing its aspect, have for their object the regulation of the flow of light into the eye. When the permitted number of rays have passed through the guarded entrance, or pupil, they traverse certain crystal-like structures, which are now to be described.

Words

affectionate, *loving.*
analogies, *comparisons.*
apparent, *manifest.*
apprentice, *assistant.*
bestowed, *expended.*
circular, *round.*
compared, *likened.*
concentrate, *bring to a focus.*
conspicuous, *obvious.*
determined, *regulated.*
endowments, *talents.*
essentially, *fundamentally.*
example, *instance.*
excelling, *surpassing.*
exposure, *subjection.*
exquisite, *perfect.*
faculty, *mental power.*
familiar, *well known.*
intelligent, *thoughtful.*
liberally, *radically.*
mechanism, *machinery.*
membrane, *tissue.*
mottled, *variegated.*
ornamental ,*decorative.*
permitted, *allowed.*
personality, *individuality.*
pliable, *easily bent.*
precious, *valuable.*
prevailing, *general.*
probably, *likely.*
projecting, *jutting out.*
provided, *furnished.*
rapidly, *quickly.*
regulation, *control.*
restless, *roving.*
sensitive, *susceptible.*
spherical, *globular.*
surmount, *rise above.*
suspicions, *distrustful.*
traverse, *cross.*
treacherous, *faithless.*
unceasingly, *constantly.*
unresting, *ever-moving.*

Questions

What is peculiar in the eyes of flies and spiders? Mention some of the lower animals that have beautiful eyes. Why does the eye of man excel all these? When is its beauty most apparent? What part of it looks like a deep, dark well? What do you always see in it? What is the shape of the whole organ as it exists in the head? Of what does the larger part of it consist? What is there in front of the eye? What purposes do the eyelids serve? What is the iris? What purpose does it serve? What flower does it much resemble? With what great difference? How may we observe the contracting of the iris? In what animal are its changes most perceptible?

眼睛是人类特享的一种恩惠。许多活着的生物都没有眼睛。而其他动物——例如，海星的眼睛，则仅仅是感光体，只能模糊地分清光和黑暗，但不能辨别出不同色彩或是各异的形状。苍蝇的眼睛是坚硬的角状灯笼，它们不能像我们的眼睛那样随意转动；而蜘蛛，要看清周围的事物则需要不止一双苍蝇这样的眼睛（见放大图），一双灯笼一样的眼睛不够，因而它们整个头部都遍布着眼睛，它们能用其中一只眼睛观测到被捉住的小昆虫，用另一只眼睛通过蛛网的孔眼来窥视。

我们的眼睛要比这些生物中任何一种的眼睛都高级，虽然我们只有两只小小的眼球可用。首先，想想看，人类的眼睛多么美丽啊，超越了所有生物的眼睛之美。许多低级动物的眼睛毫无疑问都是非常美丽的。你一定曾羡慕过鹰隼那无畏、锐利而明亮的眼睛；公牛那又大又温柔的褐色眼睛；猫那狡黠而碧绿的眼睛，那眼睛如同月亮一般或全或缺，如同太阳一样或光彩熠熠或低垂黯淡；还有麻雀那鲁莽的眼睛，狐狸那狡猾的眼睛，那如同黑色珐琅珠子一样的老鼠的眼睛，那使得蟾蜍不再显得丑陋不堪的宝石一样的眼睛，还有那像人类的眼睛一样的马和狗的眼睛，它们都含着聪慧和爱意。

这些动物美丽的眼睛以及许多动物眼睛都美丽动人。事实上，没有一种动物的眼睛是不美的，但人类的眼睛之美却超越了它们的全部。我们只有在凝望着自己深深爱着的人的脸的时候，才能完全体会到这一点。当我们靠近他们的时候，我们看到是他们的双眼，当不在他们身边的时候想到的也是他们的双眼。一张没有眼睛的脸是空洞的脸，而眼睛似乎把所有的五官特征都积聚到自身了。微笑的时候，是眼睛在微笑，而不是嘴唇；倾听的时候，是眼睛在倾听，而不是耳朵；皱眉的时候，是眼睛在惆怅，而不是眉毛；悲伤的时候，是眼睛在悲伤，而不是嗓音。每种感觉和能力似乎都向眼睛流去，并通过它表达情感，而不是在眼睛中迷失：对于所有人而言，有时候会感觉到自己的眼睛并不属于自己，而就是他自己；好像眼睛不仅仅是有生命的，而且还有人格；好像它不仅仅是一个有生命的东西，还是一个能思考的个体。

除了人类眼睛中的美超越了所有其他的生物，就像人类的精神境界超越其他生物一样。就眼睛自身而言，甚至当生命已逝，灵魂不再透过它的窗口向外张望的时候，眼睛也是非常美丽而神奇的。可能眼睛之美，最明显是在婴儿的眼中，如果你愿意的话，我们假设不是死亡的婴儿而只是睡觉时双目睁开的婴儿的眼睛。它们多么大多么圆啊，那眼多么纯净就像珍珠一般，有一条或两条蓝色的静脉如同大理石虎纹一样布在上头，彩虹圈多美啊，将它斑驳的圆圈张大向光！

瞳孔的构造多么精准，那么黑的颜色，却那么清澈，以至于你向里看的时候就像在向一口又深又黑的井望去一样，会看见有一张小小的面孔在向你回瞧着，而你都忘了那其实就是自己，于是你窃喜着那些婴儿的眼睛“向窗外望去却是黑暗一片”的日子没有来临！而那时，我们叫作眼睑的柔软的粉红色帘子，连同长长的如丝绸流苏一般的眼睫毛以及喷涌而出的泪水会冲掉一切，让一切都明亮起来！这一切多么美好啊！在上帝眼中，这些小小的圆球是多么珍贵啊，而他在它们身上赋予了如此之多的美啊！

但除了能让画家愉悦的美之外，人类的眼睛是一个神奇的构造。我们不妨来看一下它的神奇之处。

本质上，它是一个空空的球体，或者是个小的球状腔体。没有人的腔体会和它的形态相像，除非我们把人类的居所中那些超越了圣彼得和圣保罗大教堂或大教堂穹顶的伟大的球形空心建筑算在内。

眼睛是这样一个球体。其中较大的部分，当我们看着彼此脸庞的时候是看不到它的，而这一部分就是眼白，并形成了一个很强壮，厚密而结实的薄膜，有点像羊皮纸，但柔然性更佳。这个部分实际上形成了眼睛腔室的外墙。它就像橡子的外壳，或者像一个我们更加熟悉的鸡蛋壳，或者像一个圆形的矮脚葡萄酒杯。它很强韧，以至于它不会轻易受伤；它很厚密，以至于光不能穿透；它是圆形的，这样它就能向各个方向转动，而我们用一双眼睛看见的东西比蜘蛛用多双眼睛看见的要多。

眼睛前面是清晰而透明的窗户，和玻璃表盖如出一辙。如果你看着旁边的一张脸的话，就会看见眼睛像拱形窗一样发生折射，表面会有弧度，你还可能观察到它绝佳的透明性。而眼睑，也就是我之前描述成帘子的部位，对它更好的比喻可能是窗户外面的百叶窗，当我们要睡觉的时候就把它拉下，当我们醒来的时候就把它拉起。

但在白天，这些百叶窗并非一无是处，或仅仅起装饰作用。每时每刻它们都会做升降移动，或者就像我们所说的那样，眨眼。我们不断地眨着眼，以至于我们都彻底忽视了眨眼这个动作。但这种无意识的眨眼的目的，是非常重要的。外面的窗户会很快变得干涩，变脏，一个认真仔细的店员每天早晨都会擦拭自己的窗户。但我们眼睛的窗户却从来都是一尘不染，而眨动的眼睑则是一位忙碌的学徒，它不是每天仅仅一次而是一整天都保持这有生命的玻璃的整洁。因此，说到底我们在这点上和鱼类几乎无异，鱼类给自己的眼睛洗澡并每时每刻都清洗自己的眼睛。

在这扇永远清洁的窗户后面，隔着它有点距离的地方，悬挂着美丽的环形的帘子，它构成了我们眼睛中有颜色的部分，而中间是瞳孔。它名为虹膜，也就是彩虹的另外一个名字；因为，尽管我们简单地把眼睛的颜色叫作蓝色、灰色或黑色，鉴于它们有一种主要色调，所以我们不能观察到眼睛当中的圆环颜色总是在斑驳不停，点缀着或流露出彩虹一样的色彩。

这个彩虹帘子或者虹膜，它起到的功能就像威尼斯软百叶窗一样。和后者一样，它能在不同的间隔或开或闭，而且就和后者一样，它从来都不会闭合在一起。但它是比威尼斯软百叶窗神奇得多的一个机械装置，而且能以不同的方式或开或闭。

从形态和工作方式上来说，没有什么东西是和这个虹膜极其相像的，就像没有什么让人挚爱不已的花朵是和雏菊非常相像的一样。这个名字本身就解释出白天眼睛的样子；而花朵则是白天张开其花瓣，或者有的是在迟暮时分开放。莎士比亚，他看见过所有类比性的东西，把眼睛的这种机制和万寿菊的生长活动做了类比，在《辛白林》的清晨之歌中解释了它们是如何相像的：

玛丽骨朵眨着眼睛，
展露出它们金色的眼眸。

雏菊和虹膜在这一点上是一样的，因为它们的或开或闭都是由它们是暴露在光线之下还是在黑暗之中决定的，但在这一点上它们也不一样，因为雏菊在日上竿头的时候紧紧闭合；而在黑夜沉沉的时候则开放得最盛，而瞳孔当被太阳光照耀的时候，则收缩得紧成一个黑点。

如果我们希望能在自己眼中观察到这点的话，我们只需要闭上一会儿眼睛，面对着一面镜子即可，这样垂下的眼睑就可以将白天关闭在外了，和腼腆的夜晚的鸟儿一样，而那有生命的眼球则会向外扩展；至于眼睛的瞳孔，则像太阳照耀在雪上融化出的洞一样，会很快地变宽成一个又深又清晰的池子。如果现在我们睁开眼睛的话，我们就能看见彩虹圈在光线落到它身上的时候会收缩，而黑色的瞳孔则剧烈收紧，就像一口泉眼几乎被霜冻封住一样。

但很可能我描述的这些所有的变化，在一只猫的眼睛中也会有所体现，而比起我们的眼睛，猫的眼睛中的这些变化要更加明显；很可能你们曾经见过在傍晚时分，猫的宽延的虹膜会舒展开来，看起来好像在质疑什么的表情，直到柔化成温和的一瞥；而当猫咪在阳光下沐浴的时候，这正是它喜欢的事情，它会在自己频繁眨动的眼睛中间仅仅留一条小缝露出瞳孔来，就像百叶窗上的缝隙一样，或者就像窗棂中间的空隙一样。

这个有生命帘子无尽的开合，就像无限涌动的大海无时无刻不改变着自己的形态一样，根据映入眼帘的对象的不同而调整着进入的光线。当相当数量的光线进入到这守卫的入口，或者瞳孔时，它们穿过了有点像水晶一样的结构，也就是接下来我们要描述的这个结构。

Lesson 52 THE EYE (II)

第五十二课 眼 睛(二)

Behind the iris is a lens, as opticians call it, or magnifying-glass. We are most familiar with this portion of the eye as it occurs in fishes, looking in the recently-caught creature like a small ball of glass, and changing into what resembles a ball of chalk, when the fish is boiled. This lens is enclosed in a transparent covering, which is so united at its edges to the walls of the eye that it stretches like a piece of crystal between them; and in front of it, filling the space dividing the lens from the watch-glass-like window, is a clear, transparent liquid, like water, in which the iris floats.

Further: the lens is set like the jewel-stone of a ring, in what looks, when seen detached, like a larger sphere of crystal; but which in reality is a translucent liquid contained in an equally translucent membrane: so that the greater part of the eye is occupied with fluid; and the chamber, after all, which it most resembles is that of a diving-bell full of water.

Lastly: all the back part of the eye has spread over its inside surface, first a thin white membrane, resembling cambric or tissue paper, and behind that a dark curtains so that it resembles a room with black cloth hung next to the wall, and a white muslin curtain spread over the cloth. The latter curtain, or retina, seen alone, is like a flower-cup, such as that of a white lily; and, like it, ends in a stem, which anatomists name the optic nerve. The stem, in its turn, after passing through the black curtain, is planted in the brain, and is in living connection with it.

Altogether, then, our eye is a chamber shaped like a globe, having one large window, provided with shutters outside, and with a self-adjusting blind within. For the rest, it is filled with a glassy liquid, and has two wall papers, or curtains, one white and the other black.

How small this eye-chamber is we all know; but it is large enough. A single tent sufficed to lodge Napoleon and Nelson guided the fleets of England from one little cabin. And so it is with the eye: it is set apart for the reception of one guest, whose name is Light, but also Legion; and as the privileged entrant counsels, the great arms and limbs of the body are set in motion.

Within our eyes, at every instant, a picture of the outer world is painted by the pencil of the Sun, on the white curtain at the back of the eye; and when it has impressed us for a moment, the black curtain absorbs and blots out the picture, and the Sun paints a new one, which in its turn is blotted out; and so the process goes on all the day long.

What a strange thing this is! We speak of seeing things held before our eyes, as if the things themselves pressed in upon us, and thrust themselves into the presence of our spirits. But it is not so. You no more, any one of you, see my face at this moment, than you ever saw your own. You have looked at times into a mirror, and seen a something, beautiful or otherwise, which you have regarded as your face: yet it was but the reflection from a piece of glass you saw; and whether the glass dealt fairly with you or not you cannot tell; but this is certain, your own face you have never beheld.

And as little do you see mine. Some hundred portraits of me, no two the same, are at this moment hanging, one on the back wall of each of your eye-chambers. It is these portraits you see, not me. And I see none of you, but only certain likenesses, two for each of you, a right-eye portrait and a left-eye portrait, both very hasty and withal inaccurate sketches. And so it is with the whole visible world. It is far off from us when it seems nearest. Darkness abolishes it altogether. The mid-day sun but interprets it; and we know it not in the original, but only in translation.

Face to face we shall never meet this visible world, or gaze eye to eye upon it. We know only its picture, and cannot tell whether that is faithful or not; but it cannot be altogether faithless, and we must accept it, as we do the transmitted portraits of relatives we have never seen, or the sculptured heads of men who died ages before us. On those we gaze, not distrusting them, yet not altogether confiding in them; and we must treat the outward world in the same way.

What a strange interest thus attaches to that little darkened chamber of the eye! Into it the sun and the stars, the earth and the ocean, the glory and the terror of the universe, enter upon the wings of light, and demand audience of the soul. And from its mysterious abiding-place the soul comes forth, and in twilight they commune together. No one but HE who made them can gaze upon the unveiled majesty of created things. We could not look upon them and live; and therefore it is that here we see all things "through [or rather in] a glass darkly," and are permitted only to gaze upon their shadows in one small, dimly-lighted chamber......

The eye so triumphs over space, that it traverses in a moment the boundless ocean which stretches beyond our atmosphere, and takes home to itself stars which are millions of miles away; and so far is it from being fatigued by its flight, that, as the wise king said, "It is not satisfied with seeing." Our only physical conception of limitless Infinity is derived from the longing of the eye to see further than the furthest star.

And its empire over time is scarcely less bounded. The future it cannot pierce; but our eyes are never lifted to the midnight heavens without being visited by light which left the stars from which it comes untold centuries ago; and Buns which had burned out, aeous before Adam was created, are shown to us as the blazing orbs which they were in those immeasurably distant ages, by beams which have survived their source through all that time.

How far we can thus glance backwards along a ray of light, and literally gaze into the deepest recesses of time, we do not know; and as little can we tell how many ages will elapse after our sun's torch is quenched, before he shall be numbered among lost stars by dwellers in the sun most distant from us; yet assuredly it is through the eye that we acquire our most vivid conception of what Eternity, in the sense of unbeginning and unending time, may mean.

—GEORGE WILSON

Words

absorbs, *rocks in.*
acquire, *obtain.*
assuredly, *certainly.*
atmosphere, *air-ocean.*
audience, *hearing.*
commune, *convene.*
conception, *notion.*
connection, *communication.*
crystal, *fine glass.*
detached, *separated.*
distrusting, *doubting.*
immeasurably, *incalculably.*
impressed, *engaged.*
inaccurate, *incorrect.*
interprets, *translates.*
likenesses, *portraits.*
magnifying, *enlarging.*
mysterious, *hidden.*
occupied, *filled.*
privileged, *favoured.*
quenched, *extinguished.*
reception, *admission.*
regarded, *considered.*
resembles, *looks like.*
sculptured, *carved.*
survived, *outlived.*
transmitted, *handed down.*

Questions

What is behind the iris? In what is the lens set? What has the back part of the eye spread over it? What is the curtain called? What connects this with the brain? What is going on every instant within our eyes? What becomes of that picture when we look at a new object? Does one person actually see another when he turns his eyes towards him? What then does he see? What, in like manner, do we know of the world? How does the eye triumph over space? What does Solomon say of it? How does it triumph over time? Of what mystery does it afford us our most vivid conception?

☆ ☆

虹膜之后是眼科专家们称之为晶状体，或者叫作放大镜的部分。这是我们最熟悉的眼睛的部分，因为我们经常会看到鱼的晶状体，刚刚被抓的这生物的晶状体就像一个小小的玻璃球一样，而当鱼被煮熟了，它就会变成有点像白垩球一样的东西。晶状体被一层透明的覆盖物包裹着，而这层物质的边缘和眼壁紧紧连在一起，以至于它舒展的时候就像眼壁之间的水晶层一样；晶状体前面的空间把晶状体和玻璃表盖一样的窗户隔开的物质，是一种清澈而透明的液体，就像水一样，而虹膜就在其上漂动。

另外，晶状体就像镶嵌在戒指上的宝石，看起来好像是分离开来的，就像一个稍大一些的水晶球；但实际上却是一个半透明的，里面装有包裹在一层同样半透明薄膜里的液体物质。因此眼睛主要都是由液体组成的；而眼室，说到底非常像一个里头装满水的潜水钟。

最后，眼睛后面所有的部分都铺展在眼睛内部的表面，首先是一层薄薄的海瑟薄膜，很像细纱布或纸巾，之后是一层黑色的帘子，很像一个黑布悬挂在墙壁的房间上，并且还有一块白色的穆斯林帘子铺展在黑布上。后面的帘子，或者说视网膜，如果单独观察的话，很像一个花杯，比如白色百合花的花杯；而和它一样，末端呈茎状的物体，被解剖学家们称为视神经。这些茎状神经在穿过黑色的帘子之后，根植于大脑中，并和大脑实时相连。

总体而言，我们的眼睛是一个形状像球体的内室，它有一扇大窗子，外面有百叶窗，里面还有一个自动调节的百叶窗。至于剩下的部分，则充满了玻璃一样的液体，有两张眼壁或帘子，一个白色，另一个黑色。

我们所了解的眼睛个头多小啊，但它又足够大。这么一个帐篷足以容纳得下拿破仑，并且能装得下那从小木屋走出来的尼尔森指挥的英格兰舰队。这就是眼睛的神奇之处了。它和映入眼帘的对象分开，而这个对象名字叫作光，同时也是军团；而当有特权的新进入者决策的时候，那身体的强壮的手臂和肢体都在眼中动来动去。

每时每刻，我们眼睛里都是一幅外面世界的画，它是由太阳的铅笔绘就的，绘就在眼睛后面的白色幕布上；当这景象映入眼帘的时候，黑色的帘子就吸收并涂改掉这幅画，而太阳又会绘出一幅新画来，然后接着再次涂抹掉。这个过程在一整天的时间里循环往复。

这是多么奇妙啊！我们说到看见眼前的东西的时候，好像这东西自己印到了我们眼睛里似的，然后在我们脑海中凸显。其实并非如此。你和任何人，在此刻都不能看到我的脸，就像你看不到自己的脸一样。你多次向镜子里看，看到一个东西，可能漂亮可能不漂亮，你把它当作是自己的脸，然而它只是在你看到的那片玻璃上的倒影罢了；而至于那玻璃是不是清楚地照出了你的模样，这就不得而知了，但有一点是肯定的，即你永远都看不到自己的脸。

而你也几乎看不到我的脸。那几百幅我的肖像中，没有两幅是相同的，它们此时同时挂起来，每一幅都出现在你眼睛中的后壁上。你看到的只是这些肖像罢了，不是我本人。我也看不到你，而只是看到和你相像的样子罢了，是两个你的样子，一个是右眼中的肖像，一个是左眼中的肖像，两个肖像都是一挥而就、准确性不佳的素描。同样的道理也适用于整个可见世界。这世界看起来离着我们非常近的，其实离我们十万八千里。黑暗把一切统统吞噬，而正午的太阳却给了解读它的机会；但我们知道的并不是它的原始面貌，而是经过转化了的面貌。

我们永远没法面对面地看到这个可见世界，或者四目相对地看着它。我们只是知道它的画像，却不能判断这画像是否忠实于它的本来面目。但这么多的画像，不可能都是失真的，我们必须得接受，就像我们接受了那些送来的从未见过的亲戚的肖像一样，或者在我们出生前就死去多年的人的半身像雕塑一样。对于我们看到的这些东西，我们并不是完全不信任它们，也不是完全相信它们；对于外部世界，我们也必须以同样方式对待。

这样一个小小的晦暗的眼睛的内室中有太阳和星星、大地和海洋、人世间的荣耀和恐惧，还居然藏进了光之羽翼，并且把看着它们的人的灵魂都收了进去，这是多么奇妙而有趣的事啊。从它神秘的栖身地中，灵魂逸出，在迟暮时分它们合二为一。除了造出眼睛的上帝之外，没有人能盯着世间万物那毫无遮掩的威严。我们没有办法看到它们而同时活着，因此，我们看到所有的一切都是“通过一个暗色的玻璃体”，而人只有在通过一个又小又光线羸弱的小室才能凝望它们的影子……

因此眼睛能战胜空间，因为它能在一瞬间就穿越那延伸到天际的无垠的海洋，把远在几百万英里之外的群星收入眼帘。而到现在为止，它并没有为极目眺望而感到疲惫，正如那睿智的君王所说的那样，“它并不满足于只用眼睛见识。”我们对无限无穷的唯一的形态认识，就是眼睛所期望的能看到比最遥远的星星还要远的地方。

而眼睛对于时间的驾驭几乎没有什么限制。它不能穿透未来，但当我们抬起双眼眺望子夜的天穹的时候，眼睛里射入的光线是从很久远的世纪之前来到的；而那是在火开始燃烧之前，在亚当还未被创造出来的久远时代，而这些难以测算的久远时代能展现在我们面前，是通过那炽热的眼球中穿越了所有时代而来到现在的光线实现的。

究竟我们瞥见一束光线，能向之前的时代眺望多远呢？这一点我们不得而知，但从字面上来说，我们所凝望的乃是时间最深邃的隐蔽处；就像我们对于距离太阳的火炬熄灭还有多少岁月，几乎一无所知一样，通过距离我们最遥远的恒星上的栖息者来计算它还有多少时日成为陨落的群星中的一员，也同样不可知晓。然而，可以确定的一点是，通过眼睛我们获得了对永恒最丰富的认识，可能它存在于尚未开始和没有结束的时间之间。

——乔治·威尔森

Lesson 53 THE SHIPWRECK

第五十三课 大海难

There were two fathers in this ghastly crew,
And with them their two sons, of whom the one
Was more robust and hardy to the view;
But he died early: and when he was gone,
His nearest messmate told his sire, who threw
One glance on him, and said, "Heaven's will be done
I can do nothing;" and he saw him thrown
Into the deep, without a tear or groan.

The other father had a weaklier child,
Of a soft cheek, and aspect delicate;
But the boy bore up long, and with a mild
And patient spirit held aloof his fate:
Little he said, and now and then he smiled,
As if to win a part from off the weight
He saw increasing on his father's heart,
With the deep, deadly thought, that they must part.

And o'er him bent his sire, and never rained
His eyes from off his face, bat wiped the foam
From his pale lips, and ever on him gazed:
And when the wished-for shower at length was come,
And the boy's eyes, with the dull film half glazed,
Brightened, and for a moment seemed to roam,
He squeezed from out a rag some drops of rain
Into his dying child's mouth;—but in vain!

The boy expired. The father held the clay,
And looked upon it long; and when at last
Death left no doubt, and the dead burden lay
Stiff on his heart, and pulse and hope were past,
He watched it wistfully until away
'Twas borne by the rude wave wherein 'twas cast;
Then he himself sank down all dumb and shivering,

And gave no sign of life, save his limbs quivering.

'Twas twilight, and the sunless day went down
Over the waste of waters; like a veil,
Which, if withdrawn, would but disclose the frown
Of one whose hate is masked but to assail.
Thus to their hopeless eyes the night was shown,
And grimly darkled o'er their faces pale,
And the dim, desolate deep: twelve days bad Fear
Been their familiar, and now Death was here.

Then rose from sea to sky the wild farewell—
Then shrieked the timid, and stood still the brave—
Then some leaped overboard with dreadful yell,
As eager to anticipate their grave;
And the sea yawned around her, like a hell,
And down she sucked with her the whirling wave,
Like one who grapples with his enemy,
And strives to strangle him before he die.

And first one universal shriek there rushed,
Louder than the loud ocean—like a crash
Of echoing thunder; and then all was hushed,
Save the wild wind and the remorseless dash
Of billows; but at intervals there gushed,
Accompanied by a convulsive splash,

A solitary shriek, the bubbling cry
  Of some strong swimmer in his agony.

—LORD BYRON (1788–1824)

Words

anticipate, *foretaste*.
aspect, *appearance*.
assail, *attack*.
brightened, *gleamed*.
convulsive, *spasmodic*.
darkled, *grew dark*.
delicate, *weakly*.
disclose, *reveal*.
expired, *died*.
ghastly, *hideous*.
patient, *enduring*.
remorseless, *pitiless*.
robust, *strong*.
shivering, *trembling*.
squeezed, *pressed*.
universal, *general*.
wistfully, *longingly*.
yawned, *gaped*.

☆ ☆

在这个可怕的船队中有两位父亲，
他们各自有两个儿子跟随，其中
一个看起来稍壮实点儿，更鲁莽一点；
可惜他英年早逝；而他死后，
他最亲近的兄弟告诉自己的父亲，那父亲
向他瞥去一眼，他说道："上天已经注定，
我无能为力；"然后他看见父亲陷入
沉思中，既没有流泪也没有叹息。

另外一位父亲有一个稍羸弱些的孩子，
长着柔软的脸颊，清秀的面庞；
但这孩子在出生后不久，他那温和
而耐心的性格就注定了他的命运。
他说话很少，时不时还微笑一下，
好像是为了能让心理负担减轻一些，
他看见父亲的心变得越来越沉重，
他们必须要放弃那深沉而致命的想法。

他父亲弯腰向自己，目光从未
从他的脸上移开过，擦掉
他苍白的嘴唇上沾着的浮沫，当木然的眼睛快要凝固，
闪亮，有一会儿似乎要翻过去的时候，
他从一块碎布中挤出几滴雨水，
到他快要死了的孩子的口中；但一切徒然！

这孩子死了。父亲抱住他的身体，
久久地凝望着；当最后
死神离去，死去的人的身体重重
压在他的心头，脉搏和死亡都消逝，
他怀念地看着它直到消失不见。
“那是由粗犷的波浪所生，那是你的归处”；
然后他麻木而战栗地陷坐在地上，
除了肢体在发抖之外，看不出一点儿活着的迹象。

那是暮色时分，没有阳光的一天，
广漠的水域；就像一层面纱一样，
它，如果撤掉的话，就会暴露出那紧缩着眉头
的是一个心中掩饰恨意，但恨意仍在的人。
这样，黑夜出现在他们绝望的眼中，
冷酷地把他们苍白的面孔变暗，
一切都笼罩在阴郁、荒芜的深沉之中，整整十二天的时间，
可怕的恐惧都和他们相伴，而现在死神来临了。

然后从大海向上天狂野告别，
腼腆的人尖叫，勇敢的人站立，
还有人发出可怕的叫喊跳出甲板，
好像迫不及待地期待他们的坟墓似的；
大海在它周围打着呵欠，就像地狱一般，
它吮住下面卷动的波涛，
就像一个和敌人格斗的人一样，

在死之前和他搏斗到底。

那里猛地出现划破天际的尖叫声，
声音盖过轰鸣的大海，就像一声
回响的雷声，接着一切沉寂，
只剩下那狂躁的风和冷酷的
巨浪翻腾；还有那惊厥的浪花飞溅，
但时不时地，会迸发出，
一声孤独的尖叫，冒泡的哭喊，
那是某个游泳健将在濒死之际的呐喊。

——拜伦爵士（1788-1824）

Lesson 54 THE FIVE GREAT OCEANS

第五十四课 五大洋

THE ARCTIC OCEAN

A circle round the Earth at 1600 miles from the North Pole as a centre is called the *Arctic Circle*. All the land and sea within the Arctic Circle form what we call the *North Frigid Zone*. Very little is known regarding the region round the North Pole: but recent discoveries lead us to believe that it is surrounded by a vast open sea, forming the Arctic Ocean.

The lands around the Arctic Ocean form a vast treeless waste, exposed to the cold winds which sweep over it from the Polar Seas.

This dreary, desolate region, covers a space larger than the whole of Europe. It extends over the north of Europe, Asia, and America, round the globe.

In the Polar regions, the sun is one half of the year above and the other half below the horizon. There is but one long, dreary night, of six months. But the gloom of the Arctic winter is often relieved by the magnificent spectacle of the Aurora Borealis, which shines in these northern regions with a brilliancy unknown in other lands. (Sec page 114.)

In Europe, the north of Norway is within the Arctic Circle; but here the climate is milder, owing to the influence of the warmer waters of the Atlantic, and of the prevailing south-westerly winds. Lapland and a small part of Russia are also within the Arctic Circle.

The north of Asia lies within the Arctic Circle. Here three mighty rivers—the *Obi*, the *Lena*, and the *Yenisei*—pour their waters into the Arctic Ocean. These rivers flow through the dreary plains of Northern Siberia; and, as they come from a warmer to a colder region, they become more and more clogged with ice as they approach the ocean. At last they overflow their banks, and convert the regions around them into a vast dismal swamp, making the northern part of Asia a barren, desolate waste. There is no pasture for cattle, as in Norway and Sweden, and even the hardiest grains cannot grow on these desolate shores.

The Arctic portion of North America is covered with snow and ice nearly the whole year. Here another of the giant rivers of the Earth (the *Mackenzie River*) discharges its waters into the Arctic Ocean, after a course of above 1200 miles.

In winter an awful silence reigns over this vast region, as scarcely a living thing remains when the Arctic summer has ended; but in spring enormous flights of birds come from the south, and find abundance of food in the lakes and rivers, and along the fish-teeming coasts. In some places these flocks of birds are so numerous, that they may be said to darken the sun when they fly, and to hide the sea when they swim. But as soon as the first frosts announce the approach of winter, nearly all the animals of these dreary regions hasten to the south.

The ARCTIC OCEAN forms a circle bounded by the northern coasts of Europe, Asia, and America. It is studded with islands, most of which lie along the northern coasts of America, and form a vast archipelago to the west of Greenland.

For more than three centuries, successive generations of brave and skilful navigators tried to discover a north-west passage to the Pacific through this region of ice. Of all the great enterprises of the world, not one has been so enthusiastically taken up, so ably and resolutely prosecuted, and so tardily accomplished. When at length the secret was won, the victor perished in the horn of triumph. The North-West Passage was discovered by Sir John Franklin in 1847, but not until the autumn of 1859 did the news reach England. Franklin died in 1847, and his gallant company of one hundred and thirty-four tried men all perished in those dark Arctic regions.

The largest island in the Arctic Ocean is *Greenland.* Its northern shores have never been reached, but enough of its coasts has been explored to show that it is an island about ten times the size of the British Isles. The west coast of Greenland is mountainous, and its valleys are blocked up with *glaciers*.

A *glacier* is a river of ice. Though it does not seem to move, yet it slowly forces its way down the valley till it reaches the sea. As it pushes its way further and further into the sea, the projecting part begins to float, and the rising tide breaks it off in huge fragments. These glacier fragments are the icebergs which are found floating in the Arctic seas. They are of various sizes. Some of them measure only a few yards; others are miles in circumference, and sometimes hundreds of feet high. One of the sublimest spectacles that can be seen in the Arctic seas is a fleet of icebergs lighted up with the glories of the setting sun.

Many of these icebergs, formed from the glaciers of Greenland, float far away into the Atlantic, where they slowly melt as they drift towards the south.

Besides the islands on the northern coasts of America, there are, further east, *Spitsbergen* and *Nova Zembla*. *Spitsbergen* lies midway between Norway and the North Pole. *Nova Zembla* forms a group of islands lying to the north of Russia.

It is an interesting fact that at some parts the water of the Arctic Ocean is warmer below than at the surface. This is owing to the circumstance that the warmer waters of the Atlantic are constantly flowing in, while cold currents are constantly flowing out. At the surface intense cold prevails, while the water remains warm below. The severity of the Polar winter is thus unfelt beneath, and myriads of creatures find a secure retreat against the frost which reigns supreme above. They form the food of the whale, the walrus, and other creatures which abound in the Northern seas.

Though ice covers the sea for many hundreds of miles, there are always immense spaces of open water, where the whale, the walrus, and the seal are found. Without such open spaces these creatures could not exist; for they are warm-blooded animals, and constantly require to come to the surface to breathe.

THE ANTARCTIC OCEAN

A circle of 1600 miles round the South Pole as a centre is called the *Antarctic Circle*. All the land and sea within this circle form the *South Frigid Zone*. It is in extent exactly similar to the North Frigid Zone. The ocean within it is called the ANTARCTIC OCEAN. Very little is known about this part of the Earth's surface. It is a region of ice and snow.

Land has been discovered at various points, but it is even more desolate and barren than the lands of the Arctic regions. No human being, no land quadruped has been found; no plant of any kind, not even a moss or a lichen, has been seen—all is one dreary, uninhabitable waste. But though neither quadruped nor plant has been found on the land, there are innumerable *sea-birds*; and the *whale*, the *dolphin*, and the *seal* abound in the sea.

Many suppose that there is a vast continent in this part of the globe, occupying a large portion of the Antarctic regions. Sir James Ross, in an expedition to the Antarctic Ocean, made some interesting discoveries. He saw a lofty mountain-chain stretching away to the South Polo. It contained several volcanoes, one of which he called Mount Erebus, from the name of his ship. This mountain, towering up in a region of snow and ice, rose to a height of 12,000 feet above the level of the seas It was seen only from a great distance, as an impenetrable barrier of ice prevented the ship from approaching the land.

THE ATLANTIC OCEAN

The Atlantic Ocean lies between the Old World and the New. On the one side are *Europe* and *Africa*, on the other side *North* and *South America*. The waters of the Atlantic extend from Greenland to the southern extremities of Africa and South America, a distance of about 9000 miles. At the north it unites with the Arctic Ocean, between Norway and Greenland. *At the south* it joins the Pacific, the Indian, and the Antarctic Oceans.

The Atlantic Ocean exceeds all the other oceans in the number of its seas and gulfs.

PRINCIPAL SEAS—EAST

The principal Seas on the eastern side of the Atlantic are the North Sea, the Baltic Sea, and the Mediterranean with the Black Sea.

1. The North Sea is about 600 miles from north to south. Its width varies from 100 to 400 miles.

From the mouth of the Thames to Holland it is 100 miles wade, and in this part it is comparatively shallow, and beset with sand-banks. Near the mouth of the Thames are the celebrated *Goodwin Sands*, a dangerous range of shoals. Floating lights have long been fixed here, and some lofty beacons erected; still this part of the coast is the scene of numerous shipwrecks every year. It has been more fatal to life and property than any other part of the coast of England. Sand-banks also stretch all along the coast of Holland

Between Scotland and Denmark the North Sea is 400 miles wide. *Between Scotland and Norway*, it is 300 miles wide, and of great depth near Norway.

The parts of the Continent opposite Britain are:—

NORWAY (*South part*)....................opposite.......................North of SCOTLAND.
DENMARK......................................opposite.......................SCOTLAND.
HOLLAND }
BELGIUM }....................................opposite.......................ENGLAND.
FRANCE..opposite.......................South of ENGLAND.

The principal Seaports on the Continent, opposite Britain, are:—

Rotterdam.....................................opposite.......................London.
Amsterdam...................................opposite.......................Yarmouth.
Hamburg.................................... .opposite.......................Hull.
Bergen (Norway)..........................*opposite.......................Shetland Isles.*

In ancient times the North Sea was the scene of the exploits of the Scandinavian sea-kings, and across its waters sailed the various tribes that successively landed on the coasts of Britain and settled in the British Islands after the breaking up of the Roman Empire.

The Angles came from the south of Denmark, and the Saxons from Northern Germany, about A. D. 449. The Danes came from Denmark, A. D. 787.

These tribes gradually drove back the original Celtic inhabitants; whose descendants, however, to this day occupy a considerable portion of the British Islands. The inhabitants of Wales, Ireland, and the Highlands of Scotland, are chiefly of Celtic origin.

At a later period (A. D. 1066), the *Normans*—who, like the Danes, were originally Norsemen—came from the north of France across the *English Channel*, and conquered England.

2. The Baltic Sea lies between the Baltic States and Sweden. It is a long narrow sea with several branches. Its northern half is called the *Gulf of Bothnia*. Its other branches are the *Gulf of Finland* and the *Gulf of Riga*.

It is mostly very shallow, and subject to severe storms. A number of large rivers flow into it, and make its waters comparatively fresh.

The Countries on the shores of the Baltic are ESTHONIA, LATVIA, LITHUANIA, EAST PRUSSIA, DENMARK, and SWEDEN. A large trade is carried on between Britain and these countries. The chief articles received from them are *timber, wheat, flax, hemp, tallow, and hides*.

The entrance to the Baltic from the North Sea is called the *Skager Rack* on the one side of Jutland, and the *Cattegat* on the other.

3. The Mediterranean Sea is, in some respects, the most interesting sea in the world From the earliest days to the present time its shores have been the scene of many of the greatest events of history. It was the great highway of commerce among the civilized nations of ancient times. On its coasts lay ancient GREECE, ITALY, CARTHAGE, EGYPT, PIHENICIA, and PALESTINE.

The entrance to the Mediterranean from the Atlantic is by the *Strait of Gibraltar*, 11 miles wide at its narrowest part. From this point to the coast of Syria the Mediterranean is nearly 2500 miles long.

The heat on the shores of the Mediterranean is very great, and the evaporation over so large a surface of water land-locked on all sides is enormous. Though many large rivers flow into it, they are not sufficient to make up the loss caused by evaporation. A strong current therefore is found to flow into it from the Atlantic at the Strait of Gibraltar, which is only partially reduced by an under-current outwards at the same place. The Mediterranean is almost a "tideless sea;" but at some places the tide rises several inches.

The principal branches of the Mediterranean are, the *Adriatic Sea*, between Italy and Yugo-Slavia; and the *Archipelago or AEgean Sea*, between Greece and Asia Minor. The eastern portion of the Mediterranean is called the *Levant*. On the south of France is the Gulf of Lions, and at the north of Italy is the Gulf of Genoa.

The principal Rivers which flow into the Mediterranean are the *Rhone*, from France; the *Po*, from Italy; and the *Nile*, from Egypt. Besides these, the waters of the *Danube*, the *Dnieper*, and the *Don*, come to the Mediterranean from the Black Sea by the Sea of Marmora.

The Countries on the shores of the Mediterranean are:—

SPAIN.....................................*opposite*...................................MOROCCO.
FRANCE.................................*opposite*...................................ALGERIA.
ITALY.....................................*opposite*...................................TUNIS.
GREECE.................................*opposite*...................................TRIPOLI.
ASIA MINOR.........................*opposite*...................................EGYPT.

Syria and Palestine form the *eastern shore of the Mediterranean*.

The principal Islands in the Mediterranean are, *Corsica*, *Sardinia*, *Sicily*, *Crete*, and *Cyprus*. Besides these, there is a large number of smaller islands; one of which, *Malta*, to the south of Sicily, belongs to Britain. It lies about midway between Gibraltar and Egypt.

The Mediterranean is separated from the Red Sea by the narrow *Isthmus of Suez*. A great ship-canal across the isthmus was, after ten years of labour, constructed by a French engineer named Lesseps. The waters of the two seas are united, and ships can now sail from Europe to India, China, Australia, &c., without having to pass either round the south of Africa or round Cape Horn.

4. The Black Sea lies between Russia and Turkey-in-Asia. It is connected with the Mediterranean by the Bosphorus, Sea of Marmora, and the Dardanelles.

On the north of the Black Sea is the *Crimea*, a peninsula of Russia, famous for the siege of *Sebastopol*, the chief city of the Crimea, and, at the time of the war (1854-56), a great naval station of Russia.

At the entrance to the Black Sea is the *Golden Horn*, on which stands the city of Constantinople, the former capital of the Turkish Empire.

Three great Rivers flow into the Black Sea: the *Danube*, through Austria, Hungary, Yugo-Slavia, Romania, and Bulgaria; and the *Dnieper* and the *Don* (into the Sea of Azov), from Russia.

The Countries on the shores of the Black Sea are:—RUSSIA, ROMANIA, BULGARIA, TURKEY, ARMENIA, and GEORGIA.

Large quantities of wheat, grown in the *south of Russia* and in the *countries of the Danube*, are exported by way of the Black Sea.

PRINCIPAL SEAS—WEST.

The principal Seas on the western side of the Atlantic are Davis *Strait* and *Baffin Bay*, *Hudson Bay*, *Gulf of St. Lawrence*, *Gulf of Mexico*, and the *Caribbean Sea*.

1. Davis Strait and Baffin Bay (named after two great English navigators, who discovered them) lie between Greenland and the northern coasts of America. Through these seas nearly all the expeditions to the Polar regions have passed. *Baffin* Bay is now the principal resort of the whaling ships in the North Atlantic.

By *Smith Sound*, to the north of Baffin Bay, many explorers attempted to reach the Pole. Here, in 1854, were discovered the shores of an open sea free of ice, stretching away to the Pole. By the same route the Pole itself was reached by Commander Peary in 1909.

2. Hudson Bay is named from the celebrated Henry Hudson, one of the boldest and

most successful of the early English navigators. It was discovered by him in 1609, and hero that brave seaman perished. A mutiny broke out among his men, and he and several sick sailors were put into a small boat and cast adrift. The carpenter of the ship alone refused to remain with the mutineers, nobly preferring to share the fate of his brave commander. The boat was never seen or heard of more.

Hudson Bay forms a vast inland sea in the very heart of British America. Its shores are covered with ice for the greater part of the year. The principal entrance from the Atlantic is called Hudson Strait.

3. The Gulf Of St. Lawrence is one of the most important inlets on the coasts of America. It is a wide bay lying between the Island of Newfoundland and Canada. At its western extremity is the mouth o! the *River St. Lawrence*, the great river of Canada. During summer, steamers and vessels of all kinds are constantly crossing the gulf on their way to Quebec and Montreal, or from the St. Lawrence to Europe. In winter, owing to the ice, the navigation is closed. The fisheries in the Gulf of St. Lawrence are very extensive and valuable.

On the coast, to the south of the Gulf of St. Lawrence, is a long narrow inlet called the *Bay of Fundy*, remarkable for the great height and violence of its tides. These usually rise to a height of sixty or seventy feet, and are caused by the vast flow of water from the Atlantic forcing itself into so narrow a channel.

4. The Gulf of Mexico lies between Mexico and the United States. It is an immense sea, nearly 1000 miles long, and about 500 miles broad.

Into it flow the waters of the *Mississippi*, and many other smaller rivers from the United States and Mexico.

It gives its name to the celebrated Gulf Stream, the most remarkable ocean current in the world.

The *Gulf Stream* is a current of warm water which flows into the Atlantic from the Gulf of Mexico. Its water, heated under the burning sun of the tropics, first flows from the Atlantic along the northern shores of South America. It then enters the Caribbean Sea, and from it flows into the Gulf of Mexico: hence the name Gulf Stream. There, hemmed in, it sweeps round the gulf, and rushes with great force through the Strait of Florida back into the Atlantic.

Its course is so well marked, that at some places the bow of a ship may be in the Gulf Stream and the rest of the vessel out of it. This has been shown by noticing the difference between the temperature of the water at the bow of the vessel and that amidships. From Florida it flows northward to Newfoundland, gradually increasing in width. From Newfoundland its waters spread over the surface of the colder waters of the Atlantic, one branch turning southward, and another eastward. The southern branch encircles a great space called the *Sargasso Sea*, which is covered for hundreds of miles with thick sea-weed. The eastern branch slowly crosses the Atlantic to the shores of Europe.

The air over the Gulf Stream is loaded with warmth and moisture, and makes the climate of the British Islands much milder than it otherwise would be. On the opposite side of the Atlantic lies the coast of Labrador—a region of ice and snow. Were it not for the warm waters of the Gulf Stream, the harbours and rivers of Britain would be blocked up with ice for a great part of the year. The influence of the Gulf Stream is felt as far as the north of Norway, where it mingles with the icy waters of the Polar Seas.

5. The *Caribbean Sea* lies south of the Gulf of Mexico, and is connected with it. The two together form the great opening between North and South America.

BED OF THE ATLANTIC

The depths of the Atlantic have been sounded and surveyed by the British and the American navies, so that we now know, to a considerable extent, the character of its bed or bottom. Its greatest depth is about six miles. One result of these measurements is the certain knowledge we now possess that the bed of the ocean, like the land, is diversified by mountains and valleys, hills, table-lands, and plains.

Between Newfoundland and Ireland the bed of the Atlantic is remarkably level. Here, in the still waters at the bottom, lie the *Atlantic Cables*, by which messages are ever: flashing across the ocean from one hemisphere to another.

The Atlantic contains few Islands compared with the vast number in the Pacific Ocean. The principal islands in the Atlantic are Iceland (see page 100), the British Islands, Newfoundland, and the West India Islands.

The Countries which lie opposite each other on the two sides of the Atlantic are:—

GREEN LAND................................*opposite*........................NORWAY.
LABRADOR..................................*opposite*........................BRITAIN.
CANADA.......................................*opposite*........................FRANCE.
UNITED STATES, &c......................*opposite*..........................Spain and North of AFRICA.
WEST INDIES and MEXICO........*opposite*........................SAHARA.
BRAZIL &c....................................*opposite*..........................Middle and South of AFRICA

South America extends further south than Africa, so that there is no land opposite Patagonia on its eastern side.

The Atlantic is the great highway of commerce. On its waters are constantly sailing the ships of all the maritime nations of the Earth.

To the coasts of Greenland and Labrador ships sail to hunt the *whale* and the *seal*; and they return laden with *oil*, *whalebone*, and *sealskin*.

From Canada and the other British provinces ships cross the Atlantic with *timber, wheat, flour, furs*, and other productions.

From the United States come *cotton, wheat, tobacco, rice, flour*, &c.

From the West Indies we get *sugar, coffee, pepper*, &c.

From Honduras we get *mahogany* and other valuable woods, and *dyes*.

From Brazil we get *coffee, india-rubber, hides, silver*, and *diamonds*.

From the coast of Africa we get *ivory, palm-oil, wool*, and *gums*.

It is also by the Atlantic that ships come laden with *cotton* from India, *tea* and *silk* from China, *wool* and *gold* from Australia.

In a voyage from England to India, China, or Australia, ships sail down the Atlantic, then round Africa by the *Cape of Good Hope*, and across the Indian Ocean. This is one route, though most of the traffic now passes through the Suez Canal; but ships can also reach Australia by sailing to the west and passing through the *Panama Canal*. For sailing ships the route by the Cape of Good Hope was generally preferred, as in this region the winds blow chiefly from the west. But in the voyage from Australia it was usual to return by Cape Horn. It thus appears that a ship going from Britain to Australia by the Cape of Good Hope, and returning by Cape Horn, made a voyage round the world. The first voyage round the world was made by Magellan, a Portuguese navigator, in 1519-1521.

THE PACIFIC OCEAN

The Pacific is the largest of all the oceans. It is larger than the whole land surface of the globe, so that all the continents and islands of the world could lie within it.

The Pacific also forms one-half of the water-surface of the Earth, all the other oceans together being only about equal in extent to this great ocean. Its length from north to south is about 9000 miles. Its greatest breadth (*from South America to China*) is about 12,000 miles.

At the north, a very narrow channel, called *Behring Strait*, connects it with the Arctic Ocean. *At the south*, a vast expanse of water extends from *Cape Horn to Australia*.

In the middle of the Pacific lie thousands of Islands, of all forms and sizes, known by the general name of *Polynesia*, a word signifying "many islands." These islands, with some lying equally to the Indian and the Pacific Ocean, but assigned to the larger ocean, the Pacific, form part of the sixth division of the Earth's surface, called OCEANIA.

The Countries on the two sides of the Pacific are:—

ALASKA (*United States Ter.*)......................*opposite*......................SIBERIA.
BRITISH AMERICA..................................*opposite*......................SIBERIA.
UNITED STATES......................................*opposite*......................JAPAN.
MEXICO and CENTRAL AMERICA.........*opposite*......................CHINA.
ECUADOR..*opposite*......................BORNEO, &c.

PERU and CHILI..*opposite*......................AUSTRALIA.
PATAGONIA..*opposite*.......................NEW ZEALAND.

THE INDIAN OCEAN

The Indian Ocean extends from Africa to Australia, and is bounded on the north by India and Arabia. It is about 6000 miles long and 6000 miles broad. At the south its waters unite with those of the Antarctic Ocean.

Its two principal branches are, the *Bay of Bengal*, to the east of India; and the *Arabian Sea*, with its two arms, the *Red Sea* and the *Persian Gulf*.

The Indian Ocean is one of the regions of the globe frequently visited by *cyclones*, or circular hurricanes. These storms (in the Chinese seas called typhoons) are often very destructive to ships.

The principal Islands in the Indian Ocean are: *Madagascar*, near Africa; *Ceylon*, to the south of India; *Sumatra* and *Jam*, and a large chain of islands, in the Eastern Archipelago.

☆ ☆

北 冰 洋

以北极点为中心，距离北极1 600英里的点为圆周所画的圈被称作北极圈。北极圈中所有的陆地和海洋聚成了我们称之为的北寒带。我们关于北极点周围地区的了解非常有限，但最近的发现则让我们相信，它其实是由一片广阔的海洋所包围的，而这片海洋就是北冰洋。

北冰洋周围的陆地形成了一片广袤而没有植被的荒原，暴露在从极地海域吹来的寒冷风中。

这片沉闷而荒芜的地区，所占的面积要比整个欧洲还要大。它向地球的各个方向延伸，一直延伸到欧洲北部、亚洲和美洲。

在北极地区，太阳有半年的时间是在地平线之上，剩下的半年则是在地平线之下。有六个月的时间是漫长而枯燥的黑夜。但北极地区冬季的沉闷经常因为北极光的奇妙景象而得以缓解，北极光是北极地区特有的一种绚丽景象，别的地区则没有。

在欧洲、挪威北部位于北极圈之内；但那里的气候要比北极地区温和，这是由于那里受到大西洋暖流和常年西南风的影响。拉普兰和俄罗斯的一小部分地区也都位于北极圈内。

亚洲北部也位于北极圈之内。在这里有三条伟大的河流——鄂毕河、勒拿河以及叶尼塞河——它们均注入北冰洋。这些河流流过沉闷的北西伯利亚平原，因为它们是从一个较为温暖的地带向着较为寒冷的地带流淌，当它们流向海洋的时候，结的冰越来越多，河道越来越堵塞。最终它们冲出河岸，把周围的地区变成一片广阔而阴郁的沼泽，亚洲北部就成为一片贫瘠而荒芜的荒原。这里不像挪威和瑞典那样，可以作为饲养牛群的草原，甚至连最顽强的作物都不能在这些荒凉的河岸上生长。

北美洲的北极部分几乎终年被冰雪覆盖。这里，作为地球上的大河之一的麦肯齐河在奔流了一千两百英里之后，将自己的河水倾泻入北冰洋。

这些描述性的地理课课文，在平常的学校课本中见识不到，它们只能在兴趣阅读中被找到，而在传授有用知识这一点上，它和课文一样有同样的价值。冬天的时候，这片广大的地区陷入可怕的沉寂中，因为当北极的夏天结束之后，那里几乎见不到有生命的东西；而到了春天，大批的鸟儿则从南方而来，它们在湖泊和河流中找到充足的食物，海岸边的鱼群也大批涌来。在一些地方，这些飞鸟群数量非常之多，以至于当它们飞过天空的时候，据说都遮暗了太阳，而当它们从海面掠过的时候，则压黑了海面。但只要冬天的第一阵霜冻来到，这些沉闷地区几乎所有的动物都赶着去往南方了。

北冰洋由欧洲、亚洲以及北美洲的北部海岸线围成了一个圈。这其中布满岛屿，而大部分的岛屿都是沿着美洲海岸线，并形成格陵兰岛西部的一个巨大岛链。

三个多世纪以来，一代又一代勇敢而技艺高超的航行者努力探索着一条经由这片冰雪之洋到达太平洋的西北通道。世界上所有的这些探索征程中，从未有一个像探索这条通道一样热忱不倦，这样极尽所能并决心坚定地实施，这样姗姗来迟地实现。最终，当这个谜底揭开的时候，胜利的人在胜利到来的黎明前去世了。西北通道于1817年由约翰·富兰克林爵士发现，但一直到1859年的秋天，通道被发现的消息才传回英格兰。富兰克林于1847年逝世，而他那勇敢的134名勇于探索的船员在黑暗的北冰洋地区长眠了。

北冰洋中最大的岛屿是格陵兰岛。该岛北部的海岸线从未有人到达过，但已经探索过的该岛海岸线已经足够向我们展示它是一个面积差不多十倍于不列颠群岛的岛屿。格陵兰岛的西海岸是群山，而山谷则被冰川堆积。

冰川即为冰河。虽然它看起来并不流动，然而它是以缓慢的速度朝着山谷向下移动，直到大海。当它一步步推向大海的时候，其突出的部分会漂浮在海面上，翻越而起的巨浪会将其劈成巨大的碎片。这些冰川碎片就是冰山，它们漂浮在北冰洋海域。冰山大小各有不同。有的仅仅有几码大小；有的周长则达数英里，甚至有时会有几百英尺高。北冰洋海域上能见到的最美的景象之一，就是看到一列列的冰山反射着落日的余晖的景象。

许多由格陵兰岛的冰川所形成的冰山，都漂浮了很远的距离到大西洋，在那里，它们在向南漂移的过程中缓慢融化。

除了美洲北部海岸的岛屿外，与距离较远的东面是斯匹次卑尔根岛和新地岛。斯匹次卑尔根岛介于挪威和北极之间，而新地岛则是位于俄罗斯北面的一系列岛屿。

一个有趣的事实是，在北冰洋水域的部分地区，其水下温度要比其水面温度高。这是因为较为温暖的大西洋的水经常流入，而寒冷的洋流同时又流出的缘故。水面上，寒冷占据主流，而水面之下则较为温暖。因此，异常严峻的极地冬天在水下体会不到，而各种各样的生物则找到了一个安全的庇护所来躲过统治水面之上世界的霜冻。它们成为鲸鱼、海象以及其他北方海域大量出现生物的食物。

虽然这片海域被冰雪覆盖了数千英里，但总有开阔的海域没有冰封，在那里能找到鲸鱼、海象还有海豹。如果没有这些未冰封的水域，那么这些生物也就无法生存；因为它们都是温血动物，而且需要不断地到海面上呼吸。

南　冰　洋

以南极点为中心，距离南极1 600英里的点为圆周所画的圈被称作南极圈。南极圈中所有的陆地和海洋聚成了我们称之为的南寒带。从范围上来讲，南寒带和北寒带非常相似。位于南寒带中的海洋，叫作南冰洋。我们对于地球上的这个地区知之甚少。它是冰天雪地的世界。

这里各个地方的陆地都有冰雪覆盖，但它比北极地区的陆地还要荒芜和贫瘠。没有人类的迹象，也没有发现任何陆地四肢动物；没有任何种类的植物，甚至连苔藓或地衣都没有——一切都是处在一片沉闷而无生物栖息的荒原之中。但是虽然南极陆地上既没有四肢动物又没有植物，但是那里有不计其数的海鸟，而且还有鲸鱼、海豚以及海豹大量出现在南极海域。

许多人认为，地球的这一地区有一块面积广大的大陆，占据着南极相当大的部分。詹姆斯·罗斯爵士，在一次南冰洋探险中，有一些有趣的发现。他看到一纵高耸的山脉延伸到南极。其中有几座火山，他把其中的一座命名为厄瑞波斯山，这是根据他船的名字命名的。这座山，耸立于冰雪之间，高度达到距离海平面12 000英尺。只能从距离很远的地方看到它，因为有难以逾越的冰的障碍物阻止了船只靠近大陆。

大　西　洋

大西洋位于旧世界和新世界之间。其一边是欧洲和非洲，另一边则是南北美洲。大西洋的水域从格陵兰岛一直延伸到非洲和南美洲的最南端，整个距离达到9 000英里。它北接北冰洋，居于挪威和格陵兰岛之间。而南端则和太平洋、印度洋以及南极海域相通。

就海域和海湾的数量而言，大西洋超越了其他所有的大洋。

位于大西洋东侧的主要海域有北海、波罗的海、地中海和黑海。

（1）北海南北走向约600英里，其宽度从100到400英里不等。

从泰晤士河口到荷兰，北海宽100英里，而这一部分是水域相对较浅的地区有沙滩。靠近泰晤士河河口的就是著名的古德温沙滩，也是一片危险的浅滩。很早之前，水面上就安上浮灯，而且还竖起了高大的灯塔，然而这一海岸地区依然每年都会有很多船只遇难。比起英格兰其他的海岸地区而言，这一地区对生命和财产安全的威胁更加致命。沙滩也沿着荷兰海岸线一路延伸。

苏格兰和丹麦之间的北海宽400英里。苏格兰和挪威之间的北海部分宽300英里，而最深的海域靠近挪威。

和不列颠隔海相望的大陆地区有：

挪威（南部）…………… 隔海相望 …………… 苏格兰北部
丹麦……………………… 隔海相望 …………… 苏格兰
荷兰……………………… 隔海相望 …………… 英格兰
比利时
法国……………………… 隔海相望 …………… 英格兰南部

和不列颠隔海相望的主要港口有：

鹿特丹…………………… 隔海相望 …………… 伦敦
阿姆斯特丹……………… 隔海相望 …………… 雅茅斯
汉堡……………………… 隔海相望 …………… 赫尔
卑尔根…………………… 隔海相望 …………… 设德兰群岛

在古代，北海是斯堪的纳维亚半岛的君主在海上的探索之地，其水域上穿行着不同的部落民族，他们先后登上不列颠的海岸，并在瓦解了霍曼帝国之后在不列颠群岛上定居。

安格鲁人从丹麦南部迁来，而撒克逊人则从北边德国迁来，这迁徙大约发生在公元49年。丹麦人则在公元787年来到不列颠。

这些部落的人逐渐把原住民赛尔特族人向后驱赶，但直到今天赛尔特人的后裔依然占据着不列颠群岛相当大的地区。威尔士人，爱尔兰人以及苏格兰高地人，都是赛尔特人的主要后裔。

在之后的时期（即公元1066年），诺曼人——他们和丹麦人一样，祖先是古代挪威人——从法国北部横渡英吉利海峡而来，并征服了英格兰。

（2）波罗的海是一片狭长的海域，有数个支海。其北半边被叫作波斯尼亚湾。而其他的支海则是芬兰湾和里加湾。

大体而言，波罗的海非常浅，而且海上经常发生大风暴。有许多大河注入波罗的海，因此它的海水就相对淡一些。

波罗的海沿岸的国家有爱沙尼亚、拉脱维亚、立陶宛、东普鲁士、丹麦以及瑞典。英国和这些国家有着大量商贸往来。这些国家主要的出口商品有木材、小麦、亚麻、大麻、动物油脂以及动物毛皮。

（3）在某些方面，地中海是世界上最有趣的海域。从最久远的时代到现在，其海岸线见证了许多伟大的历史事件。古代的时候它是文明国度之间的商贸之路。其海岸上有古希腊、意大利、迦太基、埃及，腓尼基以及巴勒斯坦诸国。

从大西洋进入到地中海的入口是直布罗陀海峡，其最窄处只有11英里。从这里出发一直到叙利亚海岸，地中海的长度大约是2500英里。

地中海海岸的温度非常高，而这片四周都被陆地围住的广阔海域上的水蒸气非常多。虽然有许多大河汇入地中海，但注入的水量不足以抵消蒸发的损耗。因此，从大西洋经由直布罗陀海峡有一股强劲的洋流汇入地中海，这股洋流仅仅被经直布罗陀向大西洋流去的海底洋流削弱一部分。地中海几乎是“无浪之海”，但在有的地方海浪会有数英寸之高。

地中海的主要支海有亚德里亚海，它位于意大利和南斯拉夫之间，还有位于希腊和小亚细亚之间的千岛海或爱琴海。地中海东面的部分叫作黎凡特。法国南边是里昂湾，意大利北部则是热那亚湾。

注入地中海的主要河流有从法国注入的莱茵河，自意大利注入的波河，自埃及注入的尼罗河。除此之外，还有多瑙河和第聂伯河以及顿河，它们通过马尔马拉海从黑海流入地中海。

地中海沿岸的国家有：

西班牙…………………… 隔海相望 …………… 摩洛哥

法国	隔海相望	阿尔及利亚
意大利	隔海相望	突尼斯
希腊	隔海相望	的黎波里
小亚细亚	隔海相望	埃及

叙利亚和巴基斯坦构成了地中海的东海岸线。

地中海上的主要岛屿有：科西嘉岛、撒丁岛、西西里岛，克里特岛以及塞浦路斯岛。除此之外，还有大量较小的岛屿；其中位于西西里岛南面的马耳他岛，属于英国。它大致位于直布罗陀海峡和埃及中间。

地中海和红海被狭窄的苏伊士运河隔开。这条巨大的运河贯穿整个海峡，历经十年时间才建成，它是由一位叫作莱斯普斯的法国工程师设计挖掘的。两个海域的海水在这里汇集，船只能够从欧洲去往印度、中国、澳大利亚等国，而不需要绕非洲南端或者绕好望角了。

（4）黑海位于俄罗斯和土耳其亚洲部分之间。它和地中海通过博斯普鲁斯海峡、马尔马拉海以及达达尼尔海峡相连接。

黑海的北面是克里米亚，俄罗斯的一个半岛，它因克里米亚的主要城市塞巴斯托普尔，在1850到1854年间的战争中被围而著名，塞巴斯托普尔是俄罗斯的一个知名的海军基地。

位于黑海入海口的是黄金角，在这个海角上屹立君士坦丁堡，也就是土耳其王国从前的首都。

有三条大河注入黑海中：流经奥地利、匈牙利、南斯拉夫、罗马尼亚以及保加利亚的多瑙河，以及发源俄罗斯的第聂伯河和顿河。

位于黑海沿岸的国家有：俄罗斯、罗马尼亚、保加利亚、土耳其、阿美尼亚和格鲁吉亚。

生长在俄罗斯南部和多瑙河流域国家的大量小麦，经由黑海出口。

西侧主要海域

大西洋西侧的主要海域有戴维斯海峡、巴芬湾、哈德逊湾、圣劳伦斯海湾、墨西哥海湾以及加勒比海。

（1）戴维斯海峡和巴芬湾（分别以发现它们的两位伟大的英国航海家的名字

命名）位于格陵兰岛和美洲北部海岸线之间。几乎是去往极地地区探险活动的必经之地。巴芬湾现在成为北大西洋地区捕鲸船的胜地。

许多探险家企图经由巴芬湾北面的史密斯海峡到达极地。在这里，1854年的时候，发现了一片没有冰的开阔海域的海岸，一直延伸到北极。1909年，通过同样的路线，珍珠号也到达了北极。

（2）哈德逊湾是以著名的亨利·哈德逊命名的，哈德逊是英国早期航海家中最有胆识，也最成功的一位。他于1609年发现了该海湾，而这位勇敢的航海家也正是在这里去世的。他的船员中发生了一场暴动，他和几个生病的水手被放在一条小船上，放任自生自灭。只有船上的木匠拒绝和暴动者同流合污，他高尚地选择和勇敢的指挥官共生死。此后，再也没有人看见或听说过那艘小船。

哈德逊湾形成了一片巨大的内海，位于英属美洲殖民地的心脏部位。其海岸大都终年被冰雪覆盖。从大西洋通往该海湾的主要入口叫作哈德逊海峡。

（3）圣劳伦斯海湾是美洲沿岸最重要的通道之一。这片开阔的海湾位于纽芬兰岛和加拿大之间。其最西端，是加拿大伟大的河流，圣劳伦斯河的入海口。夏天的时候，各式各样的蒸汽船和轮船不断在海湾上来回穿梭，去往魁北克和蒙特利尔，或者从圣劳伦斯河去往欧洲。冬季的时候，由于冰雪的存在，航道被封。圣劳伦斯海湾的鱼类种类繁多且价值很高。

在圣劳伦斯海湾南面的海岸上，是狭长的叫作芬迪湾的入口。芬迪湾以其浪头高，力量惊人而著称。这些海浪通常会升到60或者70英尺的高度，他们是由大量的海水自大西洋向如此狭窄的海峡强行流动而形成的。

（4）墨西哥海湾位于墨西哥和美国之间。这片海域很广阔，长约1 000英里，宽约500英里。

向其内部流入的密西西比河的河水和许多其他的小河注入的河水来自于美国和墨西哥。

它以海湾洋流著称于世，其海湾洋流是世界上最引人注目的洋流。

墨西哥湾洋流是从墨西哥湾流入大西洋的暖流。其海水在热带阳光的照射下变得灼热，首先从大西洋沿着南美洲北部海岸奔流。然后进入到加勒比海，从那里流入墨西哥湾，因此它被命名为墨西哥湾洋流。在那里，它绕着海湾奔腾，以巨大的力量从佛罗里达海峡流入大西洋。

它的路线是如此鲜明，以至于在某些地方一条船的船底可能是位于海湾洋流之上，而船的其他部分则不是在洋流上漂流。这一点，根据观察到的船底水温和船腹水温的不同就可以知晓。它从佛罗里达向北流向纽芬兰岛，并逐渐地拓宽其宽度。从纽芬兰岛，它的海水又在大西洋温度较低的洋面上扩散，其中的一支转而向南，另一支则往东流去。往南的那支围绕起来的巨大的海域叫作马尾藻海，其数百英里的海面上漂浮着厚厚的海草。往东的那支则缓慢横越过大西洋到达欧洲海岸。

墨西哥湾洋流上方的空气温暖而潮湿，如此，不列颠群岛的气候就比没有该洋流的情况下变得温和了许多。与其大西洋一侧对望的是拉布拉多海岸——这是一片冰雪天地。如果不是有温暖的海湾洋流，不列颠的港口和河流一年中大部分时间都会结冰。墨西哥湾洋流的影响远在挪威北部也能够感觉到，在那里，它和来自极地海域的冰冷海水相融合。

（5）加勒比海位于墨西哥湾南面，并与之相连。两片海域共同组成了北美洲和南美洲之间的巨大海域。

大西洋海床

大西洋的深度已经由英国和美国海军通过声呐勘测得知，因此，我们现在知道大西洋海床或海底的很多特征。大西洋最深处有6英里。这些测量的收获之一是我们现在掌握了确切的关于大洋海床的知识，其海床就像陆地一样，有各种地形构造，有山峦和峡谷，有山丘、高地以及平原。

位于纽芬兰岛和爱尔兰岛之间的大西洋海床极其平坦。在这部分海底铺设着光缆，用来传输信息，这些信息横跨大洋，从一个半球传输到另一个半球。

大西洋上的岛屿同太平洋上星罗棋布的岛屿相比数量要少很多。大西洋上的主要岛屿有冰岛、不列颠群岛、纽芬兰岛以及西印度群岛。

隔海相望，位于大西洋两侧的国家有：

格陵兰岛…………………………隔海相望 ……………挪威
拉布拉多岛………………………隔海相望 ……………英国
加拿大……………………………隔海相望 ……………法国
美国………………………………隔海相望 ……………西班牙和北非
西印度群岛和墨西哥……………隔海相望 ……………撒哈拉
巴西………………………………隔海相望 ……………非洲中部和南部

与非洲相比，南美洲向南延伸得更深，因此，在其东侧没有国家和巴塔哥尼亚相望。

大西洋是繁忙的货运水路，其海面上不断有来自各个国家的船只来来往往。

沿格陵兰岛和拉布拉多岛的海岸线，有船只出海捕鲸和海豹，当它们回来的时候，上面满载着油脂、鲸鱼骨以及海豹皮。

船只从加拿大和其他英属国出发，横渡大西洋，满载着木材、小麦、面粉、皮毛以及其他物品。

从美国而来的船只则运有棉花、小麦、烟草、大米、面粉，等等。

从西印度群岛那儿我们获得了蔗糖、咖啡、胡椒等。

从洪都拉斯，我们获得了红心木和其他珍贵的木材以及染料。

从巴西那里，我们获得了咖啡、印度橡胶、动物皮、银以及钻石。

从非洲沿岸国家，我们获得了象牙、棕榈油、羊毛以及树胶。

同时也是通过大西洋，船只满载着棉花从印度而来，满载着茶叶和丝绸从中国而来，满载着羊毛和黄金从澳大利亚而来。

在从英格兰到印度、中国或者澳大利亚的航程中，船只顺着大西洋向南驶进，然后绕过非洲好望角，横渡印度洋。这是一条航线，尽管大部分的船只如今都通过苏伊士运河完成这一航行，但船只也可以通过向西航行并穿过巴拿马运河抵达澳大利亚。对于航行的船只而言，绕好望角的航线大体上是更优的路线，因为在那里风基本都是从西往东吹。但从澳大利亚出发的回程航线，则通常要绕过合恩角。因此，一条从英国到澳大利亚的船只要经过好望角，而当它回程的时候，则要经过合恩角，这样它似乎就绕行了地球一圈。首次环球航行是西班牙航海家麦哲伦于1519到1521年之间完成的。

太 平 洋

太平洋是所有大洋中最大的大洋。它要比地球表面所有陆地的面积还要大，因此世界上所有的大陆和岛屿都能放进太平洋中。

太平洋占据了地球表面水域一半的面积，而其他的大洋加起来才和这个浩瀚的大洋差不多大。太平洋自北向南约长9 000英里。最宽处（即从南美到中国）约有12 000英里。

太平洋北部一个非常狭窄的海峡，叫作白令海峡，它将太平洋和北冰洋连接，而其南部一片非常开阔的海域则是从合恩角一直延伸到澳大利亚。

太平洋中部星罗棋布着数以千计的岛屿，它们形态和大小各异，这些岛屿通常被叫作波利尼西亚，意思是“许多岛屿”。这些岛屿，其在印度洋和在太平洋上的面积相同，但它们却属于太平洋这个更大的海洋，并形成了地球表面第六大的洲，称为大洋洲。

位于太平洋两边的国家有：

阿拉斯加（美国）…………	隔海相望 ……………	西伯利亚
英属美洲国家………………	隔海相望 ……………	西伯利亚
美国…………………………	隔海相望 ……………	日本
墨西哥和中美洲……………	隔海相望 ……………	中国
厄瓜多尔……………………	隔海相望 ……………	加里曼丹
秘鲁和智利…………………	隔海相望 ……………	澳大利亚
巴塔哥尼亚…………………	隔海相望 ……………	新西兰

印　度　洋

印度洋自非洲向澳大利亚延伸，北部以印度和阿拉伯半岛为界限。它长约6 000英里，宽约6 000英里，其南部水域连接南冰洋。

印度洋的两个主要支海是孟加拉湾，位于印度以东，以及阿拉伯海，它又有两个支海，红海和波斯湾。

印度洋是地球上旋风或旋转飓风最常造访的地区。这些暴风（在中国海域叫作台风）通常对船只具有毁灭性的打击。

印度洋上的主要岛屿有：马达加斯加岛，靠近非洲大陆；锡兰岛，在印度以南；苏门答腊岛以及东部群岛的大型岛链。

Lesson 55 HEALTH OF THE BODY

第五十五课 身体健康

The human body is a machine, or system of "works," more delicately constructed than a watch, more complicated and wonderful than the most powerful steam-engine.

The "works" of the body are organs and tissues—as the heart, the stomach, the lungs, the arteries, the muscles, the nerves, the skin—each of which has a distinct function or duty to perform. When all the parts of the bodily machine are in good working order, the body is in a state of HEALTH (Old Eng. *hael*, whole).

A state of health is necessary, not only to the comfort and activity of the body, but also to the comfort and activity of the mind. It is therefore of the greatest importance that we should take every means in our power to promote bodily health.

The chief means within our power of keeping the body in a healthy state are attention to *food*, *cleanliness*, *clothing*, *ventilation*, (air and light,) *exercise*, and *rest*.

FOOD

Food keeps the body in health by making it warm, and by forming the material of which every part of the bodily frame is made.

If you read the Lesson called "Living Stoves," at page 73, you will see that our food is really the fuel of the bodily machine, just as coal is of the steam-engine; and that its end is combustion, and the production of animal heat. Food, therefore, is necessary to make warmth.

But, in the act of burning, the body wastes, by throwing off its worn-out particles. So does the stove of an engine; but there is this great difference between them—that while the engine-stove must be repaired or renewed by man, the body is self-repairing. It is replacing the worn-out tissues as fast as they are consumed. The blood is simply bone and muscle and brain in a fluid state, and each draws from it the substance required to renew itself. Food is therefore necessary to form the body.

Food must be nourishing; that is, it must be blood-making. If the body does not get a sufficient amount of blood-making food, it cannot last. A furnace fire would not last long if you fed it with nothing but bricks or iron.

Mixed food is best. The blood consists of different elements. Some of these elements are more abundant in vegetable, others in animal food. Of ordinary animal food, beef and mutton are the most nourishing, and are as easily digested as any other. In both respects, old flesh is preferable to young—beef to veal, and mutton to lamb.

Bread and porridge, as well as rice and barley, are vegetable food. They are generally classed with farinaceous or starchy foods, which are very important, as they supply the principal elements which are burned within the animal system. Stale bread digests more easily than new, and brown bread is more wholesome than white.

Whilst food is being cooked, it is often deprived of its saline and mineral elements, which are as necessary to animal life as its other constituents. These elements should be supplied in the form of uncooked food, as milk, ripe fruits, such vegetables as can be eaten raw, fresh water, and common salt.

Food should be thoroughly chewed before being swallowed. This makes it digest more easily, and lightens the work of the stomach. The peculiar uneasiness in the stomach known as indigestion is frequently caused by the food having been bolted when imperfectly chewed. Even soft food, which does not require much chewing—as bread, rice, and corn-flour—should be retained in the mouth for some time, to allow the saliva to mix with it, whereby its starchy matter is turned into sugar, and the work of the stomach is greatly lightened.

Three meals a day are usually enough; but more important than the number of meals are the intervals between them. The process of digestion requires rest for the whole body; but it especially requires that the organs of digestion should not be disturbed during the operation. The food is changed while in the stomach into a new substance. If when it is half changed you mix fresh food with it, confusion will necessarily arise. It is as if you were to mix fresh rags with the soft pulp which is ready to be made into paper. The time which food requires for its proper digestion varies, with the nature of the food, from two to four hours. No food of any kind should be taken within two hours after a meal; and the interval between regular meals should be four hours at least. Supper should be taken two hours before gonig to sleep, that the stomach, as well as the other parts of the body, may have rest while we are asleep. At the same time, we should not fast too long; and we should observe regularity in the times at which we take our meals.

Questions

What is the human body? What are its "works"? Name some of them. When is the body in a state of health? Why is this state so important? By what means may it be secured? How does food keep the body in health? What does the consumption of food produce? With what other machine may the body in this respect be compared? What great difference is there between them? What food is best? Of what elements is food deprived by cooking? How may these be supplied? How should food be prepared for the stomach? What is the use of the saliva? How many meals a day are enough? What is more important than the number of meals? Why should the body rest between meals? Why is it bad to eat between meals? Why should we sup two hours before going to sleep?

CLEANLINESS

Cleanliness—that is, keeping the whole skin of the body pure and fresh—is a great source of health. The skin, like the internal organs of the body, has work to do, and it cannot do its work unless it is kept clean.

The skin is one means of getting rid of impure, refuse matter from the blood. For this purpose it is supplied with two or three millions of small tubes, called pores, through which it sweats out the superfluous moisture. These pores also regulate the temperature of the body. When the body gets over-heated, from violent exercise or exposure to fire, it is flooded with perspiration from these pores, and so is cooled down.

The skin, besides, is kept soft and smooth by a kind of oily matter secreted in small cells over its surface.

Now, if the pores and the oil-cells become blocked up with dirt, they cannot perform their functions. In that case, either the skin itself will become diseased, or the blood will be injured by being forced to retain its impurities; or, it may be, some other organ (as the kidneys) will have to do the work of the skin besides its own, and serious disease may follow.

Washing the skin is therefore indispensable to health. A complete bath should be taken, or at least the whole body should be well sponged, every day. The face and hands, which are most exposed, should be washed three or four times a day.

Sea-bathing is the healthiest kind of washing, as it combines fresh air and vigorous exercise with its other benefits. It is a safe rule never to bathe till at least two hours after a meal. It is unsafe to go into the water when cold, or to remain in it after you begin to feel chilled.

Questions

What is the chief function or work of the skin? How do the pores regulate the temperature of the body? How is the skin kept soft? What will be the consequence if the skin is not kept clean? What is therefore indispensable to health? What is the healthiest kind of washing? What rules are to be observed in connection with sea-bathing?

CLOTHING

That the skin may properly discharge its functions, it must not only be kept clean; it must also be protected from cold as well as from heat by clothing. Clothes keep us warm by keeping in our own heat, rather than by communicating heat to us. The less clothing the body wears, the more quickly does it consume its fuel (food), and the more food does it require. Warm clothing is therefore an economizer of food. It is necessary to maintain the natural temperature of the body; for when that is reduced, the blood is driven inwards to the internal organs, which are thereby oppressed, and the health is injured. This is why we feel it necessary to put on warmer clothing at the setting in of the cold season of the year.

That is the warmest clothing which is the worst conductor of heat; hence down is warmer than wool, cotton than linen, fine cloth than coarse, light-coloured fabric than dark. Loose garments are warmer than tight-fitting ones, because the air which the former enclose is a bad conductor of heat.

We require clothing in summer, and in hot climates, to protect the skin from the heat of the sun. Those clothes are the best for this purpose which reflect or throw off external heat most. Thus, white or light-coloured clothing is worn in summer, because it is a bad absorbent of heat Under-clothing should be put off each night, and entirely changed once or twice a week.

Clothing should be made so as on the one hand not to restrain or cramp the action of any of the organs of the body, and so as not to expose them unduly to cold or moisture on the other.

Tightening the waist, whether by wearing stays or corsets, or by any other means, prevents full breathing, compresses the liver, and drives the blood to the extremities, besides giving the body an unnatural and ungraceful form.

Tight neck-ties and collars worn by men arc equally injurious. They check the flow of blood to the head, and may bring on apoplexy.

Head-dresses should be light and airy, and should not press upon the veins of the head so as to obstruct the circulation. Baldness, so prevalent among men, is said to result in many cases from wearing heavy and tight-fitting hats. The fashion once prevailing amongst women of padding the natural hair, and overloading the head with ornaments, was injurious in many ways.

The custom of exposing the legs of children, especially of infants, to cold, is a fruitful source of disease and detail. Exposing the chest and shoulders of older persons in cold weather and in cold climates is equally dangerous.

Questions

What is the purpose served by clothing? How do clothes keep us warm? How is warm clothing an economizer of food? What is the effect of allowing the natural temperature of the body to be reduced? Which is the warmest clothing? Give examples. Why are loose clothes warmer than tight-fitting ones? Why is clothing required in hot weather? What clothes are best for this purpose? What should be attended to in the making of clothes? What are the effects of tightening the waist? Why are tight neck-ties injurious? What often results from wearing heavy and tight-fitting hats? What is a frequent source of disease in the case of children?

VENTI LATION

Fresh air is as necessary to life and health as wholesome food. In fact air is food, inasmuch as our material food would be useless without air. It is the oxygen in the air we breathe, uniting with the carbon in the blood, that fits our food for wanning and nourishing the body. Every time we draw air in, our lungs deprive the air of a certain amount of oxygen. Every time we send breath out, our lungs supply the place of that oxygen by a corresponding amount of carbonic acid. Now, carbonic acid acts as a poison; and breath is therefore simply more or less poisoned air. If instead of inhaling fresh air we inhale breath, we not only deprive the blood of the oxygen which is necessary to enable it to warm and support the body, but we positively poison the blood; and if we continue this process, sooner or later disease and death will ensue.

Yet nothing is more common than for crowds of people to remain together, in churches and other public places, for hours after the air has been polluted by the breathing of the assembled people. The consequence is that many people faint from the effects of the heated and poisoned air; and if they were to be forcibly confined there for a few hours longer, many would certainly die.

The injury which is thus done suddenly and evidently, is done gradually, but not less surely, to people who spend their days in hot, crowded workshops, and their nights in small, close dwellings. Physicians tell us that such diseases as consumption and scrofula are due far more to poisoned air, breathed in our houses and factories, than to a cold or changeable climate.

All places in which people assemble in large numbers—as schools, workshops, churches, lecture-halls, and theatres—should be well ventilated; that is, should be supplied with the means of carrying off the breathed air, and of letting in a copious supply of fresh air. It is imperfect ventilation, or the total want of it, that so often makes people sleepy in church, and children listless in school.

Ventilation is on less necessary in small rooms occupied by a few persons. There also the air will, in course of time, become polluted, unless fresh supplies of oxygen are constantly being admitted. One man may be confined in a room so small and close, that in a short time he may be poisoned by his own breath!

Perhaps more injury is done from want of ventilation in bed-rooms than in any other places. They are kept closed for so many hours at a time, and people think it necessary to make them so completely airtight, that the occupants are generally dependent for the whole night upon the air that fills the room when they enter and close it. Long before morning, the sleepers are breathing their own or each other's breath over and over again. No wonder that crowded sleeping-rooms have so close and offensive a smell in the morning! Let any one of their occupants go into the fresh air for five minutes, and then return to the room in which he has spent the night, and he will in many cases be shocked if not stifled by the air on which he has been living for hours!

The air may be contaminated by other means besides the carbonic acid emitted from the lungs. The stone-cutter may inhale minute particles of stone; the iron-grinder may inhale metallic particles; the cotton-spinner, particles of cotton; and these settling on the lungs, often produce disease and death.

But the poisonous particles given off by putrefying animal and vegetable matters cause the most dangerous pollution of the air we breathe. They often produce the most fatal and destructive diseases; and such matters should never be allowed to accumulate near dwelling-houses. If they cannot be carried off by drainage, (which is the best remedy,) they should be continually disinfected with carbolic acid, or chloride of lime. There has hardly ever been an outbreak of typhoid fever in any locality which could not be traced to the diffusion of this kind of poison in the air; so true is this, that the fever referred to is now popularly called drain-fever.

The air is also frequently the medium of carrying disease-poison from a sick person to those who are well. It is thus that small-pox, scarlet fever, and other "catching diseases," often spread in a community. It is the duty of those who have charge of the patients in such cases to take every means to prevent the spread of the poison from the sick persons to those who are well. "It is," says Dr. Lankester, "a common practice, much to be reprehended, to send children to school from families where small-pox, scarlet fever, measles, and hoopings cough are prevailing; thus spreading the poison amongst those who have not been previously attacked."

Houses should be built so as to admit plenty of light as well as of fresh air. The former is not less necessary than the latter to a healthy condition of body. Just as plants, when deprived of light, become white in their stalks and leaves, so man becomes pale and unhealthy when he lives under ground. Light acts as a stimulus to the nervous system, quickens the mind, and promotes the activity of the whole body. It helps, therefore, to keep off disease; and it is a fact that consumption is often the result of living in rooms from which the light of the sun is excluded.

Questions

Why may air be considered food? What happens every time we draw in air? What do we send out to take the place of the oxygen? What is breath? What poisons it? What is the effect of inhaling breath? Where is this done very often? Where is the same injury done by degrees? What diseases result from that? How is this to be prevented? What effects of bad ventilation are often seen? Where is most injury done from want of ventilation? Why is this? What takes place long before morning? In what other ways may the air be contaminated? What causes the most, dangerous pollution of the air we breathe? How should decaying animal and vegetable matter be carried off? What diseases result from it? In what way does the air often spread disease? What should those who have the charge of patients do? What practice, in this connection, does Dr. Lankester strongly condemn? What, besides air, should, be admitted into our houses? Why? What is the effect of absence of light upon plants? And upon man? How does light act upon the body? What does it help to keep off? What disease in particular?

EXERCISE AND REST

The muscles grow and gain strength by being used. Exercise is therefore necessary to their healthy condition; and not to their healthy condition only, but to that of all the organs of the body. Muscular exercise accelerates the circulation of the blood; increases the healthy action of the heart, the lungs, and the skin; invigorates the nerves; stimulates the appetite; improves the powers of digestion, and carries healthful energy wherever the blood penetrates.

Care should be taken that the exercises we practice calls into play not one set only, but the whole of the muscles. Swimming is on this account the most healthful of all exercises. This cannot always be indulged in; but no one need be at a loss for invigorating exercises. Boys can run and leap, if they cannot play cricket or foot-ball; men can walk, if they cannot row or ride on horseback.

Systematic exercises, as gymnastics, are very useful; but boys are apt to attempt feats that are dangerous and to over-tax their energies. Young people should therefore always be superintended, while engaging in them, by an experienced person who can estimate their strength. Competition in games is most injurious, as it almost inevitably taxes the strength beyond the powers of the system, and too often causes permanent injury to the health. It is a good rule that one should never engage in any game to the extent of producing painful or continued exhaustion.

No exercise is more interesting, or more useful in quickening both mind and body, than military drill. It would be an excellent thing, both for master and scholars, if, two or three times a week, half an hour were taken from books and given to drill in the open air, under the master's leadership.

The muscles require rest as well as exercise. In this they differ from the heart and the lungs. These are always in motion, even when we are asleep; but the muscles, and the nervous system which governs the muscles, cannot work unless they have periodical seasons of total rest, during which all their functions are suspended. This rest we call sleep. We may rest the muscles to some extent while we are awake; but so long as we are awake, the brain and the nervous system, of which the brain is the seat, are at work. These latter cannot rest unless we are thrown into the state of unconsciousness called sleep.

A man usually requires to sleep eight hours out of the twenty-four. Persons whose employment does not involve much anxiety or thinking might thrive with less; but they generally take more. On the other hand, those whose brains are most active during the day, and who therefore require most rest, often obtain or allow themselves least sleep at night; but such persons are never long-lived. A young person, while growing, needs more sleep than a man; and an infant spends half its time in sleep; -which one poet calls "nature's soft nurse;" and another, " tired nature's sweet restorer, balmy sleep."

Too much sleep makes us dull, as too little exercise makes us lazy, converting our muscle into fat. Too little sleep, however, is much more injurious. A man who is forcibly kept awake will erelong become insane or will die.

Questions

Why docs the body require exercise? What is its effect on the blood and the organs of the body? What is to be aimed at in the exercise we take? What exercise is, for this reason, the most healthful? What other exercises are recommended for boys? What for men? How may gymnastics be abused? What precaution should be taken against this? Why is competition in games injurious? What exercise is recommended for masters and scholars? Wherein do the muscles and the brain differ from the heart and the lungs? What is the total rest of the former called? How much sleep does a man usually require? What persons require most rest? What do young persons need? What have poets called sleep? What is the effect of too much sleep? and of too little?

☆ ☆

人类的身体是一台机器，或是“工程”系统，它比一只手表的结构还要精细，比马力最大的蒸汽机还要复杂，还要神奇。

身体的“工程”系统即器官和组织——例如心脏、胃、肺、动脉、肌肉、神经、皮肤——它们各自有各自的功能或职责需要履行。当身体机器的所有部分都运转良好的时候，身体就处于健康状态（在古英语中，健康即是全面的意思）。

健康状态是身体所必需的，这不仅仅因为健康状态能让身体舒适，并提供身体活动的动力，还因为它能让心灵舒适，有利于精神活动。因此，我们必须采用各种力所能及的方法来增强身体健康，这一点是极其重要的。

我们力所能及保持身体处于健康状态的主要方法有注意饮食、清洁、穿着、空气流通，（空气和光），锻炼以及休息。

饮　食

食物通过保持体温以及形成我们身体各个部分所需要的养料给养身体。

如果你读过名为《有生命的火炉》这篇课文的话，你就会发现食物实际上是我们身体机器的燃料，就像煤是蒸汽机的燃料一样；而它最终会被燃烧掉，产物就是动物的体温。因此，食物是保持体温的必须材料。

然而，在燃烧过程中，身体排泄掉使用完毕的材料后就会衰弱。同样的道理也适用于蒸汽机，但两者之间有很大的不同——即蒸汽炉必须要人对其进行修理或更新，而身体则能自我修复。它在消耗衰弱的组织的同时，对其尽快地实施了替代。血液简单来说就是骨头、肌肉和大脑的液体状态，而每一滴血都有足够能进行自我更新的物质。因此，食物是长成身体的必备材料。

食物的营养一定要易于吸收，也就是说，它一定要有造血功能。如果身体不能得到足够产生血液的食物，那么它就不能继续运转。如果你只往熔炉内填砖块或铁，而不给它燃料的话，熔炉中的火就不会燃烧下去。

食物最好要合理搭配。血液中含有不同的元素。有的元素大量存在于蔬菜中，有的则存在于动物类食物中。平常的动物类食物中，牛肉和羊肉是最有营养的，并且要比其他的肉类更易于消化。这两种肉类中，成年牲畜的肉比幼年动物的肉要好——即牛肉好于小牛肉，羊肉较之羊羔肉更佳。

面包和粥以及米饭和谷类，都属于素食品。它们通常被划分为谷物制品或淀粉食物，这一类食物非常重要，因为它们提供了动物系统内部燃烧的主要材料。干面包要比新出炉的面包好消化，而全麦面包要比白面包的营养更全面。

通常，在烹饪过程中，食物所含的盐和矿物质会损耗掉，而这些物质，和其他机体所需的成分一样，是维持机体必需的。这些元素应该以未经烹饪的形式提供给身体，例如牛奶、成熟水果，可以生吃的蔬菜、淡水以及粗盐。

在吞咽之前，食物应该得到充分咀嚼。这样更有利于消化，并且能减轻胃的负担。胃部特有的不适现象，也就是通常所说的消化不良，通常是由于食物未经充分咀嚼，狼吞虎咽所引起的。即使绵软的食物，例如面包、大米、玉米粉——也应该在嘴里停留一段时间，让唾液和其充分混合，这样其中的淀粉物质就能转化成糖了，而胃部的负担就大大减轻了。

一日三餐已经足够，但比进餐次数更重要的是两餐之间的间隔。消化的过程需要在身体的休息状态下进行，尤其需要身体器官的消化过程不被打扰。食物在胃里转化成新的物质。如果食物只消化了一半，而你又吃了新的食物，就会引起混乱。这就好像你把刚裁好的碎布和柔软的绒浆混合在一起，而绒浆已经可以制成纸张了。不同食物所需的消化时间各异，从2小时到4小时不等，这取决于食物的性质。没有任何一种食物应该在一餐之后的2小时之内进食；而规律的两餐之间的间隔时间至少应该有4小时。晚餐应当在入睡前2小时进食，这样胃部以及身体其他脏器就能在我们睡着的时候休息了。同时，两餐之间不应该间隔太长时间；而且我们应该观察自己进餐的时间规律。

清　洁

清洁——就是保持身体皮肤洁净而清爽——是健康的一大源泉。皮肤和身体内部器官一样，有其独特的功能，如果它不能保持清洁的话，就没法履行自身功能。

皮肤是祛除血液中不纯净的废弃物质的一种方式。为了达到这一功能，皮肤中有200万或300万之多的被称作毛孔的小通道，通过毛孔，皮肤将多余的水分排出体外。同时这些毛孔还能够调节体温，当身体由于剧烈运动或靠近火源而过热的时候，皮肤上就布满从这些毛孔中流出的汗水，这样体温就降下来了。

除此之外，皮肤还能通过一种油类物质保持柔软而光滑，这种物质蕴藏在其表面的小细胞内。

如果毛孔和油脂细胞被灰尘堵塞，它们就不能履行自己的功能。那样的话，皮肤本身就会变得不健康，血液也会因为保留其废弃物而受到损害；或者一些脏器（例如肾脏）除了自身功能运转之外，还要承担起皮肤的功能，而这样可能会引起严重病变。

因此，清洁皮肤是保持健康不可或缺的条件。人们每天都应该好好洗澡，或者至少用海绵擦洗全身。暴露最多的脸和双手，应该每天清洗三到四次。

洗海澡是最健康的清洗方式，因为它集新鲜空气，活力运动和自身其他的好处于一身，一个安全的法则是饭后至少要2小时再洗澡。当进入到冷水中，或者你都冻得打战了还在冷水中泡着的话，是很不安全的。

穿　着

要想让皮肤履行起自己的功能来，不光要保持皮肤清洁，还必须要保护皮肤免受寒冷和炎热的伤害。衣物保持我们的体温是通过把热量阻隔在身体中，而不是通过把热量传递到我们身上来。身体所穿的衣服越少，身体消耗其燃料（即食物）的速度就越快，而我们就需要越多的食物。因此，温暖的衣物能节省食物。保持身体的自然体温很有必要，因为当体温下降的时候，血液就会流向内部脏器，对脏器产生压力，有损健康。这就是为什么我们在寒冷季节要穿上更温暖的衣物的原因。

最温暖的衣物，也是最差的导热材料。保温性次之的是羊毛，棉花的保温性优于亚麻，细布优于粗布，浅颜色材质的衣物优于深色衣物。宽松的衣物比紧身的衣服更保温，因为宽松衣服包围起来的空气是很差的导热材料。

夏天炎热时候的衣物要能保护皮肤免受太阳灼热的烘烤。能最好的达成这一功能的衣物，反射或过滤掉的外部热量也最多。因此，夏天最好穿白色或浅色衣物，因为它们的吸热性能较差。内衣则应该每天晚上脱下，并每周更换一到两次。

衣物的制作标准是既不能限制或阻碍身体任何器官的正常运转，也不能让身体暴露在过度的寒冷或潮湿的环境之中。

不论是佩戴腰带还是流苏，或者其他物件，腰带过紧除了会让身体觉得不自然，看起来不端庄之外，还会阻碍呼吸顺畅，压迫肝脏，并把血液驱赶到肢体末端，男人穿戴过紧的领带和领口的衣物同样也对身体有伤害。它们会压迫向头部流动的血液，可能会引起中风。

头饰要尽可能的轻盈，不要压迫到头部血管，这样就不会阻碍血液的循环。男人中非常普遍的谢顶现象，据说是戴了重而紧的帽子导致的。女人们曾一度风靡把头发盘起来，然后在头上装饰过多的头饰，这样造成的损伤也是多方面的。

兰克斯特博士说欧洲人和美洲人在夏天和冬天都穿着深色衣物，这是出于节省的目的，并没有考虑到舒适因素。因为穿深色衣服能节省肥皂的使用和洗衣成本了。

把孩子的腿部暴露在寒冷中的习惯，特别是在婴儿时期的时候，通常是引起疾病和不适的一个因素。而上了年纪的人把胸膛和肩膀裸露在寒冷的空气或气候下，也同样危险。

空气流通

新鲜空气对于生命和健康的必要性如同健康食品对人们的重要性一样。实际上，空气即食物，因为固体的食物如果没有空气就变得一无是处。我们呼吸的是空气中的氧气，它和血液中的碳相结合，这符合我们对于食物温暖并给养身体的定义。每当我们吸入空气的时候，肺部就将空气中的一定数量的氧气吸入殆尽。而每当我们呼气的时候，肺部就将吸入的氧气转化成相应数量的碳酸气体。而碳酸就像毒药一样污染空气。如果我们吸入的不是新鲜空气的话，那么我们不仅不能满足血液对能温暖身体并支持身体系统的氧气的需要，还会毒化血液；这样的话，疾病和死亡迟早会接踵而至。

因此呼吸不新鲜的空气所引起的伤害是很突然也很明显的，这对于那些整天在热而拥挤的商店，晚上在狭小而紧密的住所中的人的伤害是逐步发生的，但这种伤害是确定无疑的。医生告诉我们，像肺结核和淋巴结核这样的疾病，更多时候就是因为在我们的房子里和工厂内呼吸了有毒空气，而不是寒冷或变化较大的气候导致。

所有大量人群聚集的场所——例如学校、商店、教堂、演讲厅以及剧院——都应该有良好的通风设施，也就是说应该安装上输送新鲜空气的装置，并将适量的新鲜空气输入。因为不完善的通风设施，或者没有完全满足空气流通的需要，会导致人们在教堂睡着，而孩子们则在学校里无精打采。

空气流通在人较少的小房间中也同样重要。随着时间的推移，空气也会被污染，除非有新供应的氧气源源不断输入。如果有一个被困在又小又狭窄的房间内的人，不久之后也会因自己呼出的空气而中毒。

卧室空气不流通所造成的伤害，要比其他任何地方空气质量不好造成的伤害更大。人们进入卧室后，有相当长的一段时间是封闭在一个空间中的，因为人们认为把自己彻底隔绝在室内是有必要的，这样，屋子里的人所能依赖的空气就只能是他们进入并关上门之后，留在屋子里的空气了。在清晨到来之前的很长一段时间内，睡梦中的人们所呼吸的就是他们自己或其他人反复呼吸的空气。难怪拥挤的卧室到早晨起来的时候有那么一股又强又刺鼻的味道！如果其中有个人去呼吸5分钟的新鲜空气，当他再回到屋子里的时候，就会觉得非常震惊，自己居然在这样浑浊的空气中过了好几个钟头！

室内空气可能是被除了肺部呼出的碳酸气之外的其他物质所污染。比如我们接触碎石机会吸入一些石头碎屑，用绞铁机可能吸入一些金属离子；而用纺棉布机则会吸入一些棉絮；而如果这些都停留在肺部的话，久而久之就会引起疾病和死亡。

这些动物和植物所产生的有毒颗粒，会极大地危害、污染我们呼吸的空气。它们经常会产生非常致命且致死的疾病，而这些物质绝不应该被允许在靠近居民住所的地方囤积。如果它们不能进入到排污管道的话，（这是最好的解决方法），那么，应该不间断地用碳酸或者漂白粉消毒。几乎没有一种地区性伤寒症不是由于这种形式的空气毒物扩散所造成的，这种情况真实存在，因此伤寒症现在有一个通俗的名字叫作流感。

空气经常也是一种将病毒从病人身上传递到健康人身上的载体。因此，天花、猩红热以及其他的“传染性疾病”，经常会在一个社区传播开来。那些管理者们在这些情况下有责任运用各种方式阻止病毒从病人扩散到健康人群。“这是，”兰克斯特医生说道，“一种常用且备受诟病的方式，就是把儿童送到学校里，同经常感染那些天花、猩红热、麻疹以及百日咳的家庭隔离开来，这样就阻止了病毒在尚未感染的人群中传播。”

房子应该建造得尽可能光线充足且有充足的新鲜空气。光线对于健康身体的重要性并不亚于新鲜空气。如果植物缺少阳光，它们的茎和叶子就会变得苍白，和植物一样，如果人生活在不见阳光的地方，也会变得苍白而不健康。光作为一种神经系统的刺激物，能加速我们头脑的运转，提升整个身体的运作效率。因此，它能够帮助我们抵御疾病；而且事实上，肺结核经常就是因为生活在室内而缺乏阳光的照耀而造成的。

锻炼和休息

肌肉的生长和力量的获取是通过锻炼实现的。因此，锻炼对于保持肌肉的健康状态是必要的；锻炼不仅有利于肌肉健康，还对身体所有脏器的健康有利。肌肉锻炼加速血液循环，增加了心脏、肺脏以及皮肤的健康运转，兴奋神经，刺激食欲，增强消化功能，并将健康的能量带到血液能循环到的地方。

值得注意的是我们所进行的运动不只锻炼其中的一组肌肉，而是锻炼了全身的肌肉。从这个角度出发，游泳是所有运动中最健康的一种。但也不能有失偏颇，说到刺激性运动的话，大家不必不知所措。男孩子如果打不了板球或踢不了足球的话，他们可以跑步、跳跃；成年男子如果不会射箭或者不会骑马的话，可以散步。

系统的运动，或体操，是非常有用的，但男孩们倾向于尝试那些危险并且身体负担较重的运动，因此年轻人在锻炼的时候应该有一位有经验的人陪同，那位有经验的人可以预估一下他的能力。竞技运动非常容易引起伤害，因为它几乎不可避免地会超出身体系统能力所能负荷的范围，而且会经常引起身体的永久性伤害。因此，大家必须秉承的一条金科玉律是，绝对不要从事任何有害或让自己精疲力竭的运动。

没有什么运动比军事操练更能够在身心方面促进身体的运转了。对于老师和学者而言，如果一个星期能有两三次从读书的间隙抽出半个小时到户外，在老师的领导下进行操练，那会是一件非常不错的事。

肌肉需要锻炼，也同样需要休息。在这一点上，它们和心脏以及肺部有所不同。后者永远处在运动当中，即使是我们睡觉的时候；但肌肉和控制肌肉的神经系统则没法工作，除非它们经过了周期性的彻底休息，在此期间它们所有的功能都会中止。我们把这个休息的过程叫睡眠。当我们醒着的时候，我们可以在某种程度上使肌肉得到休息，但我们醒着的时间如此之长，以至于大脑和大脑所在的神经系统还在工作。而后者只有进入无意识状态，即睡眠中才能得到休息。

每天24小时中，一个人通常需要8小时的睡眠时间。那些没有从事太多需要操心或思考工作的人，即使睡眠时间少于8小时也能够保持精力充沛，但睡眠时间一般会更长。另一方面，那些大脑在白天活跃的人，也就需要更长时间的休息，他们晚上的睡眠时间经常非常少，但这样的人寿命都不会很长。一个年轻人在长身体的时候，需要的睡眠时间要比成年人多；而一个婴儿每天则有一半的时间是在睡觉曾有位诗人把睡眠比作“自然柔软的护士”，而另一位诗人则说：“疲劳的大自然的甜美修复者，就是安详的睡眠”。

睡眠时间太长会让我们反应迟钝，正如锻炼得太少会让我们懒惰一样，而且太多的睡眠会把我们的肌肉转化成脂肪。然而，睡眠时间太短，伤害则更大。一个被强迫保持醒着的状态的人，不久就会精神失常或死亡。

Lesson 56 THE AMAZON

第五十六课 亚马孙河流域

Starting from Lima, the capital of Peru, and crowing the Andes in a north-easterly direction for one hundred and twenty miles, the traveller reaches the famous silver mines of Pasco, the most elevated city in the world. Close beside it, in the very heart of the Cordilleras, there is a little lake, nearly 14,000 feet above the sea-level, and just below the limit of perpetual snow. To this little lake belongs the honour of giving birth to the mighty Amazon, the king of rivers.

At first a comparatively small stream, it flows in a series of cataracts and rapids, through rocky valleys, northwards, till it reaches the frontier of Ecuador, at a distance of eight hundred miles from its source. From this point the eye of the traveller may range, in imagination, over a vast valley clothed with impenetrable forests, stretching eastwards to the far distant Atlantic. Behind him, on the west, tower the lofty peaks of the Cordilleras; on his left, in a northerly direction, appear the highlands of Venezuela and Guiana; while to the south rise the sierras and table-lands of Brazil. In the valley before him more than half of Europe might be contained; and the tributaries alone of the mighty stream which drains it, exceed in bulk of water all the European rivers put together. The length of the main river, with its windings, is not less than four thousand miles.

The valley of the Amazon is divided into an upper and a lower basin by the Rio Negro. The region of the Upper Amazon, as the great river is called above that boundary line, in a magnificent wilderness, where civilized man as yet has scarcely obtained a footing. Though the atmosphere, from the absence of regular winds, is stagnant and sultry, the climate is wonderfully healthy; and the rich alluvial soil produces vegetation even more luxuriant than on the lower river. The Upper Amazon is navigable at all seasons by large steamers for upwards of fourteen hundred miles above the Rio Negro; but during the rainy season the navigation is dangerous, as the tearing current, one or two miles in width, bears along a continuous line of uprooted trees, and often undermines the banks, which fall into the river with a terrific crash.

The chief feature of the Lower Amazon is its vast expanse of smooth water, of a pale yellowish colour, often bearing on its bosom detached islets of floating vegetation. Sometimes the timid stag takes refuge upon one of these treacherous islands, when pursued by the fierce jaguar; and the hunter and his prey, thus entrapped, are carried out to sea together. At mom and even, flocks of parrots and yellow macaws fly backwards and forwards, uttering their hoarse cries; while all night long the screams of gulls and terns sweep over the sandy banks, where they make their home.

Now and then, dolphins and sea-cows show their backs above water, as they glide up the stream. Huge alligators, with open jaws, are basking in the sun on the banks, or leisurely swimming across the river.

The Rio Negro, the largest northern tributary of the Amazon, has a course not much inferior to that of the Danube, the greatest river of Central Europe. Rising in the highlands of New Granada, and traversing the llanoss of Venezuela, it has already, before reaching the Amazon, flowed over fifteen hundred miles. As one of its tributaries is an offshoot from the upper waters of the Orinoco, a complete circuit is established, uniting the basins of two mighty rivers in one vast system of interior navigation.

About sixty miles below the mouth of the Rio Negro, the gigantic Madeira—the largest southern affluent of the Amazon—unites its milky waters with the turbid stream of the main river. The whole length of this tributary, from the centre of Bolivia, where it has its source, is nearly as great as that of the Amazon itself; but owing to the occurrence of falls, it is not navigable for large vessels for more than five hundred miles above its mouth.

Thus enriched by vassal tributaries on the right hand and on the left—each a river in itself—this monarch of waters flows on between sue low, forest-clad banks, till, four hundred miles from its mouth, it reaches the Strait of Obydos, where it is narrowed to two thousand paces. Through this channel its waters rush with a force so irresistible as to have defied all efforts to fathom its depths, and with a volume sufficient to fill all the streams in Europe, and swell them to overflowing. Before it reaches the Atlantic its vast flood is fifty miles wide; and, in mid-channel, the opposite banks are entirely lost to view. Indeed, it resembles an ocean-current, or a constantly-rolling Baltic, rather than an inland river.

At its mouth a fierce struggle takes place between the giant river rolling down and the tide flowing up. Twice every day they strive for the mastery; and in the meeting of the enormous masses of water a ridge of surf and foam is raised to a height of 180 feet! Victory may be said to be fairly divided between them; for while the tide makes its way nearly five hundred miles up the river, the influence of the latter is felt three hundred miles out at sea. Hence the seaman approaching the shores of South America, when still out of sight of land, may lower his bucket, and draw up the fresh waters which have issued, it may be weeks before, from the rocky sides of the Andes!

So uniform is the level, in the plain of the Upper Amazon especially, that many of its tributaries are interlaced with it and with one another by a net-work of mazy

channels, or water-paths, with the intricate navigation of which the natives alone are acquainted. So narrow are these water-paths in many places, that the branches of the lofty trees meet overhead, and form a canopy, which, for miles together, shelters the traveller in his canoe from the noon-day sun. Here and there, a glimpse of the sky may be obtained through the thick foliage; while birds of gay plumage flit to and from enjoying the cool shade, or sit on the branches trimming their feathers, and uttering strange and varied cries.

Sometimes the water-path broadens into pools and lakes, filled mostly by the overflowing of the main river during the rainy season. These pools swarm with a great variety of fishes, with many kinds of turtles and alligators, with electric eels, and other curious water-creatures. Waterfowl and other aquatic birds dwell on their banks; while on the surface of their placid waters float the wide-spreading leaves and magnificent blossoms of the Victoria Regia, and other lilies and water-plants.

The inland navigation of the Amazon and its tributaries available for commerce extends to no less than fifty thousand miles. Flowing, however, through a region very scantily peopled by indolent natives and not very active colonists, there are fewer vessels upon its waters in a year than may be seen on the bosom of the Mississippi every hour of the day.

Yet there is no nobler field of enterprise in the world than the great valley of the Amazon—none which is richer in natural resources, or which holds out a more certain reward to energy and perseverance. You have only to look at the map to see that, with the exception of Chili and Patagonia, every county in South America is brought, directly or indirectly, within the range of its interior navigation.

THE VICTORIA REGIA

So varied and so abundant are the products of this wide region, that it might well become the garden and the store-house of the world. There is scarcely one either of the necessaries or of the luxuries of life which, if all other sources of supply were cut off, might not be obtained from valley of the Amazon in sufficient abundance to supply the wants of the whole habitable globe. The supply of flesh, fish, and fowl, of every description, is dimply unlimited. There is plenty of coffee and cocoa and sugar; of maize and rice; of cotton and tobacco; of bananas and grapes; of spices, drugs, and dyes; of silver and gold; of every variety of fancy-wood for the finest cabinet-work, and of timber for building houses and ships.

Yet this prolific region remains still unused, and in great measure unexplored. Here, if anywhere, is a field in which modern enterprise and enlightenment may achieve the grandest results.

Words

abundant, *plentiful.*
acquainted, *familiar.*
alluvial, *deposited.*
approaching, *going near.*
available, *practicable.*
cataracts, *torrents.*
circuit, *circular course.*
civilized, *refined.*
colonists, *settlers.*
commerce, *trade.*
continuous, *unbroken.*
detached, *separated.*
direction, *course.*
enlightenment, *intelligence.*
enormous, *vast.*
enterprise, *adventure.*
entrapped, *caught.*
established, *formed.*
expanse, *breadth.*
foliage, *leafage.*
frontier, *border.*
habitable, *fit for man.*
impenetrable, *dense.*
insolent, *lazy.*
influence, *effect.*
interior, *inland.*
interlaced, *interwoven.*
intricate, *involved.*
irresistible, *overwhelming.*
leisurely, *lowly.*
narrowed, *contracted.*
navigation, *water transport.*
occurrence, *interposition.*
overflowing, *flooding.*
perpetual, *constant.*
products, *productions.*
prolific, *fruitful.*
resources, *supplied.*
stagnant, *standing.*
tributaries, *affluent.*
turbid, *muddy.*
unexplored, *not searched.*
uniform, *regular.*

Questions

Where has the Amazon its source? How far from Lima? What is the character of its higher waters? Give some idea of the great size of the valley, and of the volume of its water? What is the length of the river? What is the region above the Rio Negro called? What is the character of the Upper Amazon? What makes its navigation dangerous? What is the chief feature of the Lower Amazon? What connection has the Rio Negro with the Orinoco? What is the largest southern tributary of the Amazon? What is the Strait of Obydos? What width does the river attain before it reaches the Atlantic? What takes place at its mouth? How far up the river does the tide extend? How far out at sea are the waters of the river perceptible? What causes the network of water-paths in the Upper Amazon? What is remarkable about them? What is the extent of the inland navigation of the Amazon? Why is so little use made of it? What do its varied products fit it for becoming? Mention some of these products.

☆ ☆

从秘鲁首府利马出发，顺着安第斯山脉向东北行进120英里，旅行者们就到达了著名的帕斯科银矿，而帕斯科城是世界上海拔最高的城市。紧邻帕斯科城，是科迪勒拉山系的最中心处，是一个海拔大约有14 000英尺的小湖泊，上边有常年不化的积雪。这个小湖泊，就是伟大的亚马孙河，是众河之河的发源地。

亚马孙河起初是一条相对小的溪流，它流淌过一系列的瀑布和湍流，穿过山石密布的峡谷，一路向北奔流，直到厄瓜多尔边境，距离其发源地800英里的地方。在这里，旅行者们想象的眼神可以极目眺望过一片覆盖了无法穿越的森林的广袤峡谷，这片森林向东一直延伸到遥远的大西洋。旅行者向后转身，向西望去的话，就能看到科迪勒拉山系耸立的高峰；在左边，向北望去，能看到委内瑞拉和圭亚那高原；而南面则是巴西的锯齿山脊和高地。其眼前的河谷可能装的下一半的欧洲，而那伟大的河流的支流水量，就超过了欧洲所有河流水量之和。亚马孙河主河的长度，如果将其蜿蜒处的长度计算在内的话，超过4 000英里。

亚马孙河河谷由尼格罗河分成上游平原和下游平原。亚马孙河上游位于分界河的北部，那里是一片伟大的原始地带，几乎没有文明世界的人踏足过。那里的气候虽然缺乏季风的吹拂，潮湿而闷热，但总体而言还是非常宜人的，而肥沃的冲积土壤则养育了比下游流域种类更丰富的植物。上游亚马孙终年都通航，大的蒸汽船可以向上游航行1 400英里，到达尼格罗河的北部，但雨季的时候，航行变得很危险，因为宽约1英里或2英里的湍急水流上面不间断地浮着连根拔起的树木，而且经常会冲毁河岸，产生可怕的撞击声。

亚马孙河下游的主要特征是其宽广平缓的水流。水带有淡淡的黄色，底部经常有浮游植物聚集的浮岛。有时候，胆小的牡鹿在受到凶残的美洲豹追击的时候，会在这些闯入河面的其中一个小岛上避难；而捕猎的美洲豹和被追捕的猎物经常一起掉入河里，一同被冲到大海去了。在早晨和傍晚时分，鹦鹉群和黄色的金刚鹦鹉群前后飞来飞去，扯着它们粗哑的嗓子叫着；而整个晚上，海鸥和燕鸥群则在沙地的河岸上掠过，在那里筑下自己的巢。时不时地，还有海豚和海牛在溯流而上的时候，背部露出水面。巨大的短吻鳄，张着大嘴巴，在河岸上沐浴阳光，或者在河里悠闲自在地游着泳。

尼格罗河，是亚马孙河北部最大的支流，它的河道宽度不逊于中欧地区最大的河流——多瑙河的宽度。它从新格拉纳达高原发源，经过委内瑞拉的大草原，在注入亚马孙河之前，已经蜿蜒流过了1 500英里。鉴于它其中一条支流也是奥里诺托河水域的支流，于是就形成了一个完整的迂回，把两条大河的流域连接成一个广大的内河航行系统。

在距离尼格罗河河口60英里的地方，是巨大的马德拉河——它是亚马孙河南部最大的支流——它把奶白色的河水和主流河道中的翻滚的水流汇合到一处。这条支流从玻利维亚中部，也就是其发源地开始流淌，它的整个长度和亚马孙河相当，但由于瀑布分布其间，大型轮船在这条河道上只能航行到距河口500英里的距离。

因此，水量由于左右两边各有一条巨大支流的存在而非常充沛，这条众河之河在地势低的森林覆盖的河岸开始奔流，一直到距离其河口400英里的位置，到达额比多斯海峡，在那里，它的河道收窄到2 000步的宽度。通过这个海峡，亚马孙河的河水势不可挡地倾泻入海，要想测量它深度是徒劳的，同时其水量足以灌满欧洲所有的河流，并吞噬掉它们的河岸。在它到达大西洋之前，它巨大的洪流可达50英里宽，而在河道中间，从一侧岸边几乎望不到对岸。事实上，亚马孙河就像一支洋流，或奔腾不息的波罗的海一样，而不像是一支内陆河流。

在河口，巨大的河流奔腾的力量和海浪向上流淌的力量进行着角逐。每天两次，它们角逐着掌控权；在大量的河水交汇之处形成的浪花和水沫会冲到180英尺的高度，应该说，两支力量平分秋色；当海浪向河流涌进差不多五百英里的时候，河流的影响力便会在海上300英里的位置体现出来。因此，从南美洲驶向海上的人，当还没有看见陆地的时候，放下桶，就能打上淡水来，而这些淡水可能是在数星期之前，从安第斯山脉陡峭的一边奔涌而来的！

亚马孙河的水面高度非常一致，特别是在亚马孙河上流平原地区，许多支流都和它错综相连，彼此之间由像迷宫一样的河道网或者水道连接在一起，只有土著人才熟悉这些错综复杂的航线。而许多地方的水道都极其狭窄，以至于河面上的高大树木的枝条彼此交错形成一个个华盖，绵延数英里，可为中午烈日炎炎时乘坐独木舟的旅行者遮阳。时不时地透过厚厚的树叶间的空隙能瞧见天空；而羽翼丰满的鸟儿则来回飞着，享受着阴凉的树荫，或者端坐在枝条上梳理自己的羽毛，用各种奇怪的叫声交谈着。

有时候，水道会拓宽成水塘或湖泊，基本上都是主河中在雨季时产生的过多的河水。这些水塘中聚集了种类繁多的鱼，还有许多种类的龟和鳄鱼，电鳗以及其他奇怪的水生生物。水鸟和其他的水栖鸟类都在岸上定居；平静的水面上则漂浮着蔓延的树叶和王莲美丽的花朵以及其他的百合类植物和水生植物。

亚马孙河及其支流的内河航行适用于商品运输，其航道长度不少于5万英里。然而，在其流经的相对人迹罕至，土著人和喜欢隐居的殖民者居住的地方，水面上一年的船只比密西西比河流域每天一小时经过的船只还要少。

然而，世界上没有一处地方比伟大的亚马孙河谷要高贵的了——无论在自然资源的丰富程度上，或是能源和资源储量上，其他地方都不能和亚马孙河谷相提并论。你只需要看一眼地图即可知晓，除了智利和巴塔哥尼亚之外，南美洲的每一个国家，直接或间接都处在亚马孙河的内河航行腹地之内。

这片广大地区上的物产是如此种类丰富且数量繁多，以至于它几乎可以成为全世界的花园和仓库了。无论是常见的动植物还是奇珍异兽，如果其他供应资源中断，它们可以从亚马孙河谷获取到数量丰富到足够支撑地球上所有栖息地的资源，各种肉、鱼以及禽类的供应都会大打折扣。这里有充足的咖啡、可可以及蔗糖；有大量的玉米和稻米、棉花和烟草、香蕉和葡萄、辣椒、药以及染料、金和银，各式各样上乘的创造家具的板材以及建造房子和轮船的木料。

然而，这片多产的地区依然未被开发，并且在很大程度上尚未探索。如果有一个能让现代管理和启蒙达到可能的最优效果的地方，那就是亚马孙。

Lesson 57 THE PACIFIC OCEAN (I)

第五十七课 太平洋（一）

When the astonishing sagacity and enterprise of the Genoese had discovered the confines of a new world across the trackless Atlantic, it was without hesitation concluded, not only by himself, but by all Europe, that the new land formed the extreme eastern shore of Asia. Hence the name of Indies was erroneously given to those islands—a mistake which has been perpetuated even to the present time.

Aware of the round form of the Earth, the geographers of that age could well conceive the possibility of reaching India by a westerly course; but, ignorant of the magnitude of the globe, they had formed a very inadequate idea of its position, being totally unaware of the vast continent, and still vaster ocean, which separated Asia from the Atlantic. But as, impelled by an insatiable thirst for gold, the unprincipled Spaniards pushed their career of robbery and murder further and further into the continent, they began to hear tidings of a boundless sea, which stretched away to the south and west, beyond the horizon of the setting sun.

Balboa, one of the reckless spirits who sought fortune and fame at all hazards in the newly-found regions, boldly determined to seek the sea of which the Indians spoke. At the head of a little band of men, guided by a Mexican, he succeeded, after severe privations and imminent dangers, in crossing the isthmus that connects the northern and southern portions of the continent.

They had arrived at the foot of a hill, from the top of which the Indian assured him he would obtain a sight of the wished-for sea, when, in the enthusiasm of the moment, leaving his companions behind, the Spanish chief ran to the summit, and beheld a limitless ocean sleeping in its immensity at his feet! With the spurious piety common to the times—a piety that could consist with the grossest injustice, the blackest perjury, and the most barbarous cruelty—he knelt down and gave thanks aloud to God for such a termination of his toils. Then, having descended the cliffs to the shore of the ocean, he bathed in its mighty waters, taking possession of it by the name of the Great South Sea, on behalf of the King of Spain.

This was in the year 1513; but it was not till seven years afterwards that its surface was ruffled by a European keel. Then Megaphones, or Magellan, a Portuguese navigator of great ability, in the service of Spain, having run down the coast of South America, discovered the straits which have since borne his name. Through these he sailed, and emerging from them on the 28th November 1520, was the first to launch out upon the broad bosom of the South Sea.

For three months and twenty days he sailed across it, during which long period its surface was never ruffled by a storm; and from this circumstance he gave to the ocean the appellation of the "Pacific," which it still retains. The immediate vicinity of the straits, however, has been considered peculiarly subject to tempests; while the almost continual prevalence of westerly winds, combined with the severity of the climate, has always given a character of difficulty and hazard to the passage from the one ocean to the other.

A remarkable feature in the Pacific Ocean, and one that distinguishes it from every other sea, is the vast assemblage of small islands with which it is crowded, particularly in the portion situated between the tropics. For about three thousand miles from the coast of South America, the sea is almost entirely free from islands; but thence to the great isles of India, an extensive belt of ocean, nearly five thousand miles in length, and fifteen hundred in breadth, is so studded with them as almost to be one continuous archipelago.

The term "Polynesia," by which this division of the globe is now distinguished, is compounded of two Greek Words signifying many islands. Very few of these gems of the ocean are more than a few miles in extent, though Tahiti, and some in the more western groups, are of rather larger dimensions; while Hawaii, the largest island in Polynesia, is about the size of Yorkshire.

The isles, which in such a vast number thus stud the bosom of the Pacific, are of three distinct forms—the coral, the crystal, and the volcanic. Of these, the first formation greatly predominates; but the largest islands are of the last description; of the crystal formation but few specimens are known.

Imagine a belt of land in the wide ocean, not more than half a mile in breadth, but extending in an irregular curve to the length of ten or twenty miles or more; the height above the water not more than a yard or two at most, but clothed with a mass of the richest and most verdant vegetation. Here and there, above the general bed of luxuriant foliage, rises a grove of cocoa-nut trees, waving their feathery plumes high in the air, and gracefully bending their tall and slender stems to the breathing of the pleasant trade-wind.

The grove is bordered by a narrow beach on each side, of the most glittering whiteness, contrasting with the beautiful azure waters by which it is environed. From end to end of the curved isle stretches, in a straight line, forming, as it were, the cord of the bow, a narrow beach, of the same snowy whiteness, almost level with the sea at the lowest tide, enclosing a semicircular space of water between it and the island, called the lagoon.

Over this line of beach, which occupies the leeward side, the curve being to windward, the sea is breaking with sublime majesty. When the long unbroken swell of the ocean, hitherto unbridled through a course of thousands of miles, is met by this rampart, the huge billows, rearing themselves upwards many yards above its level, and bending their foaming crests, "form a graceful liquid arch, glittering in the rays of a tropical sun as if studded with brilliants. But, before the eyes of the spectator can follow the splendid aqueous gallery which they appear to have reared, with loud and hollow roar they fall, in magnificent desolation, and spread the gigantic fabric in froth and spray upon the horizontal and gently broken surface."

Contrasting strongly with the tumult and confusion of the hoary billows without, the water within the lagoon exhibits the serene placidity of a mill-pond. Extending downwards to a depth varying from a few feet to fifty fathoms, the waters possess the lively green hue common to soundings on a white or yellow ground. The surface, unruffled by a wave, reflects with accurate distinctness the mast of the canoe that sleeps upon its bosom, and the tufts of the cocoa-nut plumes that rise from the beach above it.

Such is a coral island; and if its appearance is one of singular loveliness, as all who have seen it testify, its structure, on examination, is found to be no less interesting and wonderful. The beach of white sand, which opposes the whole force of the ocean, is found to be the summit of a rock which rises abruptly from an unknown depth, like a perpendicular wall. The whole of this rampart, as far as our senses can take cognizance of it, is composed of living coral! and the same substance forms the foundation of the curved and more elevated side which is smiling in the luxuriance and beauty of tropical vegetation. The elevation of the coral to the surface is not always abruptly perpendicular; sometimes reefs of varying depths extend to a considerable distance, in the form of successive platforms or terraces.

Words

appellation, *name*.
aqueous, *watery*.
assemblage, *collection*.
astonishing, *marvelous*.
cognizance, *knowledge*.
compounded, *made up*.
confines, *borders*.
desolation, *loneliness*.
emerging, *issuing*.
enthusiasm, *excitement*.
environed, *surrounded*.
extending, *stretching*.
extrusive, *wide*.
gracefully, *elegantly*.
horizontal, *level*.
immensity, *vastness*.
imminent, *threatening*.
inadequate, *insufficient*.
insatiable, *unquenchable*.
interesting, *attractive*.
luxuriant, *exuberant*.
navigator, *sailor*.
perjury, *faithlessness*.
perpendicular, *vertical*.
perpetuated, *continued*.
placidity, *quietness*.
platforms, *terraces*.
predominates, *preponderates*.
privations, *straits*.
remarkable, *striking*.
sagacity, *penetration*.
semicircular, *half-circular*.
spurious, *mock*.
sublime, *imposing*.
trackless, *pathless*.

Questions

What did the earliest discoverer of the western continent suppose it to be? To what mistake has this given rise? Who was the European discoverer of the Pacific Ocean? In what year did he discover it? Who first sailed over it? Why did he call it "Pacific"? What feature distinguishes it from every other sea? "What name is given to the island sea? What does "Polynesia" mean? What is the formation of most of these islands? What is the usual shape of a coral island? What stretches from end to end of the curve? What is the water between it and the island called?

☆ ☆

当热那亚人以惊人的才智和行动找到无边无际的大西洋彼岸的封闭新世界的时候，不光是发现者本人，甚至整个欧洲都毫不犹豫地下定结论，认为新世界就是亚洲最东端的海岸了，而印度这个名字被错误地加在这些岛屿头上——这个错误一直保留到了现在。

那个时代的地理学家们已经意识到地球是圆形的，认为通过一条向西的航线到达印度是很有可能的，但他们并未意识到地球之大，因而对于印度位置的认识并不准确，对于大陆的广袤知之甚少，而对于那分隔开亚洲和大西洋更加浩瀚的海洋则更是一无所知。然而，在永不满足对获取黄金的欲望的驱使下，道德沦丧的西班牙人通过烧杀抢掠将自己的手向大陆伸得越来越深，手从能听到一片无垠大海的潮起潮落，到这片海向西向南延伸开去，绵延到落日地平线的尽头。

巴尔博亚是在这些新建地区不惜代价追名逐利的无畏的人之一，他大胆决定要寻找那片印度人所说的海域。他带领一小队人马，由一个墨西哥人做向导，在经历了几次生死垂危的海盗袭击和危急时刻之后，终于成功横渡了连接大陆北部和南部的海峡。

他们到达了一座山的脚下，从山顶望去，看到了印第安人向他许诺的期盼已久的大海，而就在他们热情高昂的时候，这位西班牙船长独自跑到山巅，看到那无边无际的大海在他脚下，在一片广袤无垠中沉睡！用当时那个时代常见虚伪的虔诚——可以和最粗俗的不公正，最黑心的伪证以及最野蛮的残忍行径相适应的虔诚——他跪了下来，并大声感谢上帝终结自己的辛苦。之后，他从悬崖下山，走到海岸边，沐浴在大海浩瀚的海水中，代表西班牙国王将这片海命名为伟大的南海，并将其占有。

这发生在1513年；但直到7年之后，才有另一个人下跪在这片海岸的地面。麦格福恩尼斯，或麦哲伦，一位能力卓绝的葡萄牙航海家，在他为西班牙皇室服务，沿南美海岸线南下期间，发现了并且之后以他的名字命名的海峡。他航行于海峡中，并于1520年11月28日驶过这些海峡，成为进入南海开阔海域的第一人。

在3个月零20天的日子里，麦哲伦航行在这片大洋上，而在此期间，海上没有任何风暴的来袭，鉴于这一点，麦哲伦将这片大洋命名为“太平洋”，并一直沿用至今。然而，这些海峡之间的宽度非常有限，被认为是特别容易受到暴风侵袭的地区；再加上几乎不间断的盛行西风的吹拂和恶劣气候的影响，从这里穿越到另一个大洋，总是困难重重，危险迭出。

太平洋的显著特征，也是和其他所有大洋的不同之处，就是它是一片数量众多的小岛集合之地，众多的小岛密布在海面上，特别是在其热带的海域上。从南美洲海岸出发大约三千英里的距离，那里的海域几乎没有任何岛屿；之后是伟大的印度岛，它是太平洋绵延的一条腰带，长约5 000英里，宽约1 500英里，周围星罗棋布着几乎一条连续的岛链。

术语“波利尼西亚”，它是由两个希腊词语组成的合成词，即许多岛屿，而根据波利尼西亚的存在，能把地球清晰地划分为两个半球。海洋上这些宝石一般的岛屿，其岛上距离一般都不过几英里，虽然塔西提岛和一些位于西部岛群的岛屿面积要更大；而夏威夷岛，也就是波利尼西亚中最大的岛屿，大小则相当于约克郡。

这些岛屿，数量巨大地星罗棋布在太平洋的怀抱中，它们可以清晰地划分为三类——珊瑚礁岛、水晶岛以及火山岛。在这些岛屿中，第一种形式的岛屿数量最多，然而最大的岛屿都属于第三类的火山岛，而我们已知的水晶岛则鲜有存在。

在一片广阔海域上的陆地组成的带子，宽不过一英里，而其不规则的长度则绵延了10英里，或20英里，甚至更长；其高度，最高不过高出水面一码或两码，但大量的葱郁的植物生长在上面。时不时地，在这些生长繁茂的植物的温床上，会耸立起一小片椰子树，它们挥动着自己高高飘在空中的轻盈树叶，并优雅地弯下自己又高又细的树干呼吸那吹拂而来的宜人的风。

椰子树周围都围有窄窄的沙滩，沙子是最闪亮的白色，和包裹着它们的美丽而蔚蓝的大海形成了鲜明对比。从这个形状蜿蜒的岛屿一端到另一端，有一个形状好像弓弦的狭窄海滩，也是一片同样的雪白色，绵延着几乎和大海退潮的时候一样低的距离，在它和岛屿之间围出一个半圆形的水域空间，名字叫环礁湖。

这片占据在下风向的沙滩和处在上风向的岛屿把这片海洋分隔开来。当那长长的未被切分的海洋因此向前涌动了数千英里的路程和这堡垒相遇的时候，巨大的浪潮腾起高于海面数码的距离，将那吐着白沫的浪头向前猛拍，“形成了一个优雅水的拱形桥，在热带的阳光照耀下熠熠闪光，好像上面布满了宝石一样。但是，就在观看者看到这似乎是它们形成的壮丽的水廊的时候，它们惊天动地地呼啸着落下，偃旗息鼓，将那巨大的波涛推向前方，散落在平整而温和，没有断开的海面上。”

环礁湖中的水，和外面呼号的巨浪的翻腾和旋转形成了鲜明的对比，它带有一种池塘的宁静氛围。海水向下延伸的深度从几英尺到50英尺不等，呈现出一抹生动的绿色，那是很常见的萦绕在白色或黄色土地周围的颜色。水面上没有一个海浪激起的涟漪，大致能准确而鲜明地映衬出睡在它怀抱中的独木舟的桅杆以及沙滩上耸立的椰子树的形状。

这就是珊瑚岛，而如果其形貌是它的一个可爱之处的话，因为所有见过它的人都能证明，仔细观察之下，其形态的奇妙有趣之处丝毫不比环礁湖逊色。白色的沙滩和整片海洋相对，那是一块岩石顶端，那岩石则是从一个不知深度几何的地方突然冒出来的，就像一个垂直方向的墙壁。我们极尽自己的感官去认识整个的壁垒，它是由活着的珊瑚组成的。而正是这种相同的生物形成了那曲折而更高的岛屿的边线，在那繁盛而美丽的热带植物的簇拥下微笑着。珊瑚朝水面的上升过程并不总是突兀垂直的，有时候位于不同深度的礁石会绵延到非常远的距离，它们会以逐步过渡的平台的方式或形式呈现。

Lesson 58 THE PACIFIC OCEAN (II)

第五十八课 太平洋(二)

In these regions may be seen islands in every stage of their formation: "some presenting little more than a point or summit of a branching coralline pyramid, at a depth scarcely discernible through the transparent waters; others spreading, like submarine gardens or shrubberies, beneath the surface, or presenting here and there a little bank of broken coral and sand, over which the rolling wave occasionally breaks." Others, again, exist in the more advanced state that I have just described, the main bank sufficiently elevated to be permanently protected from the waves, and already clothed with verdure, and the lagoon enclosed by the narrow bulwark of the coral reef.

Though the rampart thus reared is sufficient to preserve the inner waters in a peaceful and mirror-like calmness, it must not be supposed that all access to them from the sea is excluded. It almost invariably happens that in the line of reef one or more openings occur, which, though sometimes narrow and intricate, so as scarcely to allow the passage of a native canoe, are not infrequently of sufficient width and depth to permit the free ingress of large ships.

The advantage to man of these openings is very great. Without them, the islands might smile invitingly, but in vain,—no access could be obtained to them by shipping, through the tremendous surf by which their shores are lashed; but by these entrances the lovely lagoons are converted into the most quiet, safe, and commodious havens imaginable, where ships may lie and water and refresh their crews in security, though the tempest howl without.

It is scarcely less beneficent provision, that the position of the openings is in most cases indicated so as to be visible at a great distance. Had there been merely an opening in the coral rock, it could not have been detected from the sea, except by the diminution of the foaming surf just at that spot,—a circumstance that could scarcely be visible unless the observer were opposite the aperture. In general, however, there is on each side of the passage a little islet, raised on the points of the reef, which, being commonly tufted with cocoa-nut trees, is perceptible as far off as the island itself, and forms a most convenient landmark.

Notwithstanding that the highest point of these narrow islets is rarely more than a yard above the side, it is a remarkable fact that fresh water is frequently found in them. It is probable that the coral rock acts as a filter, allowing the sea water to percolate through its porous substance, but excluding all the saline particles held in solution.

A stranger is forcibly struck with the remarkable fearlessness which the natives of these islands have of the sea. They appear almost as amphibious as seals, sporting about in the deep sea for many hours, sometimes for nearly a whole day together! No sooner does a ship approach a large island than the inhabitants swim off to welcome her; and long before she begins to take in sail she is surrounded by human beings of both sexes, apparently as much at home in the ocean as the fishes themselves. The children are taken to the water when but a day or two old; and many are able to swim as soon as they are able to walk. In coasting along the shore it is a rare thing to pass a group of cottages, at any hour of the day, without seeing one more bands of children joyously playing in the sea.

The natives have several games which are played in the water, and which are followed with exceeding avidity, not only by children, but by the adult population.

One of these is the fastening of a long board on a sort of stage, where the rocks are abrupt, in such a manner that it shall project far over the water; then they chase one another along the board, each in turn leaping from the end into the sea. They are also fond of diving from the yardarm or bowsprit of a ship.

But the most favourite pastime of all, and one in which all classes and ages, and both sexes, engage with peculiar delight, is swimming in the surf. Mr. Ellis has seen some of the greatest chiefs, between fifty and sixty years of age, large and corpulent men, engage in this game with as much interest as children.

A board, six feet long and one foot wide, slightly thinner at the edges than at the middle, is prepared for this amusement, stained and polished, and preserved with great care by being constantly oiled and hung up in their dwellings. With this in his hand, which he calls the wave-sliding board, each native repairs to the reef, particularly when the sea is running high and the surf is dashing in with more than ordinary violence, as on such occasions the pleasure is the greater.

They choose a place where the rocks are twenty or thirty feet under water, and shelve for a quarter of a mile or more out to sea. The waves break at this distance, and the whole space between it and the shore is one mass of boiling foam. Each person now swims out to sea, pushing his board before him, diving under the waves as they curl and break, until he has arrived outside the rocks.

He now lays himself flat on his breast along his board, and waits the approach of a huge billow. When it comes, he adroitly balances himself on its summit, and, paddling with his hands, is borne on the crest of the advancing wave, amidst the foam and spray, until within a yard or two of the shore or rocks. Then, when a stranger expects to see him the next moment dashed to death, he slides oft his board, and, catching it by the middle, dives seaward under the wave, and comes up behind, laughing and whooping, again to swim out as before.

The utmost skill is required, in coming in, to keep the position on the top of the wave; for if the board get too far forward the swimmer will be overturned and thrown upon the beach, and if it fall behind he will be buried busiest the succeeding wave: yet some of the natives are expert as to sit, and even to stand upright, upon then board, while it is thus riding in the foam!

—P. H. GOSSE

Words

adroitly, *cleverly*.
adult, *grown up*.
amusement, *time*.
aperture, *opening*.
avidity, *eagerness*.
beneficent, *bountiful*.
bulwark, ram *part*.
commodious, *roomy*.
corpulent, *stout*.
diminution, *lessening*.
discernible, *perceptible*.
favourite, *popular*.
imaginable, *conceivable*.
inhabitants, *denizens*.
invariably, *uniformly*.
joyously, *merrily*.
paddling, *rowing*.
permanently, *lastingly*.
pyramid, *cone*.
required, *needed*.
substance, *material*.
succeeding, *following*.
surrounded, *thronged*.
tremendous, *terrific*.
violence, *fury*.
whooping, *jelling*.

Questions

In what different stages of formation may coral islands be seen In the Pacific? What means of access there generally to the lagoons? How is the opening in most cases indicated? What peculiarity of the natives most strikes a stranger? What is their favourite pastime? What apparatus do they use for it? Describe the game. What danger attends it?

☆ ☆

在这些地区可以看到岛屿在形成过程中的各个阶段的形态：有的像一个伸展的珊瑚金字塔的顶点，其深度透过透明的海水几乎不可见；有的则伸展着，像海底花园或海底灌木林似的，隐藏在水面下，或者在这里或那里呈现出一点破损的珊瑚和沙子筑成的堤岸，堤岸之上，翻腾的海浪偶尔会把它击断；还有的则以一种比上述更高级的形态呈现，其主堤从水面上抬升得十分充分，这样就能够永久地将海浪阻挡在外了，并且上面已经生长了许多绿色植物，环礁湖则被狭窄的珊瑚礁壁垒环绕着。

虽然那如此高耸的堡垒足够让其中的水保持波澜不惊的状态，我们还是不能假设海洋所有通向里面的通道都被堵塞了。几乎不可避免会出现的情况是，在珊瑚礁的一边或周围会有缺口出现，虽然有时候这些缺口狭仄而紧密，但一只土著人的独木舟依旧能够从中穿行，而且它们通常的宽度和深度足够让大船自由进入。

这些缺口对人的好处是非常大的。如果没有它们的存在，小岛即使是宜人地微笑着，也都是枉然，因为没有入口能让船只进入，从那拍打着它们堤岸的波涛汹涌中穿行。但有了这些入口之后，迷人的环礁湖就变成了想象中的最静谧、最安全，也最宽敞的天堂，虽然环礁湖之外暴风呼啸，但在湖里，船只能安全地歇息，让船员补给淡水，重新恢复体力。

同样让人获益匪浅的是这些缺口的位置，它们在大多数情况下都是在很远的距离就能被发现。如果一块珊瑚石上只有一个缺口，那么从大海望去的话，基本是发现不了的，除非是通过对那吐着白沫的浪头的减小来判断，而这种情况要发现缺口，必须是观察者正好处在缺口的对面才行。然而，总体而言，在通道的两边各自有一个小岛，一直升到和珊瑚礁平行，而那通常耸立着椰子树的珊瑚礁，则远在岛屿之上就能看得到，并形成了最易于辨认的地标。

尽管这些狭窄小岛的最高点也很少会比周围高出一码，但其中却经常存有淡水，这一点着实了不起。这很可能是因为珊瑚石充当了过滤器，让海水通过的时候，用它多孔的岩体过滤了海水，将所有的盐分都阻隔在外了。

陌生人会对这些岛屿上的土著人对大海的无畏精神感到惊诧不已。他们看起来几乎就和海豹一样，像两栖动物一般，在深海中玩上好长时间，有时差不多一天的时间都在海里嬉戏。一艘船只要一靠近大型岛屿，岛上的居民们就会游过去欢迎船只的到来；而早在船只起航之前，它就被男男女女包围了，这些人在大海中就像鱼儿一样如鱼得水。小孩子只有一两岁大的时候，就被带到水中，许多孩子一会走路就能游泳了。在沿着哈南的地带，从一个村落的房子走过，几乎随时都会看到一两拨小孩在大海里高兴地嬉戏着。

土著人有好几种在海里玩的游戏，而这些游戏不光小孩子喜欢玩，大人也非常热衷。

这些游戏中有一项是将一个长长的板子绑紧在一个平台上，平台上有突兀的岩石，深深地延伸就大海中，然后他们会一个接一个沿着板子，轮流从板子的一端跃入大海。而且它们还喜欢从船的横杆端或船首斜桅潜入大海。

但所有人最喜欢的消遣项目，也是所有阶层和年龄层，所有男男女女都特别青睐的活动，就是冲浪游泳。埃利斯先生曾见到过有些身居高位的酋长，年纪已经有五六十岁了，身形庞大又肥胖，还和小孩子一样兴趣盎然地进行这种运动。

一块长六英尺、宽一英尺的板子，末端比中间稍窄一些，已经为这次的娱乐准备就绪，它被染好颜色，抛了光，还经常用油漆粉刷后高高吊在居民的住所，得到精心的保养。土著人手里拿着板子，也就是他们叫作滑浪板的东西，每个人都向着礁石而去。这种活动尤其会在海浪汹涌，海浪比平时的拍打力度更胜的时候举行，因为在这样的情况下，得到的愉悦更多。

他们选定了一处岩石的位置，这岩石在水下的部分大约有20到30英尺，它向海面延伸的距离约四分之一英里或更长。海浪在这个距离会被拍散，而海浪和海岸之间的空间就成为一片沸腾的泡沫。此时游泳，人们把板子推在自己身前，当他们翻转身体乘风破浪的时候，就潜入海浪之下，直到他到达岩石之外的地方。

他们趴在板子上，等待着一个巨浪的到来。当浪打过来的时候，他灵巧地平衡身子攀爬到浪头，同时双手作桨滑动着，跟着向前推进的巨浪顶端向前行进，周围都是泡沫和飞溅的浪花，直到离着海岸或岩石不到一码或两码的距离。当一个陌生人以为接下来会看到他被海浪拍打至死的时候，他从板子上滑下，抓住板子中间，潜到海浪之下，然后从海浪后面浮出水面，大笑着，叫着，再次像之前一样畅游。

当海浪涌来的时候，需要有卓绝的技艺才能将身体保持在海浪的顶部，因为如果板子太向前离游泳的人太远，那么游泳的人就会被掀翻身子甩到沙滩上；而如果板子落后的话，游泳的人也会被其后的海浪结结实实地压在下面。然而有的土著人技艺如此高超，以至于他们能够坐在，甚至能够直着身子站在板子上，穿越在那飞浪之间！

——P.H. 高斯

Lesson 59 THE HIMALAYAH (I)

第五十九课 喜马拉雅（一）

Northward of the great plain of India, and along its whole extent, towers the sublime mountain region of the Himalayan, ascending gradually till it terminates in a long range of summits wrapped in perpetual snow. There may be traced, for the space of 1000 miles, a continuous line 20,000 feet above the sea; from which, as a base, detached peaks ascend to the additional height of 8000 or 9000 feet. The inhabitant of the burning plain contemplates, not without wonder, this long array of white pinnacles, forming the boundary of the distant horizon. In this progressive ascent, nature assumes a continually changing aspect; and hence it will be necessary to view in succession the different stages through which she passes.

The Himalayan range, where it touches on the champaign country, is almost everywhere girt with a peculiar belt or border, called the Tarryai. This term is applied to a plain about twenty miles broad, upon which the waters from the higher regions are poured down in such profusion that the river-beds are unable to contain them. They accordingly overflow, and convert the ground into a species of swamp; which, acted on by the burning rays of a tropical sun, throws up an excessively rank vegetation, whereby the earth is choked rather than covered.

The soil is concealed beneath a mass of dark and disma foliage, while long grass and prickly shrubs shoot up so densely and so close as to form an almost impenetrable barrier. It is still more awfully guarded by the pestilential vapours exhaling from those dark recesses, which make it, at certain seasons, a region of death. Beneath these melancholy shades, too, the elephant, the tiger, and other wild animals prowl unmolested; while the few human beings who occupy the vicinity present a meagre, dwarfish, and most sickly aspect.

On emerging from this dark and deadly plain, and beginning to ascend the lower mountain-stages, the visitor enjoys a much more pleasing scene. He passes now through smiling and fruitful valleys, overhung by the most romantic steeps, and covered to a great extent with the noblest forests. Amid trees similar to those which spread their majestic foliage on the banks of the Ganges, various species of the more hardy oak and the pine begin to appear. The prospects obtained from commanding points in those regions—consisting in a foreground of smiling and cultured vales, hills behind crowned with natural plantations, steeper and loftier ranges beyond, and in the distance the snow-clad tops of the highest mountain-chain—form a combination of the most sublime and enchanting scenery.

The Himalayan, as it ascends above the picturesque slopes which diversify its lower border, assumes a much bolder and severer aspect. The lofty ridge, the deep valley, the dashing torrent, produce a resemblance to the most elevated portions of the Highlands of Scotland; and Scottish officers, accordingly, who have happened to serve in that remote province, have fancied themselves wandering amid the romantic glens of their native country.

Generally speaking, the character of this mountain-chain is rugged and stern; its ridges rise behind each other in awful array, but they enclose no rural scenes, nor present any gentle undulations. Their steep sides, sometimes wooded, sometimes presenting vast faces of naked rock, dip down abruptly, forming dark chasms and ravines, at the bottom of which there is only room for the torrent to force its way through rude fragments fallen from the cliffs above.

In consequence of this peculiar structure, these loftier regions of the Himalayan do not present that tranquil grandeur, and those picturesque views, which render the mountain scenery of Europe so enchanting. They are rugged, gloomy, and monotonous. The mighty summits overhang no soft, pastoral valleys, nor wave with varied foliage, nor are reflected in the bosom of still and transparent lakes. The traveller, hemmed in between their steep precipices, sees only the dark grandeur of the chasm through which he winds.

Sometimes, however, on reaching a clear point, he finds himself in possession of a prospect bearing a character of the most awful sublimity. A spot raised almost to an immeasurable height above the plain beneath, proves only the base whence seven or eight successive ranges rise towards heaven, and terminate at length in a line of snowy pinnacles.

Mr. Royle, in his work on the botany of the Himalayan, divides that region, in respect to vegetation, into three tones or belts.

The first he considers as rising to the height of 5000 feet The general temperature is here lowered, as usual, in proportion to the elevation, yet without the disappearance, to the extent that might be expected, of tropical plants. The southern exposure, the intense force of the sun's rays during the hot season, and the tropical rains falling in undiminished abundance, enable these to be brought to almost equal maturity with those in the upper part of the central plain.

In Nepaul, and other favourable situations, rice as a summer, and wheat as a winter crop, form the regular course of cultivation. But some of the more delicate plants are unable to bear exposure to the keen atmosphere and the nightly breezes; among which are the choicest of fruits, the mango and the pine-apple. At the same time, in the colder season, on elevated peaks, the plants of Europe and other temperate climates are seen springing side by side with those of the tropics. Snow is scarcely ever observed on this lower stage of the mountain territory.

The second belt is considered as reaching to the height of 9000 feet. Snow here falls constantly in winter, often to a great depth, but melts in early spring. Although the vegetation becomes more and more that of the temperate zone, yet the causes already stated enable tropical plants to climb beyond their natural height, and to mingle with those of a very different clime. In sheltered, well-watered valleys, crops of rice are still successfully raised, while wheat grows on the heights above. But though the herbaceous plants are able to mount thus high, it is otherwise with trees, exposed to every vicissitude of the seasons. The palms and other Indian species are seen no longer, and the foliage appears exclusively European.

The third and most elevated belt reaches from the border of the latter to the summit of the Himalayan. The climate here is that of the more northern part of Europe and America, terminating in the perpetual snows of the arctic world. These, even in the lower districts, do not melt till May or June, when the extreme cold of winter is suddenly succeeded by the most intense heat. The rays of the sun, indeed, beat fiercely and painfully, even when the atmosphere is so little affected by them that the thermometer stands many degrees below the freezing point! and hence the traveller is scorched amidst almost unbearable cold—extremes which always prove distressing, and sometimes fatal.

The territory called Bhutan, constituting the most elevated portion, has the severity of the climate aggravated by its rocky surface, so that not above one-sixteenth part of it is fit for cultivation. Yet even here, under circumstances not at all favourable, vegetation displays a luxuriance which could little be expected at so great a height. Buck-wheat and barley are generally raised with success. At 12,000 feet, Captain Webb saw the finest grain; and at 11,680, he observed forests of oak, and beds of strawberries and currants in full blossom!

The pasturage, in consequence probably of copious moisture, combined with the power of the sun's rays, grows with a luxuriance almost unequalled. A productive field, however, is occasionally ruined by the descent of glaciers, or beds of snow, which do not melt for several years.

Notwithstanding the shattered and rocky aspect of those precipices, they are covered with vast masses of hanging wood. Amidst the wilds, tall and majestic forests of pine, larch, spruce, and silver fir, sometimes even of cypress and cedar, grow, flourish, and decay; for there are no means of conveying the timber to any spot where it might be subservient to human use or ornament.

With these trees are intermingled numerous bushes loaded with the fruits which form the luxury of the northern regions of Europe; gooseberry, raspberry, strawberry—all unknown to the plains below. In sheltered spots, the wild rose, the lily of the valley, cowslip, dandelion, and various other flowers, are seen bursting through the green carpet. The trees and rocks in the higher districts are richly clothed with moss and lichen—the vegetation of the countries bordering on the arctic circle.

Words

aggravated, *intensified.*
arctic, *north-polar.*
ascending, *rising.*
contemplates, *regards.*
continuous, *unbroken.*
cultured, *cultivated.*
disappearance, *absence.*
distressing, *painful.*
unchanging, *captivating.*
excessively, *extremely.*
exclusively, *entirely.*
exhaling, *arising.*
fiercely, *violently.*
fragments, *pieces.*
glaciers, *ice rivers.*
immeasurable, *immense.*
impenetrable, *not to be pierced.*
intermingled, *mixed.*
melancholy, *gloomy.*
monotonous, *same.*
pasturage, *herbage.*
pinnacles, *peaks.*
plantations, *forests.*
profusion, *abundance.*
progressive, *gradual.*
resemblance, *likeness.*
romantic, *picturesque.*
sheltered, *proceeded.*
subservient, *contriblitary.*
suddenly, *abruptly.*
temperate, *cool.*
terminates, *finishes.*
territory, *region.*
thermometer, *heatmeasurer.*
tranquil, *calm.*
unbearable, *insufferable.*
undiminished, *not lessened.*
undulations, *Irregularities.*
unmolested, *undisturbed.*
vegetation, *plant-life.*
vicissitude, *change.*

Questions

What is the height of the continuous line of the Himalayan? To what height above that do some of the peaks rise? What is the Tarryai? What are its dangers? What is the nature of the country immediately above that? To what is the bolder scenery still higher up compared? Into how many zones, as to vegetation, has the Himalayan been divided? What are their limits? What is remarkable in the vegetation of the first zone? What is the character of that of the second zone? How are tropical plants able to grow in those elevated regions? To what extremes is the traveller often exposed in the third zone? Why is the pasturage so luxuriant there? What European fruits and flowers are found there?

印度北方的平原沿着其整个基线，矗立着宏伟的喜马拉雅山脉，它的海拔逐渐升高，直到那绵长的高峰山顶被永久积雪所覆盖。在那里能看到1 000英里长、绵延在海岸线2 000英里高度之上的群山，以这个山脉作为基准线，与世隔绝的山峰在此基础上又向上耸立了2 000或者9 000英尺的高度。这片阳光灿烂的高原上的居民，心存敬仰地把这一座座白色的山峰看作是遥远地平线的边界。在这不断攀升的高山上，自然呈现出不断变换的景致，因此，我们要依照大自然的变换流转观看这些不同的景致。

喜马拉雅山脉似与天堂相接，这里几乎处处都是独特的地带或边界，这些地方叫作雅依。这个名字是用来称呼一个宽约20英里的高原区的，上面奔流着从更高的地区一泻而下的洪流。那水流极其湍急，以至于河床都容纳不了那么多水流。因此水都被冲出了河床，并把周围的土地变成沼泽，而这在灼热的热带阳光的作用下，形成了种类极其丰富的植被，那里的土地与其说是覆盖着植被，不如说是被植被紧紧地裹在那里。

土壤隐藏在黑暗而阴郁的植被下面，而高草和真叶状植被则耸立得又密集又紧凑，形成了一个几乎穿越不过的屏障。更糟糕的是从这些黑暗的庇荫处蒸腾而起的有害气体。在特定季节的时候，这气体让这一地带成为死亡之地。在这些阴郁的阴影下，大象、老虎以及其他的野生动物不受烦扰的觅食；而占领附近地区的极少数的人类，则呈现出一种贫困、胆小以及最战战兢兢的状态。

这片黑暗而致命的高原上，出现并开始耸立起较低的山体，旅行者能够观赏到一片更愉悦的景色。现在旅行者穿过了宜人的硕果累累的山谷，那山谷被最浪漫的陡峭山峰所环绕，上面覆盖着广袤的原始森林。在那些生长在恒河岸边的树木相似的树木中，各式各样的树质坚硬的橡树和松树开始出现。从居高临下俯视看到的景色——那宜人的、经过耕耘的山谷的前部，位于高海拔的自然平原之后的山丘，远处更加陡峭海拔更高的山峰以及遥远地方积雪覆盖其顶端的高耸山峦——形成了最崇高而迷人的景致。

随着喜马拉雅山向风景如画的山坡攀爬，那山坡把它较低的边界线分化成不同的样子，而喜马拉雅山则呈现出越来越荒凉和庄严的景象。高耸的山脊、幽深的山谷、湍急的水流，都和苏格兰高地的最高海拔地区的景象非常相像；而恰好在那一偏远地区服役的苏格兰的军官们，能够想象自己是在他们祖国浪漫的山野中漫步徜徉。

总体而言，这个山系的特点就是崎岖不平，其山脊依次排列的形态非常险峻，但它们并没有营造出任何的乡野风光，也没有呈现出任何温和的起起伏伏。山系险峻的一侧，有的地方有树木生长，有的地方则呈现出光秃秃岩石嶙峋的景象，这一侧突兀地向下伸展，形成黑暗的缝隙和山涧，而在其底部的空间仅仅够水流奔流向前，从上方悬崖掉落下来的粗犷的碎石上流过。

这种特殊的形态之下，喜马拉雅山系这些海拔较高的地区没有呈现出一种静谧的巍峨，也没有那些如画的景致，而正是这些景致让欧洲的山野风光如此迷人。它们崎岖不平、晦暗阴郁且单调乏味。巍峨的峰巅没有环绕着柔和或有田园风光的山谷，也没有各种不同植被错落其间，亦没有在那精致而透明的湖泊倒映出来的美景。旅行者在它们陡峭的峭壁之间哼着歌儿，看见的只有他蜿蜒走过晦暗的峡谷。

然而有时候，当到达了一个视野清晰地点的时候，他发现自己看到的是一片拥有最巍峨而崇高的景象。这个点虽然要比下面的平原高出几乎不可测量的高度，但实际上只不过是在七八座连续绵延的山脊之间的盆地罢了，那山脊一直向着天穹上升，直到最后终止在积雪覆盖的山峰。

罗勒先生，在他对喜马拉雅山系的植物学研究中，把这一地区，根据植被覆盖的不同，分成了三个植物带。

他认为第一个植物带高度上升有5 000英尺。总体而言，这里的气温相对于平常这个海拔高度的气温来说要低一些，然而和预料的情况不同的是，热带植物并没有在这里消失。南部的向阳坡，在气候炎热季节的密集阳光照耀下以及在频繁的热带降雨的作用下，这里的植物的繁茂程度几乎可以和那些生长在中部平原海拔较高地区的植物没什么差别。

而尼泊尔和其他气候宜人的地区，使夏季作物的大米和冬季作物的小麦形成了有规律的耕作制度。但有些生命力较弱的植物则不能适应在这样的大气之中，并被夜风吹拂，其中就有一些最娇贵的水果，如芒果和凤梨。同时，较为寒冷的季节，在海拔很高的山峰上，能够看到欧洲其他温带地区的植物和热带地区的植物肩并肩地摇曳生长。在山区这一较低海拔的地区，几乎见不到积雪。

第二个植物带被认为到达了9 000英尺的高度。冬天的时候，大雪不断降落，经常会积得很深，但在早春时节就会融化。尽管这里的植被变成越来越多的温带地区植物，但前文提到的原因使得热带植物能在高于它们自然生长海拔的地方，和不同气候下的各种植物混杂生长。在阳光充足、水源充足的峡谷中，稻米作物依然能够成功种植，而小麦则在海拔更高的地区生长。尽管草本植物能够在这么高海拔地区生长，适应在这样的环境中，树木则要另当别论了。这里看不到棕榈树和其他印度树木，全部都是欧洲大陆的植被了。

第三个也就是海拔最高的植物带从第二个植物带的上边界一直延续到喜马拉雅山系的顶峰。这里的气候比欧洲和美洲北部地区更寒冷，最终以北极世界的永久积雪为其终点。这些积雪，即使是在海拔稍低一些的地区，也不见融化。直到到了5

月或者6月的时候，当彻骨的寒冷突然被最灼热的高温取代，这些积雪才会有所融化。要知道，这里的气候几乎不受阳光影响。的确，太阳光线猛烈的照耀照样使温度计还是显示在冰点若干刻度之下！因此，旅行者在几乎难以忍受的寒冷中还被阳光所灼伤——这样极端的情况总是让人沮丧的，而有的时候这样的情况是致命的。

有个名叫不丹的国家，处在海拔最高的地区，那里岩石嶙峋的地形则让本已严峻的气候变本加厉。因此，能够适合耕作的面积不过占整个国土的十六分之一。然而，即使是在这里，环顾那并不十分宜人的四周环境，也能够看见植物繁茂地生长着，而植物能生长在这样的高度出乎人们的想象。荞麦和大麦通常能在这里成功种植。在海拔12 000英尺的高度，韦伯上校曾看到最好的谷物；而在海拔11 680英尺的高度，他看到有橡树林，草莓田还有花朵盛放的黑加仑。

而草场，在这种湿气丰富的气候的影响下以及太阳光的作用下，几乎无与伦比地茂盛地生长着。然而，一块多产的田地，偶尔会因为数年未能融化的冰川的下移，或者冰雪从高海拔落下而遭到毁坏。

尽管这些悬崖峭壁岩石嶙峋且支离破碎，但上面覆盖了大量的树木。在这些野生植物中有高大而肃穆的松树林、落叶松、云杉、银杉，有时甚至还有柏树和雪松在林子里生长、繁茂和衰败，因为没有任何可能把这些木材运输到可为人类所用或装饰的地方去。

和这些树混杂生长在一起的还有不计其数的灌木丛，里面有大量的果树，这些果树形成了欧洲北部地区的繁盛景象：醋栗、覆盆子、草莓——在下面的平原上都无人知晓。在荫庇的地方，能看到野玫瑰、山谷百合、流星花、水仙花，还有其他各种各样的花，在“绿毯”的映衬下怒放着。较高海拔地区的树木和岩石则都被苔藓和地衣包裹着——它们是北极圈周边国家标志性的植被。

Lesson 60 THE HIMALAYAH (II)

第六十课 喜马拉雅（二）

The animal world in this higher region undergoes a change equally striking with the vegetable. The elephant and the tiger, kings of the forests beneath, disappear, or are very seldom seen. Depredations are chiefly committed by the wild cat, the bear, and the hog. The chamois bounds from rock to rock, and the forests are filled with deer of various species; of which the most rare and precious is that producing the musk. It is found only in the loftiest heights, amid rocks which the human foot scarcely dares to tread. The most intense cold is so effectual to its life, that the young, on being brought down to a warm situation, usually perish in a few days.

The forests, at all the more moderate elevations, are filled with flocks of such fowls as are elsewhere domesticated, here running about wild, tempting the pursuit of the sportsman; but, as they very seldom take wing, they are with difficulty reached by the gun. The peacock displays his glittering plumage only on the lower hills. The sovereign eagle is seldom descried amid the cliffs, which are inhabited by kites, hawks, and others of the minor predatory birds. Partridges and pheasants are numerous, and of various species; the latter are even seen flying amid the snows at a great elevation.

THE MUSK-DEER

The domestic animals, fed by the natives on their rich pastured, are the common black cattle of India, combined with the yak of Thibet. Sheep and goats are also reared in large numbers, not only for the ordinary purposes of food and clothing, but for the conveyance of merchandise, which they alone are fitted to transport over the steep mountain-passes. Besides the common sheep, there is another breed, powerful and long-legged, and able to bear more than double the burden of the former.

The most elevated part of this stupendous range is that to the north of Bengal, along the heads of the Gogra, the Ganges, and the Jumna, and westward as far as the Sutlej. Above fifty peaks rise about 20,000 feet; and Kanchenjunga, 28,180 feet; Karakoram, 28,278 feet; and Everest, 29,000 feet, are the highest known points of the globe.

THE YAK

Notwithstanding the gloomy aspect of these mountain scenes, there are a few places in which they open out into smiling plains of considerable extent. The valleys of Nepaul, indeed, besides being very narrow, belong rather to the region of the lower hills. Considerably higher is found the Rama Serai, or the Happy Valley, where little eminences, villages, and richly-cultivated fields, combine to form a delightful scene. The most extensive opening, however, takes place at its western extremity, where these great ridges enclose the little kingdom of Cashmere, which, beyond any other spot on Earth, seems to merit the appellation of a terrestrial paradise.

The passes which extend across this tremendous ridge into Thibet are of extreme and peculiar difficulty. From the structure of the mountains, the roads must generally be carried nearly over their summits, rising sometimes as high as 20,000 feet They are, in most cases, formed by a precarious track along the alpine torrent, which dashes in an unbroken sheet of foam, through dark ravines bordered by precipitous mountain walls ascending above the clouds.

Down the perpendicular faces of these stupendous avenues descend almost continual showers of stony fragments, broken off from the cliffs above. Occasionally, large portions of rock are detached, and roll down in heaps, effacing every path which has been formed beneath, filling the beds of the rivers, and converting them into cataracts. The whole side of a mountain has been seen thus parted, and spread in fragments at its base. Trees, torn up and precipitated into the abyss, lie stretched with their branches on the earth and their roots turned up to the sky. Yet through these tremendous passes, and across all these mighty obstructions, the daring industry of man has contrived to form tracks,—narrow, indeed, as well as perilous, but such as to enable Thibet and India to exchange commodities.

In proceeding along these stupendous heights, the traveller occasionally experiences a distressing sensation. The atmosphere, rarefied to excess, becomes nearly unfit for supporting respiration. The action of the lungs being impeded, the slightest fatigue overpowers him; he stops at every three or four steps, gasping for breath; the skin is painful, and blood bursts from the lips.

The natives, who are also seized with these symptoms, without being able to divine the physical cause, ascribe them to *bis*, or *bish*; meaning air poisoned, as they imagine, by the deleterious odour of certain flowers. A little observation would have shown them that the flowers in these regions have scarcely any scent; while it is in the most elevated tracts, where all vegetation has ceased, that the feelings in question become most oppressive.

Amid these awful scenes there are two spots peculiarly sacred and sublime; those, namely, where the Jumna and the Ganges, the two rivers which give grandeur and fertility to the plain of Hindustan, burst from beneath the eternal snows. No mortal foot has yet ascended to their highest springs, situated in the most elevated recesses of the mountains. There they issue forth as torrents, amid broken masses of granite, to force their way through the deep glens of the middle Himalayan.

—HUGH MURRAY

Words

fertility, *fruitfulness*.
abyss, *depths*.
appellation, *name*.
avenues, *passes*.
conveyance, *transport*.
deleterious, *poisonous*.
depredations, *plunder*.
domesticated, *tamed*.
elevated, *lofty*.
eminences, *heights*.
experiences, *encounters*.
gloomy, *sombre*.
inhabited, *occupied*.
intense, *severe*.
merchandise, *goods*.
obstructions, *hindrances*.
oppressive, *painful*.
paradise, *Eden*.
plumage, *feathers*.
precarious, *dangerous*.
precipitated, *hurled*.
precipitous, *steep*.
predatory, *preying*.
producing, *yielding*.
respiration, *breathing*.
stupendous, *tremendous*.
terrestrial, *earthly*.
undergoes, *suffers*.

Questions

What animals disappear as we reach the higher region? What the chief animals found there? What is remarkable about the musk-deer? What birds are found there? What domestic animals are reared by the natives? What are the highest peaks in the range? What is the height of Everest? What Is the character of Cashmere? What is the nature of the passes across the Himalayan ridge? What makes travelling by them very dangerous? What painful sensation does the traveller often feel in the higher altitudes? To what do the natives ascribe this? To what is it really owing? What are the two spots which are peculiarly sacred and sublime?

☆ ☆

高原上的动物所经历的剧烈变化，和植物经历的剧烈变化并没有什么差别。大象和作为丛林之王的老虎都消失了，或者非常少见了。掠夺和破坏植被的主要是野猫、熊以及山猪。岩羚羊在岩石间大量出没，森林中则充满了各式各样的鹿，而其中最罕见也最珍贵的一种鹿能产生麝香。这种鹿只能在这样高海拔的地方才能找到，它们出没在岩石间，那里很少有人类胆敢踏足。它们对于这里高寒的气候非常适应，以至于如果把它们的幼崽带到温暖的地带，通常不出几日就会死亡。

在气候更温和地区的森林，有许多的鸟类，那些在其他地方都已经被驯化或豢养的鸟类，在这里却自由自在地飞翔，惹得运动员都要去追逐它们了；但因为它们很少展开翅膀飞翔，要用枪打中它们也就十分困难。孔雀只在海拔较低的山丘上才舒展它那美丽的羽毛。鹰隼则很少在悬崖上出现，在悬崖上生存的是鹞、鹰，和其他较小的猎食性鸟类。鹧鸪和野鸡数量庞大，它们的种类也是各式各样；而后者则是在高海拔地区的雪上飞翔。

有土著人在他们丰美的草原上圈养动物，有常见的印度黑牛以及西藏的牦牛。这里圈养的绵羊和山羊的数量也很大，它们不仅可以作为平日的食物和衣物供给，更能方便商业往来，因为这些动物能穿越陡峭的山间要塞，驮载物品。除了常见的羊之外，还有另外一种动物，它力量更大，腿更长，而且能够承受前者所能载重的两倍的重物。

这个庞大的山系中海拔最高的部分是位于孟加拉国以北的，沿着高格拉河、恒河、亚穆纳河以及一直向西延伸的萨特累季河的源头的地区。大约有五十座山峰的高度达到2万英尺，干城章嘉峰的高度则达到28 180英尺，喀喇昆仑山脉有28 278英尺，珠穆朗玛峰有29 000英尺，它们都是地球上已知的最高点。

然而，这些山区景色荒凉，当然还有一些地方，它们开阔地延伸进微笑的高原中，那高原面积非常巨大。尼泊尔山谷，除了的确非常狭窄以外，其实更应该属于较低海拔山区。海拔高得多的峡谷则出现在罗摩谷，或者幸福谷。那里有小高寨、村庄以及耕耘良好的田地，它们共同形成了一片愉悦景象，然而最开阔的空地，却是在它的最西端。在那里，伟大山峰裹挟下的是克什米尔王国，这个地方似乎比地球上任何其他国家更能够当得起人间天堂的称号。

这些延伸进西藏巍峨山峰之间的通道是极难通过的。根据山峦的地形特点，这些路大都修在山巅，有时高度会达到海拔2万英尺。大多数情况下，这些路沿着高山险峻的湍流修成。这些湍流以一种气势磅礴、飞沫四溅、从险峻而高耸入云的山壁围成的暗黑的山洞中穿过。

顺着这些庞大的大道垂直的岩壁向下走，不断有石头碎片如大雨一样倾盆而下，它们是从上面的悬崖掉落下来的。偶尔会有很大的岩石部分剥离下来，大堆大堆地滚落下来，把下面已经形成的所有小路都弄得面目全非，填满河床，将河流变成了瀑布。这样，整个山峦的一侧被分离开来，碎片在其基准线上蔓延飘落。树木被折断了并沉沦进深渊之中，树枝伸展着躺在地上，它们的根部则朝向天空。然而人们却能从这些危险的通道中，还有那些高耸的障碍物上通过，他们无畏的勤劳精神造就了这些小路——这些小路的确很狭窄，也很危险，但这样就能在西藏和印度间进行商品贸易了。

沿着这些巍峨的高山向前走，旅行者会不自然地产生沮丧情绪。那里的大气变得非常稀薄，几乎不足以支持呼吸。肺部的运动受到阻隔，轻微的疲劳感就能让人疲惫不堪；旅行者每走上三四步就得停一下，大喘着气呼吸；他们的皮肤变得疼痛，血液从嘴唇上渗透出来。

土著人也会出现这样的症状，如果没有确切原因的话，他们会将其身体反应归因于碧斯或碧史，意思是空气中毒，正如他们想象的那样，这症状是由某种花的有毒气味引起的。只要稍作观察就能发现，这些地区的花朵几乎都没有什么气味；而在那些海拔最高，所有的植物都不再生长的地区，这种疑惑的心情就变得更加压抑了。

在这些可怕的景象中，还有两处特别神圣而崇高的地方，这两处地方分别是亚穆纳河和恒河，这两条河流给了印度高原庄严和生机，它们从永久积雪那里奔流而下，流过大片裂纹的花岗岩地，一路奔流着穿过深邃的喜马拉雅中间的幽谷，还没有人踏足过它们最高的发源地——那海拔最高的群山的隐秘之处。

——休·穆雷

Lesson 61 LONDON AND ITS FOOD

第六十一课 伦敦和伦敦食品

If, early on a summer morning, before the smoke of countless fires had narrowed the horizon of the metropolis, a spectator were to ascend to the top of St. Paul's, and take his stand upon the balcony that with gilded rail flashes like a fringe of fire on the summit of the dome, he would see sleeping beneath his feet the greatest camp of men upon which the sun has ever risen. As far as he could distinguish by the morning light, he would behold stretched before him the mighty map of the metropolis; and could he ascend still higher, he would note the stream of life overflowing the brim of hills which enclose the basin in which it stands.

In the space swept by his vision would lie the congregated habitations of two and three-quarter millions of his species,—but how vain are figures to convey an idea of so vast a multitude! If Norway, stretching from the Frozen Ocean down to its southern extremity in the North Sea, were to summon all its people to one vast conclave, they would number little more than half the souls within the London bills of mortality! Switzerland, in her thousand valleys, could not muster such an army; and even busy Holland, within her mast-thronged harbours, humming cities, and populous plains, could barely overmatch the close-packed millions within sound of the great bell at his feet.

As the spectator gazed upon this extraordinary prospect, the first stir of the awakening city would gradually steal upon his ear. The rumbling of wheels, the clang of hammers, the clear call of the human voice, all deepening by degrees into a confused hum, would proclaim that the mighty city was once more rousing to the labour of the day; and the blue columns of smoke climbing up to heaven would intimate that the morning meal was at hand.

At such a moment the thought would naturally arise in his mind,—In what manner is such an assemblage victualled? By what complicated wheels does all the machinery move by which two and three-quarter millions of human beings sit down to their meals day by day, as regularly and quietly as though they only formed a snug little party at Lovegrove's on a summer afternoon?

As thus he mused respecting the means by which the apply and demand of so vast a multitude are brought to agree, so that every one is enabled to procure exactly what he wants, at the exact time, without loss to himself or injury to the community, thin lines of steam, sharply marked for the moment, as they advanced one after another from the horizon and converged towards him, would indicate the arrival of the great commissariat trains, stored with produce from all parts of these isles and from the adjutant continent. Could his eye distinguish in addition the fine thread of that far-spreading web which makes London the most sensitive spot on the Earth, he would be enabled to take in at a glance the two agents—Steam and Electricity—which keep the balance true between the wants and the supply of London.

The inadequacy of figures to convey a clear impression to the mind of the series of units of which the sums are composed, renders it impossible to give more than a faint idea of the enormous supplies of food required to victual the capital for a single year. But the conception may be somewhat assisted by varying the process. Country journals now and then astonish their readers by calculations to show how many times the steel pens manufactured in England would form a chain around their own little town, or how many thousand miles the matches of their local factory would extend if laid in a straight line from the centre of their market-place. Let us try our hand on the game sort of picture, and endeavour to fill the eye with a prospect that would satisfy the appetite of the far-famed Dragon of Wantley himself.

If we fix upon Hyde Park as our exhibition-ground, and pile together all the barrels of beer consumed in London in a single year, they would form a thousand columns not far short of a mile in perpendicular height.

Let us imagine ourselves on the top of this tower, and we shall have a look-out worthy of the feast we are about to summon to our feet.

Herefrom we discover the Great Northern Road, stretching far away into the length and breadth of the land. Lo! as we look, a mighty herd of oxen, with loud bellowing, is beheld approaching from the north. For miles and miles the mass of horns is conspicuous winding along the road, ten abreast; and even thus, the last animal of the herd would be seventy-two miles away, and the drover goading his shrinking flank considerably beyond Peterborough.

On the other side of the park, as the clouds of dust clear away, we see the Great Western Road, as far as the eye can reach, thronged with a bleating mass of wool; and the shepherd at the end of the flock (ten abreast), and the dog that is worrying the last sheep, are just leaving the environs of Bristol, one hundred and twenty-one miles from our beer-built tower.

Along Piccadilly, Regent Street, the Strand, Fleet Street, Cheapside, and the eastward Mile End Road line, for seven and a half miles, street and causeway are thronged with calves (still ten abreast); and in the great parallel thorough-fares of Bayswater Road, Oxford Street, and Holborn, we see nothing for nine long miles but a slow-pacing, deep-grunting herd of swine.

As we watch this moving mass approaching from all points of the horizon, the air suddenly becomes dark—a black pall seems drawn over the sky—it is the great flock of birds (game, poultry, and wild-fowl) that are come up to be killed. As they fly wing to wing, and tail to beak, they form a square whose superficies is not much less than the whole enclosed portion of St. James's Park, or fifty-one acres. No sooner does this huge flight clear away than we behold the park at our feet covered with hares and rabbits. Feeding two thousand abreast, they extend from the marble arch to the round pond in Kensington Gardens—at least a mile.

Let us now pile up all the half-quartern loaves consumed in the metropolis in the year, and we shall find they form a pyramid which measures two hundred square feet at its base, and rises into the air a height of one thousand two hundred and ninety-three feet, or nearly three times that of St. Paul's.

Turning now toward the sound of rushing waters, we find that the seven companies are filling the mains for the day. If they were allowed to flow into the area of the adjacent St. James's Park, they would in the course of the twenty-four hours flood its entire space with a depth of thirty inches of water, and the whole annual supply would be quite sufficient to submerge the City part of London (one mile square) ninety feet.

Of the fish we confess we are able to say nothing: when numbers mount to billions, the calculations become too trying to our patience. We have little doubt, however, that they would be quite sufficient to make the Serpentine one solid mass.

Of ham and bacon, again, preserved meats, and all the countless comestibles, we have taken no account; and, in truth, they are little more to the great mass than the ducks and geese wore to Sancho Panza'scelebrated mess—"the skimmings of the pot."

The railways having poured this enormous amount of food into the metropolis, as the main arteries feed the human body, it is distributed by the various dealers into very quarter of the town: first into the wholesale markets, or great centres; then into the sub-centres, or retail-shops; and lastly into the moving centres, or barrows of the hawkers. By this means nourishment is poured into every corner of the town, and the community at large is supplied as effectually as are the countless tissues of the human body by the infinitely divided net-work of capillary vessels. These food distributors amount to about 100,000. Among them are no less than 7000 grocers, early 10,000 bakers, and 7000 butchers.

—DR. WINTER.

London, as a city, is in its arrangements and regulations perhaps the most complete in the world. All seems in the most perfect order,—everything in its place, like the brooms, brushes, dusting-cloths of a perfect housekeeper; and for that prime virtue, cleanliness, it is, perhaps, more remarkable than any other. Even the air of London is sweet, save in a few localities. The atmosphere is often, indeed, thick with mingled smoke and fog, but the sense of smell is rarely offended; and this is the best evidence of an all-pervading cleanliness. As a remarkable example of arrangement, nothing can be conceived more complete in all its parts than the management of the Post Office department in London. Several times every day throughout London there is a delivery of letters, newspapers, and parcels; and notes, often scarce bigger than the wax that seals them, are conveyed with exactness and rapidity to and from every street, lane, and alley of the vast metropolis.

Words

adjacent, *neighbouring*.
appetite, *hunger*.
arrangements, *plans*.
balcony, *gallery*.
calculations, *estimates*.
celebrated, *famous*.
cleanliness, *purity*.
community, *public*.
complicated, *involved*.
conception, *idea*.
conclave, *meeting*.
congregated, *assembled*.
conspicuous, *prominent*.
consumed, *swallowed*.
countless, *numberless*.
department, *section*.
distributed, *dealt*.
effectually, *thoroughly*.
environs, *outskirts*.
exactness, *accuracy*.
extraordinary, *unusual*.
habitations, *dwellings*.
inadequacy, *incompetency*.
infinitely, *endlessly*.
localities, *districts*.
management, *administration*.
mortality, *death-rate*.
nourishment, *sustenance*.
patience, *entrance*.
perpendicular, *vertical*.
poultry, *domestic fowl*.
proclaim, *announce*.
rapidity, *speed*.
regulations, *rules*.
respecting, *regarding*.
sensitive, *susceptible*.
submerge, *overflow*.
sufficient, *enough*.
superficies, *surface*.
thoroughfares, *streets*.
victualled, *supplied with food*.

Questions

What is the population of London? Illustrate its extent by comparison with Norway. With Switzerland. With Holland. What are the two agents which keep the balance true between the wants of London in the matter of food, and the supply? If all the barrels of beer consumed in London in a year were piled together, what would they form? How far would the oxen trench, ten abreast? And the sheep? And the calves? And the swine? What area would the birds cover? And the hares and rabbits? Of what size would a pyramid of the loaves consumed in a year be? Give an idea of the annual water supply. How is this food distributed In London? How many do the food-distributors number?

☆ ☆

如果在一个夏日的清晨，在那不计其数的炊烟冒起，把都市的地平线变得狭窄之前，一个观察者登上圣保罗教堂的顶部，站在教堂穹顶上，站在镀金把手如同火焰光圈一样熠熠生辉的阳台上，他就会看见在太阳升起前，他脚下沉睡着数量最多的人。他尽可能地透过清晨的光线来辨别，就会看见在他面前绵延着一幅雄伟的大都市地图；如果他能登得更高些，就会发现生命的溪流已经溢出了山峦的边缘，而那山峦则包裹着它所在的盆地。

在他目所能及的空间中，有聚集而居的200万到325万的同胞们，而现在用这个数字来传达出那么多的芸芸众生是多么虚妄啊！如果挪威，从北冰洋向南延伸到挪威国境位于北海中的最南端，把所有这个广大地区上的人都召集起来的话，他们的数量也不过是伦敦现在人数的一半！如果是那拥有数以千计峡谷的瑞士的话，它也召集不起来数量如此之众的军队；甚至是繁忙的荷兰，在它那桅杆攒动的海港，熙熙攘攘的城市以及人口众多的平原，也几乎不能和他脚下的大钟的声响所传播的地区紧密聚集的百万之众相提并论。

当这位观察者凝望着这了不起的景象的时候，唤醒城市的第一声响动会逐渐传入到他的耳中。车轮的辘辘声，锤子的当当声，人说话的清晰声音，全部都一点点深化成一种混沌的嗡嗡声，它们预示着这座伟大的城市再次醒来迎接一天的忙碌了；蓝色的烟柱爬上天空，这说明早饭已经快准备好了。

此时此刻，他头脑中很自然地会产生一个想法，这样一个聚居地是如何产生的呢。那200万甚至325万的人要如何运转这复杂的系统啊，他们每天坐着吃早餐，非常有规律也非常安静，好像他们只是为了组成在那洛夫格罗夫的夏日下午一个小小的窃喜的聚会呢。

于是他思考，如何才能满足数量如此庞大的人群的需求呢？如何才能让每个人都正好得到他们所需要的东西，并且又不会有所损失，或者对社会产生什么危害呢？那细缕的蒸汽，此时此刻鲜明凸显，它们一个接一个从地平线冒出并吹向他的时候，合并成了一缕蒸汽，看到它就说明那伟大的补给所需的火车到来了，上面屯满了从岛国和临近大陆各个地方而来的琳琅满目的产品。如果他的眼睛能辨识出这让伦敦成为地球上最敏感的地方的细微而密布的铁路网的话，那么他只消看上一眼就能看到两个伟大的中介——蒸汽和电力——是它们让伦敦在需求之间能真正保持平衡。

数字不足以向头脑传达出一个清晰的印象，即这个数字究竟是由多少的物品组成的，这样，除了需要大量的食物供应来供养这座城市，满足其一年的需求之外的模糊观念之外，不可能再形成更清晰的概念了。但概念在一定程度上会有变化的过程。乡村记者们时不时地会为他们的读者计算出一个令人惊奇的事实：全英格兰生产的钢笔可以打造成一个环绕过他们小镇的一条钢链，或者读者们会计算出当地工厂生产的手表，如果一块块连接成直线，从商场中心开始摆放的话，它们的长度会延伸几千英里，这也让记者们惊诧不已。让我们也来试试这样的游戏，并努力地把能满足声名在外的万特雷之龙的胃口的景象尽收眼底。

如果我们把海德公园作为我们展览的基地，然后把伦敦消耗一年的啤酒桶摞在一起，那么它们就会形成一千个柱子，其垂直高度一点不小于1英里。

让我们来想象一下自己站在这个啤酒桶高塔的顶部，那么我们看到的美景，能和我们即将要赴的盛宴相媲美。

从这里我们发现了大北方路，它远远地向远方延伸，其长度和宽度都延伸进了这片土地上。我们在看的时候，一大群牛大声地哞哞叫着，正从北方而来。这一大群的牛在数英里之外就非常醒目地沿着弯弯的路走着，十头牛并排着走；而即使是这样，牛群中的最后一头牛已经在72英里之外了，而赶牛人则赶着他那数目明显减少的牛群走在彼得伯勒之外。

在公园的另一侧，当乌云散去的时候，我们就能看到大西方路，放眼望去，上面是一大簇的羊毛；在羊群（十头一排）的后面则是放牧人，还有驱赶着羊群向前的狗，他们正离开布里斯托尔的市郊，那里离着我们用啤酒桶堆成的高塔有121英里之远。

顺着皮卡迪利大街、丽晶大街、斯特兰德大街、佛里特街、齐普赛街以及米勒恩德大街的东侧，走上7英里半的路程，就会看到大街和堤道上都挤满了小牛（依然是十头一排）；而在同样著名的大道如贝斯沃特路、牛津路以及霍尔伯恩路上，我们走了9英里的路，除了形迹缓慢，低声哼叫的猪群没看见什么其他的东西。

当我们看着这一大群动物从地平线各处走来的时候，天空霎时间变得晦暗起来——似乎有一块黑色的遮挡物拉开，遮住了天空——那是一大群飞鸟（有猎鸟、家禽还有野禽）它们聚集而来，最终要被猎杀。它们翅膀挨着翅膀地飞着，首尾相接，形成了表面积一点不小于整个圣詹姆斯公园内部面积的方形，或者说面积不小于51公顷。不一会儿，这巨大的鸟群就散开了，我们看到了脚下的公园里到处是野兔和家兔。它们2 000只并排着进食，从大理石拱形桥一只绵延到肯辛顿花园的圆形池塘那边至少有1英里的长度。

现在我们把所有今年大都市里消费的超两磅重的面包排起来，就会发现它们能排成一座底部200平方英尺，高1 293英尺，或差不多三倍于圣保罗大教堂那么高的金字塔。

现在把目光转向奔流的河水，我们就会发现有七条河流来供应一天的水消耗。如果它们被允许流入到圣詹姆斯公园附近区域的话，那么它们就能在24小时之内将整个公园的区域占满，水的深度达到30英寸；而整个一年的水供应能达90英尺深，足足能吞没伦敦城（方圆1英里）。

关于鱼，我们承认无话可说：当它的数量以亿万来计算的时候，我们已经没有那么多的耐心来计算了。然而，我们几乎没什么疑问，它们将足以把蛇形湖填满。

关于火腿和培根以及能保存的肉类，还有所有不计其数的食物，我们已经没法计算了。事实上，它们的数量并不比堂吉柯德大街上的名流们头上戴的鸭毛和鹅羽少多少，这只不过是杯水车薪罢了。

铁路不断地把这些数量庞大的食物输送到这座大都市中，而这些主要的动脉又提供着人类的需求，食物被分配给城市中各个区域的不同的商贩，首先它们进入到批发市场，或者大型集散中心，然后进入到次级批发中心，或批发商店，最后到流动中心或者商贩的手推车上。通过这样的方式，营养物质就输送到了伦敦城的每一个角落，而这个大城市就像人类身体数之不尽的组织一样及时得到了给养，人类身体是通过不间断工作的毛细血管的分化合作达成正常运作。这些食物分销商们的数量达10万人之多。他们中有不少于7000个杂货商，差不多1万个面包师，还有7 000千名肉商。

——温特博士

伦敦，作为一座可能拥有世界上最完善的设施和法规的城市，一切看起来都非常井然有序，一切都按部就班，就像一个完美的管家，他的扫帚、刷子、工作服都摆放得井井有条；而在其所有的美德中，整洁要比其他的美德更加令人瞩目。即使是伦敦的空气也是甜美的，除了少数一些地方之外。大气层的确经常会厚厚地掺杂着烟和雾气，但气味闻起来却不怎么令人生厌，这就是整个城市整洁的最好例证。作为设施完善的最典型例子，没有什么能比伦敦邮政部门的管理更难能看出其设施的完备了。每天都有许多穿越在伦敦各处的送信件、送报纸以及包裹的人，还有票据，它们通常比封口的蜡大不了多少，但也被准确而快速地在这座大都市的大街小巷来来回回传送着。

Lesson 62 THE WATERS OF THE GLOBE

第六十二课 地球上的水

Water is one of the most widely diffused bodies in nature, about three-fourths of the surface of the globe being covered by it. The benevolence of the Creator is manifest in the wide diffusion of this element. It is indispensable both to the animal and to the vegetable worlds. It serves in valuable purposes in the arts and manufactures; in the form of rivers, lakes, and seas, it becomes a medium of intercourse among the nations of the Earth. To the vast reservoir of water in the ocean, moreover, we are indebted for the clouds, which carry moisture from the sea and let it down upon the parched and thirsty earth in refreshing rain.

There is a river in the sky a hundred times larger than the Amazon or the Mississippi; and not only one, but many. These rivers come to us in the spring rains, the summer showers, the nightly dews, and the winter snows. The water which thus falls from the sky every year would cover the earth, if it were level like a field, to the depth of fully five feet.

All the waters of our mighty rivers and lakes were once clouds, and the clouds are but vapour lifted into the sky from the sea by the secret engineering of the sun. The winds, by the flapping of their mighty wings, drive the vapour over the land to the hills, and the mountains, and the thirsty fields; and there the clouds pour their blessings on the farms, and pastures, and orchards, and the dusty roads and the wayside grass, bringing greenness and gladness everywhere.

The sea is in the sparkling dew-drop, and it falls in the summer shower. It makes the grass grow and the flowers unfold their gay banners—red, white and blue. It ripens the peach and the apple, and loads the fields with the yellow harvest. It spins our thread and weaves our cloth. It is harnessed to mighty engines, and does more work than thousands of men and horses. It saws our timber, lifts our coal from the bowels of the earth, and steams in the iron horse. The sea clothes and cools us, and carries us and works for us. All the water in our rivers, lakes, fountains, in the dew, fog, snow, sleet, and rain, comes alike from the sea.

From whatever source water is procured, whether from ocean, river, lake, or spring, it is always the same. It is true that water from the sea has a different taste from that of rain or river water; but the difference does not lie in the water, but in the substances dissolved in it.

Water is composed of two gases, oxygen and hydrogen, in the proportion of eight parts of oxygen to one of hydrogen, by weight.It is one of the most marvellous facts in the natural world, that though hydrogen is highly inflammable, and oxygen is a supporter of combustion, both combined form an element destructive to fire.

Pure water is destitute of colour, taste, and smell. It seldom, however, occurs in this state, but usually contains various ingredients, derived either from the atmosphere or from the earth. Rain water is the purest that can be obtained, except by distillation.

The waters of the globe are divided into fresh and salt. The fresh water includes all streams and rivers, and nearly all the springs and the greater number of the lakes, on the Earth's surface. They are called fresh, because they contain no amount of saline matter unfitting them for use. It is supposed that the lakes of North America contain more than half of all the fresh water on the face of the globe.

Salt water is that which fills the vast basin of the ocean, besides numerous lakes and springs. It forms much the larger portion of the liquid element. The proportion of saline matter which the ocean contains is about three and a half per cent. Supposing the sea to have a mean depth of one thousand feet, it has been calculated that the amount of common salt it contains is equal to five times the mass of the Alps, or about one-third less than that of the Himalayan Mountains!

Near the equator and towards the poles the ocean is less salt than in other parts. This is probably owing to the abundant rains at the equator, and to the melting of the ice in the polar regions.

The saline ingredients render sea water much heavier than fresh water, and, consequently, better adapted for navigation. Fresh water freezes at the temperature of 32 degrees; salt water, at that of 28½ degrees. The healthfulness of the ocean is partly ascribed to its constant motion, which prevents its waters from becoming stagnant and corrupt.

Words

ascribed, *attributed.*
benevolence, *bountifulness.*
consequently, *therefore.*
distinctive, *ruinous.*
difference, *diversity.*
dissolved, *decomposed.*
engineering, *contrivance.*
greenness, *verdure.*
harnessed, *yoked.*
healthfulness, *salubrity.*
includes, *computes.*
indebted, *obliged.*
indispensable, *essential.*
inflammable, *combustible.*
intercourse, *communication.*
marvelous, *wonderful.*
medium, *channel.*
moisture, *water.*
procured, *obtained.*
proportion, *ratio.*
refreshing, *reviving.*
reservoir, *store.*

Questions

What proportion of the surface of the globe is covered by water? What important purposes does it serve? What amount of water falls upon the earth in a year? Whence does all the water of the globe come? How is it diffused over the land? Of what is water composed? In what proportions? What is the purest water that can be obtained in nature? What does the fresh rater include? What are the North American lakes said to contain? What proportion of saline matter does the sea contain? Where is the ocean least salt? Why is sea water better adapted for navigation than fresh? To what is the healthfulness of the ocean partly ascribed?

☆ ☆

水是自然界分布最广泛的东西，地球表面大概四分之三都被水覆盖。造物主的仁慈在水的广泛分布上体现得一览无余。水，无论对动物世界还是对于植物王国来说，都是不可或缺的。在艺术创作和工业生产中，它都起着举足轻重的作用，它以河流、湖泊以及海洋的形式成为地球上各个国家之间交往的中介。我们不仅要感谢海洋中储存的大量的水资源，而且还应该感谢云朵，因为它们从海洋中汲取水分，然后降甘霖于干涸和皴裂的土地上。

天空中有一条河，比亚马孙河或密西西比河还要大百倍，但其实这样的河有很多。这些河以春天的降雨、夏天的倾盆大雨、夜晚的露水以及冬季的降雪来到我们身边。以这样的形式从天空坠落的水，每年都能覆盖地球。如果把地球看成一个平面的话，其覆盖深度能达到整整5英尺。

我们所有大河和湖泊的水都曾经是云朵，而云朵其实不过是因为太阳的秘密蒸馏而蒸发到天空中的水蒸气。风，拍打着它强劲的翅膀，将布满大地上空的水蒸气赶往山丘或山区以及其他缺水的地带；而在那里，云朵会降甘霖于农田、草场以及果园，还有那风尘仆仆的马路和路边草地，把葱郁和欢乐带到各处。

大海在那闪闪的露珠之中，而露珠随着夏日的倾盆大雨降到海中。它让草木生长，花朵绽放笑颜——无论是红色的、白色的还是蓝色的花朵。它催熟了桃子和苹果，促成了田野中沉甸甸的金黄的大丰收。它给我们绕线织布。它启动巨大的机器，做的活儿比一千个劳动力和马匹做的还要多。它锯着我们的木材，从矿井中把煤炭升到地面上，让汽车产生蒸汽。大海包裹我们，让我们凉爽，带我们去远方，为我们服务。河流中、湖泊中、喷泉中所有的水以及露珠、雾气、雪、冰雹和大雨同样都来自大海。

无论水是从哪种途径中得来，不管是从海洋中、河流中、湖泊里还是泉水中来，水都是一样的。的确，大海里的水，味道和雨水或者河水有所不同，但这种不同并不在于水本身，而是在于水中融化的物质。

水能被分解成两种气体，氧气和氢气，比例为每八分氧气对应一分氢气。这是根据重量的不同来划分的。水是自然世界最神奇的存在之一，虽然氢气非常易燃，而氧气又是助燃物，两种元素组合起来的物质却能够灭火。

纯净水没有颜色，没有味道，也没有气味。然而，水很少以这种形式存在。通常，它都含有各种成分，这些成分不是来自于大气，就是来自陆地。除了蒸馏水之外，雨水是能获取的最纯净的水了。

地球上的水，分为淡水和咸水。淡水包含地球表面所有的溪流和河流以及几乎所有的泉水和大部分的湖泊。它们被称为淡水，因为这其中不包含超出它们使用范畴的盐分。据估计，北美洲的湖泊包含了地球表面一半以上的淡水资源。

咸水则指的是广阔的海洋当中以及许多的湖泊和泉水中的水。它占据了水的大部分。海水中盐分的比例大约是3.5%，假设大海有1 000英尺深，那么据计算，其中含有的粗盐数量相当于阿尔卑斯山的5倍，或者差不多是喜马拉雅山脉的三分之一。

靠近赤道以及趋近两级的海域，盐分含量要小于其他海域。这很可能是因为赤道地区雨量丰沛，而极地地区则有冰雪融化的缘故。

盐分让海水变得比淡水重很多，因此，也就更适合航行。淡水的结冰点是华氏三十二度，而咸水则是三十八度。海洋的健康，部分归功于其永不停歇的运动，这使得它的水质不会沉滞或变坏。

Lesson 63 THE OCEAN

第六十三课 大 海

Who ever gazed upon the broad sea without emotion; Whether seen in stern majesty, hoary with the tempest, rolling its giant waves upon the rocks, and dashing with resistless fury some gallant bark on an iron-bound coast; or sleeping beneath the silver moon, its broad bosom broken but by a gentle ripple, just enough to reflect a long line of light—a path of silver upon a pavement of sapphire;—who has looked upon the sea without feeling that it has power "to stir the soul with thoughts profound"?

Perhaps there is no earthly object—not even the cloud-cleaving mountains of an alpine country—so sublime as the sea in its severe and naked simplicity. Standing on some promontory whence the eye roams far out upon the unbounded ocean, the soul expands, and we conceive a nobler idea of the majesty of that God who "holdeth the waters in the hollow of his hand." He has set bars and doors, and said, "Hitherto shalt thou come, but no further; and here shall thy proud waves be stayed."

—Gossz

Roll on, thou deep and dark-blue ocean—roll!
  Ten thousand fleets sweep over thee in vain:
Man marks the earth with ruin—his control
  Stops with the shore;—upon the watery plain
The wrecks are all thy deed, nor doth remain
  A shadow of man's ravage, save his own,
When, for a moment, like a drop of rain,
  He sinks into thy depths, with bubbling groan,
Without a grave, unknelled, uncoffined, and unknown.

The armaments which thunder-strike the walk

Of rock-built cities, bidding nations quake,
And monarchs tremble in their capitals;
The oak leviathans, whose huge ribs make
Their clay creator the vain title take
Of lord of thee, and arbiter of war;—
These are thy toys, and, as the snowy flake,
They melt into thy yeast of waves, which mar
Alike the Armada's pride and spoils of Trafalgar.

Thy shores are empires, changed in all save thee.
Assyria, Greece, Rome, Carthage—what are they?
Thy waters wasted them while they were free,
And many a tyrant since: their shores obey
The stranger, slave, or savage: their decay
Has dried up realms to deserts. Not so thou:
Unchangeable save to thy wild waves' play,
Time writes no wrinkle on thine azure brow—
Such as Creation's dawn beheld, thou rollest now.

Thou glorious mirror, where the Almighty's form
Glasses itself in tempests; in all time—
Calm or convulsed—in breeze, or gale, or storm
Icing the pole, or in the torrid clime
Dark-heaving,—boundless, endless, and sublime—
The image of Eternity!

—BYRON

Words

alpine, *mountainous.*
arbiter, *umpire.*
armaments, *fleets.*
control, *Jurisdiction.*
convulsed, *agitated.*
emotion, *intense feeling.*
eternity, *endless duration.*
glorious ,*splendid.*
monarchs, *sovereigns.*
pavement, *floor.*
profound, *deep.*
promontory, *headland.*
ravage, *devastation.*
remain, *survive.*
resistless, *irresistible.*
tremble, *quake.*
tyrant, *despot.*
unchangeable, *immutable.*

有谁曾不带感情地凝望过宽广的大海！在它看起来庄严而恢宏的时候，古老的海面在暴风雨的推动下，卷着巨大的海浪拍在岩石上，以势不可挡的雷霆之势扑向岩石嶙峋的海岸上的几棵大树；或是它在银色的月光下睡着，宽阔的胸膛上被一串温柔的涟漪打开，波光粼粼足以反射出长长的光线——一条银色的小径铺在宝蓝色的路面上；有谁看着大海的时候，感觉不到它那“深沉的思想激荡心灵”的力量？

可能，世间没有什么——甚至连那阿尔卑斯山区云朵萦绕的群山也算在内——能像大海一样，在静谧和不加修饰的简朴中表现得如此崇高。站在某个海角上，当眼睛极目眺望向那无垠的海洋的时候，心灵随之开阔，而我们了解到上帝恢宏的一个更高贵的说法，即上帝“把水捧在自己的掌心里”。他设上闸栏和门，并说道：“你此刻来到这里，但不能再向前奔涌；而这里将是你骄傲的海浪的栖身之所。”

——高斯

继续翻腾吧，你这深沉而蔚蓝的海洋，翻腾吧！
万艘舰船徒劳地在你身上驰骋；
人类用毁坏来标示疆界，他的控制
停留在岸上，在那流水冲刷过的平原上
遗墟残垣是你的杰作，没剩下一丝一毫
人类蹂躏的阴影，除了他自己的孽迹，
曾有一刻，他如沧海之一粟，
潜入你的深邃之中，吐气呻吟，
没有坟墓栖身，没有丧钟奏鸣，没有棺材裹体，亦无人所知。

那雷霆般袭击，
磐石筑起的城池之路的武器，撼动世人，
君王们在自己的城堡里瑟瑟发抖；
身躯巨大的海中怪兽，
使得它们血肉之躯的锻造者浪得虚名，
称你为主人，战争的主宰；
它们都是你的玩具，而且就像雪花一般，
它们融化进你海浪的泡沫中，那海浪击毁了，
无敌舰队的荣耀和特拉法加的虚荣。

你的岸即为各国疆土，变化永恒，只有你不曾改变。

亚述国、希腊、罗马、迦太基无论它们名字几何，
它们是自由国度时，你的水曾冲刷过，
此后它们在暴君统治下，你也曾造访过：它们的海岸顺从
陌生人，奴隶，或蛮夷；它们的衰败
将王土干涸成沙漠。你依然如故；
除了玩弄你那狂野的巨浪，毫无改变，
时间没有在你单薄的蔚蓝眉头上写下皱纹；
于是在造物主的暮色中见到如此景象，你现在极其猛烈地翻腾。

你荣耀的镜面上啊，上帝把自己的形象；
在暴风雨中映衬在上面，在所有岁月中，
宁静或是痉挛，在微风中，或大风下，抑或暴风雨里，
将南北极冰冻，或者在气候炎热之地，
深邃起伏，无垠，无尽，
而崇高的永恒之形象！

——拜伦

Lesson 64 THE VISION OF MIRZA

第六十四课 米尔扎的想象

When I was at Grand Cairo I picked up several Oriental manuscripts, which I have still by me. Among others, I met with one entitled "The Visions of Mirza," which I have read over with great pleasure. I intend to give it to the public when I have no other entertainment for them; and shall begin with the first vision, which I have translated word for word as follows:—

"On the fifth day of the moon, which, according to the custom of my forefathers, I always keep holy, after having washed myself and offered up my morning devotions, I ascended the high hills of Bagdat, in order to pass the rest of the day in meditation and prayer. As I was here airing myself on the tops of the mountains, I fell into a profound contemplation on the vanity of human life; and passing from one thought to another, 'Surely,' said I, 'man is but a shadow, and life a dream.'

"Whilst I was thus musing, I cast mine eyes towards the summit of a rock that was not far from me, where I discovered one in the habit of a shepherd, with a little musical instrument in his hand. As I looked upon him, he applied it to his lips and began to play upon it. The sound of it was exceeding sweet, and wrought into a variety of tunes that were inexpressibly melodious, and altogether different from anything I had ever heard. They put me in mind of those heavenly airs that are played to the departed goals of good men upon their first arrival in Paradise, to wear out the impressions of their last agonies, and qualify them for the pleasures of that happy place. My heart melted away in secret raptures.

"I had often been told that the rock before me was the haunt of a Genius, and that several who had passed by it had been entertained with music; but I had never heard that the musician had before made himself visible. When, by those transporting airs which he played, he had raised my thoughts to taste the pleasures of his conversation, I looked upon him like one astonished. Thereupon he beckoned to me, and directed me by the waving of his hand to approach the place where he sat.

"I drew near with that reverence which is due to a superior nature; and as my heart was entirely subdued by the captivating strains I had heard, I fell down at his feet and wept. The Genius smiled upon me with a look of compassion and affability that familiarized him to my imagination, and at once dispelled all the fears and apprehensions with which I approached him. He lifted me from the ground, and taking me by the hand, 'Mirza, 'said he, 'I have heard thee in thy soliloquies;follow me.'

"He then led me to the highest pinnacle of the rock, and placing me on the top of it, 'Cast thine eyes eastward,' said he, 'and tell me what thou seest. I see,' said I, 'a huge valley, and a prodigious tide of water rolling through it.' 'The valley that thou seest,' said he, 'is the Yale of Misery; and the tide of water that thou seats is part of the great tide of Eternity.' 'What is the reason,' said I, 'that the tide I see rises out of a thick mist at the one end, and again loses itself in a thick mist at the other?' 'What thou seest,' said he, 'is that portion of Eternity which is called Time, measured out by the sun, and reaching from the beginning of the world to its consummation.

"'Examine now,' continued he, 'this sea that is bounded with darkness at both ends, and tell me what thou discovers in it,' 'I see a bridge,' said I, 'standing in the midst of the tide.' 'The bridge thou seest,' said he, 'is Human Life; consider it attentively.' Upon a more leisurely survey of it, I found that it consisted of threescore and ten entire arches, with several broken arches, which, added to those that were entire, made up the number to about an hundred. As I was counting the arches, the Genius told me that this bridge had consisted at first of a thousand arches, but that a great flood had swept away the rest, and left the bridge in the ruinous condition in which now beheld it.

"'But tell me further,' said he, 'what thou discovered on it?' 'I see multitudes of people passing over it,' said I, 'and a black cloud hanging on each end of it.' As I looked more attentively, I saw several of the passengers dropping through the bridge into the great tide that flowed underneath it; and, upon further examination, perceived that there were innumerable trap-doors that lay concealed in the bridge, which the passengers no sooner trod upon than they fell through them into the tide, and immediately disappeared.

"These hidden pit-falls were set very thick at the entrance of the bridge, so that throngs of people no sooner broke through the cloud than many of them fell into them. They grew thinner towards the middle, but multiplied and lay closer together towards the end of the arches that were entire.

"There were, indeed, some persons, but their number was very small, that continued a kind of hobbling march on the broken arches; but they fell through one after another, being quite tired and spent with so long a walk.

"I passed some time in the contemplation of this wonderful structure and the great variety of objects which it presented. My heart was filled with a deep melancholy to gee several dropping unexpectedly, in the midst of mirth and jollity, and catching at everything that stood by them, to save themselves.

"Some were looking up towards the heavens in a thoughtful posture, and in the midst of a speculation stumbled, and fell out of sight. Multitudes were very busy in the pursuit of bubbles that glittered in their eyes and danced before them; but often when they thought themselves within the reach of them, their footing failed, and down they sank.

"In this confusion of objects, I observed many with scimitars in their hands, who ran to and fro upon the bridge, thrusting several persons on trap-doors which did not seem to lie in their way, and which they might have escaped had they not been thus forced upon them.

“The Genius, seeing me indulge myself on this melancholy prospect, told me I had dwelt long enough upon it.

‘Take thine eyes off the bridge,’ said he, ‘and tell me if thou yet seats, anything thou dost not comprehend?’ Upon looking up, ‘What mean,’ said I, ‘those great flights of birds that are perpetually hovering about the bridge, and settling upon it from time to time? I see vultures, harpies, ravens, cormorants, and, among many other feathered creatures, several little winged boys, that perch in great numbers upon the middle arches.’ ‘These,’ said the Genius, ‘are Envy, Avarice, Superstition, Despair, Love, with the like cares and passions that infest human life.’

“I here fetched a deep sigh. ‘Alas,’ said I, ‘man was made in vain! How is he given away to misery and mortality, tortured in life, and swallowed up in death! ’

“The Genius, being moved with compassion towards me, bade me quit so uncomfortable a prospect. ‘Look no more,’ said he, ‘on man in the first stage of his existence, in his setting out for Eternity; but cast thine eye on that thick mist into which the tide bears the several generations of mortals that fall into it.’

“I directed my sight as I was ordered, and (whether or no the good Genius strengthened it with any supernatural force, or dissipated part of the mist that was before too thick for the eye to penetrate, I know not, but) I saw the valley opening at the further end, and spreading forth into an immense ocean, that had a huge rock of adamant running through the midst of it, and dividing it into two equal parts.

“The clouds still rested on one half of it, insomuch that I could discover nothing in it; but the other appeared to me a vast ocean planted with innumerable islands, that were covered with fruits and flowers, and interwoven with a thousand little shining seas that ran among them. I could see persons dressed in glorious habits, with garlands upon their heads, passing among the trees, lying down by the sides of fountains, or resting on beds of flowers; and I could hear a confused harmony of singing birds, falling waters, human voices, and musical instruments.

“Gladness grew in me upon the discovery of so delightful a scene. I wished for the wings of an eagle that I might fly away to those happy seats; but the Genius told me there was no passage to them except through the gates of Death, which I saw opening every moment upon the bridge.

“‘The islands,’ said he, ‘that lie so fresh and green before thee, and with which the whole face of the ocean appears spotted as far as thou canst see, are more in number than the sands on the sea-shore. There are myriads of islands behind those which thou here discoverest, reaching further than thine eye, or even thine imagination, can extend itself. These are the mansions of good men after death, who, according to the degree and kinds of virtue in which they excelled, are distributed among these several islands, which abound with pleasures of different kinds and degrees, suitable to the relishes and perfections of those are settled in them. Every island is a paradise accommodated to its respective inhabitants. Are not these, O Mirza! habitations worth contending for? Does life appear miserable, that gives thee opportunities of earning such a reward? Is death to be feared, that will convey thee to so happy an existence?

Think not man was made in vain, who has such an eternity reserved for him."

"I gazed with inexpressible pleasure on these happy islands. At length I said, 'Show me now, I beseech thee, the secrets that lie hid under those dark clouds which cover the ocean on the other side of the rock of adamant.'

"The Genius making me no answer, I turned about to address myself to him a second time, but I found that he had left me. I then turned again to the vision which I had been so long contemplating; but instead of the rolling tide, the arched bridge, and the happy islands, I saw nothing but the long, hollow valley of Bagdat, with oxen, sheep, and camels grazing upon the sides of it."

—JOSEPH ADDISON

Words

accommodated, *adapted.*
adamant, *diamond.*
affability, *courtesy.*
attentively, *closely.*
avarice, *greed.*
beckoned, *motioned.*
comprehend, *understand.*
concealed, *hidden.*
consummation, *completion.*
contemplation, *meditation.*
contending, *striving.*
conversation, *discourse.*
delightful, *charming.*
despair, *hopelessness.*
devotions, *prayers.*
discovered, *descried.*
dispelled, *dissipated.*
entertainment, *amusement.*
envy, *jealousy.*
garlands, *wreaths.*
imagination, *fancy.*
inexpressibly, *unutterably.*
interwoven, *interlaced.*
manuscripts, *writings.*
melancholy, *sadness; sad.*
melodious, *sweet.*
multiplied, *Increased.*
multitudes, *crowds.*
oriental, *eastern.*
passengers, *travelers.*
prodigious, *enormous.*
raptures, *transports.*
relishes, *tastes.*
speculation, *train of thought.*
structure, *erection.*
subdued, *charmed.*
supernatural, *miraculous.*
superstition, *fanaticism.*
threescore, *sixty.*
transporting, *captivating.*
uncomfortable, *disagreeable.*
unexpectedly, *suddenly.*

Questions

What does this story profess to be? Where did the vision appear to Mirza? For what purpose had he gone there? On what was he reflecting? Who appeared to him? By what did he captivate him? Where did the Genius lead him? What did he show him? What did the valley represent?

And the tide of water? Why was the tide enclosed between thick mists? What stood in the midst of the tide? What did the bridge represent? How many arches had it? Of how many had it at one time consisted? To what is this an allusion? What lay concealed in the bridge? Where were they set most thickly? What does this represent? How are very old persons represented in the vision? How, sadden deaths? How, the devastations of war? What was the meaning of the flights of birds about the bridge? How was the region of Eternity divided? Which part was Mirza not allowed to see? Of what did the other consist? What did the Genius say the islands were? What Lessons was Mirza to draw from what he had seen?

☆ ☆

当我在大开罗的时候，我偶然发现了几卷东方手稿，现在这些手稿还在我手上。在这些手稿中，我发现一卷名为“米尔扎的想象”的手稿，我兴趣盎然地将其通读完毕。我打算既然自己没有什么好的处理方式，就把它们公之于世。现在我将开始讲述第一个想象，我将其逐字翻译如下：

“在第五个月夜，根据我祖先的习俗，我在洗漱完毕并奉上我早晨的供奉之后，总是怀着神圣的心情，向巴格达的高山攀登，这样我一天中剩下的时间就能在冥想和祈祷中度过了。当我站在山巅的时候，我陷入了对人类之虚妄的深深的沉思中；头脑中一个思绪接着另一个思绪，当然，我说道，人不是只是幻影，而人生不过是梦一场罢了。

“当我如此想着的时候，我放眼望去，看见山巅的一块离我不远的石头，在那块石头上我发现有一个从穿着看像是一个牧童的人，他手里还拿着一个乐器。我看着他的时候，他把这乐器放在唇边，开始吹奏。那乐声当真是美妙极了，其袅袅变幻的音符悦耳动听之处，难以用语言表述，而它们和我曾经听过的其他乐曲非常不同。它们让我进入了一种天堂一般的氛围中，而这是为那些初次到达天堂的好人所演奏的，以荡涤他们前世的苦难印记，让他们有资格来享用这快乐福地的愉悦。我的心在窃喜中融化了。

“经常有人告诉我说，我眼前的这块石头是有精灵附身的，而那些从它面前经过的人都会被它的乐声吸引，但我从未听过那位音师曾经现过身。在他演奏的这余音绕梁的乐声中，当我看着他的时候，我一脸惊讶。因此，他召唤我，并摆手引导我走近他坐着的位置。

“我满怀着对某种超越自然之物的崇敬心情走进他，而当我的心完全被这迷人音乐吸引的时候，我倒在他脚下，哭泣了起来。那精灵对我微笑着，脸上是同情和蔼的神色，这和我对他的想象很像，于是我走近他时的所有的恐惧和担忧都打消了。他把我从地上扶起来，拉住我的手，说道，米尔扎，我听到你的独白；跟着我来吧。

“之后他就带我到了那石头最高的一角，让我坐在石头顶部。放眼向东望去吧，他说道，然后告诉我你看到了什么。我看到，我说，一个巨大的山谷以及一条奔涌的大河翻腾着从山谷中流过。你看到的这个山谷，他说，名叫苦难谷，而那条你看到的大河属于永恒之河的一部分。是什么原因呢？我说，那条我看到的河流一端从浓雾中奔腾而来，而在另一端又消失在浓雾之中了呢？你说的现象，是叫作时间的永恒的一部分，它用太阳来测量，从开天辟地之初到它的终点。

“现在看看，他继续说道，这片两端被黑暗所包裹着的河流，然后告诉我你在里头发现了什么。我看到一座桥，我说道，那桥就在河中间。你提到的那座桥，就是人生；仔细想一想，在一次对它更自在的检视中，我发现它由三个内核和十个完整的拱形桥组成，并且其中还有几个破损的拱形桥，而这些拱形桥和那些完整的拱形桥一起，差不多有一百个。我正数着拱形桥的时候，精灵告诉我，这座桥起初包含一千个这样的拱形桥，但一场大洪水将剩余的拱形桥都冲走了，只剩下这座破败的桥，也就是你现在看到的这个样子。

“再和我说说，他说，你在上面发现了什么？我看到许多人从桥上经过，我说道，而且还有一片乌云笼罩在桥头。当我看得更仔细些的时候，我看见有几个过桥的人从桥上掉落到桥下那奔流不息的洪流之中；而再看得更仔细些，就能看到有不计其数的陷阱藏在桥身，不一会儿那些走在桥上的人就会从陷阱口掉落到水中，接着很快消失了。

“这些隐藏的坑洞在桥头的时候设置得非常厚实，这样那些过桥的人群还没等他们走过云朵覆盖的范围就掉落下桥了。到桥中间的时候，这些坑变得越来越单薄，但数量越来越多，且都靠着完整的拱形桥的末端。

“的确有些人能继续在那些破损的拱形桥上颠簸前行，但他们的数量极其微小；当他们在走了如此之长的路程之后，还是会一个接一个掉落下去，因为他们走了这么久，已经太劳累了。

“我用了一些时间思考这个了不起的结构以及它所呈现的林林总总的景象。我的心里充满了深深的忧伤，看到那么多的人在愉悦和欢快时，毫无先兆地掉落下去，他们抓住身边能抓住的一切东西来拯救自己。

“有的人是抬头望着苍天的姿势，若有所思，然后在他们思考的过程中绊倒了，之后掉落不见了。许多人在忙着追逐眼前闪动的气泡，但通常的情况是，当他们想到自己能够得着气泡的时候，他们就脚底不稳了，然后向下陷落了。

“在这么多混杂的景象前，我观察到有许多手里拿着半月刀的人，他们在桥上来回跑动着，把那些似乎没有步入自己应该走的路的人推到陷阱口上，而那些人如果没有他们的推搡本来可以逃过一劫的。

“那精灵看见我沉浸在这种忧伤的景象中，告诉我，我在上面沉思的时间太长了。

“把你的眼睛从桥上移开吧，他说道，然后告诉我你向上看的时候，有没有看到什么你不理解的东西。什么意思？我说道，这大群大群的飞鸟一直都在桥上方盘旋，而且我时不时地看到有秃鹫、鸟身女妖、渡鸦、鸬鹚还有其他有羽毛的生物会落在桥上，有很多小小的有翅膀的男孩，在中间的拱形桥上栖息着。它们代表的意思是，精灵说道，是嫉妒、贪婪、迷信、绝望和爱，用相同的关怀和激情滋养人生。

“我看到这里长长叹了一口气。唉，我说道，人类真是虚妄啊！他要经历不幸和死亡，在生活中遭受苦难，还要被死亡吞噬！

“那精灵因出于对我的同情而心生感触，因为他给我看了这样一个让我不舒服的场景，‘别再看了’，他说道，‘别再看人向永恒进发的第一阶段的存在形态了；你放眼去看看那浓厚的迷雾，在里头大水承载着许多代掉落到里头的人。’

“于是我照着他的吩咐转移视线，而且不管是不是这好心的精灵用什么超自然的法力增强了我的眼力，或者将之前我看不透的十分浓厚的迷雾散开了一些，我不知道，但我看到山谷在很远的那端开阔而向前绵延到广阔的海洋，而海洋中有一块巨大的磐石在中间涌动，将其分成了两片大小均匀的海域。

“云朵依然在其中的一半海域上空停留着，因此，我看不到里面的任何东西，但另一半则好像是一片浩瀚的海洋，里面有数不尽的岛屿，岛屿还被各式各样的水果和花朵覆盖，它们和岛屿之间的数千个小小的闪亮的海域交织在一起。我看到有穿着艳丽的人，头上还带着花环，他们从树林中穿行，在喷泉边躺着，或者在花坛中休憩；而且我能够听到鸟儿的歌唱，瀑布的磅礴，人们的交谈声以及乐器奏鸣交错在一起的和谐乐声。”

“发现了这样令人愉悦的景象之后，高兴的情绪在我心中滋长。我希望能有鹰隼一样的翅膀，这样我就能飞跃到那些我看到的福地，但精灵告诉我说没有到那里的路，除非是经过死亡之门，也就是在那桥上每时每刻发生的景象。

“这些岛屿，他说道，在你面前显得如此新鲜而葱郁，而且在整片海域的映衬下，你极目远眺就会发现它们的数量要比海滩上的沙子还要多。还有大量的岛屿在那些你看得到的岛屿之后，它们比你眼睛能看到的最远的地方还要远，或者甚至比你的想象延伸得更远。这些就是好人死后的居所，它们根据他们高出美好品德的程度和种类，被划分居住在这些岛屿上，这些岛上充满了各式各样的欢乐，适合那些生活在上面的人们完美生活和享受。每一座岛屿都是一个天堂，它们各自的居民相映衬。那不是吗，米尔扎，值得拥有的归宿，难道生活给了你得到如此丰厚归宿的机会，你还能认为它是悲惨的吗？难道还应该害怕死亡吗？而死亡将会给你如此幸福的生活，不要再想人皆虚妄了，他们面前有永恒在等待着他们。

“我以难以言表的愉悦看着这些幸福的岛屿。最后我说道，给我看看吧，求你啦，这些乌云之下隐藏着的秘密，就是那些笼罩在磐石另一侧的岛屿之上的那些乌云。

“精灵一言不发，我又跟他重述了一遍自己的请求，但我发现他已经离我远去了。然后我又转入了自己曾长时间冥想的想象，但我没有看到翻腾的大海，没有看到拱形桥，也没有看到幸福的岛屿，我什么也没有看到，除了又长又空洞的巴格达山谷，山谷边上的牛，羊以及正在吃草的骆驼，我什么也没有看到。”

——约瑟夫·艾迪森

Lesson 65 A PSALM OF LIFE

第六十五课 生命礼赞

Tell me not, in mournful numbers,	勿用悲伤的口吻对我诉说，
Life is but an empty dream!	那人生不过是梦幻一场！
For the soul is dead that slumbers,	因为沉睡中的灵魂已经逝去，
And things are not what they seem.	万物并非他们显现的模样。
Life is real! life is earnest!	生命真实可感！生活严肃真诚！
And the grave is not its goal;	其终点绝不是坟场；
"Dust thou art, to dust returnest,"	尘归尘，土归土，
Was not spoken of the soul.	然而灵魂并未灭亡。
Not enjoyment, and not sorrow,	我们宿命的结局和道路，
Is our destined end or way;	既非丝竹享乐，亦非悲伤悲鸣；
But to act that each to-morrow	而应行动起来，每一个明天，
Find us further than to-day.	都比我们今天走得更长远。
Art is long, and Time is fleeting,	韶光飞逝，艺术弥坚，
And our hearts, though stout and brave,	心虽勇敢坚毅，
Still, like muffled drums, are beating	然仍如低沉的鼓声阵阵，
Funeral marches to the grave.	向着坟墓，哀乐奏鸣。
In the world's broad field of battle,	在世界辽阔的战场上，
In the bivouac of life,	在生命露宿的营地上；
Be not like dumb, driven cattle!	勿要默默无声，作那任人驱逐的牛羊，
Be a hero in the strife!	而要是战斗中骁勇善战之猛将！
Trust no Future, howe'er pleasant!	莫依赖未来，不管它怎样欢畅！
Let the dead Past bury its dead!	让逝去的岁月将死者埋葬！

Act—act in the living Present!	行动吧，就在活着的此刻行动！
Heart within, and God o'erhead!	胸内有红心，头顶有上苍！
Lives of great men all remind us	伟大人物的生平提醒我们，
We can make our lives sublime;	我们能使自己的一生变得高尚，
And, departing, leave behind us	在离开人间时，也能让
Footprints on the sands of time,—	足印遗留在我们身后时间的沙滩上。
Footprints that perhaps another,	呵，足印！也许另一位兄弟，
Sailing o'er life's solemn main,	当他航行在生命庄严的海洋上，
A forlorn and shipwrecked brother,	不幸遇难，看见了这些足印，
Seeing, shall take heart again.	他的勇气定会新增长。
Let us, then, be up and doing,	那么，让我们振奋起来吧，
With a heart for any fate;	准备迎接任何命运的风浪；
Still achieving, still pursuing,	永远要有所作为，不断追求，
Learn to labour and to wait.	学会劳动，也学会等待和期望。
—H. W. LONGFELLOW	——亨利·沃兹沃斯·朗费罗

Words

achieving, *accomplishing*.
bivouac, *campaign*.
destined, *appointed*.
earnest, *serious*.
enjoyment, *pleasure*.
fleeting, *transient*.
footprints, *traces*.
forlorn, *desolate*.
goal, *end*.
mournful, *doleful*.
muffled, *dull*.
pursuing, *striving*.
remind, *suggest to*.
slumbers, *sleeps*.
sublime, *noble*.

Lesson 66
THE TIDE-WAVE IN THE BAY OF FUNDY
第六十六课　芬迪湾大潮

The tide-wave that sweeps to the north-east, along the Atlantic coast of the United States, entering the funnel-like mouth of the Bay of Fundy, becomes compressed and elevated as the sides of the bay gradually approach each other. In the narrower parts, the water runs at the rate of six or seven miles an hour, and the vertical rise of the tide amounts to sixty feet or more! At some points these tides, to an unaccustomed spectator, have rather the aspect of some rare convulsion of nature than of an ordinary daily occurrence.

At low tide, wide flats of brown mud are seen to extend for miles, as if the sea had altogether retired from its bed; and the distant channel appeal's as a mere strip of muddy water. At the commencement of flood, a slight ripple in seen to break over the edge of the flats. It rushes swiftly forward, and, covering the lower flats almost instantaneously, gains rapidly on the higher swells of mud, which appear as if they were being dissolved in the turbid waters.

At the same time the torrent of red water enters all the channels, creeks, and estuaries; surging, whirling, and foaming, and often having in its front a white, breaking wave, or "bore," which runs steadily forward, meeting and swallowing up the remains of the ebb still trickling down the channels. The mud flats are soon covered; and then, as the stranger sees the water gaining with noiseless and steady rapidity on the steep sides of banks and cliffs, a sense of insecurity creeps over him, as if no limit could be set to the advancing deluge. In a little time, however, he sees that the flat, "Hitherto shalt thou come, but no further," has been issued to the great bay tide: its retreat commences, and the waters rush back as rapidly as they entered.

Much interest attaches to the marine sediment of the Bay of Fundy, from the great breadth of it laid bare at low tide, and the facilities which it in consequence affords for the study of sun-cracks, impressions of rain-drops, foot-prints of animals, and other appearances which we find imitated on many ancient rocks. The genuineness of these ancient traces, as well as their mode of preservation, can be illustrated and proved only by the study of modern deposits. We quote a summary of facts of this kind from a paper on Rain-prints by Sir Charles Lyell, who was the first to direct attention to these phenomena as exhibited in the Bay of Fundy.

"The sediment with which the waters are charged is extremely fine, being derived from the destruction of cliffs of red sandstone and shale, belonging chiefly to the coal measures. On the borders of even the smallest estuaries communicating with a bay in

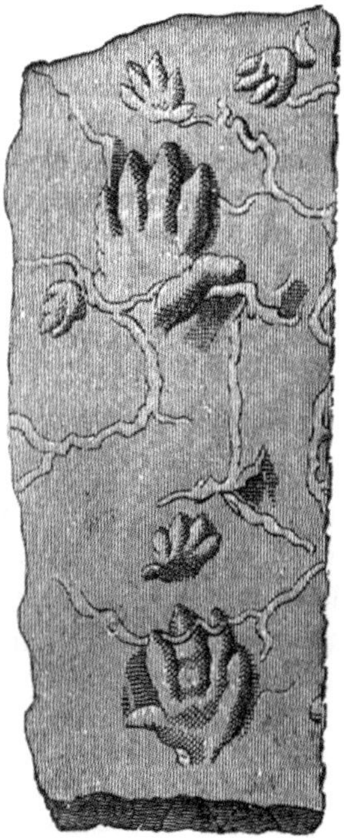

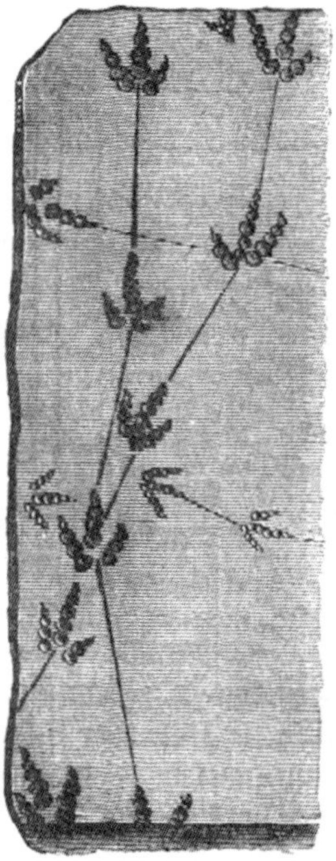

which the tides rise sixty feet and upwards, large areas are laid dry for nearly a fortnignt, between the spring and the neap tides; and the mud is then baked in summer by a hot sun, so that it becomes solidified and traversed by cracks. Portions of the hardened mud may then be taken up and removed without injury.

"On examining the edges of each slab, we observe numerous lay era, formed by successive tides, usually very thin—sometimes only one-tenth of an inch thick; of unequal thicksness, however, because, according to Dr. Webster, the night-tides, rising a foot higher than the day-tides, throw down more sediment.

"When a shower of rain falls, the highest portion of the mud-covered flat is usually too hard to receive any impressions; while that recently uncovered by the tide, near the water's edge, is too soft. Between these areas a space occurs almost as smooth and even as a looking-glass, on which every drop forms a cavity of circular or oval form. If the shower be transient these pits retain their shape permanently. being dried by the sun, and being action of the succeeding tide, which deposits upon them a new layer of mud. Hence we find, on splitting open a slab an inch or more thick, on the upper surface of which the marks of recent rain occur, that an inferior layer, deposited perhaps ten or fourteen tides previously, exhibits on its under surface perfect casts of rain-prints which stand out in relief, the moulds of the same being seen in the layer below."

After mentioning that a continuous shower of rain obliterates the more regular impressions, and produces merely a blistered surface. Sir Charles adds:—

"On some of the specimens there are seen the winding tubular tracks of worms, which have been bored just beneath the surface. Sometimes the worms have dived, and then reappeared. Occasionally the same mud is traversed by the foot-prints of birds, and of musk-rats, minks, dogs, sheep, and cats. The leaves also of elm, maple, and oak trees have been scattered by the winds over the soft mud, and, having been buried under the deposits of succeeding tides, are found on dividing the layers. When the leaves themselves are removed, very faithful impressions, not only of their outline, but of their minutest veins, are left imprinted on the clay."

We have here a perfect instance, in a modern deposit, of appearances which we notice in some of the most ancient rocks; and it is only by such minute studies of existing nature that we can hope to interpret those older appearances. In some very ancient rocks we have impressions of rain-marks quite similar to those which occur in the alluvial mud of the Bay of Fundy. In those old rocks, also, and especially in the coal formation, we find surfaces netted with sun-cracks precisely like those on the dried surfaces of the modern mud flats, and faithful casts of these taken by the beds next deposited.

A striking geological fact connected with the marshes, is the presence beneath them of stumps of trees still rooted in the soil, and other indications which prove that much, if not the whole of this marine deposit, rests on what once was upland soil supporting forest trees; and that, by some change of level, these ancient forests had been submerged and buried under the tidal deposits.

—From DAWSON' S Acadian Geology.

Words

preservation, *projection*.
recently, *lately*.
cavity, *hollow*.
commencement, *beginning*.
compressed, *narrowed*.
conversion, *commotion*.
estuaries, *firths*.
examining, *inspecting*.
genuineness, *authenticity*.
impressions, *copies*.
Indications, *symptoms*.
insecurity, *danger*.
instantaneously, *immediately*.
interpret, *explain*.
imitates, *finest*.
obliterates, *effaces*.
occasionally, *sometimes*.
permanently, *lastingly*.
phenomena, *appearances*.
retreat, *retirement*.
sediment, *deposit*.
solidified, *hardened*.
specimens, *examples*.
swallowing, *absorbing*.
transient, *passing*.
unaccustomed, *unfamiliar*.

Questions

To what does the vertical rise of the tide in the Bay of Fundy amount? What appearance does the coast present at low tide? What has the torrent of red water often in its front? What does the stranger feel as he sees its advance? For what does the sediment in the Bay of Fundy afford facilities? What do these appearances illustrate? Why is the sediment extremely fine? At what time are large areas of it exposed to the sun? What portion of it is best adapted for receiving impressions? Of what did Lyell find casts between the layers? Of what are these perfect instances? What it inferred from the presence of stumps of trees rooted in the soil?

沿着美国大西洋海岸，向东北方向掠去的大潮，在进入到隧道一样的芬迪湾湾口的时候，由于海湾两边变得愈来愈向彼此趋近，海水受到挤压高涨起来。在更狭窄的部分，海水以每小时6到7英里的速度奔流，而大潮垂直方向的上涨幅度居然达到60英尺或更高的高度！这些潮汐在某些地方，在不习惯于观看大潮的人看来，更像是自然界难得一见的痉挛现象，而不是每天都会发生的平常景象。

在低潮区，能看到宽阔的棕色泥土层绵延数英里，好像大海从其海床上隐退了一样，而远处的海峡看起来则不过是浸泡在泥水中的狭窄地带。洪水开始的时候，会稍微出现一些涟漪打散泥土层的边缘。然后迅猛地冲刺向前，几乎在一瞬间就盖住地势较低的平地，快速激荡起喷得越来越高的泥土，看起来好像它们溶进了浑浊的海水中了。

同时，红色海水的湍流进入到所有峡口、溪流和入海口中；它高涨着，旋转着，涌起白沫，还经常在浪头涌起白色的分开的浪花，或者“波浪”，它稳健地奔流向前，和剩余的在峡口依然缓慢移动的退去的潮水交汇并吞并它们。不一会儿工夫，泥土层就被完全覆盖了；之后，当陌生人看着海水积聚着无声而稳健的速度，在河岸和悬崖陡峭的一侧的时候，他心中会油然而生出一种不安全感来，好像那先前奔涌的巨浪会无限向前似的。然而，不一会儿，他就会看到，那泥层，“你将来到这里，但不能再往前奔流”，已经留住了这伟大的海湾大潮。它开始退潮，而海水以它涌来时的速度快速退去。

芬迪湾的海洋沉积物引起人们极大的兴趣，这些沉积物在其伟大的浪潮之下，会在它退潮的时候露出来，而这些沉积物上的图样非常多，有太阳裂隙，雨滴的形状，动物足印，还有其他我们发现的古代岩石上模仿的形象。这些古迹的真实性以及它们的保存方式只有通过研究现代收藏的相关沉积物才能说明并加以佐证。因此，我们引用一段关于这一类沉积物说明的总结，这个总结出自查尔斯·莱尔爵士关于雨石的研究论文，莱尔爵士是关注芬迪湾此类现象的第一人。

“海水中所携带的沉积物非常秀美，它们是从红砂石和泥板岩质的悬崖上剥落下来的，大都属于煤炭层。在即使是和海湾相通的最小的河口边缘，那里的潮汐也会升到60英尺甚至更高，在大潮和小潮之间会留下大约干涸两个星期的大片区域；而泥土之后会被夏天的骄阳炙烤，这样它就变得很坚固并有了裂纹。之后，部分变硬的泥土会被毫发无损地吸入潮汐中并移走。

“仔细检查一下每块石板的边缘，我们就会发现它有很多层，非常薄，是由浪潮不断冲刷形成的——有时候它的厚度仅有十分之一英尺；然而它们厚度不一，这是因为，根据韦伯斯特博士的说法，夜晚的潮汐升到的高度要比白天的潮汐高1英尺，因而会抛落下更多的沉积物。

“当倾盆大雨降落的时候，绝大部分泥土覆盖的海床都因太坚硬而不能再被刻上什么印记；而当海潮退去的时候，靠近水域的边缘，它则变得非常软。在这些区域之间是一片几乎平滑得甚至像镜面一样的空地，上面每一滴雨滴都形成一个圆形或椭圆形的小坑。如果大雨转瞬即逝的话，那么这些小坑就会永久保持它们的形状，它们在阳光下灼干，而在一波又一波海浪的作用下，它们上面会形成一层新的泥土。因此我们发现，当把一块石板撬开1英尺或更厚一点的时候，它上面的一层表明最近有降雨发生，而里面的一层，可能是之前十次或十四次海浪沉淀下的，显示出底部的表面有清晰的雨滴烙印，这些烙印非常突出，同样的印记在下面的一层也能看见。”

在陈述完持续的倾盆大雨会冲刷掉较为规则的印记，并仅仅形成一个模糊的表面之后，查尔斯爵士补充道：

“在一些标本上，可以看见蜿蜒的虫子挣扎的痕迹，这些痕迹恰好位于表面之下。有时候这些虫子向内沉去，之后又重新出现。偶尔的一种情况是同样的泥层会同时出现鸟、麝香鼠、貂、狗、羊以及猫的爪印。而榆树、枫树以及橡树的树叶被风吹拂散落在柔软的泥土表层，然后被一波又一波涌来的海潮中的冲积物埋在了下面，这些树叶被发现位于不同的岩层中。当树叶本身不存在之后，会有和它们本来面目非常相像的印子，烙印在土层中，而这些印子不仅和它们外形轮廓形似，而且连它们细微的脉络也保留了下来。”

我们这里有个绝佳的范例，是一个现代收藏物，它上面的印记我们在一些最古老的石头上曾经见过，而我们只有寄希望于通过细致入微的对现存自然界的研究，来揭示这些古老的印记。在一些年代非常久远的石头上，我们发现一些雨滴的印记和芬迪湾冲积泥层上的石头印记非常相似。在这些古老的岩石上，特别是煤炭中，我们还发现了其表面密布着太阳痕，和那些现代泥土层干涸表面的裂纹非常像，也是那些在之后沉积了的海床上的物质的忠实投射。

地质学上关于沼泽的一个惊人事实是，沼泽下面依然有扎根于土壤中的树桩存在，而其他的现象则证明事实差不多如此，如果不是有整个这层海洋沉积物的话，那些曾经滋养森林树木的上层土壤依然会在沼泽表面，而这些古代的森林，由于土层的改变，已经被海潮沉积物覆盖并被埋葬在下面了。

—摘自汤森的《阿卡迪亚地质学》

Lesson 67 COAL

第六十七课 煤 炭

Who can sum up the benefits we derive from coal? It warms and lights our dwellings, cooks our food, illuminates our streets. Coal develops and sustains the force which propels the locomotive along the railway and the ship across the sea; works the printing press, wields the hammer, lifts the weight, draws the load, moves the machinery, grinds the com, spins the cotton, weaves the cloth, pumps the mine, deepens the river, covers the land with a network of railways, forges the electric wire, and, submerging the ocean telegraph, "will put a girdle round about the Earth in forty minutes." Who shall set bounds to the power of Coal, Iron, and Steam?

The economical and industrial importance of the union of coal and irons in the British Isles cannot be over-estimated. To the abundance of these minerals in the deposits of the coal formation are owing the increase and prosperity of the British people, their wide-spread mercantile enterprise, their rapid intercourse with all parts of the world, their boundless territories abroad, their opulence and influence at home.

From its proximity to a mere patch of the English coal measures—a detached portion not exceeding the area of one of the larger Scottish lakes—Birmingham has risen to the rank of the first iron manufacturing town in the world. Manchester and Glasgow have equally derived their manufacturing and commercial importance from being placed each in the centre of a great coal basin.

The vegetable origin of coal is no longer a matter of doubt. The leaves of ferns, reeds, and other plants, are frequently found between layers of shale or slaty clay, beautifully perfect, but converted into coal. And in many kinds of coal, by means of very thin sections, and by the employment of the microscope, the cells of a vegetable structure become visible; thus affording us a distinct proof that coal is really a vegetable substance, and produced by vegetable decay.

The coal plants flourished in the widely extended forests of the primeval world; and as they fell and decayed, they left their remains imbedded in sandstone and shales, accumulating in lakes and the deltas and estuaries of rivers, to become transformed into coal in the lapse of ages, by the united influences of heat and pressure.

The trunks of the trees, being covered with water, were kept from contact with the air, and gradually decayed, until they were converted into a blackish-brown substance resembling peat, but which still retained more or less of the fibrous structure of wood. The decomposed mass became gradually covered with a deposit of sediment, the great pressure of which, when accumulated into beds of clay or sand of some thickness, gave to this substance the hardness and density of a true mineral. It thus became stored up for future employment in the service of man.

The trees which grew in the swamps and forests of the coal period derived their carbonaceous substance from carbonic acid gas and water, existing in the soil and floating in invisible currents in the air. They imbibed the gas by their fronds, leaves, and roots; and separating the solid carbon from the oxygen gas with which it was combined, they appropriated the former for the purposes of their nourishment and growth, and restored the latter to the atmosphere. But the plant can only decompose carbonic acid and water with the aid of the light and heat of the sun—the process ceases in the dark.

IDEAL VIEW OF A MARSHY FOREST OF THE COAL PERIOD

In helping the plant to appropriate and deposit carbon in its tissues, the sun parted with so much of its light and heat, which became latent in the vegetable. This long dormant light and heat are set free by the process of combustion.

When the Yule log is laid on the blazing hearth of the baron's hail, and the fagots are piled on the peasant's fire, they shed upon the radiant faces of the festive circle light and heat which were borrowed from the sun while the seed sprang into a sapling, and at length became a goodly tree, a century or two old.

But the coal glowing in the cheerful fires of our town dwellings, and diffusing light by means of the gas-pipes of our streets, is composed of vegetables in which are stored up, in another form, light and heat originally derived from the sunshine of distant ages. In the grate we liberate this ancient heat for our comfort; in the geometer we take advantage of the light for our convenience; in our boilers and engines we convert the latent heat into mechanical force.

"Wood fires," says a distinguished philosopher, "give us heat and light which have been got from the sun a few years ago. Our coal fires and gas lamps bring out, for our present comfort, heat and light of the primeval sun, which have lain dormant beneath seas and mountains for countless ages."

—Sketches in Natural History—ELLIS' S Chemistry.

Words

accumulating, *gathering.*
appropriated, *adopted.*
composed, *made up.*
decomposed , *decayed.*

develop, *evolves*.
dormant, *sleeping*.
economical, *wealthsaving*.
employment, *use*.
flourished, *grew*.
geometer, *gas-measurer*.
illuminates, *lights*.
imbibed, *drank in*.
industrial, *pertaining to the arts*.
liberate, *set free*.
locomotive, *steam-carriage*.
opulence, *wealth*.
over-estimated, *exaggerated*.
prosperity, *success*.
proximity, *nearness*.
radiant, *glowing*.
submerging, *sinking*.

Questions

Mention some of the great things done by means of coal. What other mineral is generally found near coal? Mention great cities which owe their importance to coal. What is the origin of coal? How is this proved? How have the coal plants been transformed into coal? Whence did they derive their carbonaceous properties? What are latent or dormant in coal? Whence were they derived? When do they again become active?

☆ ☆

有谁能总结一下我们从煤炭那里得到的好处？它能产生热量，还能照亮我们的住所，能帮助我们烹饪，还能照亮我们的街道。煤炭产生并提供了使火车在铁轨上跑动和轮船穿越海洋的动力；它能使印刷机运转、挥动斧头、举起重物、拉动货物、移动商品、研磨谷物、纺织纱线、织造布匹、抽送矿产、挖深河道，在土地上建造铁路网，锻制电线以及安装海底通信设备，“能在40分钟之内绕地球一周。”有谁能对煤炭、铁还有蒸汽的力量设限？

煤炭和铁的组合对于不列颠群岛有着极高的经济和工业价值。不列颠人口增长和生活富足，多亏了煤炭中包含大量的矿物，同时也造就了他们林立的商业公司，快速增长的同世界各个地区的贸易往来，无止境的境外领地以及国内的富足、影响力和繁荣。

紧紧因为靠近一个英国煤场——一个人烟罕至，大小不超过苏格兰最大湖泊的地方——伯明翰就已经跻身世界上一流钢铁生产城市的行列。曼彻斯特和格拉斯哥都因位于最大的煤炭盆地中心获得的生产价值和商业价值而闻名于世。

煤炭来源于植物，这已经不再是令人质疑的观点了。蕨类植物、芦苇以及其他植物的叶子，经常会出现在岩层和板岩之间，保存完好，但它们已经被转化成了煤炭。在许多种类的煤炭中，通过非常细小的部分以及显微镜的使用，植物纤维细胞就变得清晰可见，这样就呈现给我们一个清楚的证据，即煤炭的确是植物，而且是植物死亡后产生的。

形成煤炭的植物在原始时代的广袤森林中繁茂生长。当它们倒下并死亡的时候，会将剩余的部分嵌入到砂石中和岩层间，并在湖泊和河流三角区和入海口不断积聚，之后随着时间的流逝，在热量和压力的共同作用下转化成煤炭。

树干表面被水覆盖，这样就隔绝了空气，渐渐腐烂，直到它们转化成为黑褐色的泥状物质，但这种物质还是或多或少保留了木头的质地结构。这些被分解的物质逐渐被一种沉积物覆盖，而在这种沉积物的巨大压力下，当这些物质在土层间或较厚的砂石间聚集的时候，它们就会形成一种在硬度致密度上能真正称得上矿石的物质。它们被储存起来，在未来为人类所用，服务人类。

煤炭时代生长在沼泽和森林中的树木，从一氧化碳和水中汲取碳，而这种叫作碳的物质既存在于土壤中，也漂浮于不可见的空气流中。树木通过自身的枝、叶和根吸收这些气体。通过把一起吸收的固体碳和氧气分离开来，植物将前者用于自身营养供给，将后者归还到大气层中。但只有在太阳光和热的帮助下，植物才能够分解一氧化碳和水——这个过程在黑暗中无法进行。

为了能帮助植物使用并储存碳到自身组织中，太阳将相当大的光和热分配给植物，而光和热则潜藏在植物中。这种长期潜藏的光和热会在燃烧过程中被释放出去。

当男爵家的壁炉烧着圣诞柴火，农民家的火堆上也燃起木柴的时候，人们就展现出一张张红光满面的节日笑脸，而那光和热则是在植物从种子生长成树苗并最终经过一两个世纪，长成参天大树的过程中从太阳那里吸收来的。

但在我们城镇房中的欢快火堆中燃烧的煤炭，那通过街上的烟囱管道释放光的煤炭，是植物形成并以另外一种形式，以源自远古时代的太阳光的光和热的形式储存的。壁炉中，我们把这种来自远古的热量释放出来，给我们提供舒适的温度；在水壶和蒸汽机中，我们将这种潜藏的热量转化成机械动力。

“木火”，一位享誉盛名的哲学家说，“给我们从若干年前的太阳那里得来的光和热。煤炭的火焰和煤气灯产生了，带给我们当下的舒适，和来自远古时期太阳的光和热，它们曾经在海洋底部和山峦之下沉睡了无数岁月。”

——“自然历史素描”——《艾利的化学》

Lesson 68 THE AIR-OCEAN

第六十八课 大气海洋

Enveloping this solid globe of ours are two oceans—one partial, the other universal. There is the ocean of water, which has settled down into all the depressions of the Earth's surface, leaving dry above it all the high lands—as mountain-ranges, continents, and islands; and there is an ocean of air, which inwraps the whole in one transparent mantle. Through the bosom of that ocean, like fishes with their fine and whales with their flippers, birds and other winged creatures swim; whilst, like crabs and many shellfish, man and other mammalia creep about at the bottom of this aerial sea.

The air-ocean, which everywhere surrounds the Earth, and feeds and nourishes it, is even more simple, more grand, and more majestic than the "world of waters"—more varied and changeful in its moods of storm and calm, of ebb and flow, of brightness and gloom. The atmosphere is, indeed, a wonderful thing—a most perfect example of the economy of nature. Deprived of air, no animal would live, no plant would grow, no flame would burn, no light would be diffused. The air, too, is the sole medium of sound. Without it, mountains might fall, but it would be in perfect silence—neither whisper nor thunder would ever be heard.

The atmosphere is supposed to become inappreciable at the height of between forty and fifty miles from the Earth.

A philosopher of the East, with a richness of imagery truly Oriental, thus describes it:—" It surrounds us on all sides, yet we see it not; it presses on us with a load of fifteen pounds on every square inch of surface of our bodies, or from seventy to one hundred tons on us in all, yet we do not so much as feel its weight. Softer than the softest down, more impalpable than the finest gossamer, it leaves the cobweb undisturbed, and scarcely stirs the slightest flower that feeds on the dew it supplies; yet it bears the fleets of nations on its wings around the world, and crushes the most refractory substances with its weight.

"When the air is in motion, its force is sufficient to level the most stately forests and stable buildings with the earth; to raise the waters of the ocean into ridges like mountains, and dash the strongest ships to pieces like toys. It warms and cools by turns the Earth, and the living creatures that inhabit it. It draws up vapours from the sea and the land, retains them dissolved in itself, or suspended in cisterns of clouds, and drops them down again, as rain or dew, when they are required. It bends the rays of the sun from their path, to give us the twilight of evening and of dawn; it disperses and refracts their various tints to beautify the approach and the retreat of the orb of day.

"But for the atmosphere, sunshine would fail us at once; and, on the other hand, at once remove us from midnight darkness to the blaze of noon. We should have no twilight to soften and beautify the landscape, no clouds to shade us from the scorching heat; but the bald Earth, as it revolved on its axis, would turn its tanned and weakened front to the full and unmitigated rays of the lord of day. It affords the gas which vivifies and warms our frames, and receives into itself that which has been polluted by use and is thrown off as noxious. It feeds the dame of life exactly as it does that of the fire;—it is in be the cases consumed, and affords the food of consumption; in both cases it becomes combined with charcoal, which requires it for combustion, and which is removed by it when this is over."

"It is only the girdling, encircling air," says another philosopher, "flowing above and around all, that makes the whole world kin.' The carbonic acid with which today our breathing fills the air, to-morrow seeks its way round the world. The date-trees that grow around the falls of the Nile will drink it in by their leaves; the cedar of Lebanon will take of it to add to their stature; the cocoa-nuts of Tahiti will grow rapidly upon it; and the palms and bananas of Japan will change it into flowers.

The oxygen that we are breathing was distilled for us some short time ago by the magnolias of the Susquehanna, and the great trees that skirt the Orinoco and the Amazon;—the giant rhododendrons of the Himalayan contributed to it, and the roses and myrtles of Cashmere, the cinnamon-trees of Ceylon, and the forest, older than the Flood, buried deep in the heart of Africa. The rain we see descending was thawed for us out of the icebergs which have watched the polar star for ages; and the lotus lilies have sucked up from the Nile, and exhaled as vapour, snows that rested on the summits of the Alps.

"The atmosphere, which forms the outer surface of the habitable world, is a vast reservoir, into which the supply of food designed for living creatures is thrown; or, in one word, it is itself the food, in its simple form, of all living creatures. The animal grinds down the fibre and the tissue of the plant, and the nutritious store that has been laid up within its cells, and converts these into the substance of which its own organs axe composed. The plant acquires the organs and nutritious store, thus yielded up as food to the animal, from the air surrounding it.

"But animals are furnished with the means of locomotion and of seizure: they can approach their food, and lay hold of and swallow it. Plants must wait till their food comes to them. No solid particles find access to their frames. The restless ambient air, which rushes past them, loaded with the carbon, the hydrogen, the oxygen, the water, everything they need in the shape of supplies, is constantly at hand to minister to their wants; not only to afford them food in due season, but in the shape and fashion in which alone it can avail them."

There is no employment more ennobling to man and his intellect than to trace the evidences of design and purpose in the Creator, which are visible in all parts of the creation. Hence, to him who studies the physical relations of earth, sea, and air, the atmosphere is something more than a shoreless ocean, at the bottom of which he creeps along.

It is an envelope or covering for dispersing light and heat over the surface of the Earth; it is a sewer, into which, with every breath we draw, we cast vast quantities of dead animal matter; it is a laboratory for purification, in which that matter is recompounded and wrought again into wholesome and healthful shapes; it is a machine for pumping up all the rivers from the sea, and conveying the waters from their fountains in the ocean to their sources in the mountains; it is an inexhaustible magazine, marvellously adapted for benign and beneficent purposes.

—MAURY

Words

ambient, *surrounding.*
beautify, *adorn.*
begin,*kindly.*changeful, *benign.*
breathing,*inhaling.*
changeful,*fickle.*
depressions,*cavities.*
deprived, *destitute.*
diffused, *shed abroad.*
distilled, *liberated.*
economy, *systematic arrangement.*
employment, *occupation.*
ennobling, *elevating.*
enveloping, *surrounding.*
exhaled, *breathed out.*
gossamer, *film.*
impalpable, *intangible.*
inexhaustible, *exhaustless.*
intellect, *mind.*
laboratory, *chemists room.*
locomotion, *changing place.*
mantle, *garment.*
minister, *attend.*
noxious, *hurtful.*
nutritions, *nourishing.*
polluted, *poisoned.*
purification, *cleansing.*
refractory, *stubborn.*
remove, *transport.*
reservoir, *magazine.*
retains, *holds.*
transparent, *clear.*
vivifies, *enlivens.*

Questions

Name the two oceans which envelop the globe. What effects would follow if the globe were deprived of air? With what weight does it press upon our bodies? What is its force able to do when it is in motion? How does twilight depend upon it? How does it " make the whole world kin"! Of what is the atmosphere a vast reservoir? Wherein do plants differ from animals in regard to food? How does the air minister to plants? Why may the atmosphere be compared to a sewer? Why to a laboratory? Why to a pumping-machine?

包裹我们这个固体星球的是两个海洋——一个有固定的体积，另一个则无处不在。水的海洋，最终形成了地球的表面特征，让那些高于它的高地——诸如山脊，大陆以及岛屿成为干燥的陆地，而大气的海洋则像一个透明的穹盖包裹在一起。大气的海洋中部，有鸟儿和其他有羽翼的生物畅游其间，就好像鱼类用鱼鳍以及鲸鱼用短鳍游泳一样，而在这个空气的海洋底部，则有人类和其他的哺乳动物行走和爬行，就好像螃蟹和许多壳类生物在海洋底部一样。

大气海洋包裹在地球周围，无处不在，并且供养着地球。这个海洋要比“水世界”更加简单，更加壮大，更加壮观，更加多变和复杂，时而风暴骤降，时而风平浪静，时而退潮时而涨潮，时而明媚和煦时而晦暗阴沉。事实上，大气是非常神奇的，它是大自然法则的绝佳范例。没有空气，动物就不能生存，植物也不会生长，火焰会熄灭，也就不会有光亮。同时，空气还是声音的唯一介质。没有了空气，山峦可能会倒塌，但一切会在绝对静谧之中进行——既不会有窃窃私语，也不会有雷声轰鸣。

在距离地面40到50英里的高度，大气层变得很稀薄了。

一位拥有真正东方世界的丰富想象的东方哲学家曾描述道：“它在各个方向包围着我们，然而我们却看不到；它在我们身体表面每平方英尺的压力是15磅，或者整体压在我们身上的压力是70到100吨，然而我们并没有感觉到它有那么大的重量。它比最柔软的绒毛还柔软，比最细微的蛛丝还要细微，它不会吹动蛛网，几乎不会颤动含苞未放的骨朵，那花朵靠着它提供的露珠得到给养，然而它把世界上所有国家的船都载在自己的翅膀上，同时又能用自身的重量压垮最坚硬的物质。

“当空气流动的时候，它的力量足以将生长最挺拔的森林和最稳固的建筑物夷为平地，足以将沧海抬高成为群山的屋脊，并将最强健的船只像玩具一样撕得粉碎。它的温暖和凉爽交替着造访地球，而生物则在它中间生存。它从海洋和大陆上汲取水蒸气，滞留住它们并对它们进行转化，或者将它们阻隔在云朵组成的贮水池中，然后在需要的时候，把它们像雨或露一样抛向地面。它能扭转太阳光的路线，给我们早晨的晨光和傍晚的暮光；它分散并折射不同的光彩来美化我们这个星球的晨曦或是傍晚。

“要是没有大气层的存在，阳光会马上伤害到我们；而另一方面，我们将经历从子夜的黑暗到中午的明亮的骤然变化。我们将没有暮光来柔化并美化我们的风景，也不会有云朵为我们遮蔽灼人的烈日；相反，我们会只有光秃秃的地球。如果地球顺着其地轴旋转的话，人们会被晒黑，暴露在完全未经过滤的太阳光之下。它丰富了并温暖了我们身体的气息，并接受被污染的或是排放进大气层的有毒气体。它供养了生命的呼吸就如同它供给了火焰的燃烧一样；前者是供呼吸消耗，后者是提供以供消耗的燃料；在两种情况中，它都和碳相结合，因为燃烧过程需要碳的参与，同时在结束的时候，大气中的碳就被移除了。

“它仅仅是环绕在空中并包裹着地球的一层气体，”另一位哲学家说道，“它在地球上空漂浮并萦绕着一切，让整个世界都亲如一家。”我们今天呼吸的碳酸充斥在大气中，明天它就会游荡在全世界。沿着干涸的尼罗河河岸生长的枣树会通过自己的叶子吸收它，黎巴嫩的雪松则会吸收它来增加自己的巍峨长势，塔希提岛的椰子树的快速生长依赖于它，而日本的棕榈树和橡胶树会把它转化成盛开的花朵。”

我们呼吸的氧气在不久之前，已经由萨斯奎哈纳的木兰，和生长在奥利诺科河和亚马孙河流域的参天大树为我们过滤过了；还有喜马拉雅山巨大的雪莲以及克什米尔的玫瑰和桃金娘，锡兰的肉桂树以及年代比大洪水还久远的，深深掩埋在非洲中心地带的森林，也都在这一过程中发生过作用。我们看到掉落的雨滴是从冰山中融化来到我们面前的，这些冰山已经守望北极星很久了，而在尼罗河边释放出气体的莲子百合，它吸收的其实是曾经环绕在阿尔卑斯山顶峰的气体。

“构成我们这个适于生存的世界外围表层的大气层，是一个巨大的保存层，里面供养生物和他们的食物；或者换句话说，它简单的形态本身就为所有生物提供了食物。动物把植物的纤维和组织磨碎，把营养储存进它们的细胞中，之后营养又会转化成构成它们器官的物质。植物则从周围的空气中生长出组织并获取营养，因此也就成为动物的食物。

“但动物是通过移动和捕捉的形式来获取营养的：它们可以获取食物，抓住食物然后吞咽下去。植物则必须等待它们的食物送上门来。没有固体物质能够进入到它们的系统中。不停运动在周围的大气，从它们身边一闪而过，满载着碳，氢和氧气以及水分，还有它们需要的各种形式的给养，都不断地送到它们面前，满足它们的需要。大气不仅在合适的季节提供给它们食物，而且这些食物以它们唯一能吸收的形式和形态存在。”

没有什么人类行为比造物主的设计痕迹和设计目的更能让人类变得高尚，让他们的智慧变得崇高的了，而造物主在所有他的创造物中都清晰可见。因此，对于研究陆地、海洋和大气的物质关系的人而言，大气层不仅仅是一片无岸的海洋，不仅仅是人们在其底部爬动向前的海洋。

大气层是一个外衣或覆盖层，它包裹住分散在地球表边的光和热。它是一个排污处，我们吸进的每一口气，都呼出到它里头，我们把大量的死去动物的物质投放在其中；它是一个净化的实验室，里面有重新复合的物质和重新转化成无害和健全形态的物质；它是一个巨大的水泵，把海洋中所有河流的水都抽走，然后把水从其喷涌的海洋中，转移到它们在群山中的发源地；它是一个用之不竭的机器，它被用来作善意和有益之事时，神奇无比。

——毛瑞

Lesson 69
UNWRITTEN HISTORY, AND HOW TO READ IT

第六十九　非文字记载的历史及其解读方式

It cannot be discovered in what age of the world Britain first became a scene of human habitation. There is nothing in all history, no written record of any kind, to yield us any information concerning the original possessors of the land.

But the history of the early Britons, though it was never written, may be read. A curious history it is; and the way in which the materials of it have been gathered and put together is a fine example of the triumphs of patient thought. The historian of other periods finds his materials in books, in written records and documents. The materials for the history of this period have been found on waste moors and in deep mosses, in caves and on hills, under ancient burial mounds and cairns, by the margins of rivers and on the beds of drained lochs.

Here, for instance, is an ancient boat, found a few years since on the south bank of the Clyde, when excavations were being made for the purpose of enlarging the harbour of Glasgow. It is of oak, not planked or built, but hewn out of the trunk of a single tree. The hollow has been made with fire, as the marks still show. Within it,

when it was discovered, there lay an axe-head of stone.

Now, that fire-hollowed boat and stone axe tell their story as plainly as a printed book. The savage on the shores of the Pacific cuts a groove in the bark round the root of the tree of which he intends to form his canoe. Into this groove he puts burning embers till it is charred to some depth. Next he deepens the groove by hewing out the charred wood with his stone hatchet. Then he applies the fire again; and so on, until, by the alternate use of fire and axe, the tree is brought to the ground. By the same process it is hollowed out, and shaped into a canoe. The ancient boat-maker of the Clyde had used exactly such a method of forming his little vessel. The stone axe, brought to light after untold ages, bears mute but expressive witness that its owner was a savage.

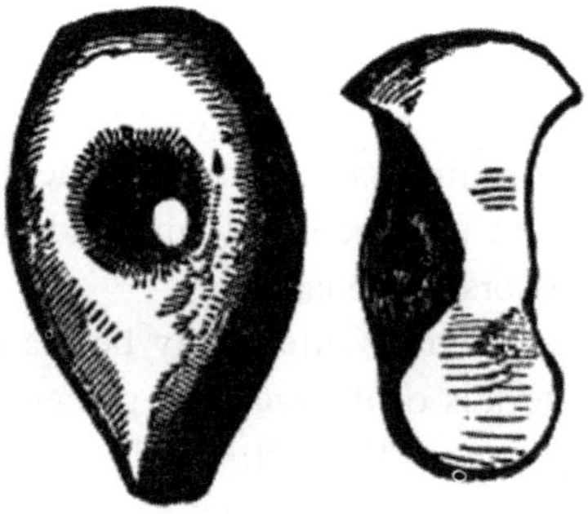

STONE AXES

The axe with which the ancient Briton hollowed his canoe, served him also as a weapon in battle. Under a large cairn, on a moor in the south of Scotland, a stone coffin of very rude workmanship was found. It contained the skeleton of a man of uncommon size. One of the arms had been almost severed from the shoulder. A fragment of very hard stone was sticking in the shattered bone. That blow had I been struck with a stone axe. When the victor, after the fight, looked at his bloody weapon, he saw that a splinter had broken from its edge. Thousands of years passed, the cairn of the dead was opened, and that splinter was found in the bone of the once mighty arm which the axe had all but hewn away. What a curious tale to be told by a single splinter of stone!

On yonder lea field the ploughman turns over the grassy sward. At the furrow's end, as he breathes his horses for a moment and looks at his work, his eye is caught by some object sticking in the upturned mould. He picks it up. It is a barbed arrow-head, neatly chipped out of yellow flint. How came it there? It is no elf-arrow, shot by the fairies. It was once, when tied to a reed with a sinew or a strip of skin, an arrow in the quiver of an ancient British savage hunting the deer.

There are spots where the flint arrow-heads have been found in such numbers as to show that the barbarian tribes had met there in battle. Spear-heads, too, and knives of flint, have been dug up from time to time in various parts. The ancient race who employed such weapons must have existed before the use of iron, or any other metal, was known.

That period when the rude inhabitants of a country were ignorant of metals, and formed their tools and weapons of stone, is called the *Stone Period*.

Had this ancient race any idea of religion and a future state? We shall see. Here is an earthen mound, heaped over the grave of some chief. When dug into, it is found to contain a rude stone coffin. In the coffin with the skeleton are flint arrow-heads, a spear-head, also of flint, and perhaps the stone head of a battle-axe, the wooden portions of these weapons having long since moldered away.

Now we know that the savage expects to go after death to the happy hunting-grounds, and to follow again the warpath. His implements of war and the chase are therefore buried with him, that he may start up fully equipped in the new state of being. His favourite horse or dog, and perhaps his favourite attendants, are laid beside his grave, that at his rising he may appear in a manner fitting his rank. The contents of the burial-mound unmistakably proclaim that the men of these long-forgotten ages had the same rude idea of a future state which the Red Indian still has.

In all probability, this ancient race occupied the country, with unchanging habits and with little or no progress, for many centuries. At length, however, the elements of a great change were introduced: the savage tribes became acquainted with the use of metals.

The introduction of metals is the first great stage in the history of civilization. Armed with an axe of metal, instead of the old axe of stone, the savage can go into the forest and cut down trees at will. He can split them, and hew them into planks. He needs not now to pile up overlapping blocks of stone to roof in his dark, underground abode. He can make a far more convenient dwelling of rough, axe-hewn boards.

He needs not now to hollow out a log-canoe, for his new tools have given him the power of building boats of plank. He can now increase the size of his little vessel, and thus make further and bolder ventures out to sea. The trees nearest his village fall first by his axe; but, year by year, he cuts his way deeper into the forest. The clearings extend, and the soil, which will be corn-land by-and-by, is laid open. He now can form a variety of tools suited to a variety of purposes. New wants are created with the increased facility of meeting them. In a word, with the introduction of metal among a savage race, stationary till then, the march of improvement has begun.

The discovery of copper, silver, and gold, naturally takes place before the discovery of iron. The smelting of iron is an art much too difficult for the savage to master, till he has been long familiar with the working of the softer and easier metals. Accordingly, we find that the earliest metallic implements used in Britain were not of iron, but of bronze. Copper and tin are soft metals; but if a portion of tin is mixed with copper, the result is bronze, a metal harder than either of the two of which it is composed. Tools and weapons made of this metal are a great advance upon those made of stone or flint. Bronze, however, is but a poor substitute for iron and steel, and we may be very sure that the people who made use of bronze tools knew nothing of iron.

That period during which the ancient inhabitants of a country, ignorant as yet of iron, made use of bronze tools and weapons, is called the *Bronze Periods*.

Let us again suppose ourselves present at the opening of an ancient British tomb. It is under a cairn heaped on the top of a hill which overlooks a wide tract of moorland. The stone coffin is very short—not over four feet in length. From the position of the bones, the body has evidently been placed in a sitting or folded posture. There are cups or bowls of pottery, one or more. There is a bronze sword, but it has been broken in two before it was laid beside its owner in his long rest. And what is that which glitters among the warrior's dust? It is an ornament of gold—a bracelet or a collar—which he had worn.

The skeleton of a dog is found beside the coffin; for the warrior knew hunting-craft by lake and wood, and loved to pursue his game with hound and bow. So they laid his four-footed favourite, which had licked his hand and followed his halloo, in his long home beside him.

Now observe the cup or bowl, which has contained drink or food—friendship's last gift to the dead. This cup is very different from the unshapely hand-made and sundried pottery of the Stone Period. It has been rounded on a wheel. It is made of fine baked clay, and is neatly ornamented with a simple pattern. There has been progress, then, in the mechanical arts since the ruder and older time.

Let the broken sword next tell its story. The last honour paid to the buried warrior was to break his sword and lay it beside him, ere his companions-in-arms piled over him the memorial cairn. The warrior of the Stone Period was buried with axe, lance, and bow, in barbarian anticipation of warfare beyond the grave; but the warrior of the Bronze Period was laid in his narrow bed with his broken sword, in token of warfare accomplished and of expected rest. This speaks in no obscure language of some better and higher ideas which this ancient race had acquired.

—J. MACKENZIE

Words

accomplished, *completed.*
acquainted, *familiar.*
acquired, *obtained.*
alternate, *by turns.*
anticipation, *expectation.*
attendants, *followers.*
barbarian, *savage.*
civilization, *refinement.*
contained, *held.*
convenient, *suitable.*
curious, *strange.*
discovered, *ascertained.*
documents, *papers.*
employed, *used.*
equipped, *furnished.*
evidently, *apparently.*
excavations, *cuttings.*
expressive, *emphatic.*
facility, *ease.*
hollowed, *scooped.*
implements, *instrument.*
improvement, *advancement.*
information, *knowledge.*
mechanical, *manufacturing.*
moldered, *wasted.*
obscure, *dark.*
observe, *notice.*
pattern, *device.*
ploughman, *husbandman.*
posture, *position.*
probability, *likelihood.*
quiver, *arrow-case.*
shattered, *broken.*
skeleton, *bones of the body.*

splinter, *fragment*.
stationary, *standing still*.
substitute, *exchange*.
uncommon, *unusual*.
unmistakably, *clearly*.
workmanship, *execution*.

Questions

Where are the materials for unwritten history found? How had the ancient boat found near Glasgow been hollowed out? What was found within it? For what purpose had the axe been used? Where is the same plan followed still? To what, then, does the axe bear witness? For what other purpose did the axe serve the ancient Briton? How can you show this? What other stone implements have been found? What is that period of history called? What shows that the ancient Britons believed in a future state? What is the first great stage in the history of civilization? What work does the introduction of metals enable the savage to improve? What metals are first discovered? Why? What is the period therefore called? How is bronze made? What is its character, compared with copper and tin? What are often found within coffins of the Bronze Period? What difference is observed in the cup, as compared with that of the Stone Period? What story does the broken sword tell?

☆ ☆

没有人知道不列颠从什么时候起成为人类的聚居地。关于这片土地上原始居民的信息，没有任何形式的书面记录，也没有任何方面的历史记载。

虽然早期不列颠人的历史没有以文字的形式记载，但这段历史还是可以被解读的。这是一段很有意思的历史，而搜集和汇集其中相关史料的过程，则是经过耐心思考从而得到胜利果实的绝佳范例。其他历史时期的史学家们通过书本、书面材料和文献来发掘素材。但这一历史时期的史料，则是隐藏在无人的荒野和深仄的苔藓地上，隐藏在洞穴中或在山头上，在古代的墓穴中或是石冢里，在河流的边缘地带或是干涸的河床之上。

比如说，这是个古代的船只，它几年前在克兰德河南岸被发现。当时人们为了扩大格拉斯哥港的吞吐能力，在那里进行挖掘。这艘船是橡木的，但不是由橡木拼起来或是由橡木打造的，它是从整根木头中间挖掘出来的。挖空处是用火烧出来的，从船上的印子依然能辨别得出来。被发现的时候，这艘船内部放着一个石头的斧头。

现在通过被火烧空内部的船只和石斧，我们就能清楚地讲出这艘船的故事，这和印刷的书本没有区别。住在太平洋海岸上的土著要造一条独木舟，于是就沿着树干底部砍出一个凹槽来。在这个凹槽中，他放上燃烧着的灰烬，直到凹槽被碳化进一定深度。接着，他就用石凿子把碳化的木头砍掉，这样凹槽的深度就进一步加深了。然后他再次借用火的力量。如此反复，直到通过火和斧头的交替使用，大树倒了下来。根据同样的原理，树木被挖空，并被塑造成独木舟的样子。克兰德河的古船建造者正是使用这个方法建造了自己的小船。经过了漫长的岁月，石斧成了无声胜有声的见证者。

古代不列颠人用来挖空独木舟的斧头，也是他在战场上的武器。在苏格兰南部的一片沼泽地的一个巨大的石冢下，人们发现了一个石头打造的棺木。它的制造工艺非常粗劣。棺木中躺着一个身形不太正常的人的骸骨。这个人的一只胳膊几乎从肩部被砍断。一个非常坚硬的石块卡在破碎的骸骨中。我想那是被石斧击打造成的创伤。当胜利者在战斗之后看到自己沾着鲜血的兵器的时候，他会看见斧头刀刃处有一个缺口。数千年过去了，死者的石冢被打开，石斧的碎片被发现嵌在那曾经强而有力的手臂骨头中。仅仅一片石头碎片，居然告诉了我们这样一个离奇的故事！

在那边的农田里，农民正在杂草丛生的土地上耕耘。犁头边上，当他牵着马喘息着，看着自己的劳动成果的时候，他发现了有个什么东西粘在了犁开的土中。于是他把它捡起来。那是一个倒钩形的箭头，这个箭头被黄褐色的打火石整齐地切下。它是怎么到这来的呢？这不是精灵们射出的精灵之箭，而是曾经被一根或是一条皮子绑在一颗芦苇上，装在猎鹿的古代不列颠的土著的箭袋之中。

有些地方会有燧石箭头大量出现，这表明蛮夷部落的人曾经在那里发生过战争。矛头和燧石刀具也时不时会被从不同地方挖掘出来。古代使用这些武器的民族，一定在已知的使用铁器和其他金属器的时代之前就已经存在了。

而我们把先民们对金属一无所知，用石头打造工具和兵器的时期，称作石器时代。

古人有没有形成宗教观念呢，对来生他们又有怎样的想法呢？我们将在下文中见分晓。这是一个土丘，它的顶部直指某位酋长的墓穴。当向里掘进的时候，人们发现里面是一尊粗制的石棺。石棺里除了骸骨之外，就是若干燧石箭头和一个矛头，当然矛头也是燧石做的，此外还有一些疑似石制的战斧。这些武器的木质部分已经在很久之前就被腐蚀掉了。

现在我们知道，蛮夷人想死后去往幸福的狩猎地，然后继续进行战争。他对战争的实施和追逐都随他葬在一处了，这样当他重新开始来生的时候，就有齐全的装备了。他最喜欢的马或狗，还有他最喜欢的随从，都可能同他一起躺进了墓穴。这样，当他重生的时候，就能享受到前世的待遇了。墓室中随葬的物品明确表明，这些生活在久远的被遗忘的年代的人，对于来生的粗略设想和红种印第安人如出一辙。

机缘变换，这支古老的民族占据了这片土地，他们生活习惯始终不变，生活水平几乎没什么提高，他们就这样生活了许多个世纪。然而，最终出现了一个巨大的变化：蛮夷部落变得能熟练使用金属器了。

金属的出现，是文明史上的第一次巨大变革。蛮夷人装备上金属质的斧头，而不再使用古老的石斧，他们就能够到森林中随意砍伐树木了。他可以把树木劈开，可以把他们砍成木板，更不用说把这些木板一块块摞起来，覆盖在他地下暗处房屋的石头屋顶上。他用斧头砍下结实的木板，就可以建造出一座远比以前的房屋舒适得多的住所。

现在，他不必再挖空一根木头造独木舟了，因为他的新工具让他可以用木板来打造船只。现在他能掌握自己船只的大小，因此也就能向更深的海域前进，进行更冒险地航行。离村落最近的树木先被他砍下；但是，年复一年，他一路砍伐，越来越向森林深处进发。空地的范围扩大了，空荡荡的土地上将逐渐种植上玉米。他现在能打造不同的工具，以适应自己不同的需要。随着新需求的产生，新的工具也应运而生。总而言之，金属在蛮夷族人中出现，标志着一次巨大的进步，而在此之前，蛮夷人的发展则是举步不前的。

铜、银以及金子的发现，很自然地都发生在铁的发现之前。对于蛮夷人而言，在对那些更软更容易获得的金属有相当长时间的熟悉和使用之前，铁的冶炼是一门极其难以掌握的技术。据此，我们发现，不列颠人最早使用的金属器并不是铁，而是青铜。铜和锡都是软金属。但如果一定比例的锡和铜混合在一起，就会产生青铜，一种比这两种金属都坚硬得多的金属。用青铜打造的工具和兵器与之前用石头或燧石打造的工具和兵器相比，是巨大的进步。然而，青铜与铁和钢相比则是一种质量较差的替代物，我们可以肯定地认为，使用青铜工具的人们对于铁一无所知。

我们把先民们对铁一无所知，使用青铜工具和兵器的时代叫作青铜时代。

我们不妨再来假设一番，我们处在一座不列颠古墓的入口处。古墓位于一个石冢之下，石冢被堆砌在能俯瞰一片广阔沼泽地的山头。石棺非常短，长度不到4英尺。从骨头的位置可以看出，遗体是明显被摆放成坐着或者屈着的姿势。石棺里面有若干杯子，一个或多个陶制的碗，还有一把青铜剑。但这把剑在被放在它长眠的主人身边之前，就已经一分为二了。而在战士的骨灰中闪闪发亮的东西是什么呢？原来是一个金质装饰品——一个手镯或袖环——是佩戴到他身上的东西。

棺材旁边是一条狗的骸骨，因为这位战士知晓湖边和森林里的狩猎技术，并喜欢用狗和弓箭来追逐自己的猎物。因此，他们把他最爱的四条腿的宠物放进墓穴，这条狗曾经在他身边，在他回家的路上，曾经舔过他的手，跟随他的高声吠叫。

现在看看那只杯子或碗，它们盛着饮品或食物——这是友人们给死者最后的礼物。这只杯子和石器时代形状不规则的手工制品以及经日晒干燥而成的陶器非常不同。它下面有个轮子。它是由细腻的烘焙土制成的，上面整齐地装饰着一个简单的图形。从这个手工制品中，可以看出其较之更手工粗糙的远古时代的进步。

接下来让断裂的剑来讲讲它的故事。最后献给下葬的战士的荣耀就是把他的剑弄断，然后放在他身边，而他携带武器的同伴则堆砌起纪念他的石冢。石器时代的战士是用斧头、长矛还有弓箭等工具完成下葬的，下葬地点不是在墓穴中而是在蛮夷人的战场上。而青铜器时代的战士则躺在自己狭窄的床上，身边是把断剑，以此纪念他曾经完成以及将要参与的其他战事。这些非常清楚地表明，这支远古民族的人们已经形成了某种更好、更高深的概念。

——J. 麦肯锡